WHAT'S WRONG WITH MANAGEMENT AND HOW TO GET IT RIGHT

WHAT'S WRONG WITH MANAGEMENT AND HOW TO GET IT RIGHT

THE MUST-DO STRATEGY PRACTICES THAT MAKE THE
DIFFERENCE BETWEEN WINNING AND LOSING IN BUSINESS

Tony Manning

PENGUIN BOOKS

Published by Penguin Books
an imprint of Penguin Random House South Africa (Pty) Ltd
Reg. No. 1953/000441/07
The Estuaries No. 4, Oxbow Crescent, Century Avenue, Century City, 7441
PO Box 1144, Cape Town, 8000, South Africa

www.penguinbooks.co.za

First published 2015

1 3 5 7 9 10 8 6 4 2

PUBLISHER: Marlene Fryer
MANAGING EDITOR: Robert Plummer
EDITOR: Alison Lowry
PROOFREADER: Genevieve Adams
COVER DESIGNER: Sean Robertson
TEXT DESIGNER: Ryan Africa
TYPESETTER: Monique van den Berg
INDEXER: Sanet le Roux

Set in 10.5 pt on 14 pt Minion

Printed and bound by CTP Book Printers, Duminy Street, Parow, 7500

ISBN 978 1 77022 899 3 (print)
ISBN 978 1 77022 900 6 (ePub)
ISBN 978 1 77022 901 3 (PDF)

For Calum.
Your curiosity about how the world works, and your ability to
find the words for concepts, are a wonder and a delight.
And you're only four. So watch out, world!

CONTENTS

INTRODUCTION

Great news! There's less to making a business competitive than you might think. We know what works – what brings results. And since most firms *don't* do it, do only some of it, or do it badly, the way is open for you to gain the advantage you want more easily than you might think.

Of course, understanding the world around you is more important than ever – and more difficult. Constant change is normal. Growing complexity entangles every decision, and a bewildering array of factors and actors tilt outcomes one way or another. Circumstances, timing, and luck matter enormously. But when it comes to what *managers* can and must do to gain and sustain an edge, everything hinges on just eight critical strategy practices – which I will come to in Chapter 1.

These practices give you the best possible chance of coping with whatever the world throws at you, of exploiting emerging opportunities, and of out-innovating your competitors.

They are what the winners *do* that puts them ahead in the race for customers and profits.

They are the critical core.

Together they comprise a "strategy system" in which each of them is a source of competitive strength.

This system frames strategic conversation, focuses attention on what really matters, and helps managers combat what is undoubtedly the most prevalent and pernicious destroyer of value – what I call "the tyranny of tools."

Over the past century or so, the management advice industry – whose purpose, you'd think, is to help managers improve their performance – has churned out more theories, methods, models, frameworks, concepts, and questionnaires than any executive can ever use.[1] And they keep coming. Yet efforts to push forward the boundaries of management thought and practice have been largely futile.

In only the past decade, astonishing progress has been made in science, medicine, computing, advanced materials, energy, agriculture, and countless other fields.

Genomic mapping, 3D printing, wearable technology, driverless cars, and mobile computing have arrived with astonishing speed, and their impact on how we live and work will be mind-boggling. Meanwhile, many astonishingly fundamental questions about management remain unanswered.

So here we are, in a time of unprecedented challenges, when so much is expected of managers and the pressures on them are so great, when so many smart people have so much to say on the topic of management, still grappling with how to define competitive advantage.[2] Still unclear about what strategy is, why we need it, and how best to "do" it. Still quibbling about the difference between strategy and tactics, and worrying that our strategic conversations are too operational.

Here we are, questioning the importance of leadership,[3] what it takes to be a leader, and how best to lead.[4] Hooked on visions, missions, and values, but up in the air about what they mean, why we might need them, or what effect, if any, they might have on business results. Hoping against hope that someone can tell us how to design our organizations for best results. Desperate to know how to get the best performance from people, accelerate innovation, and execute our plans. Yet at the same time overwhelmed by opinion that often is based on no more than cursory observation, uninformed speculation, or pure guesswork – in fact, is no more than a figment of someone's imagination.

Some of the tools we have are clearly valuable. Most, however, add nothing to what you need, and if truth be told, are worth more to the experts who produce them than to the firms that fall for them. But there's so much hype that it's hard to know which to go for and which to ignore. And it's a fair bet that like most managers you'll try too many and inadvertently throw sand in the gears of your business.

Organizations are complex systems, and never in a "perfect" state. They're always in tension between stability and chaos, repetition and renewal. It's easier to screw them up than make them hum, and managers are at the mercy of many factors they cannot control. Learning how to apply any new tools, how they fit and interact, and how they'll pan out always takes longer than anyone imagines, and every intervention has unanticipated consequences, good or bad.

But there's more to worry about.

As managers strive for growth in conditions that are more testing by the day, it's essential that they bring as much stability as possible to their organizations. But it's equally essential that they also keep their teams on edge, constantly alert, challenging the status quo, reinventing every aspect of what they do and how they do it, and exploring possibilities that may be fraught with risk. As managers grapple with the complexities of their business amid a hail of surprises, they have to keep questioning their own assumptions, rethinking the best way forward, adjusting their plans, shifting the deck chairs. All this is deeply unsettling to everyone, and its full impact on business performance may only be evident long after the event.

It's perplexing, then, that managers so zealously amplify this disruption and turbocharge their troubles. That they waste as much time, effort, and money as they do complicating their lives, making work more difficult than it need be, and shoving the results they want further and further out into the future.

The first and ongoing task of a leader – a strategist – is to frame the way they and others see the world. To craft and conduct a strategic conversation that makes sense of today's realities and shines a light on tomorrow's possibilities. To inspire a common purpose among disparate stakeholders who see things from their own perspectives, coloured by their own assumptions, experiences, values, and interests. And to define, drive, and facilitate the actions that will lead to a desired future.

Management ideas are key to this process. They're at once a language[5] and a lens. More than just a basis for *discussing* and *doing,* they also affect *seeing* and *being.* So they have a profound impact on what gets attention in an organization; what gets talked about and how; the way that strategy is thought about, created, and executed; and where resources are applied. All of which makes them far too important to be toyed with.

The aim of strategy must be to deal with a clearly defined challenge – either a problem or an opportunity. Similarly, management ideas should only be adopted for a specific purpose. So they should be carefully evaluated and chosen, well understood, and sparingly used.

Too often, though, executives settle on answers before they've clarified their questions. They're drawn to "solutions" they don't need and won't be able to use to best effect. They trigger a bullshit alert when they pepper their conversations with buzzwords, and they undermine their own credibility when they trot out half-baked thoughts on "best practices," picked up from who knows where, without being able to properly explain them. And when they foist what they find onto their already stretched firms, they set themselves up for failure.

This is utter madness. But it gets worse.

Instead of focusing on one idea and helping their people get their heads around it, they quickly become excited by something else. And because new challenges keep arising, they keep grasping.

Ignoring the fact that their people are under pressure and struggling with current problems, let alone trying to make sense of the latest ideas, they keep changing priorities and generating new work. They rewrite vision and mission statements, revise goals, restructure, and reengineer. They dump projects that only yesterday were "essential to our success" and announce new ones that will "bring a step change in our competitiveness" – while allowing no slack or delay or deviation from budget. They demand "out of the box" thinking and overnight results. And when they get together with their colleagues in a strategy retreat, they assure them, "This is not *my* strategy, it's *our* strategy."

But "our strategy" is too often *no* strategy, because no one knows what it is. The overall picture is hazy and the bits don't hang together. And chances are it'll be different tomorrow. And again the day after that.

This rat-tat-tat of random, unclear, and mixed messages undermines understanding, morale, and performance. It leads to any number of pointless activities, creates chaos and confusion when these should be fought tooth and nail, and locks people into a toxic spiral of poor performance (Figure 1).

These habits are fuelled by an assortment of management gurus, including scholars, consultants, writers, and speakers. And by business schools. And the media. And by almost anyone with an opinion on what makes firms tick. There's no shortage of people keen to grab your attention and tell you how to run your business. And who in their right mind would want to pass up a chance at some miracle fix? After all, if you try enough new stuff you just might hit on what you need!

Figure 1

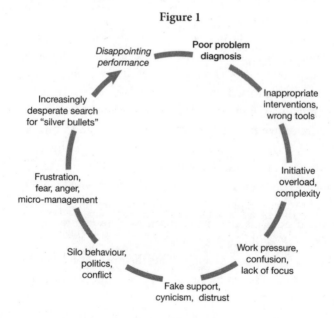

Being keen to learn is an important strength. But impatience and a short-run orientation are serious weaknesses. They "lead to fads," cautions MIT professor emeritus Edgar Schein, "a preoccupation with instant solutions, a blind faith that if we put in enough effort and money anything is possible, and an unwillingness and inability to see the long-range consequences of some of the quick fixes which we try."[6]

But if easy answers are what the market wants, that's what it will get. So the formula of choice for management books is to promise salvation. Rescue from reality. Insights and advice you've never had before, which will take you and your firm to unprecedented heights. Immediately. Painlessly. Effortlessly.

This book is different.

Instead of promising yet another "groundbreaking" theory, tool, or technique, I'm going to tell you why you don't need one; why you should instead get back to a few critical strategy practices that are well known; and why they offer you the best chance of getting the results you want.

In saying this, I'm making a long-overdue but now especially timely argument – one that flies in the face of fashion and has serious implications for managers and for those who advise them. I do this not to play down the importance of management ideas, or to take potshots at well-intended efforts to advance management thinking, but in response to six worrying facts:

1. Business is the engine of society, and will fund or otherwise facilitate most of the progress we need. So the future of humankind depends on managerial performance – and that performance overall is disappointing.

2. Most companies do not achieve even average results, and certainly not with any consistency. Their life expectancy is falling. Their financial returns have flattened or declined. And since global economic growth is likely to be slower than in the past, and lead to increasingly vicious competition, better sales and profits will be increasingly hard to come by.

3. Managers are overloaded with advice, much of which is clearly failing them. The use of just about any management tool is arbitrary, and as there are many ways to do things there's no evident downside to *not* using almost any popular tool.

4. Hype about "reinventing management" has not translated into reality. Most changes in management practice over the past 100 years have come in response to social, technological, or other contextual shifts. Not only has a small set of basics – the critical core – endured, but most seemingly "new" ideas are actually just more of the same.

5. Although yet-to-be-discovered management ideas may have some impact on business performance, no one knows what these might be or when to expect them. Meanwhile, failure to excel in *known* practices will ensure that firms do not exploit the opportunities that exist all around them, and that profits keep "falling through the cracks."

Finally – and this is the one that should concern us the most:

6. The most vocal critics of management scholars' research methods, the relevance and practical value of their outputs, their inability to add much that's new to management thinking, and the offerings and teaching methods of business schools are *insiders*, not *outsiders*. They include some of the world's most respected management professors and a growing number of business school deans.

As I'll show, there's compelling evidence that the way to build your competitive advantage, capture and keep customers, and stay ahead in the profit game lies in what you may already know but just don't focus on. That if you want to be a serious competitor today and tomorrow, less really is more and simpler is better.

What's Wrong With Management and How to Get It Right identifies the practices that have been shown to matter most, and explains why you need to master, embed, and relentlessly apply them in your company. This will guide you towards doing the right things right away, and ensure that your strategic conversation is properly framed and focused. It will also help you put whatever new ideas you come across into perspective, and evaluate them sensibly before you try them.

As in other fields, each of the practices is a *bundle* of routine behaviours, concepts, tools, or techniques.[7] If the practices are the *what* you must do, these are the *how*. There's a rich array of them, and there will be even more in the future because this is where most study and experimenting occurs. The material I refer to here offers a wealth of how-to advice, and I provide references to help you access it.[*] There's also plenty more from other sources. But I urge you to treat it with caution, and keep your toolkit as light as you can.

Your company is most likely to be successful if you get back to the principal drivers of business results – what you absolutely must obsess about, and why – and then apply them in the simplest, most practical way possible. You have to free up time to think. You have to move fast. You have to keep innovating and improving. So start doing that right now.

---

[*] Wherever possible, I've cited opinions and examples in chronological order, so you can track how management thinking has advanced. I've also spelled out whether these came from books, articles, or other sources, so you don't have to keep searching the endnotes for this information. In many instances, I could have cited numerous sources to support a particular point, but this work is not intended as a complete history of management thought, and doing that would have made it unnecessarily long.

Who needs another book?

This is a book for anyone who develops or uses management ideas. It's longer than I would like it to be, but since no one else has made the same argument, and it has implications for various audiences, I felt it necessary to set out the complete message.

The book is divided into two parts. The first looks at why management ideas matter, where they come from, and why we should be suspicious about their apparently magical powers. The second provides some practical advice for managers, and also suggests what my findings mean to business schools.

Here's the map:

PART ONE: WHERE WE ARE

Chapter 1: What Really Matters – A summary of what I sought to learn, how I went about it, and what I found.

Chapter 2: Reset! – The new business environment, why global economic growth could remain sluggish, why it's imperative that companies improve their performance, and why they cannot rely on management innovation as a game-changer.

Chapter 3: Hoping and Groping and **Chapter 4: Blockbusters Bust** – The seduction of management tools, and why you should avoid fads and flavours-of-the-month.

Chapter 5: Think Generic, Act Specific – Why management ideas matter, why managers chase after them, and why it's hard to know what works and what doesn't.

Chapter 6: The Thinkers – Who creates management ideas, and why they so often fail.

Chapter 7: Strategy Stalled, Chapter 8: People First, and **Chapter 9: Leadership Lost** – An overview of the origin and evolution of key ideas about strategy, people management, and leadership, and the lack of real progress in all of them.

Chapter 10: So Far, So Blah! – How the champions of "management innovation" have failed to change the fundamentals of management.

PART TWO: THE WAY FORWARD

Chapter 11: Essential Principles and **Chapter 12: The Critical Practices** – Important principles of management, and further explanation of the eight critical strategy practices.

Chapter 13: Implications for Business Schools – What the argument in this book could mean for the future of business education.

Appendix: What Popular Studies Tell Us – Checklists from recent bestselling management books.

If you're a manager in a hurry for answers, you might want to skip straight from Chapter 1 to Chapters 11 and 12, but you'll miss out on many insights that way, so perhaps take things more slowly. Scholars and consultants would do best to read it all.

My learning journey

Arriving at the conclusions I'll share with you here has been a long and arduous process of observation, study, reflection, and trial and error.

As a senior executive in two multinational companies, I learned first-hand how hard it is to shape strategy, align and motivate people, and deal with everyday pressures, dilemmas, and corporate politics.

As a strategy consultant, I get to see companies, warts and all. My work gives me an unclouded view of what they actually do or don't do, and what separates winners from losers. For three decades I've had a ringside seat from where I've watched managers wrestle with strategy. I've listened to them debate the best way to design it, been there as they struggled to frame and sell their views, and learned how hard it is to turn good plans into action. And I've seen them skip from fad to fad, searching desperately for "The One Big Answer" that would bring them success.

I've also lectured at various business schools, spoken in hundreds of conferences, facilitated hundreds of workshops, and written 10 other books (12, if you count complete rewrites of two of them) and many articles. The pressure to learn, and the interaction and feedback have been invaluable.

Like many other people, I got my first sense of what management is about from Peter Drucker. I devoured his books, and was awed by the breadth of his knowledge, his insights, and his ability to reduce complex matters to "one moving part."* And, of course, his incisive writing style made reading him a pleasure.

Later, I started to follow other experts such as Alfred Chandler, Richard Beckhard, Edgar Schein, Douglas McGregor, Abraham Maslow, Chris Argyris, Kenneth Andrews, Bruce Henderson, and Igor Ansoff. In marketing, I studied

---

* He once said, "All my best ideas have one moving part." (Jack Beatty, *The World According to Peter Drucker*, New York: The Free Press, 1998)

Philip Kotler and Theodore Levitt, and read avidly about advertising and selling. I was particularly taken by the work of Malcolm Knowles, a pioneer in the field of adult education, and by that of the psychologist Carl Rogers. I bought every business book I could lay my hands on, and subscribed to a range of business publications, including *Business Week, Fortune, Harvard Business Review, Sloan Management Review, California Management Review, Business Horizons, Organizational Dynamics, Human Resources Journal, Fast Company, Financial Times, The Wall Street Journal, Strategic Management Journal, Journal of Strategy, Strategy & Leadership, Wired, Inc., New Management,* and the various journals of the Academy of Management.

At the same time, I attended conferences, courses, and seminars, and visited and talked to prominent academics to better understand their ideas. And I spent hours every day studying the business environment – the economy, politics, social trends, technology, and the host of other factors that impact on companies and competitiveness.

When I began consulting in 1987, I used tools that were popular at the time – vision and mission statements, SWOT analyses, values exercises, and so on. I worked with ideas like Michael Porter's generic strategies and five forces, and explored systems thinking, idealized design, and scenarios. And then there were chaos and complexity theory, appreciative inquiry, core competence, knowledge management, lean processes, speed, resilience, reframing, blue oceans, disruption ...

I spent years working on change management, worker participation, productivity and quality improvement, and customer service – helping design strategy at the highest levels, and turning it into action on the front line in factories, mines, and offices. Along the way, I dealt with corporate boards, C-suite teams, and trade unionists; and with scientists, sales people, accountants, university administrators, and government officials who came to me with different problems requiring different interventions. I worked across almost every industry, on a range of assignments, from strategy development and execution to facilitating mergers; from resolving clashes between senior executives to improving sales and cutting costs.

My interest in a broad gamut of management topics has given me a keen sense of where key ideas came from, how they evolved and spread, and where they led – and of the *connections* between them. My interest in global issues helps me see those ideas in context, and appreciate the importance of context in the management of organizations. And my everyday experience provides a stream of rich lessons in what works in the real world and what doesn't.

Whenever I've come across a new management idea, I've asked: "What is the central message here?" And I've spent endless hours – often even weeks or months – thinking about what was different or special about them and how they fitted with other ideas. I filled notebooks with reflections and drawings to help me get to grips with what was there.

This book is the result.

A debt to Drucker

One thing you'll notice in these pages is my frequent references to Peter Drucker. I make no apologies for this, since he's an invaluable resource.

Drucker was a controversial figure. Despite being attached to various universities for much of his life, he produced little "academic" research, so he was never fully accepted as an academic and was always regarded as something of an outsider. His views on management – whether original or based on the work of others – were both wise and prescient. His social and economic predictions, on the other hand, were either brilliant or startlingly wrong. But whatever his flaws, his immodest claim to have "made a discipline" of management is hard to dispute.[8]

Not for nothing is he called "the father of modern management" – or, as Warren Bennis put it, "The most important management thinker of our time."[9] He made my job easy because almost anything worth saying about the subject today was first said by him – and usually said better than by anyone else. He made it more difficult too, because I could trace the roots of various "new" ideas to him more often than I needed to, and I didn't want to quote only him.

"Drucker's work, imaginative and iconoclastic, has provided a motherlode of thought within which members of the management academia quarry for the nuggets that will make them rich and famous," says John Tarrant in his 1976 biography *Drucker: The Man Who Invented the Corporate Society.*[10]

"The new gurus aren't rewriting Drucker," writes John Byrne in a 1992 *Businessweek* article. "More often than not, they're updating him by adding new ideas and tools to what Drucker has called 'the practice of management.'"[11]

Nothing has changed in more recent years. Drucker's ideas are everywhere in the latest books and articles about management. Few of today's authors will admit this, although since his death in November 2005 he has been getting more of the credit he deserves.

But let me be clear: this isn't a eulogy to Drucker or his ideas. Rather, it's about management today, what we need to know, and how much we already know.

In tracing the origin and evolution of ideas – and showing why so many of them are less than they're cracked up to be – I hope to persuade you to abandon any illusion that there are silver bullets for all your business problems. And to help you unclutter your management toolkit, develop a clear point of view about how to take your firm into the future, and frame your strategic conversation for success.

My focus here is on strategy and people, because strategy is the business activity that determines all others and is inextricably linked to all others, and people play a pivotal role in every function and process. So this book is, in effect, about the overall management of enterprise.

Although it refers a lot to theory, it's also rich in practical advice. There are no buzzwords here (except other people's). No wacky claims. No simplistic answers or snappy slogans. Just plain common sense drawn from the best management minds of the past century. So it's a book for people who want to make stuff happen, make a difference, and leave a positive legacy.

For the rest of you – well, there are plenty of gurus around with promises of magic, and the shelves of bookstores and libraries bulge with titles that will let you indulge your fantasies, but might cost you everything.

"The thought-fox"

When management ideas are reduced to their essence – to sound bites – subtlety and nuance are leached out of them. Their connectedness to each other and to their context is broken. The infinite possibilities of humanity and the accidental nature of achievement and progress are lost.

I happen to love poetry and Ted Hughes is my favourite poet. For me, his poem "The Thought-Fox" describes not only the process of writing a book – yes, even a "technical" book – but also the process of making strategy and running a business.

A prominent literary critic, Richard Webster, said this of the poem:

"The thought-fox" is a poem about writing a poem. Its external action takes place in a room late at night where the poet is sitting alone at his desk. Outside the night is starless, silent, and totally black ... a metaphor for the deeper and more intimate darkness of the poet's imagination in whose depths an idea is mysteriously stirring. At first the idea has no clear outlines; it is not seen but felt – frail and intensely vulnerable. The poet's task is to coax it out of formlessness and into fuller consciousness by the sensitivity of his language.[12]

The manager's task is much the same.

You might see it as being mostly about techniques, processes, systems, and structures, and take comfort from the promise of a clinical view of the practices you need. But that would be a bad mistake, and it's not my intention to have you make it.

Management is not simply a matter of pressing a few buttons or pulling this lever or that. It's a complicated and messy social process – a fusion of facts and feelings, decisions and discovery, certainty and serendipity, commitment and adaptability. There's a balance to be struck between purposefulness and opportunism.

The process of managing is obviously helped by knowing what produces results. But there's more to it. Like poetry-writing, it's about striving for results … and allowing results to come to you.

PART ONE

WHERE WE ARE

1

WHAT REALLY MATTERS

The most pressing management need of our time is *to know and apply the practices that make the difference between winning and losing in business.*

There's nothing new about this. But there's an urgency now to get it right. The role and responsibilities of companies are different today than they were in the past. Many of the challenges they face are unprecedented. They, more than any other social institution, determine our future. Troubled firms must be quickly fixed, and the strategies of those that are doing well must be sharpened or changed.

But merely improving what is won't suffice. Given rapidly changing external conditions, firms find themselves constantly at what Andy Grove, the former chairman of Intel, famously called "a strategic inflection point" – a moment of both extraordinary possibilities and significant risks.[1] Choices made today, tomorrow, and next week determine their long-term prospects. And as the world continues to change, and competition becomes ever more hostile and the need for growth more pressing, all have to keep adapting and progressing to produce new results.

Over the past century, countless people have claimed to understand what makes companies tick and what makes some more competitive than others. They've produced, packaged, and peddled a truly astonishing amount of advice. But the outcome of their efforts is more often than not another minor tweak to existing knowledge rather than the invention of something new.

It is true that significant insights and ideas have been produced in areas such as finance, accounting, marketing, operations, and decision-making. But in the two whose impact on business performance overshadows all others – strategy and people management – we've seen little progress. Our understanding of how to compete and win evolves at a glacial pace. The breakthroughs would fill a thimble.

Most of what's touted as "thought leadership" is, in fact, "thought *follower-ship.*" It hitches a ride on what we already know, perhaps from a slightly different angle, or dressed up with a new name or information from a new study, but adds little to our understanding of how to manage for advantage. With few exceptions, "new" ideas are at best marginal when it comes to utility. The language describing them might change, but the foundational concepts hold firm. "In thought leadership terms," says Fiona Czerniawska, an expert on the management consulting business, "2012 was the equivalent of 1916: stuck in the mud."[2]

Bluntly put: in one of humankind's most crucial areas of knowledge and practice, we're going nowhere slowly.

Most of what spews forth never reaches managers. Much of what does reach them is confusing rather than enlightening; distracting at best, useless at worst. All too often, this results in unnecessary costs and work rather than better business results.

This should be a crisis, but it doesn't have to be.

As Max Bazerman and Michael Watkins point out in their book *Predictable Surprises*, "a predictable surprise arises when leaders unquestionably had all the data and insight they needed to recognize the potential for, even the inevitability of, a crisis, but failed to respond with effective preventative action."[3] We know what we need to know about management. It is clear what practices we need. We have them already. There is no need to create nasty surprises for ourselves by persisting in a hunt for different truths.

Finding the right question

The most important question in management is, "What is the question?" If you don't start there, you have no focus and are sure to wind up with unhelpful answers. So strategy begins with clarity about the specific problem or challenge you need to deal with.

Starting in the early 1980s, I became interested in knowing:

- Why do some companies, facing similar challenges to others, stand out from the crowd and consistently get superior results?
- Why is failure – of products, projects, and firms themselves – so common?
- Why, with so much information and advice about management so easily, widely, and quickly available, is corporate performance so erratic?
- Why do popular management ideas seem to work in some organizations, but not others?
- How can various management ideas be made more useful to more executives?

These issues have challenged many people. You don't have to look far to find opinions on all of them. But you need to carefully weigh those up and not be too quick to assume that any answer is either right or final. Strong views are sure to prompt further research, bringing new information and interpretations. What appears to hold true at one moment, and to make absolute sense, will inevitably be disputed and possibly refuted.

As the business context changes, so do fashions in business thinking. At any time, certain ideas hold the high ground and crowd out others; then those are displaced and different ones hold sway. Overarching themes such as globalization, outsourcing and offshoring (and now, *reshoring** and next-shoring†), sustainability, diversity, or emerging markets take hold and shift strategic conversations in new directions. Ideas about how to manage burst onto the scene, stir a flurry of activity, then give way to others. What's "trending" today is ho-hum or forgotten tomorrow.

One way to deal with my questions was to stay with them, perhaps even add more, and keep probing. Another was to get more specific and ask fewer questions. The first option would be interesting but unlikely to produce what I wanted any time soon, so I quickly abandoned it. The second would cut to the chase. So I asked, "What's the *intent* of my initial questions? What exactly am I trying to find out and explain?" This enabled me to narrow my search and explore three new questions:

1. What do winning companies do that also-rans don't?
2. Does success depend on particular management practices, and are they necessary in all companies?
3. Do we know what we need to know about them?

Concentrating my efforts refuelled my belief that we were overcomplicating things, repeating ourselves, and searching for answers we didn't need. That in our desperation to pump up business performance, we were overreaching.

In most organizations, too many concepts, tools, and initiatives compete for attention. Managers themselves create too much work. And much of it doesn't meld into a coherent process.

So I began to wonder if there were *imperatives* – things that firms *must* do, not what they say they do or would like to do. Ideas that had stood the test of time and mattered everywhere. Practices that would focus management attention where it was most needed and would have the most impact.

This brought me to just one question:

Are there *must-do* practices that make companies competitive, and if so, what are they?

But where to start looking for *that* answer?

---

* Bringing operations back to a home country.

† A McKinsey term invented to highlight the need to decide whether to manufacture close to sources of innovation or to customers.

The truth is well hidden

It would be impossible to consider every shred of knowledge about a subject as broad as management, or every factor influencing business outcomes. There are many aspects to managing, and they're bound up with each other and with a host of exogenous factors over which executives have little or no control. Part art, part craft, part science, management involves analysis and logic, imagination, instinct, attitude, skill, luck – and more. The fortunes of a business are, in large part, a consequence of what happens outside its walls. All of which makes it hard to put your finger on the exact causes of specific business results.

Inevitably, one element such as culture or strategy gets highlighted, while others such as resource endowments, patents, past commitments, timing, or luck are overlooked or downplayed. Or a leader's humility, decisiveness, or foresight is singled out as his great strength – and the reason for his success – when the truth lies elsewhere. Or executives claim that one or other theory or tool worked for them, when in reality it played only a minor role in their success. So it's common for firms held up as exemplars one year to hit the skids the next (think Enron, ABB, Nokia, Bear Stearns, Kodak, Dell, Tesco, or Monitor Consulting – the list is endless). Even analysts whose job it is to study particular firms and tell investors about their prospects are often hopelessly wrong.

The influence and longevity of management ideas have differed greatly. Some had a short shelf life: they took off fast, but never gained traction and quickly vanished. Some came and went, then reappeared. Very few have topped the charts and stayed there. You'd think those that made it would be worth paying attention to.

But maybe not.

Misleading promises

There are more fads and flaky ideas in management than reliable guidance, so finding the good stuff is a challenge. A wealth of studies claim to tell us what works, but their rigour and value vary. There are gems among them, certainly, but there's also dross. A lot of what passes for "management research" is deeply flawed, and even apparently thorough efforts to get to the truth can yield dodgy results (see Chapter 4).

Many success recipes are rustled up by people who skim over the surface of organizations and scoop up stories, analogies, or other "evidence" to make a point. The greatest strength of these authors is their ability to coin aphorisms that grab attention and stick in your mind, to spin a gripping yarn, or to weave seductive arguments from the flimsiest of raw material.

The fact that some idea is put on a pedestal or appears to be widely used doesn't mean it leads to whatever results are attributed to it. Hype often outweighs common sense. Popularity contests are unlikely to yield the answers managers crave.

The fact that a business book becomes a bestseller is no assurance of new thinking, and may say nothing about the practical worth of the contents. You can't assume that reprint orders for journal articles – or even citations – are a testimonial to either originality or merit. Or that success on the speaking circuit is evidence of a useful message. For once any halfway decent idea becomes public its author will inevitably be joined by others, many with their own take on it. But what appears to reflect "the wisdom of crowds" might be no more than opportunism or a herd mentality at work.

When something is repeated often enough or loudly enough, there's a chance it'll come to be seen as reality. This happens a lot in the management ideas industry. What seems to get results for one business is copied by others, and gets some press. Someone picks up on what's happening, and claims to know the reason. This gets more attention, and triggers more "studies." The next thing you know, a "theory" is born.

The noise rises. Managers clamour for information about this new "silver bullet." As the numbers using it grow, it gains "best practice" status. If anyone is bothered by its dubious pedigree, they either say nothing or voice their concern in some academic journal where it's unnoticed and soon forgotten.

So what are harried executives to believe?

Are the practices they need the eight from *In Search of Excellence*?[4] The nine from *Built to Last*?[5] The three from *The Discipline of Market Leaders*?[6] The seven from *Good to Great*,[7] or the six from *Great by Choice*[8] (both books authored by Jim Collins)? Or what about the five from *Staying Power*?[9] Or perhaps the "four + two" from *What Really Works*?[10] The seven from *Vanguard Management*?[11] The nine from *The Agenda*?[12] "The Four Principles of Enduring Success," advocated by Christian Stadler in a *Harvard Business Review* article?[13]* Or the "Three Rules for Making a Company Truly Great," from another *HBR* article, by Michael E. Raynor and Mumtaz Ahmed?[14]

All these formulas are the outcome of hard labour by really clever people. But who's right? The criteria for "success" and the methodology for understanding it differ from one of these studies to the next. There is sound advice in all of them. But although there are some overlaps, there are sharp differences too. So how might we decide what list to go with? Can we choose, or do we need them all? Do *all* companies need to go the same route? Would it make sense to cherry-pick the ideas we fancy, and cobble them together into a new list?

---

* He added a fifth rule in a follow-up book (*Enduring Success*, Stanford: Stanford University Press, 2011), but I'm only including four here.

Or – here's a worry! – maybe *none* of these is what we need. After all, there's a plethora of advice hidden in the dark corners of management literature. Maybe there are other ideas we haven't heard of, that haven't been sexily packaged, or that haven't been given the recognition they deserve.

Opinions are everywhere. But which to consider?

I have no doubt that many people will swear they were helped by these books and articles. Many more will read them in future and join their fan clubs.

But consider this:

Between them, those publications list a total of 67 practices that apparently give winning firms their edge (see Appendix). Their authors make a persuasive case for each of them, and it's easy to see why they've proved attractive to a great many managers. However, only a handful of them qualify for the "must-do" label. The rest are optional extras you may be tempted to adopt and that might boost your business – or not. They might be usefully *added* to a more fundamental practices, but are no substitute for them. None will do you much good if you don't have the basics in place first, and work at them relentlessly.

And it's those basics I'll tell you about here.

Towards a hypothesis

When scholars in any field set out to study a topic or a phenomenon, they need some focus. They typically have one or more questions in mind, and maybe some sense of what the answers might be. From these they develop an initial theory or hypothesis which frames what they see and suggests what it means. Then, to substantiate it, they cycle through a process – perhaps a lengthy one – of gathering more information, refining their views, sharing them to get feedback, and making further adjustments.[15] Any discrepancies or anomalies – gaps between what they first imagined and what they discover – lead to reframing.[16]

When I began studying management, I had only the vaguest idea of what it was about. I had no preconceived ideas about it and no focus. I just wanted to learn. My only interest was in what leading authorities in various aspects of management could tell me. So I didn't proceed in a structured or disciplined way. Gathering information was a haphazard matter, in which I simply soaked up whatever I could lay my hands on.

At first, not surprisingly, I learned a great deal. But quite soon, I noticed that many of the same ideas were cropping up again and again. In different contexts and guises, to be sure, but there they were: a handful of practices that ran through many decades. Often, they were dealt with in a novel way, or artfully presented in new language, using new examples and bolstered by new data. But when I asked, "What is the underlying message?" it was clearly just a repeat. And as the same few ideas were reaffirmed, from this angle and that, so did evidence of their value pile up. They clearly mattered to both management thinking and corporate performance.

When I started working on this book in 2006, I had a different theme in mind. But the more research I did, and the more I thought about what needed saying about management, the more apparent it became that this should be the story. No one else was telling it.

Many other people have torn into theories or warned that managers are overloaded with them. Many have written at length about one or more of the practices I have identified as critical. But to the best of my knowledge, no one has surveyed the management field in the way I've done, or labelled certain practices critical, or explained why that is so. Nor has anyone suggested that there is a "strategy system" which must be applied in its totality.

So I had to dig even deeper into what we knew. I had to look back more systematically at the origins and evolution of management thought and practice, while also keeping pace with current work to be sure some whizz-bang new idea didn't escape me.

Critical practices

My method wasn't scientific. It didn't involve cutting-edge research methodologies, extensive fieldwork or data analysis, or statistical wizardry. Instead, I combined years of intensive and wide-ranging study with lessons from the school of hard knocks, to look at what management thinkers say through the lens of what practising managers do.

As you can imagine, it would be possible with little effort to mention countless concepts and cite hundreds of renowned experts, and even more examples and stories of what apparently worked where, when, and how, and what didn't. But since strategy and people, more than anything else, stood out as the most important determinants of business results, they became my focus.

As I progressed, I filtered what I learned through a fine "sieve" (Figure 1.1) to identify insights or ideas that:

1. Were *original* – not repeated, rehashed, or re-branded;
2. Had *endured* over multiple years;
3. Had *been rigorously studied and validated*;
4. *Underpinned the latest thinking* about management;
5. Were *critical* to the performance of a company;
6. Were *generic* in that they applied across countries, companies, and industries;
7. Were *required in all circumstances*;
8. Were likely to *remain* critical in the future.

Figure 1.1

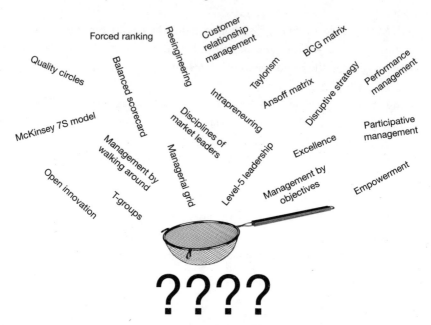

What fell through as I trawled the history of management ideas were eight practices – the essence of 100 years of management thought:

#1. **Growth leadership** – Effective leadership that's committed to growth, and to achieving it by growing people.

#2. **Fast learning and adaptation** – The ability to sense and make sense of change and act on it and learn from it faster than competitors.

#3. **Focus, value, costs** – Clarity about where and how to compete, and a relentless effort to drive value up and costs down for the "right" customer.

#4. **Business-model innovation** – Continual reinvention of the way value is created, delivered, captured, and shared.

#5. **Resource and capability development and leverage** – Accessing, attracting, acquiring, and building the strengths needed to compete, and using them to maximum effect.

#6. **Stakeholder alignment and support** – Persuading individuals and organizations with any interest in a firm to "vote" for it rather than against it.

#7. **Smart sequencing and pacing** – Doing the right things in the right order and at the right time.

#8. **Disciplined execution** – Having a deliberate and systematic way to turn intentions into action with sound outcomes. (Figure 1.2.)

Figure 1.2

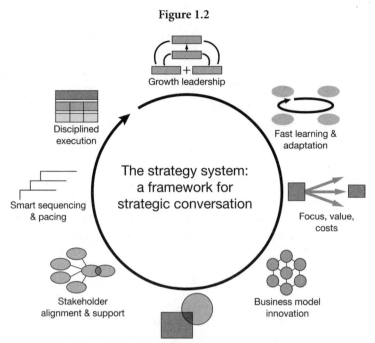

These practices appeared time and again, in different guises or explained in different ways. There was no escaping them. And if one expert or observer after another was saying much the same thing – sometimes decades apart, and maybe couched in different terms and presented from a fresh angle, in a different context, or with fresh evidence and reasoning – then surely that meant something.

And indeed it does.

The eight practices encompass virtually everything a firm does to compete. They've always been key to business performance, and always will be. They apply to every company in every industry and every part of the world. Singly or collectively, they underpin almost every "new" idea about management. This is what managers have to excel at.

Together, they help you frame your strategic conversation, and ensure that you focus on the activities that really will produce superior results. They also provide a useful means by which to unpack and understand your competitors' strategies. And they can be used by investors, analysts, and journalists to make sense of a firm's current situation and its prospects.

These practices add up to *a way of working* that involves all your people. So they must be understood across your organization. And you have to keep drumming home the need not only to work at all of them, but also to work at them as *an interdependent system*.

23

At first glance, you might see this as an obvious and underwhelming list. You might argue that the airtime given to a practice proves nothing (for reasons I've already provided). But such concern doesn't hold when an idea is validated by copious research and confirmed by many experts coming at it from different perspectives, and when it survives wave after wave of additional study, thoughtful debate, and harsh criticism. Or when it obviously is the essence of other ideas and proves useful to managers in a range of firms and over many years. Or when there is no logical case *against* it, no sensible alternative, and no apparent reason *not* to apply it.

You might, as one professor did, dismiss these practices as mere "tickets to the game," so rudimentary as to not be worth a second glance. But that would be a huge mistake. They not only get you into the game, but also keep you there, and enable you to win. And hardly a day goes by without news of businesses that have lost their way or failed because:

1. Their leaders lack the will or skill to grow, and the growth of their people is not their priority;
2. The world around them changes faster than they do;
3. They're unfocused, don't make a difference that matters to customers, don't keep offering them new value, and don't keep driving their costs down;
4. Their business models become obsolete;
5. They don't develop the resources and capabilities they need, and don't get the most bang for their buck;
6. Their stakeholders are at odds with them;
7. They act without a sense of what to do and when to do it;
8. They're unable to implement their plans.

On the other hand, it would be a stretch to argue that any firm failed as a direct result of not using some high-profile tool such as a BCG matrix or five-forces analysis, *kaizen*, CRM, or a balanced scorecard. Helpful though any of these may be, *not* using them might not matter. They're means to an end, not an end in themselves. And there are many other ways to skin a cat.

Success, insofar as managers can determine it, depends 100 per cent on the eight critical practices. The same cannot be said of almost any other management idea.

The way the practices were *applied* 100 years ago – or even a month or a week ago – was unquestionably and often radically different than the way they're applied today. But you can't get away from the fact that the practices in essence are now more critical than ever. In fact, they're *obligatory*.

But aren't there many strategic practices besides these eight that you need to consider?

You're probably itching to add others. But when you subject them to the various tests I used, it'll be apparent to you that they don't warrant being termed "critical." They may help you *implement* these practices, but if that is not your express intention, you don't need them. Blurring the distinction between *must-do* and *nice-to-do* leads you straight into the trap you should avoid: of jamming too many tools into your management toolkit, and too much onto your action list.

This is not to say that mastering the practices will on its own guarantee your success. Of course it won't. Strategy isn't a simple paint-by-numbers process. It's dynamic and surpriseful, as it occurs within a complex environment and is subject to countless variables. The ideas you use are only as good as the human skills with which you apply them.

But what is clear is that what we need to know about management is a lot less complicated than it's made out to be.

When Peter Drucker got his first consulting assignment, a massive study of General Motors, in 1943, he "knew nothing about management. I gave myself a quickie course," he recalled, "finding to my surprise that I could read all of the significant books about management in two days. There were just seven books on general management, in all languages except Japanese, and most of them repeated each other."[17]

Now, 70 years later, we have more information about the topic than Drucker would ever have imagined. But "significant"? Less than you might think. Repetition? Volumes of it.

Intensifying my search

While I was thinking about all this and bouncing my thoughts off various people, three things happened that caused me to wonder whether I was on the right track.

First came a number of articles, books, seminars, and conferences about "management innovation," which generated a great deal of excitement.

Then came the global financial crisis, which turned into a deep and protracted economic slump, forcing companies to rethink their management beliefs and scramble for salvation in both emergency surgery and new ideas.

And third, it became evident that the business models which had worked so well for many firms were suddenly under threat from challengers who were upending the status quo in one industry after another.

All this spurred me to yet more study and reflection, and brought me to the hypothesis on which this book is based:

> *What firms need today is not new ways to manage, so much as to apply what's already known and proved to work. There is a core set of eight management*

practices that have been around for decades, and have been shown positively to affect business results. They're "generic," in the sense that they apply to all companies worldwide, and they're critical, not optional. Together they comprise a "strategy system" in which various tools and techniques can be used to achieve specific aims, and provide a frame for effective strategic conversation.

Of course, a statement like this wouldn't go unchallenged. It would irk anyone involved in the study of management, and disappoint managers itching for breakthroughs.

But consider why each practice is necessary … and what the alternative might be.

Figure 1.3

THE CRITICAL STRATEGY PRACTICES	WHAT THEY MEAN	THE ALTERNATIVE
#1. Growth leadership	Leadership that is committed to growth, and to achieving it by growing people	Leaders not driven by growth, or obsessed with delivering it through the growth of their people
#2. Fast learning & adaptation	Understand and act on change – and learn from the process – faster than your competitors	Fail to see or understand changes in your world, and respond to them in your own good time
#3. Focus, value, costs	Focus on the "right" customer and relentlessly drive value up and costs down	Chase everyone ("spray and pray") with offerings they don't value, and let your costs keep rising
#4. Business model innovation	Constantly redesign the way value is created, delivered, and captured	Stick with business as usual – more of the same even when it no longer works
#5. Resource & capability development & leverage	Acquire, access, and grow the resources and capabilities you need to compete, and get the most from them	Go into battle with forces that are ill-equipped and lack the skills to win, and fail to use all your firepower
#6. Stakeholder alignment & support	Create win-win relationships to get all stakeholders on your side	Leave stakeholders to pursue their own agendas … maybe to work against you
#7. Smart sequencing & pacing	Do the right things in the right order, and at the right time	Do everything all at once, as fast as you can or as slowly as you like
#8. Disciplined execution	Have a systematic way to get the right things done	Set vague goals, assign no clear responsibilities, apply no pressure for results, shift priorities, and tolerate non-delivery

Testing the theory

How sure can you be that all this is true? Because the best evidence we have about management says so.

Whether it's from executives, employees, academics, consultants, journalists, books, peer-reviewed journals, or wherever, nothing contradicts it. So I'm as sure as anyone can be that my search criteria enabled me to come to a sound and useful point of view.

The eight practices that meet those criteria are the core of all management thinking and recur constantly in management literature. But that alone couldn't be a reason to highlight them.

So I turned to five well-known tests of management ideas. And I added two more because the practical nature of the topic means that knowledge for the sake of knowledge cannot be enough. Visible, meaningful results must follow (Figure 1.4).

Figure 1.4

TESTS OF MANAGEMENT THEORY

The accepted criteria

1. **It should have a sound base.** The sample size, methodology, and evidence should provide confidence in it.
2. **It should have predictive power.** ("If you do A you'll get B.")
3. **It should have explanatory power.** ("This is why A causes B.")
4. **It should "travel."** It should lead to similar outcomes across different organizations, in different industries and countries.
5. **The circumstances in which it works or doesn't work, and the reasons, should be clear.** ("It works when A, B, or C are happening; but not D, E, or F – and this is why.")

My additional criteria

6. **It should be practical.** Managers need to be able to use it.
7. **It should significantly advance the practice of management.**

Every one of the practices passes every test.

Still not satisfied? Well, turn back to page 21 and apply my initial eight-point test. Or consider the alternatives to these practices (Figure 1.3).

Every one of the eight critical strategy practices passes on all counts.

Now, combine those practices into one approach and apply those tests to it.

Again a 100 per cent pass!

Given the many decades of research and thought that had gone into identifying and explaining these practices, I felt no need to do further "primary" studies[*]

---

[*] Original, formal research based on established scholastic methodology.

myself. Nor did I see any need for a "meta-study"* to validate prior studies by other people.

This book isn't based on interesting commonalities among a few companies. Nor have I picked a tool or technique that seemed to work here or there, and suggested it could work for everyone. But what I have got to is a set of practices that have been shown, again and again over many decades, by countless experts, to apply across companies, industries, and countries. A set of practices that, separately and together, meet every accepted test of a management theory – plus two of my own.

Although I continue to hunt for new information and insights, constantly test my own assumptions, and keep thinking about these matters, I find no reason to change my hypothesis. I'm confident that the eight practices I've focused on are the ones managers need most.

I'm confident too that these practices are not just necessary, but *critical* to every organization. I've found no example of any firm – in books, articles, annual reports, case studies, business school classes, or wherever – that did well while flouting them. And of the hundreds of companies I've consulted to, I can't think of one that might have done better by doing something else.

There is no time, place, or circumstance in which the practices don't matter or won't assist management performance – except when managers fail to apply them well.

Everything you know about strategy and management – every concept, tool, technique, model, framework, or whatever – is peripheral to the eight critical strategy practices. If you don't work at these, nothing else matters. If you do, all those other things become more useful and more effective.

No manager can afford to turn up the potentially positive impact of these practices.

No manager can rationally say, "The practices don't apply to me," or "They won't work in my industry," or "I have better things to do."

Nor can they afford to wait for some guru to come up with smarter answers. For much as the possibility of a great leap forward might excite executives under pressure to improve results, the likelihood of one appearing is slim to zero.

Learning made simple

The development of managerial skills is a major challenge to any firm, yet it's mostly an unstructured, ad hoc, and sporadic process which leaves people with an array of tools, no linkage between them, and no clear understanding of how to use them. Through an array of courses, seminars, and workshops, exposure to experts,

---

* A study of studies.

reading, workplace socializing, and experience, they pick up ideas and develop their own points of view about how to manage. Little of what they learn is transferred into the workplace, so there's no way to calculate the return on investment.

Given what's at stake, this makes no sense. If, instead, companies used the strategy system I've described as a framework for management development, they would be better off in three ways:

1. Their approach to development would be consistent and coherent, and their people would learn what really matters. With everyone exposed to the same set of ideas, they'd have a common language and communication would be improved.
2. By promoting one management approach rather than letting everyone go their own way, they'd be able to give their full attention to deepening the expertise in the critical practices of individuals and of their organization as a whole.
3. They would facilitate faster, more effective learning. "In order for someone to capture complex, experience-based knowledge," say Dorothy Leonard and Walter Swap in their book *Deep Smarts*, "the person's brain has to contain receptors – neural structures that are the physical representations of frameworks, domain knowledge, or prior experiences – to which the current inputs can be connected."[18] Similarly, Lev Semyonovich Vygotsky, a 20th-century developmental psychologist, wrote of the importance of "scaffolding" or systematic support in helping children learn. Initially, he said, it would come from an outsider, but later should be a product of internal conversations.[19]

The eight critical practices provide the "receptors" or "scaffolding" people need to receive, stack, and store information and experience. Give them these as a starting point, and they have something to build on.

In a 1959 *Harvard Business Review* article, "Thinking Ahead: The Potential of Management Science," Drucker wrote:

Managing will always remain somewhat of an "art"; the talent, experience, vision, courage, and character of the managers will always be major factors in their performance and that of their enterprise. But this is true of medicine and doctors, too. And, as with medicine, management and managers – especially the most highly endowed and most highly accomplished managers – will become the more effective as their foundation of organized systematic knowledge and organized systematic search grows stronger, and as their roots in a real discipline of management and entrepreneurship grow deeper. That such a discipline is possible, the work already done in management science proves.

But no one, I am also convinced can survey the work to date without being worried at the same time. The potential is there – but it is in danger of being frittered away. Instead of a management science which supplies knowledge, concepts, and discipline to manager and entrepreneur, we may be developing a "management gadget bag" of techniques for the efficiency expert.[20]

Fifty years later, when terms like speed, agility, resilience, responsiveness, and adaptability trip so freely from the tongues of managers, that "management gadget bag" has become a dead weight on their performance. Yet life doesn't need to be so hard. We have the foundation of knowledge that we need. What's left is to apply it.

First steps to new results

Albert Einstein famously said, "It is insanity to keep doing the same thing and expect different results." So if you want new sales and profits, you need to start by asking, "What must we do differently to get new results?"

My answer:

Embed the critical strategy practices into your organization, by using them to frame your strategic conversation

This probably means you need to change many things.

During the years I've worked to learn about management, clarify what we know about strategy, simplify how we make and implement it, and help my clients craft and conduct effective strategic conversations, I've become increasingly sure that if leaders want to make a difference, they should:

- **Dump a lot of what they *think* they know about managing and get to work with what we really do know.**
- **Sweep aside most of their current theories, fads, themes, and tools, "clear the decks," and make a fresh start.** Clutter is distracting and slows things down.
- **Fight complexity for all they're worth.** Simplicity is their friend and they need to embrace it, worship it, and live it.
- **Accept that great results come slowly and settle in for the long haul.** Business success is hardly ever an overnight matter. For most firms, it comes over time, through relentless practice, experimentation, learning, improvement, adaptation, and resource and capacity building.

We'll return to some detail about the eight critical practices in Chapter 12. Meanwhile, test your strategic fitness using the following score sheet (Figure 1.5), and keep checking your performance over coming months.

Figure 1.5

TEST YOUR STRATEGIC FITNESS

PRACTICE	RATING					SCORE
	1	2	3	4	5	
#1. Growth leadership						
#2. Fast learning & adaptation						
#3. Focus, value, costs						
#4. Business model innovation						
#5. Resource & capability development & leverage						
#6. Stakeholder alignment & support						
#7. Smart sequencing & pacing						
#8. Disciplined execution						
TOTAL						/40

Rate your company on each practice, using the 1–5 scale, where 1 = poor and 5 = excellent. Total the scores – maximum 40 points.

2

RESET!

The global financial crisis that blew up in late 2008 caused panic in companies selling everything from computer chips to luxury cruises. The "rules of the game" in virtually every industry were overturned by the "Great Recession"* that followed. "The new normal" and "business unusual" became the mantras of CEOs everywhere.

There's no way to know how many firms explicitly concern themselves with strategy, or have explicit strategies, but it's probably fair to assume that most large ones and even many smaller ones do. And that most of them put a great deal of time and effort into crafting those strategies – often aided by consultants, market researchers, economists, industry experts, trendspotters, and scenario gurus.

But it's an equally fair bet that when the crunch came, most of them were caught off guard. As headlines told us, the best-laid plans of some of the best companies in the world were suddenly wrong for the times.

Economic uncertainties

It seems only yesterday that forecasters talked of a "long boom" fuelled by factors such as the spread of democracy, new technologies, new forms of energy, a "European Renaissance," a growing middle class, and "the emergence of women."[1] Today, however, the picture is not as rosy.

Seven years after the Great Recession started, the world remains in what the military calls a VUCA state – volatile, uncertain, complex, and ambiguous. Current events will have severe social, political, and economic implications for many years to come.

The outlook for the global economy is murky. Recovery from the crisis is taking much longer than from any other in recent history – and certainly longer

---

* Also termed "The Great Contraction."

than anyone foresaw. Despite some positive signs here and there, and upward revisions in some indicators, uncertainty remains high. It seems that as soon as there's a hint of better times almost anywhere, hopes are dashed by new reports showing all is not well.

In fact, fears are rising that we're stuck in an era – *decades* long, perhaps – of weak demand and anaemic growth. Few observers see a quick, sharp, or sustained upturn almost anywhere.

A gigantic global economic experiment is under way, whose results won't be known for many years. Economists are at odds about how to get the world out of its deep funk. Policymakers are nervous about doing what sounds necessary, lest their angry citizens vote them out of office. Pension funds and personal wealth have been decimated. Unemployment is soaring; tens of millions of young people, especially, can't find jobs and they face a bleak future. Although poverty levels have fallen steeply since 1981, new data shows that 2.8 billion people – one-third of the global total – exist just above the poverty line on $2 to $10 per day. Fewer people in work means less income and consumption, less demand growth, lower confidence, and less investment. All these things together put a further brake on recovery.

In recent decades, economic rebalancing saw wealth and power shifting from the US, Europe, and Japan towards the developing world. But optimism that this would continue was overblown. Many poor countries benefitted from a surge in demand for commodities, thanks largely to China's rapid growth, but as the Chinese economy cooled, so have its imports slowed. Some countries enjoyed a quick boost from manufacturing; but new technologies have made that sector more dependent on finance and skills, and global competition even for low-end products is white-hot. Falling oil prices provide a windfall for some nations, but strangle others.

Meanwhile, despite the efforts of the World Trade Organization, and of talks that have gone on for years in hopes of creating a new and more open trade regime, protectionism is increasing. "Globalization has clearly paused," says *The Economist* in an October 2013 special report. "A simple measure of trade intensity, world exports as a share of world GDP, rose steadily from 1986 to 2008 but has been flat since. Global capital flows, which in 2007 topped $11 trillion, amounted to barely a third of that figure last year. Cross-border direct investment is also well down on its 2007 peak."[2]

Productivity growth, which is the key to prosperity, is also under threat. The US Conference Board warns that the world's ability to turn labour and capital into goods and services is declining.[3] For the past four years, says *The Observer*, "British businesses have struggled on, producing largely the same things with

33

the same labour force. Where they have gained is by shelving plans to buy new equipment and paying people less – either by reducing their wages in real terms or by reducing their hours."[4]

In an op-ed piece in *The New York Times*, Stephen King, chief economist at HSBC, points out: "Even before the Great Recession, rich countries were seeing their tax revenues weaken, social expenditures rise, government debts accumulate and creditors fret thanks to lower economic growth rates.... We are reaching end times for Western affluence.... It's now abundantly clear that forecasters have been too optimistic, boldly projecting rates of growth that have failed to transpire." The reason, he says, is that five one-off developments – the rapid expansion of global trade, financial innovations, social safety nets, the arrival of women in the workforce, and improved education – led to rapid growth in the last century, but will not be repeated. "Policy makers simply pray for a strong recovery," says King. "They opt for the illusion because the reality is too bleak to bear."[5]

King's comments appeared in October 2013, just as politicians in Washington drove a recovering US economy into gridlock. And at the World Bank/IMF annual meeting which began just then, the IMF's chief economist, Oliver Blanchard, warned of "potentially major disruptions in financial markets, both in the US and abroad." This at a time when "Advanced economies are gradually strengthening" while "growth in emerging-market economies has slowed."[6]

Less than a month later, at the IMF annual research conference, Larry Summers, the former US Treasury Secretary, who had just been beaten to the job as Governor of the US Federal Reserve by Janet Yellen, argued that "secular stagnation" might have set in.[7] Commenting on Summers' speech, Nobel laureate Paul Krugman wrote: " the evidence suggests that we have become an economy whose normal state is one of mild depression, whose brief episodes of prosperity occur only thanks to bubbles and unsustainable borrowing."[8]

A resurgence in demand in developed markets is obviously vital to future growth – and the prospects for that aren't good. Equally important is a resurgence of *innovation*. But here too, notwithstanding excitement about breakthroughs coming out of headline-making firms like Samsung, Amazon, Tesla, Google, and Dyson,[*] there are signs of malaise.

Robert Gordon, an economics professor at Northwestern University, believes growth is close to stalling and may never get back to previous levels. The pace of

---

[*] These firms get a lot of media coverage, though in the *Forbes* list of " The World's Most Innovative Companies," Amazon ranks 7th, Google 47th, and Apple 79th, and neither Tesla nor Dyson feature in the top 100. (Jeff Dyer and Hal Gregerson, "How We Rank the World's Most Innovative Companies 2013," *Forbes*, 14 August 2013)

innovation is slowing, he says, and transformational breakthroughs such as we've seen in the past 100 years won't be repeated.[9]

From available evidence, says Nobel Prize winner Edmund Phelps, America no longer produces "the rate of innovation and high job satisfaction it did up to the 1970s."[10] And another Nobel laureate, Joseph Stiglitz, says it's puzzling that while there's worldwide admiration "for the type of technological innovation symbolized by Silicon Valley ... it is difficult to detect the benefits of this innovation in GDP statistics ... when all is said and done, the contribution of recent technological innovations to long-term growth in living standards may be substantially less than the enthusiasts claim."[11]

Falling education standards in many countries won't help. An October 2013 OECD report on adult literacy, numeracy, and problem solving found that "in the United States, as in Britain, the literacy and numeracy skills of young people coming into the labor market are no better than those who are about to retire. Americans who are 55 to 65 perform about average in literacy skills, but young Americans rank the lowest among their peers in the countries surveyed."[12] Other countries, too, are battling to lift their educational standards and prepare youngsters for the jobs of tomorrow.

"So far," says economist Kenneth Rogoff, "every prediction that mankind's lot will worsen, from Malthus to Marx, has turned out to be spectacularly wrong. Technological progress has trumped obstacles to growth." But that's "no guarantee that a broadly similar trajectory can be maintained throughout this century." Challenges he foresees include "externalities" such as environmental degradation; perceived unfairness of the economic system, which could make it politically unsustainable; ageing populations; and the many technological issues that require government regulation – from governments that may not be up to the job.[13]

Globalization and a scramble for customers mean that competition is becoming more and more hostile. "The Eurozone, Japan and emerging markets are all trying to export their way out of trouble," says BlackRock, the world's biggest investor. "Who is going to buy all this stuff? The maths does not work."[14]

Meanwhile, even as firms try to make the numbers work for themselves, stakeholders are becoming increasingly outspoken and powerful, there are more of them to worry about, and new ones raise their voices every day. New technologies, a rash of new regulation, workforce diversity, demographics, climate change, shifting social values and behaviours, geopolitical tensions, and many other factors add to this bewildering mix.

In a 1999 article in *Sloan Management Review*, Sumantra Ghoshal, Christopher Bartlett, and Peter Moran predicted: "If downsizing, cost-cutting, and 'getting lean and mean' were the mantras of the past decade, the desire for growth and renewal will be the major concern of the next."[15] Yet while it is true that many firms are working hard at growth and renewal, the business media tell us daily about swingeing job cuts, asset sales, and other measures to get slim and fit.

Economic cycles have persisted for centuries. If the past replays itself, the current slump will end sooner or later, and better conditions will return. Companies will invest more of their vast cash hoard, and customers will open their wallets.

But even if that happens, systemic changes on many fronts will inhibit growth. The frenzied business environment will not calm down, and the stresses and demands on managers won't abate.

A worrying possibility, now being floated by a growing number of economists and analysts, is that sometime soon we'll be hit by another serious downturn. If they're right, there are even more testing times ahead.

Of course, many positive things *are* happening. There *is* plenty of good news. Progress *is* being made on many fronts. But whatever scenario plays out, the future for business will be tougher than the past. And it's likely to be a lot tougher.

So there's no time to rest, no place to hide. And the case for the critical strategy practices will never be stronger.

Radical shifts

"In the three short decades between now and the twenty-first century," said Alvin Toffler in the opening chapter of *Future Shock*, his 1970 bestseller, "millions of ordinary, psychologically normal people will face an abrupt collision with the future."[16]

In a similar vein, Drucker wrote in 1993: "Every few hundred years in Western history, there occurs a sharp transformation ... Within a few short decades, society rearranges itself – its worldview; its basic values; its social and political structure; its arts; its key institutions. Fifty years later, there is a new world."[17]

And indeed, the tectonic plates have shifted. That new world is in the making, and we stand on unfamiliar ground. The first years of the new century have been momentous. There are more changes to come. There is no turning back.

Speaking to the Canadian Club in 2009, Jeffrey Immelt, chairman and CEO of General Electric, said: "If you think this is only a cycle you're just wrong. This is a permanent reset. There are going to be elements of the economy that will never be the same, ever. Smart businesses are the ones that are going to hunker down in the cycle, which you've got to do, but that also understand we're going to come out of this in a different world."[18]

In this new environment, running just about any business is nerve-wracking, gut-wrenching, energy-sapping work. Companies are bombarded by major challenges and managers are battered by "wicked" problems.* There's a lot to keep them awake at night.

The complexity they have to deal with, both inside and outside their walls, is mind-boggling. Paradoxes abound, many questions seem unanswerable, and many issues seem intractable. Making sense of the world is increasingly difficult – and just as you think you've got the picture, things change. As fast as you decide how to cope with one dilemma, another appears. The pressure is relentless.

Managing a firm of any size has never been easy. Now, managers have to produce consistent, sustainable results under awful pressure in a world that gets messier by the nanosecond. Their customers are informed, price-conscious, vociferous, and skittish. Their organizations and processes are increasingly complex. They function within a dense ecosystem of stakeholders with shifting – and often conflicting – agendas and growing clout. They're ever more reliant on costly and unfamiliar technologies. Risk is all around. And with a growing premium on the imagination and spirit of human beings, and with the global "war for talent" growing fiercer, they must put more effort into people matters. Their employees' lives are changing, so the new world of work must accommodate their personal needs while also enabling them to be more effective on the job.

This collision of factors keeps managers constantly unsettled. Their need for order, control, and predictability is at odds with the barrage of novel challenges they face. This makes them naturally eager to find the management tools and techniques that will save their skin.

Creating the future

The advance of business is essential to humankind. Everything depends on it. So it's of utmost importance that companies should attain and sustain new levels of both improvement and innovation. They must urgently ratchet up their sales, productivity, quality, and profitability, and at the same time shape new strategies, explore new opportunities, develop new offerings, accumulate new resources, and build new capabilities for tomorrow. And they must do it all in the face of headwinds which, rather than dying down soon, will surely get stronger.

This will be incredibly difficult. "What is striking about the market system," says economist Tim Harford, "is not how few failures there are, but how ubiquitous failure is even in the most vibrant growth industries."[19] Across business cycles, the performance of individual companies tends to be uneven and unexciting. Even before the Great Recession, we knew that consistently delivering exceptional results was not the norm.

---

* Problems for which there are no easy solutions, and when "solved" lead to other problems.

- In their often-quoted book *Creative Destruction*, McKinsey's Richard Foster and Sarah Kaplan point out that "the golden company that continually performs better than the markets has never existed. It is a myth ... As a general rule, companies that have survived over the long term do not outperform their industries."[20]

- Clayton Christensen and Michael Raynor tell us in *The Innovator's Solution* that nine out of ten firms fail to grow strongly enough over more than a few years to produce above-average shareholder returns. When growth grinds to a halt or falls, only about four out of ten firms are able to resume it.[21]

- A 2007 McKinsey study of big global firms found that "less than 1 percent of them outperformed their competitors on both revenue growth and profitability over a decade."[22]

- Research by Accenture shows that "only 5 percent to 20 percent of companies, depending on the industry, are able to sustain top performance over time."[23]

- According to Société Générale, profit growth from the early 1990s held at around 12 to 14 per cent a year. Yet as *The Economist* soberly noted, "Over the long run, profits cannot grow much faster than economic output, which has been growing at a nominal rate of roughly 6–8% a year."[24] (And that was before the financial crisis.)

- Deloitte's 2011 *Shift Index* showed that from 1965 to 2009, the return on assets (ROA) of US firms fell by two-thirds, while labour productivity improved only slightly. This reflected "a decline in firm performance that has been playing out for decades." A minor uptick in ROA in the 2011 study was due mostly to layoffs and other belt-tightening measures.[25] The 2013 update confirmed 'companies' decreasing ability to find and capture attractive opportunities relative to the assets they have." It also pointed to the fact that "the topple rate, a measure of how rapidly companies lose their leadership positions, has increased by 39 percent since 1965."[26]

The message is clear: consistently outperforming competitors and the overall economy is a rare feat. One that smart managers in most firms are unable to achieve.

Even when companies are able to stand out from the herd and improve on key measures such as sales, market share, productivity, quality, innovation, and ROI – sometimes quite sharply – few sustain the pace. By definition, "outperformance" is neither normal nor widespread; and it tends to occur in spurts. Often, it's a result of a specific event such as an economic upturn, the arrival of new technology, the invention of a new product or service, a merger or acquisition, drastic cost-cuts, or competitor missteps. Such transient occurrences may provide a one-time lift, but they don't come around every day. And you can't rely on them for long-term success. "Something will happen" is not a strategy. Managers can't leave the future of their organizations to chance. *They must manage.*

In the past six years, many companies have been able to sustain their profits only through draconian cost-cuts rather than revenue growth. They've sliced through fat and into muscle, and are now down to bone. They may be leaner, meaner, and more agile than ever, but further gains will be harder to come by. In most cases, these will depend on hefty investment, innovations in products and services, and new strategies to lure elusive customers. This means there are cost hikes to come – at the very time when margins are squeezed, inflation is down, and competitiveness depends ever more on falling prices.

Weak firms can't expect quick relief. Just working harder, necessary though it may be, is unlikely to get them back to past performance levels, let alone help them do much better. Their "fit" with the world has been disrupted by profound changes in one industry after another. Many of them failed to see or understand what was happening, and laboured their way to irrelevance. So if they haven't already taken harsh medicine, they need it urgently. If they haven't begun reinventing their strategies, and made wrenching changes to their business models, it may be too late and they may not pull through.

Successful firms, too, need to rethink everything they do and the way they do everything. They may have absorbed a great deal of change, and reinvented their strategies, but pausing for breath will be fatal.

Across the board and across the world, managers have to become more effective. They have to use their resources better. The way they manage today won't get them the different results they want tomorrow. Random stabs at this or that won't put them on the path to sustainable high performance.

The only way to get there is by changing their management practices.

It might seem that the best way forward would be to decisively break with the past; toss aside the management theories, tools, and techniques that brought them this far; and fast-track radically new ways to operate. To make what Thomas Kuhn calls "a paradigm shift"[27] in their thinking – and to do it without delay.

This is a sexy notion and the latest refrain of a number of management experts. And the logic is compelling. By the end of what *Harvard Business Review* calls "The Management Century" (1911–2011),[28] management practices had reached maturity, bringing business to where it is today. We've reached "the end of management," declares Gary Hamel, one of the brightest and most prominent of gurus. Nothing less will do than the replacement of "Management 1.0" by "Management 2.0."[29]

But the managerial innovations we yearn for are nowhere in sight.[*]

---

[*] More on this in Chapter 10.

They are not what we need most and they are not our priority.

So while they might belong on someone's to-do list, they shouldn't be everyone's obsession. Creating or finding them, testing them, and learning to use them will take longer than we can wait, and be costly distractions. There are businesses to run.

Besides, we already know what to do.

The false promise of management innovation

The most compelling argument for management innovation is that human history is a story of progress, not stasis. The Club of Rome's gloomy scenarios for the world, developed as "The Project for the Predicament of Mankind," between 1968 and 1972,[30] turned out to be nonsense. "The true heroes of our time," says economist John Kay in a March 2014 article in *The Financial Times*, "are the philosophers who see that messages can be made to travel at the speed of light, and the entrepreneurs who see that the best way to do things better is usually to do them differently."[31]

We must assume there are new possibilities in the world of work. It's inconceivable that we've hit the upper limits of business performance. The "step-change" that managers aspire to must lie ahead for some firms.

But this won't occur without the critical strategy practices. The future lies not in ignoring them or finding a way around them, but only *in different and better ways of implementing them.*

To compete and win – and to have the transformational impact expected of them – companies must offer their customers "a difference that matters." They can do this through distinctive products or services, or ways of doing things – or, even better, a combination of both. Whatever their choice, innovation is required in the way they create, deliver, and capture value.

Achieving this in conditions of uncertainty, as Drucker pointed out, depends on "the talent, experience, vision, courage, and character" of managers. But important as those traits are, alone they are not enough. For managers to excel, they need a "foundation of organized systematic knowledge and organized systematic search" and "a real discipline of management and entrepreneurship."[32]

So let's agree. *You absolutely should look for better ways to manage.*

But before you get too carried away, stop and think for a moment. What exactly might that mean? What exactly should you look for? A way of managing people that's quite different to your current way? A new perspective on customers, technology, or collaboration? Ways to improve a *process*? Or maybe to drive new *outcomes* such as quality, productivity, innovation, sales, or service? If you're not specific, your search will be frustrating and a waste of effort.

The "better way" you're after could be a tool or technique that you read about in *Harvard Business Review* today. Or something you're not doing that you should be doing. It could be a way of thinking or one of acting. Or all of the above. If you know what you're searching for, you improve your chances of discovering it.

But don't bet everything on some sensational new management tool. The chances of finding one are slim – and even less so of keeping it to yourself for long enough to make the effort worthwhile. We've been chasing this mirage for a long time. The results are dismal.

It is highly unlikely that some scholar or consultant will have an "Aha!" moment that suddenly changes everything. The best you can hope for is that, somewhere in the organizational maelstrom, the collective efforts of millions of minds will yield an insight here and an idea there, and gradually nudge us towards a new reality.

Henry Ford's legacy

For a sense of how little progress we've made in producing new management ideas, you only have to look at what Henry Ford was up to a century ago, around the time management became a distinct discipline. The founder of the Ford Motor Company was one of the greatest entrepreneurs ever. And a management innovator with few peers.

As a serial experimenter, Ford put every accepted business assumption on trial for its life. His story is one of constant invention and reinvention, not just of motor cars, but of every aspect of how he made them and how he ran his company. Strategy, structure, finance, supplier relationships, production systems, employee relations, pay – all were challenged, re-thought, changed, and changed again.[33]

Look at some of Ford's innovations:

- **Control over the entire value chain** – "Other carmakers put the bits together," wrote Robert Lacey in *Ford: The Man and the Machine*, "but Ford wanted to go right back to the earth, to quarry out the raw materials that made up his cars." So he bought coal and iron mines in northern Michigan. He bought land in Brazil to grow rubber, and established a Ford settlement near the Amazon, called Fordlandia. He bought pine forests for the timber he needed in his station wagons. He built a fleet of trucks to transport these raw materials back to Dearborn.[34] And he built a steel factory, a glass factory, and an iron-ore foundry at the Rouge.[35]
- **Mass production** – His giant Rouge plant was "the most awesomely integrated plant in industrial history," according to biographer David Halberstam. It comprised 93 buildings on 1,100 acres. There were 93 miles of railroad track and 27 miles of conveyor belts. Some 75,000 men worked there.[36]
- **Mechanization and a moving assembly line** – "The first step forward in assembly came when we began taking the work to the men instead of the men

to the work," said Ford.[37] Stationary chassis assembly had allowed one man to put a car together in 728 hours. With a moving line, it took just 93 minutes.[38]

- **Delivering parts to workers rather than have workers fetch them** – "Save ten steps a day for each of twelve thousand employees and you will have saved fifty miles of wasted motion and misspent energy."[39] So "The greatest distance any material has to be trucked is twenty feet."[40]

- **Just-in-time management** – "Having a stock of raw material or finished goods in excess of requirements is waste." So Ford ensured that departments worked closely together to get the right parts to where they were needed, at the right times.[41]

- **Elimination of waste** (what the Japanese call *muda*) – It began with "economy of design" of Ford's products and was aided by other steps: "90% of our equipment is standard ... The whole plant has been built with the single thought of simplifying the handling of material ... "[42]

- **Cycle-time reduction** – "The easiest of all wastes, and the hardest to correct, is the waste of time," said Ford, "because time does not litter the floor like wasted material." He cut the production cycle to "three days and nine hours instead of the fourteen days which we used to think was record breaking."[43]

- **Continuous improvement** (now catchily known as *kaizen*) – "We must regard every process employed in manufacturing as purely experimental," said Ford.[44] "We try everything in a little way first – we will rip out anything once we discover a better way." By splitting the work of one person into 29 operations, assembly times were cut from 20 minutes to just over 13; by raising the height of the production line by eight inches, it was further cut to seven minutes; and changing the line speed got it down to just five minutes.[45]

- **Platform manufacturing** – Ford launched his Model T in 1908–09, and on the same chassis "mounted a town car at $1,000, a roadster at $825, a coupe at $950, and a landaulet at $950."[46]

- **Target pricing** – "Our policy is to reduce the price, extend the operations, and improve the article. You will notice that the reduction of price comes first. We have never considered any costs as fixed. Therefore we first reduce the price to a point where we believe more sales will result. Then we go ahead and try to make the price. We do not bother about the costs."[47]

- **Continuous price reductions** – The price of a car fell from $825 in 1908 to $440 by October 1914, and $345 in August 1916.[48] "[T]rue prosperity is marked by a reduction in prices," said Ford, "and that is the only way by which prosperity can be made the normal condition and prevented from being merely spasmodic." He hiked the minimum wage from five dollars a day to six, yet sold cars at 40 percent less than in 1914, when the average wage was $2.40 a day.[49]

- **Mass customization through a value ecosystem** – While aggressively promoting mass production, Ford was also aware that value means different things to different people. So at the height of the Model T Ford's popularity, the Sears Roebuck catalogue "featured no less than 5,000 different items that could be bolted, screwed, or strapped to the vehicle."[50]
- **Suggestion schemes** – "The whole factory management is always open to a suggestion," said Ford, "and we have an informal suggestion system by which any workman can communicate any idea that comes to him and get action on it."[51]
- **Pay for performance** – "The right wage is not the lowest sum a man will work for ... the right wage is the highest wage the employer can steadily pay ... we think it is good business always to raise wages and never to lower them."[52] Ford introduced variable pay in 1908, profit sharing in 1913, and stock options in 1946.[53]

To anyone who stays abreast with current thinking, Henry Ford's innovations must ring bells. Weren't you reminded of them when you read about some whizz-bang new idea in the latest issue of a respected management journal? Aren't they what today's bestselling business books tell you? Didn't you just hear them at some conference or seminar, or from some consultant?

Ford's principles of just-in-time management, continuous improvement, cycle-time reduction, and the elimination of waste were applied in the 1970s by Taiichi Ohno, the legendary *sensei* behind the Toyota Manufacturing System. After years of work, he and his team were able to cut the time it took to change dies on a production line from around 16 hours to 60 seconds – and he then said, "If we can do it in a minute, we can do it in thirty seconds."[54] Those same principles are the essence of what we now know as lean thinking.

Japanese companies used continuous price reduction and target pricing to attack western markets in the 1970s, forcing firms elsewhere to do the same. Now, these are common practice in almost every industry.

A century after Ford, Volkswagen's Touareg, the Audi Q7, and the Porsche Cayenne share a chassis. Platform manufacturing is normal in the production of TV sets, PCs, mobile phones, and much more. And Apple's software operating system, iOS, is the platform on which all its mobile devices are built.

Value ecosystems are another key factor in strategy today. Again, look at Apple, whose developer and supplier networks, fan base, retail stores, and growing array of apps and accessories have made it the world's most valuable company.

For more examples of the influence of early management thinkers, look no further than the innovations that shaped four other large companies – Du Pont, General Motors, Standard Oil, and Sears, Roebuck – early in the last century. As told by business historian Alfred Chandler in his magisterial book, *Strategy and Structure*, the story of these firms and their leaders is one of change as an obsession, long before change became fashionable. And many of the practices developed by those pioneers have been astonishingly durable.[55]

We're often reminded of the words of Edmund Burke, a British statesman and philosopher (1729–1797), who said, "Those who don't know history are destined to repeat it." But that's not necessarily a bad thing, and it's exactly what's happening in some areas of business today. More commonly, though, an absence of historical perspective – or denial of what's in the books – keeps lots of people busy reinventing the wheel.

So what are you hearing now that's significantly different to what Ford was doing 100 years ago, or Chandler saw happening 50 years ago? Turns out much of the old stuff is the new stuff.

Management stuck

Of course, the way cars are made today differs significantly from the way Henry Ford did it. Innovations in technology, materials, supplier linkages, and business models have made possible processes he could not have imagined. Regulations have compelled companies to change their approach to environmental, health and safety issues, and people management. Ford would be astounded at the all-round improvements that have been made in production and at the consequent leaps in quality, productivity, and waste elimination. But the fundamental management practices I've just described are alive and well at most auto companies. And there's no reason to think they'll be dumped any time soon. A century on, they're entrenched as "best practice."

Reinventing management will be easier said than done. An untold number of very smart people have been trying since Ford's time to find better ways to manage. Yet despite their best efforts, and despite the self-promotion by those who produce and hawk ideas, little headway has been made.

The global ideas industry has produced few really significant ideas – game-changers, if you will – about managing. There have been long gaps between them. None has emerged because someone said, "We need a new way to manage, and we need it by Monday."

Despite surging interest in management post World War II, hardly any significant ideas about strategy have emerged since then. John Von Neumann and Oskar Morgenstern developed their theory of games in 1947. The Ansoff matrix appeared in 1957. Jay Forrester gave us "systems dynamics" – now better known as systems thinking – in 1958. Edith Penrose introduced the "resource-based view of the firm" (RBV) in 1959. Alfred Chandler alerted us to the need to balance strategy and structure in 1962, and shortly afterwards Bruce Henderson began using the experience curve* and the growth-share matrix to promote the Boston Consulting Group. Michael Porter's five-forces model arrived in 1979. All of these are still taught as key elements of business school courses.

It's the same with people management.

In a scathing article in *Academy of Management Perspectives* in May 2012, Bruce Kaufman, a professor of economics at Georgia State University, declared that strategic human resource management researchers "as a group deserve a D to F grade." Their output, he said, was "seriously flawed and inaccurate in its theory, findings, and managerial implications … too broadly or amorphously framed to provide actionable principles for practitioners, and/or … [did] not deal with HRM subject areas that are germane and add value for practitioners."[56]

And indeed, since pioneering work by Chris Argyris, David McClelland, Douglas McGregor, Frederick Herzberg, and Edgar Schein, there's been no meaningful movement. Decades of additional poking around in companies, deep thought, and hard-won experience have barely moved the needle. No amount of creative packaging and marketing of ideas can hide the fact that whether it's leadership, motivation, change management, performance management, succession planning, development, empowerment, or any other such topic, we're out of gas.

Textbooks "from half a century ago," says Kaufman, are in some ways "a more useful and insightful (if less colorful) guide to people management than many of the textbooks today … I realize that Rome was not built in a day, but after 30 years and many millions spent we might reasonably expect more progress than this."[57]

Around and around we go

No doubt you'd like to refute what I'm saying by adding a long list of other gurus and their concepts to those I've mentioned. Fifty-odd years of management opinion should provide plenty of ammunition for an argument. But if you're tempted to trawl through it to make your case, be sure to ask these questions of any theory or concept you come up with:

1. Is the essence of what it says original, or a re-hash of earlier thinking?
2. Has it profoundly altered management practice?
3. Is it likely to show up in future ideas about management?
4. Is it a must-do or a nice-to-do?

---

* It was noticed at Curtiss Aircraft in the 1920s and was originally called the "learning curve"; Henderson resuscitated and renamed it. (Art Kleiner, *The Age of Heretics*, San Francisco: Jossey-Bass, 2008)

What you dredge up might well address an issue from a fresh perspective. It might explain something in a novel and helpful way. And it might have inspired scholars to pursue new studies, and even caused managers to try new things. But look again. Chances are, it wasn't *transformative*, didn't add *essential* knowledge, and didn't clearly or significantly improve business *results*.

Gary Hamel and C.K. Prahalad made the resource-based view of the firm The Big Idea of the 1990s by renaming it core competence. Clayton Christensen acknowledges that he produced "disruption" on the back of research by Robert Burgelman,[58] but there's also a clear link to much earlier insights from Peter Drucker, Theodore Levitt, and others. The rush to "employee engagement" has its roots in the Hawthorne studies of 1924–1932. Newfound interest in purpose as a motivator evokes the message of Viktor Frankl's book, *Man's Search for Meaning*, which was first published in German in 1946.[59]

Each of these recent "breakthroughs" grabbed attention, incited huge hype, dominated managerial and academic conversations, and shifted executive priorities. But if you never heard about them and tried them, and instead just *applied the underlying thinking*, you'd surely be no worse off.

I'm not the only one lamenting the lack of progress. There is no shortage of critics telling the same woeful story. You have only to read Art Kleiner's wonderful review of management thought since World War II, *The Age of Heretics*[60] – or explore the views of so many others, many of them mentioned in this book – to get a sense of how little has been achieved.

In the strategy area, listen, for example, to Hamel and Aimé Heene as editors of *Competence-Based Competition*, a book published in 1994 by the Strategic Management Society:

> After almost 40 years of development and theory building, the field of strategic management is today, more than ever, characterized by contrasting and sometimes competing paradigms … the strategy field seems to be as far away as ever from a "grand unified theory" of competitiveness. Indeed, there is still much divergence of opinion within the strategy field on questions as basic as "what is a theory of strategic management about?" and, more importantly, "what should a theory of strategic management be about?"[61]

Three years after that article, Hamel went even further. "The dirty little secret," he wrote in the *Financial Times*, "is that we don't have a theory of strategy creation. We don't know how it's done."[62]

But that's apparently not the only gap in our knowledge about strategy. In early 2014, the Strategic Management Society called for papers for a special issue on "New Theory in Strategic Management." Here's the appeal:

While we continue to make progress in refining our understanding of these theories, one wonders if there aren't important questions in the field that are not well covered by existing theories. A *few* of many possible examples include: (1) Every major change in a firm's strategy involves significant organizational change, yet we have very little theory about how to effectively manage such change; (2) although we now know that many concepts and processes in strategy, such as firm-strategy-environment "fit", involve highly complex interdependencies, we have made little progress adapting complexity-based concepts to strategic theory; (3) We have relatively little theory that applies to strategy questions in the public sector (including public policy); to non-market strategy, and to the broader social consequences of strategic decisions; and (4) fifty years after the publication of *A Behavioral Theory of the Firm* and with a wealth of new psychological theories appearing in the interim, behavioural theories of strategy remain underdeveloped.[63]

This can't be an exhaustive list of what we don't know about strategy. There are many more unknowns. Researchers have a lot of exploring to do. This will keep them busy, but it remains to be seen how it helps humankind progress.

These doubts naturally affect management education. So a 2003 article titled "Searching for a Strategy to Teach Strategy" in *Academy of Management Learning and Education*, confesses that "Ironically, we continue to invest in a questionable strategy curriculum for which there is little empirical evidence to support its current direction and learning value."[64]

I disagree with Hamel's assertion that we don't have a theory of strategy creation. We do know all we need to know about how it's done. Yet we keep searching for an alternative. We second-guess our decisions about what processes to use, and what we should do next. We choose not to accept that we know as much as we need to about how to get results, and forget that we're dealing with a complex process full of twists and turns and surprises.

The strategy framework developed by the Harvard business policy group in the early 1960s makes as much sense today as it did back then. Based on the assumption that the goal of strategy was a "fit" between an organization and its environment, it identified the issues managers needed to consider to make this possible. And it mapped out the process that by many accounts is still the one most used by firms around the world.

Michael Porter got his academic start in that Harvard unit, and his "five forces," "generic strategies," and "activity systems" have all been lauded as conceptual breakthroughs. But none of these replaces the earlier framework on which he cut his teeth. All are useful only in the context of the original. All are "add-ons," which can be used to enrich the conversation described by Porter's elders.

The notion of "strategic fit" has taken blows in recent years, as various gurus have spread the gospel of "out of the box thinking," "stretch," "market space," "blue oceans," and so on. But as we'll see, these, too, are useful add-ons rather than disruptions. They may assist in reframing a market opportunity, but no firm – not Google, not Twitter, not IDEO or BMW or JP Morgan or any other – will survive for long as a *misfit*.

Now turn to the people area.

"Competence in the human aspects of management is no longer seen as a luxury but as an essential ingredient of business success," says Paul Lawrence, a professor at Harvard Business School, in a 1987 article. "The theory and practice of organizational behavior have come a long way since its inception nearly fifty years ago, but there would probably be little argument that its work is barely started. Our theory ignorance and our practice mistakes are still great even as our phenomenon of study is rapidly changing."[65]

Lawrence may be right to say we still lack theory that will help us manage people, and thus make "practice mistakes," but whatever might we be missing? What more do we need to know? Does its absence really hold us back? How much difference will it make?

Our problem is not that we're short of theories. Rather, it's that we're dismissive of what we know, averse to using it, and poor at doing it. We simply fail to acknowledge the value of hard-won knowledge and put it into practice.

There will always be attempts to reinvent management, and new slants on how to use what we know. The advice industry will see to that, and it's a good thing. But the advice industry has run amok – encouraged, ironically, by its clients: busy managers struggling to make sense of an increasingly troublesome world and trying to guide their people through it.

These managers are the losers. The very experts who should be explaining matters to them add to their confusion. Those who should be making life easier are actually making it harder.

So what of the future?

My bet is on more of the same.

Here we are, in a time of unprecedented turmoil and change, when organizations are more important to society than ever, when our future rests on their effectiveness and their results, and when it's clear that anything less than a "reset"[66] of how we think about the way forward won't do – and there's not much to be excited about in management.

Here we are, thinking away, and hoping against hope, while the wheels spin.

Look at the contents page of any "A-level" management journal and ask which of the topics you see there will importantly change the way we think about management and enable any executive to raise her game. Ask the same of the business books that keep pouring forth, or articles you read in the business press. Or listen to the gurus.

You will be disappointed.

The good news, however, is that all this need not be as troubling as we might imagine. For the right answer to our growth challenge is one we already have. The way through our difficulties and towards a better future lies in what we already know.

Thinking inside the box

In company after company, frazzled executives are failing to do as well as they could for a simple reason: not because they desperately need some newfangled way to manage, but because *they don't understand or don't apply what's already there.* So they operate without a sound foundation, trying instead to ramp up their results with salvos of interventions that devour resources, don't hang together, don't do what's expected, and eventually fizzle out.

The better route would be to focus on what's already known rather than obsess over what may never be known – *and what probably won't matter anyway.* Firstly, it would be easier and cheaper, and secondly, it would immediately improve their prospects of success.

By starting with a tried and true conceptual framework, they would be able to sensibly evaluate whatever "new" ideas come their way, and know which to adopt and which to ignore. And they'd undoubtedly find plenty of new ways to fine-tune and enhance their basic practices, and thus keep improving their overall performance.

This would result in less flailing about in search of the next silver bullet. Fewer costly interventions. And fewer risks from unproven ideas.

And best of all, it would mean not having to wait for some sage to make the breakthrough that would turbocharge their competitiveness and save them from decline.

Surely, then, it would make sense to pause and look back at the insights and ideas the world's best management thinkers have brought us over the past century. To agree, once and for all, what we need to do and how to do it. And then to throw ourselves into becoming excellent at doing it.

Let me put it this way:

Managers are not being held back by a lack of theory. They should resist getting into a blind rush to replace "Management 1.0" with "Management 2.0." Their priority should be to grab hold of "the basics," become damned good at them, and apply them with 100 per cent commitment.

If the dreams of management thinkers were to come true, the next leap forward would come from "out of the box" – from ideas about management not yet imagined or developed. The reality, however, is that advances in competitiveness, productivity, quality, costs, sales, service, profits, and the rest will mostly come from practices that are "*in* the box" – and that are available right now.

These practices are what you might call the real basics of management.* They're critical to business, not just interesting or helpful. They are must-dos, not optional extras. And they add up to a holistic, integrated management approach that will work for every company, everywhere.

The bottom line

No doubt, what I've said so far will draw cries of outrage and provoke a lot of vitriolic responses. That's understandable. The management ideas industry is a big one, and lots of fine thinkers are involved in it. Their livelihoods and reputations – not to mention their egos – depend on their being able to convince you that their intellectual output matters.

But let's get real.

- Decline rather than growth is natural for companies.
- Outperformance is hard to achieve and harder still to sustain.
- Management innovation is uncommon, has never happened at the flick of a switch, and is unlikely to radically change how firms operate or the results they get.

You probably agree with the first two points. But the third – which is the real issue here – may give you palpitations. So if you wish to challenge it, try this:

Name one key idea managers <u>must use</u> in the areas of strategy and people that we did not know about 50 years ago.

Just one.

(Notice that I ask for an idea managers *must* use, not one they can elect to use or ignore. Even most of those that Ford introduced fail this test: although they may have become best practice, nobody *has* to apply them.)

If you're still not convinced, try this:

Suggest how any new idea might do more to improve results than the practices we already have.

Will it transform your ability to create and execute strategy? Will it light a fire under your people and cause them suddenly to become more energized, innovative, and

---

* Not the same as the basics of your industry – the "rules of the game" – which are also important.

cooperative? Will your sales and profits shoot up faster and higher than those of your peers?

Not a chance.

Sure, customers will get wealthier, more educated, and more adventurous. Firms will find new ways to satisfy customers' hunger for new value. New markets will emerge and take shape. New technologies will be a kicker. Managers will become cannier.

But nothing will replace the fundamental management practices we have, and nothing will come along to serve us better.

Meanwhile, we're drowning in management guff. We're swamped by purportedly new theories and tools that promise to improve sales and profits while at the same time improving our lives, saving the planet, and more. And all this, while things go crazy around us.

The management advice industry causes managers to lurch frantically from one "new, new thing" to the next, seize them with manic speed, and layer one upon the other, until they paralyze themselves and their organizations with too many priorities. Yet prominent industry insiders are critical of its conventions, its methods, and its output.

This cannot make sense.

3

HOPING AND GROPING

Management is undoubtedly the pivotal function in human affairs. Yet it's hard to think of another field where there's such ready acceptance of so many half-baked ideas and seat-of-the-pants practices. Where the lure of novelty is such a common diversion from the value of what's tried and tested. Or where complexity, costs, and risks are so carelessly – yet *deliberately* – introduced by the very people who complain about them and seek to fight them.

One reason is that for all the attention management gets, there remain many unanswered questions and conflicting views about it. What is the purpose of a company? Which stakeholders matter most? Do companies become great through focus or diversification? Should they think local or act global? Should they make or buy what they sell? Are there ideal business models for particular industries? What structure works best? Is the "first-mover" advantage a reality or should you be a fast follower? What's the role of luck? Does leadership matter? And so on.

The answer to all these questions is, "It depends." But that's not an answer that lets executives sleep easier. So they keep searching, keep changing their minds, and keep second-guessing themselves and stepping on their own toes.

A second reason is that managing is an extremely dynamic activity. The causes of business success are many and varied, and they change from time to time. The context of business is always in flux, and making perfect sense of it is impossible. When choosing a response, it's hard to be sure what action will get what result and unintended consequences are inevitable. For these reasons decisions are always hazardous. What's more, they're always influenced by the mental baggage we cart around. Human factors like experience, assumptions, biases, cognitive skills, agendas, and emotion all colour our thinking.[1] An amalgam of traits such as confidence, openness, empathy, imagination, courage, persistence, and persuasiveness – and yes, even much-disputed charisma – all affect the choices that get made. Power, trust, and culture all affect the way things play out.

Third, most managers are unsure about exactly how to manage. Pummelled by circumstances and tangled within a Gordian knot of issues, largely of their own tying, they don't know where to slice or what to do next. Nor does it help that they're slaves to fads which, while consuming time and energy, may not bring the results they want.

Fourth, the people who should be guiding them – business scholars and management consultants – are themselves groping for answers. They strain at the boundaries of knowledge, but make few breakthroughs. Most of their output adds nothing to what's already known, and is of little help to anyone struggling to make and sell things and fend off competitors. Yet like Pied Pipers, these soothsayers have managers excitedly following them.

A fifth issue is economics. Inventing and selling new managerial ideas takes time and costs money. Recycling or rebranding them, or adding a few wrinkles, is less painful.

Academics under pressure to publish and carrying a heavy teaching load may see the production of new knowledge as an unwarranted investment of their time. So they settle for reviewing or reinterpreting each other's work or producing studies that have little or no impact. Irrelevance feels like their most sensible option.

Consultants typically use insights gained in one assignment across many others. It also makes financial sense for them to panel-beat and repaint their currently favourite tool or approach to satisfy any and every client need. Sometimes this works. But there's always the risk that "when you have a hammer, everything looks like a nail," and that reconstituted advice won't resolve whatever specific issue prompted a call for help.

The lure of easy answers

In the scramble to survive and thrive in a radically changing world, one thing stays constant: the search by managers for easy-to-apply instruction that will make them winners. For quick fixes that will rescue them from slumping sales and profits. For effortless ways to boost innovation, crack new markets, and win customer loyalty.

And help is at hand. There are plenty of gurus circling with solutions. They smoothly seduce anxious managers with their "unique," "groundbreaking," and "proprietary" tools and techniques. "Thought leadership" is their stock in trade. They promise that their "three rules," "seven steps," or some other formulaic approach will lead straight to profits.* According to Fiona Czerniawska, a consultant who tracks trends in the consulting industry, almost one-third of firms

---

* *What's Wrong With Management and How to Get It Right* differs in identifying what managers *must* do, rather than giving them yet another optional package.

use thought leadership as one of their criteria for choosing consulting firms. And clients rate it as one of the best ways for consultants to market themselves.[2]

The management ideas industry has enjoyed a "long boom" and there's no sign of it ending anytime soon. Its sprawling ecosystem includes academics, consultants, executives, writers, and speakers who peddle their insights, ideas, and opinions through articles, books, white papers, courses, training programmes, conferences, business breakfasts, business associations, newspaper reports, magazine columns, radio and TV shows, websites, blogs, YouTube, Facebook, Twitter, and anywhere else they can. The volume of output is astounding, and much of it is free.

The number of business schools worldwide has jumped from zero in 1910 to about 10,000 today, with the fastest growth coming in Asia. Publishers of business books churn out more than 11,000 new titles a year,* and in November 2014 Amazon.com listed 1,051,191 titles on management, 233,155 on strategy, 154,020 on leadership. An index of scholarly journals saw the number of management articles rise from fewer than 200 a year in the late 1980s to almost 1,500 by 2005.[3] Many management websites encourage comment on their content, and everyone and his dog seems to have an opinion and want to share it. When I recently googled "corporate performance," I got 107 million links. A search for "management journals" in June 2015 yielded more than 247 million links.

Czerniawska reports that in 2007 the 40 biggest consulting firms had "around 3 500 reports, articles, white papers, and books on their Web sites which can be considered as thought leadership."[4] Her company, Source, offers links to more than 20,000 articles.[5]

In "The Management Theory Jungle," a 1961 article in the *Academy of Management Journal*, Harold Koontz of the University of California suggests that the "deluge of research and writing from the academic halls" might be "nothing more than a sign of the unsophisticated adolescence of management theory ... It is important that steps be taken to disentangle the management theory jungle. Perhaps it is too soon and we must expect more years of wandering through the thicket of approaches, semantics, thrusts, and counter-thrusts. But in any field as important to society where the many blunders of an unscientifically based managerial art can be so costly, I hope that this will not be long."

This variety of approaches to management theory, he says, "has led to a kind of confused and destructive jungle warfare."[6] However, more than 50 years later, the jungle is denser and more impenetrable than ever, and the war rages on.

In his article, Koontz identified six schools of management thought: 1) the

---

* Eric Spitznagel, "How to Write a Bestselling Business Book," *Business Week*, 19 July, 2012.

management process school, 2) the empirical or "case" approach, 3) the human behaviour school, 4) the social system school, 5) the decision theory school, and 6) the mathematics school. In a 1980 follow-up, he expanded his list to 11: 1) the empirical or case approach, 2) the interpersonal behaviour approach, 3) the group behaviour approach, 4) the cooperative system approach, 5) the sociotechnical systems approach, 6) the decision theory approach, 7) the systems approach, 8) the mathematical or "management science" approach, 9) the contingency or situational approach, 10) the managerial roles approach, and 11) the operational theory approach.[7]

While the jungle war continues around busy managers, they face the daunting task of trying to decide what in the tangled mass of information and opinion is worthwhile, and what's not. Most of it is based on a few core ideas, so there's a lot of repetition. You'll be familiar with some of what you come across, and may not want to hear it again.

A great deal of confusion, said Koontz, arose from the fact that the experts themselves could not agree on what various terms meant. Even "organization" was used in different ways. "By some, decision-making is regarded as a process of choosing from among alternatives; by others, the total managerial task and environment. Leadership is often made synonymous with managership and is analytically separated by others. Communications may mean everything from a written or oral report to a cast network of formal and informal relationships. Human relations to some implies a psychiatric manipulation of people, but to others the study and art of understanding people and interpersonal relationships."[8]

Evidence about the relevance or efficacy of ideas can be hard to come by, and in any event may be no indicator of their value or staying power. Some of them may be – or turn out to be – significant. For the rest, the dustbin of history waits.

Like much else in our fast-changing world, management ideas tend to have a short shelf life. But while they're in vogue they can make a big impact. As Joel Best, professor of Sociology and Criminal Justice at the University of Delaware, tells us in his book, *Flavor of the Month: Why Smart People Fall for Fads*, "the time between a fad's introduction and its abandonment is growing shorter, yet each successive fad seems to generate more enthusiasm – more media coverage and the like. The peaks are growing higher and sharper."[9]

This was clearly illustrated by Richard Pascale in *Managing on the Edge*.[10] And by Google's Ngram Viewer, which shows sharp increases over the past two or three decades in the use of management terms such as "core competence," "balanced scorecard," "Six Sigma," and "reengineering."[11] And it's confirmed again and again by the *Management Tools* surveys put out every year or two by Bain & Company, a global management consultancy.[12] The usage and satisfaction rankings of what the firm calls "tools" bob up and down, though there are some perennial favourites.

What's probably unnoticed is that the survey also offers an implicit warning: *managers' opinions about what works for them may be utterly inaccurate and misleading – so of no help to other managers seeking to do better.*

Consider, for example, how many respondents say they use vision and mission statements – obviously because they think these boost their performance. But how on earth do they *know* that? Is there really a link between cause and consequence? What *else* was happening that affected results? On what basis could they single out these "tools" for credit? Would other executives also see an uptick in their results if they used vision and mission statements? If so, why do so many companies that use them perform so poorly?

Over the past 30 years, vision and mission statements have become *de rigueur* in strategy documents. You'd think they were required by law. They're item No. 1 on the agenda of most strategy workshops, and the first step in the popular "vision, mission, values" template for strategic planning. But surely, if they're such wonderful tools, there would at least be agreement – backed by solid proof – about the value they bring to strategic thinking. Surely, they'd be even more widely used and every company using them could say, "They did X for us because of Y." Surely *any* company using them could expect an improvement in its performance.

In fact, there's widespread *disagreement* about what the terms mean, and how to use them. Early definitions had vision meaning a big dream or ambition, and mission describing where and how a firm would compete. Yet read what firms say about themselves. Some put vision first, then mission; others switch the order. All too often, both statements say more or less the same things, and are a jumble of ideas – too fluffy and imprecise to guide anyone. So it's no wonder that these "tools" are the butt of so many jokes, and cause as much confusion and cynicism among employees as they do.

A lack of evidence for the efficacy of many fashionable management ideas should be a warning to be wary of them. Claims that they've helped companies succeed should carry a "Caution!" label. Managers often ascribe results to some theory or tool when other factors actually played a bigger role.

Or they espouse one thing, but do another.

"We use scenarios," they'll say, when what they actually do from time to time is a SWOT analysis. Or they'll claim to empower their people, when in fact they allow few of them access to important information, involvement in important discussions, or responsibility for important work. Or they'll boast about their commitment to innovation, customer service, people development, or lean production, while focusing time, effort, and funding on something quite different.

Despite this, some of them do well. You might criticize their behaviour, but you can't criticize their results.

So what you can do is ask: what did they *actually do* that seemed to work? That's what I looked for. That's what I believe I've found.

Mumbo jumbo

Every manager comes to work with a point of view about how to manage. Some can explain themselves clearly and make sense, but most either don't bother or are hopelessly imprecise.

In every company, you'll find a jumble of ideas about setting goals, getting the right things done, tracking performance, and so on. Some of it apparently makes a positive difference; the rest just gets in the way.

I'm constantly struck by the readiness of executives to underrate the need to be explicit about their beliefs, and by their assumption that people will somehow read their minds. And I'm also struck by their rush for concepts they obviously don't understand, and which are patently wrong for them – and by the fervour with which they champion them. Many business problems are caused by bright, serious people espousing "best practices" that in reality are just currently *popular* practices, and by interventions that are inappropriate or poorly applied.

Some examples:

- The head of one large industrial firm opens a strategy session with a lengthy speech about the need to change the company's culture. But she doesn't understand what culture is, and fails to make clear what changes she has in mind, or how they'll be made. Nor does she realize how difficult it will be and how high the chances are of failure. The result is she leaves people unsure and uneasy.
- A divisional leader in a mining company announces a new initiative to drive a "step change" in productivity. He tosses around notions like "lean thinking" and "short-interval controls," but quite obviously doesn't know what he's talking about, and neither does anyone else in the room.
- The CEO of a chemicals business makes a big thing about why the firm should be "values-driven." Then he throws in comments about "value-driven" management. He doesn't understand that these are completely different topics, so fails to explain why either of them might be important, which of them he wants his team to focus on, or what he expects people to do about them.*

---

* "Values-driven" means that everything you do is guided by your values. "Value-driven management" is a financially focused approach to delivering as much shareholder value as possible.

- The chairman of a food company talks about the need for "disruption," but when I probe to find out exactly what he means, it turns out that he doesn't have a clue. He came across the term somewhere, and bandies it about to mean anything and everything.
- The boss of an IT company gets passionate about "customer-centricity," but has no idea how to make it the way of life that he says he wants it to be. Even worse, his own behaviour shows why it will never take hold in his firm. He stays as far away from customers as he can, treats their feedback with contempt, refuses to invest in training or CRM systems,* and insists on policies or practices that prevent his people from responding rapidly to customer requests or complaints.
- Another CEO lays out her view of a growth strategy, but is unconvincing when she's challenged on the detail. One minute she talks about spending more on marketing, the next she's going on about product innovation. She doesn't understand the dynamics of her market, and knows little about her customers and even less about how to keep them and win more.†

Time and again, when I'm called to help an organization with strategy, I'm taken aback by the top team's lack of understanding or agreement about this most vital function and how to approach it. And by their conviction that strategy is a mysterious matter, distinct from other management activities, and that only a few rare people can "do" it.

"What process should we follow?" they ask. "Who should we involve?" "What outcomes can we expect?" They treat strategy as a ritual to be tackled once a year – usually around budget time – and keep changing the way they tackle it. Most of them have worked with a succession of consultants, each with their own ideas about strategy, and thus advocating a different way of thinking, a different toolkit. Yet nothing sticks. When offered yet another approach, they readily grasp it.

But perhaps this shouldn't be a surprise. As Columbia Business School professor Eric Abrahamson says, management fads tend to come with "emotionally charged, enthusiastic and unreasoned discourse."[13] When executives discover anything new, they go gaga. Their judgment becomes clouded. They erase their prior beliefs about management and forget that only yesterday they were committed to another tool, concept, or process.

Managing does require flexibility and improvisation. You have to make things up as you go along. But just as it's a serious mistake to constantly change your

---

* Customer relationship management systems.

† All real examples, with details changed to protect confidentiality.

strategy and the priorities and activities that flow from it, it's equally unwise to constantly change the *process* by which you develop it.

For one thing, you never get to practise any approach enough to master it – you have to keep re-learning what to do. This always involves more than what comes first, second, or third on some template, for strategizing is complicated by history and current circumstances, people's world views, your business philosophies, the place of strategy in your firm, and its connections to culture, capabilities, stakeholders, and past experiences, among many other factors.

Second, when there's no strong link from one strategy session to the next, you have to start pretty much from scratch each time. This ensures that no one takes a long view and sees decisions and commitments as building blocks for the future. Working in stop-start mode is extremely disruptive, and can make it hard for employees across your organization to see a bigger picture and understand the importance of what they do.

And third, your flip-flops make you seem foolish and indecisive, and sow confusion. Everything you say becomes suspect. Following you looks risky, and from previous experience will surely turn out to be an exercise in futility.

When you change any process, you inevitably also change the *language* you use to explain what you're about. Words mean different things to different people, so communication is easily fouled up. Mixed messages cause mayhem.

As a manager, you can never be clear enough. It's an ongoing battle to spell things out and drive shared understanding through your organization. Just one careless word can throw your strategy off course, your people off balance, and your efforts into disarray.

Without a clear point of view, it's inevitable that suspect practices will creep into your company. After all, if you create a vacuum, something will fill it. So if you even hint that you're not 100 per cent sure of your management approach or about your tools, your doubt will trump your good intentions. And you can be sure that someone will suggest an alternative. Chances are it'll be some newfangled, untested notion – because that's what happens to be in the headlines at the moment. And even if it did bring results somewhere else, it may not do the same for you.

Tools galore

Management ideas can either oil the wheels of an organization or be like sand in the gears. You need to pick them – and switch them – with extreme care.

There's no shortage of interesting possibilities. If you want a sense of what's out there, look no further than Bain's *Tools Survey*. The firm compiles a list of "tools," identifies the top 25 according to mentions in academic and business articles, and asks a sample of several thousand executives around the world which they use and how satisfied they are with them.

The 2007 study lists no fewer than 66 tools. They include old favourites like strategic planning, scenario planning, self-directed teams, and reengineering. Also in there are some newer ideas like permission marketing and "Gung-ho!" (Whatever that may be!)

When you run your eye down the list, it's hard to discern much that you haven't seen before, and it's even harder to see why a lot of the words belong there.

PIMS analysis* came along in the 1970s, and lost its shine years ago. "New science" has never entered mainstream thinking. "Growth strategies" is such a vague term it covers anything and everything. And isn't "Baldrige Award" a contest?

And anyway, what is the justification for applying the "tools" label to these and other management ideas? Take micro-marketing, for example. Or merger integration teams, customer retention, or strategic alliances. Aren't these just ways to go about your business? Or key themes? Or projects?

The top 25 tools in Bain's 2009 survey are mostly old hat. And once again, you have to ask how "voice of the customer innovation," "collaborative innovation," or "decision rights tools" find a place on the list.[14]

They make it because, says Bain, "The term 'management tool' now encompasses a broad spectrum of approaches to management – from simple planning software, to complex organizational designs, to revised philosophies of the business world."[15] But this sweeping definition isn't helpful. It allows so much licence that you could include in your management toolkit pretty well anything from a discussion about your firm's social role to one about executive pay; from the reminder list on your smartphone to your belief that you should provide Google-quality food in your company cafeteria; or from lean production to your policy on bringing dogs to the office or working from home.

I've no doubt that readers of the survey enjoy it, and many would say they find it useful. But sloppy language is a cause of many problems in organizations. There's no need to nitpick, but being clear and precise makes for good communication and also helps unclutter organizational life. When you start out unsure about what is or is not a tool, you're well on the way to trouble. When you jam up your company with a mishmash of verbal garbage, you *deserve* trouble. When you put your people to work on stuff you don't really understand, you just have to hope for the best.

Cast your eye down the list below (Figure 3.1). Do you know what it all means? Where should you start in order to change your firm's fortunes? What will actually

---

* "Profit Impact of Market Strategy."

make a difference – and why? How do you know? Can you safely dip into this pile and "mix-and-match" the concepts you fancy? Can you *explain* what you're talking about? Do you know what it'll take to make your weapons of choice *work*? Can you *do* it?

Figure 3.1

SOME TOOLS, TECHNIQUES, AND APPROACHES TO MANAGEMENT		
• Core competence	• Portfolio management	• CRM
• Reengineering	• Outsourcing	• ABC
• Six Sigma quality	• Appreciative inquiry	• TQM
• Self-managing teams	• Complexity theory	• JIT
• Knowledge management	• Chaos management	• OVA
• Learning organization	• System dynamics	• SVA
• Organizations as orchestras	• Concurrent engineering	• CPR
• Strategic intent	• Creative destruction	• SPC
• Vision & mission	• New science	• EVA
• Value-chain analysis	• CRM	• ROI
• Diversity management	• Data mining	• ROA
• Mass customization	• ABC	• CFROI
• Strategic alliances	• EVA	• 7-Ss
• Intrepreneuring	• Excellence	• 5-Forces
• Balanced scorecard	• Scenarios	• 3-Cs
• One-to-one marketing	• New options pricing	• 1-Minute managing
• Zero defects	• Cycle-time reduction	• Growth strategies
• PIMS analysis	• Benchmarking	• Baldrige Award
• Experience curves	• Merger integration teams	• Micro marketing
• Cycle-time reduction	• Competitive gaming	• 2x2 matrices
• Conjoint analysis	• Gung-Ho!	• Nominal group technique

Adapted from Bain & Company, *Tools Survey 2007*

The Bain survey shows that about 200 tools and frameworks are in use in any one year. More surprising, says Bain partner Chris Zook, "is the short life span of many of these tools that arise through a popular book or management fad, only to fail to be the magic elixir, constantly disappointing their Ponc de Leóns in search of the fountain of eternal business life. Moreover, these elixirs frequently have limited empirical support (they are new, so how can they be?) and therefore rest on only a few reports of sightings of miracle cures."[16]

According to Bain, the average large firm used 10 tools in 2000, 16 in 2003, 13 in 2004, 13 in 2005, 15 in 2006, 11 in 2008, 10 in 2009, and 10 in 2011. Strategic planning held top spot from 1993 when the project started, but was shoved into second spot by benchmarking in 2009 when the global economy soured. Yet strategic planning had the highest satisfaction rating that year, while benchmarking only made 14th. And it was back on top in 2013.[17]

Other tools also come and go and enjoy different usage ratings in different parts of the world. Satisfaction scores also rise and fall.[18] In the 2000 survey, 77 per cent of respondents said tools promise more than they deliver.[19] Only one of the top ten tools from 1993 made it onto the 2007 list.[20]

This may be because a particular tool isn't all it's cracked up to be. But mostly, it's because managers don't understand them, don't know when or how to use them, or don't use them well. Often, they grab too many, too fast, and plug them in one upon another. Their organizations are never allowed time to get a firm grasp of anything, to develop a coherent "theory of success" or a language to explain it, or to bed down initiatives so they become "the way we do things around here." While people are struggling to make sense of one idea, their bosses dash off after the next hot thing, thus keeping them constantly befuddled, unsettled, and over-loaded.

Problems also occur because the cruel capitalist system demands rapid results, whereas it takes time to implant new initiatives and see the benefits. So the short-term cost of change might outweigh whatever payoff is promised for the longer term. And when managers' careers and bonuses are on the line they're likely to put themselves first. It's hard to blame them when they focus on quick returns rather than launching long-term initiatives that may not work for them.

Three of the biggest ideas of recent years are the balanced scorecard, bench-marking, and reengineering. Let's take a look at their origins and impact – and where they are now.

If you can't measure it ...

A continuing challenge to business is what to measure and how. Financial indicators have always come first. But financial results are driven by many factors, and firms have many responsibilities; they must satisfy not just shareholders, but other stakeholders too. So non-financial goals and results, which in the past were treated as something of an afterthought, are increasingly important.

Perhaps the most widely used tracking method today is the balanced scorecard (BSC), which was introduced in a 1992 *HBR* article by Robert Kaplan and David Norton, and built into a sizeable industry through other articles, books, news-letters, courses, and consulting services. For many managers it's an indispensable tool for setting goals and executing strategy, as it directs attention not only to financial performance, but also to customers, internal processes, and learning and growth.[21]

But just how new is it?

Go all the way back to General Electric in 1951, when CEO Ralph Cordiner assigned a task force to identify key performance measures. The giant company was decentralizing so "the need for more realistic and balanced measurements became visibly more acute," he said.[22] The team came back with "profitability, market share, employee attitudes, public responsibility, and the balance between short- and long-term goals."[23]

Or go to Drucker in 1954, when he pointed out that a business had to meet eight objectives: 1) market standing, 2) innovation, 3) productivity, 4) physical and financial resources, 5) profitability, 6) manager performance and development, 7) worker performance and attitude, and 8) public responsibility.[24]

Or to William Ouchi's 1981 bestseller *Theory Z*, in which he said: "The statement of objectives should include more than financial objectives such as the rate of growth and of profitability. It should also include less tangible objectives such as the rate of technological advance and the quality of service to customers."[25]

You might also turn to Michael Porter's 1980 book, *Competitive Strategy*, in which he used "the wheel of business strategy," which had been developed in the 1960s for Harvard's business policy course, to show that firms must perform in a range of areas to meet their goals.[26] Or to the 1986 book by Porter's colleague, Richard Hamermesh, *Making Strategy Work*, in which the wheel appeared again.[27] (While not strictly a goal-setting or measurement tool, it does show what you need to manage and measure. And incidentally, it's still used at Harvard.)*

Some of this doubtless contributed to the development of the BSC by Kaplan and Norton. But they were influenced, above all, by the work of Art Schneiderman, vice president of quality and productivity at Analog Devices, a semiconductor firm. He produced a "corporate scorecard" in 1987, and in 1990 shared his thinking with participants in a year-long study, "Measuring Performance in the Organization of the Future," by the Nolan Norton Institute, the research arm of KPMG.[28]

So the balanced scorecard certainly had a lot of parents. It has legions of committed users worldwide, and has, in turn, spawned many other measurement systems. But there are reasons to think twice before adopting it.

In a *Harvard Business Review* piece in December 2007, Darrel Rigby, the Bain partner in charge of that firm's tools survey, noted that the BSC – among other ideas – has had a rather chequered history.[29] When I asked him why, he wrote back:

The challenges we hear most frequently are, theoretically, it all makes so much sense. However,

1. The wide range of metrics required is complicated and cumbersome. A few end up mattering, but people can't keep track of the others. Trying to push all of them at once doesn't seem to work well.

---

* For an excellent explanation of how to use it, see Cynthia Montgomery, *The Strategist*, New York: HarperBusiness, 2012.

2. The senior executives determine what really matters by the metrics they stress day in and day out.

3. Developing and tracking all of the metrics often creates more costs than benefits.[30]

Many of the firms I deal with use balanced scorecards, and all these issues have been borne out in my conversations with them. The people responsible for adopting BSCs are bound to voice approval of them, and do. But those who have to work with them are often vehemently opposed to them – mostly because of the work they generate and the questionable benefits they bring. I had one organization bring a *250-page scorecard* to me, concerned that "it wasn't working." This was an obvious extreme. But most of what I see is much too long and complicated to be helpful. The tool has taken over, leaving no time to even try to get results.

What isn't mentioned, and may be even more problematic, is blind acceptance of the four headline measures that Kaplan and Norton advocate – financial, customers, internal processes, and learning and growth – even when a company's strategy hinges on performance in other areas. This initial error is compounded when executives then create laundry lists of goals and actions in each area, which often are so vague as to be useless.

That said, the BSC can be helpful in setting goals and tracking performance. But is it the only tool for that? Not by a long shot. Is it one that managers *must* use? Absolutely not. Can they do without it? Of course.

When benchmarking backfires

Another practice that's attracted a big following is benchmarking. And a good idea it is too. Comparing your company to others, activity by activity, tells you how you rate, and where you might want to improve. Learning from other firms makes perfect sense.

The idea behind benchmarking is that you gauge your performance in various tasks against that of your competitors, or even against firms outside your industry, and thus hopefully highlight functions that you need to improve, change your perception of what's possible, and spur your team to set higher targets. So, for example, you might compare your materials usage, process times, production costs, or productivity to theirs. Or you might track how much revenue they get from new products, how many calls their sales people make each day, or how fast they fulfil orders.

Benchmarking has happened literally forever. Companies have always watched each other and learned from each other. But the idea really took hold after Japanese firms made a fetish of doing that when they started to invade the West in the 1970s.

Gradually, others saw the merit in picking apart their competitors' activity systems, measuring their performance in each element of them, and comparing it against their own.

Benchmarking was originally a way to check *operational effectiveness*. But as firms have found it harder and harder to develop unique advantages, it has inevitably leached into the area of *strategy*.[31] Now, when managers say, "Let's benchmark ourselves," their intention is often ambiguous. They not only watch and copy each other's activities, but also hope to discover new ways to do business altogether.

If there appears to be any advantage in copying someone else's tools – scenarios, team-building activities, Six Sigma, or whatever – then that's what happens. When one company identifies a new market, sees a product opportunity, or hits on a marketing idea, others soon follow. Low-cost airlines all learn from Southwest. Zara has become a role model for fashion retailers. Makers of mobile phones take their cue from what Apple does with its iPhones. Google shows the way in search-based advertising.

It's easy to see where this will lead. When everyone does the same things the same way, they all rush down the same path, straight into the "me too" trap. And the more pressure they feel and the harder they work, the faster their strategies converge and the more sharply their margins decline. So in their desperation to become more competitive, they deliberately and systematically commoditize themselves.

All firms can benefit from comparing themselves to others. You have to know what you're up against, and there's obviously much to gain from knowing how another company does things, and how well it does them. But is benchmarking a tool managers must use? Absolutely not. Can they do without it? Of course.

Remember reengineering?

For an example of the potential downside in "big ideas," look no further than the reengineering "revolution." It was sparked when Michael Hammer, an IT expert, coined the term "reengineering" in 1987, then published "Reengineering Work: Don't Automate, Obliterate," in *Harvard Business Review* in July–August 1990,[32] and followed this up with *Reengineering the Corporation*, written with James Champy, which arrived on bookshelves in 1992 and quickly became a bestseller.[33] Soon, every manager you bumped into talked reengineering. But two years and three million book sales later, it was clear that most of them used the term as a metaphor for downsizing, and that those who drank the Kool-Aid were killing morale in their firms and damaging their long-term prospects by cutting too far, too fast. So they hurriedly backtracked.

Sensing a new opportunity, Champy quickly produced another book. "If I've learned anything in the past 18 months," he admitted in *Reengineering Management*, "it is that the revolution we started has gone, at best, only halfway. I have also learned that half a revolution is not better than none. It may, in fact, be worse."[34]

His efforts to finish the revolution failed to breathe life back into reengineering. Many critics see it as one of the most toxic fads ever. Many managers are nervous even to mention the word.

Hammer, too, offered a *mea culpa*. In the Preface of his own follow-up to *Reengineering*, he wrote: "the popularity of the book and success of the concept led some to see it as a panacea, which in turn encouraged others to promote their favorite silver bullets. For nearly a decade, business people have been deluged with books promising eternal victory. Perhaps part of my atonement for this unintentional transgression has been to write *The Agenda*."[35]

Bain ranked reengineering No. 13 for usage in its 2001 survey of management tools[36] and 19th in 2003.[37] It showed some recovery to eighth in 2009, when cost-cutting had shot to the top of corporate agendas because of the economic slump that started in 2008.[38] However, even as tough times continued, and companies kept hacking away at their costs, mostly by cutting jobs, it fell to No. 14 in the 2013 survey.[39]

Reengineering wasn't all bad. It got managers thinking about how to trim their operations to drive down costs, which was critical in a hyper-competitive world. Champy cites many successes. And for many firms today, the tough measures proposed by him and Hammer are more urgent than ever.

All firms need from time to time to take strong, decisive, and systematic action to raise their game. They may do this for narrow reasons such as cutting costs, or more broadly because their strategy has to change. But the fact that "reengineering" is a label you could apply to any change doesn't mean you should attach it to every change.

4

BLOCKBUSTERS BUST

In 1978, two consultants and two business school teachers got together to hatch a way to sell a major consulting firm's expertise in organizational issues. Their first problem was how to rein in one of the consultants, "a crazy guy ... the driving force, the intellectual leader ... messianic and great fun." An agenda would help. So one of the academics suggested a scheme with three elements that had been developed by someone at Harvard. The other added two more items. By talking about one piece a day, they figured, they'd be able to keep their five-day meeting on course.

The consulting firm was McKinsey. The academics were Anthony Athos and Richard Pascale. The "crazy guy" was Tom Peters. The other consultant was Bob Waterman. The five topics became seven, and the famous "7S" model was born. "It was nothing more than a tool to control Tom Peters," says Pascale.[1]

While Peters remembers things slightly differently, the point is that a marketing project led to a meeting that needed an agenda that became the model at the heart of *In Search of Excellence*, and of Pascale and Athos's book, *The Art of Japanese Management*.[2] The model has been widely used, and McKinsey recently reminded managers of its value.[3] But according to the people who knocked it together, it was intended to control a conversation, was based largely on general experience and anecdote, and its usefulness is questionable.[4]

So what about the equally famous eight "basic principles" described in *Excellence*?

As Peters tells it, he'd spent many months on the road, visiting successful companies to learn their secrets. He'd produced a 700-slide presentation for Siemens, a McKinsey client, and was asked to do another, shorter one, for PepsiCo. This is what happened next:

The time was drawing near for the Pepsi presentation to take place. One morning at about 6, I sat down at my desk overlooking San Francisco Bay from the

48th floor of the Bank of America Tower, and closed my eyes. Then I leaned forward, and I wrote down eight things on a pad of paper. Those eight things haven't changed since that moment. They were the eight basic principles of Excellence.[5]

Those "principles" quickly became gospel. But listening to Peters reflect on their birth must raise questions. And listening to him reflect on their validity raises more. "A positive guarantee would say, Follow these eight principles and you will win – guaranteed. I'd never say that – not then, not now ... But what I would say is, Ignore these eight principles, and you will fail – guaranteed. If you do none of these things, I promise you that your company will never come close to being an excellent one."[6]

What might this mean? If you read Peters literally, he's saying you'll fall short if you don't apply *all* eight principles. So how many is enough? How many can you skip? What if you apply one ... five ... six ... seven? Will you be doomed? And can it really be true that using none of them will close off any hope of excellence? After all, other authors offer other counsel.

Buyer beware!

In Search of Excellence was the first of a kind and is a remarkable book. Putting "excellence" in the title was a stroke of genius. The McKinsey brand name lent it immediate credibility. It tackled the challenge of understanding business performance in an innovative way, boiling down apparently exhaustive field and desk research to breezy anecdotes, and interesting insights. Its optimistic message offered hope at a crucial moment, thus influencing millions of executives. And as a result, it inspired numerous copycat studies, thus turbocharging the business book business.

But the speed with which many of the "excellent" firms became *un*-excellent[7] after the book appeared was a nasty blow, and gave critics much ammunition. And Peters' own comments about how the book was created have been damaging. For all its merits, much of the book's advice smacks of being concocted rather than discovered.

As one reviewer observed: "the solutions' worth inescapably depends on the quality of the supporting evidence, which in the case of all eight is based neither on the excellent companies nor for that matter on any described research." And he goes on to note that "there are at least as many nonexcellent companies cited in support of the attributes as excellent companies."[8]

Another analysis, in *Academy of Management Executive*, pointed out, "The criteria chosen to measure excellence substantially affect the value of the results

... only three 'excellent' firms had higher market returns than the average returns of all 162 of the *Fortune* 1,000 firms ... the excellent firms identified by Peters and Waterman may not have been excellent performers, and they may not have applied the excellence principles to any greater extent than did the general population of firms ... the data call into question whether these excellence principles are, in fact, related to performance ... the work may be one of advocacy rather than of science."[9]

And according to Michael Cusumano, a professor of management at MIT, "What was enduring excellence and what was luck – or bad luck – seem hard to distinguish, in retrospect ... We might also wonder why Peters and Waterman choose these companies and not others. How do we really know that the factors they talked about and not other factors were responsible for the performance, good and bad, of these firms?"[10]

In fact, Peters had already revealed how they picked companies to look at. In a 2001 *Fast Company* article he said, "We went around to McKinsey's partners and to a bunch of other smart people who were deeply engaged in the world of business and asked, Who's cool? Who's doing cool work? Where is there great stuff going on? And which companies genuinely get it?" Then, in the tradition of McKinsey, he and Waterman added several quantitative measures to demonstrate rigour.[11]

Sadly, writes Matthew Stewart in *The Management Myth*, "it has since become evident that Peters and friends' intuitions concerning the excellence of companies are about as bankable as the average fortune cookie."[12] Their approach, said Julia Kirby in "Toward a Theory of High Performance" in *HBR*, "reads like something out of the *Journal of Irreproducible Results*."[13]

But despite these and other barbs – and despite Peter's own disclaimer in the first line of his next work, *Thriving On Chaos* in 1987, that "there are no excellent companies"[14] – *Excellence* established a new genre. A spate of copycat "studies" followed, offering yet more lists. Some were based on reasonably sound research, but you could pick holes in all of them if you wanted to. And that's a problem for any management writer.

Beyond excellence to greatness

The "really big business book" after *Excellence* was *Built to Last*, which arrived in 1994. In a six-year research project at the Stanford University Graduate School of Business, the authors, Jim Collins and Jerry Porras, sought to explain why some firms outlived others and performed well for many decades. They compared 18 "visionary" companies with an average age of 100 years to a not-so-visionary peer group, and reduced their findings to a set of memorable nostrums like "Clock building, not time telling," "No 'tyranny of the OR,'" and "Big hairy audacious goals" (BHAGs). Their book immediately seized the attention of managers, has been reprinted numerous times and translated into many languages, and is still immensely popular.[15]

Not content with those answers, though, Collins got right back to work. Seven years later, he produced *Good to Great* – another bestseller, and one that catapulted him from prominence to superstardom.

The question at the heart of this book was: "Can a good company become a great company, and if so, how? Or is the disease of 'just being good' incurable?" Collins and a team of 21 researchers spent five years looking for companies that had delivered 15 years of returns at or below the general stock market, followed by 15 years of returns "at least three times the market." They began with 1,435 companies that featured on *Fortune*'s listing of America's biggest in 1965, 1975, 1985, and 1995, and after a "death march of financial analysis," cut the list to 126, then to 19, and finally, to 11. The project "consumed 10.5 people years of effort," says Collins, underscoring the care that went into the book's prescriptions. "We read and systematically coded nearly 6,000 articles, generated more than 2,000 pages of interview transcripts, and created 384 million bytes of computer data."[16]

However, two articles in *Academy of Management Perspectives* challenge the findings of *Good to Great*. "Our test results provide no empirical evidence for Collins' claim that applying the GTG concepts leads to 'sustained good results,'" report the authors of one article. "Collins provided no evidence that his five principles are anything other than five 'fleeting random patterns.'"[17]

The second article's authors found that "only one of the 11 companies continues to exhibit superior stock market performance according to Collins' measure ... not a single company exhibits sustained success when measured by statistically significant abnormal stock market performance."[18]

And again, Cusumano voices concern. The structure of the study, he says, makes it impossible "to determine which concepts represent enduring practices and which do not ... Collins made no attempt to measure and test these attributes, such as to correlate one or more of them with stock performance or any other measures. As a result, we have no way to determine *statistical* significance or prioritize the factors, or control for other companies that might have exhibited the same or most of the same factors but did not have comparably good or great stock performance."[19]

Collins has a huge global following, and is considered "one of the world's most important management thinkers."[20] His books are often cited by other writers in the field. No doubt there are hordes of executives who'll swear his advice worked for them. But has it really advanced our understanding of management? And are the managers who say it "works" really right?

Commenting on *Built to Last*, Richard D'Aveni, a professor at Dartmouth's Tuck

School of Business, warned that its advice was too broad and thus "so slippery, it's like grabbing a frog." James O'Toole, research professor at the USC Marshall School of Business, said: "If Collins is to be faulted, it is that he ignores Aristotle's advice not to try to scientifically measure those things that don't lend themselves to quantification."[21] And here's psychologist and Nobel laureate Daniel Kahneman, writing in his own bestseller, *Thinking Fast and Slow*:

> The basic message of *Built to Last* and other similar books is that good managerial practices can be identified and that good practices will be rewarded by good results. Both messages are overstated. The comparison of firms that have been more or less successful is to a significant extent a comparison between firms that have been more or less lucky. Knowing the importance of luck, you should be particularly suspicious when highly consistent patterns emerge from the comparison of successful and less successful firms. In the presence of randomness, regular patterns can only be mirages.[22]

Tom Peters was much less polite: "I find the idea of 'built to last' ... offensive," he said. And he dismissed Collins's approval of "self-effacing, quiet, reserved, even shy leaders" in *Good to Great*, with "More Collins, more clap trap."[23]

When a book grabs the limelight, however, no amount of expert censure seems to put managers off.

The flaws in *In Search of Excellence* have been well documented,[24] yet it keeps on selling – around 10 million copies so far.[25] *Business Week* called *Good to Great* "the world's bestselling guide to taking companies to the next level,"[26] and in January 2015 it still ranked as the No. 153 bestseller on Amazon.com.

Given that these titles are the most successful of their ilk, in terms of both sales and the buzz around them, and have been so mindfully produced yet apparently have such serious defects, you have to query what's being offered in others that were dashed off with less care.

The formula of choice behind much management advice seems to be suspect "research," contentious assumptions, weak linkages, disregard for contextual factors, and a healthy dose of speculation and hype. Books and articles that attract the most fans are often the most questionable.

These few examples show how easily managers can be led astray. So what exactly are you to make of the handy checklists in books like *In Search of Excellence*, *Built to Last*, or *Good to Great*? Should you take them at face value, or write them off immediately? Should you follow them slavishly, or can you pick parts that you like? Can you mix advice from one with that of another? Which ideas can you safely ignore – and which should you know more about? What really will do the trick for your company?

Management ideas are to be found in many places. Some are intellectually sound, and their positive effect on business results can be isolated and demonstrated. But many more should be viewed with a critical eye. When you consider using them, you should ask: "What's the 'pedigree' of this idea? What does it depend on?" That'll help you clarify your thinking, and perhaps change your mind and have you do something more sensible.

Before you rush off and plug in the newest, coolest breakthrough concept, listen again to Peters, this time in a 2003 interview: "Anyone who read our book as if it were the Talmud," he said, "deserved their sorry fate."[27]

Such candour is rare among management gurus. Which is a good reason to keep your bullshit detector up!

Uncritical choices

Managers labour under enormous and unrelenting pressure to produce results. The rewards for success are lavish, and failure is quickly punished. Yet they're astonishingly imprudent about the tools they choose and use. (Or maybe they have little choice in the matter, as when a missive from Head Office instructs them to adopt *kaizen* or a new CRM system, or to send their key people off to be trained in a new approach to change management.)

It doesn't seem to bother those who fall for management voodoo that much of it is just common sense, cunningly packaged. Or that much of it is as likely to kill as to cure. Or that turning "solutions" into results is almost always harder than it seems. Or that many of their competitors will buy the same nostrums, thus nullifying their effect.

It doesn't occur to them that, as Bain cautions, "A tool will improve results only to the extent that it helps discover unmet customer needs, helps build distinctive capabilities and helps exploit the vulnerabilities of competitors – or a combination of all three."[28]

Nor does it occur to them that the *language* they use to talk about performance improvement – the terms, models, frameworks, and so on – has a profound effect on their strategic conversation, making it either an effective tool or useless twaddle.

It's both easy and tempting to introduce what *The Economist* called "a slapdash set of potted theories"[29] that'll confound even the most senior executives, rather than aid them. Before you know it, debate about visions, missions, values, and similar verbiage can sidetrack even the most competent team. But why stop there? Toss in reengineering, disruption, cost leadership – or a *clutch* of other favourites if you're really keen to make a difference. Add a sprinkling of "synergy," "leveraging," "out of the box," "blue sky," "empowerment," "granularity," "resilience," "human capital," or other popular jargon, and in no time you have a real mishmash. After that, getting the right things done is sure to be far harder than it need be – if it can be done at all.

The sheer difficulty of understanding managerial success, coupled with research methods that range from excellent to hopelessly flawed and even blatantly misleading, make it hard for executives to know what to spend their time on and what to ignore. Different people within a management team will be attracted by different books or articles. Some are sure to lobby hard for the ideas they fancy. In no time at all, no one can remember where an idea came from or why it was adopted.

So let's ask: what *is* likely to get attention?

"Practising managers seem to like books that have a strong central message with practical implications, and often that are inspirational," says Phil Rosenzweig, author of *The Halo Effect*. "Many of these books have the virtue of good storytelling, which is fine, except that some of them claim to be rigorous science, but are not … There's no particular need for all business books to meet the test of science, but I do think they should meet a basic test of honesty and not claim to be something they are not."[30]

A study of strategy tools by the Advanced Institute of Management Research found that "managers do not choose tools because of their relevance to the topics they intend to address, but those that are *easier to understand and use*, as well as those that hold the highest level of legitimacy with their peers i.e. the *best known and most frequently used*."[31] (My italics.)

D'Aveni is snarkier. Success, he says, rests on three factors: "One, tell people what they want to hear and give them hope. Two, make it a Rorschach test,* and three keep it so simple that it really doesn't examine the truth of the world in enough depth so people get a false sense of clarity."[32]

This explains the extraordinary sales of books like *Who Moved My Cheese?* and *Fish!* And why you hear executives parroting snappy formulas – "A bias for action," "Hands on, value driven," "Level five leadership," "First who, then what," "The flywheel effect" – from *In Search of Excellence* or *Good to Great*.

Like the Bain Tools surveys, the AIMR study also found that the most used tools are not the most *valued* ones. So, for example, SWOT analysis ranked as the most used tool but was not very highly valued. Scenario planning was highly valued but not commonly used.[33]

Slogans and symbolism are more necessary in management than most executives recognize. But substance is essential. And too often, substance gets short shrift.

When the acerbic *Financial Times* columnist Lucy Kellaway announced in

---

* A psychological test in which people say what they see in inkblots.

November 2009, "The bear market in management bullshit is over,"[34] it should have been cause for celebration. But clearly, she was wrong.

Suckers galore

If you're like most managers, you already have a toolkit with a lot of stuff in it. You learned about what's in there from books or magazines or business school, from consultants or other gurus, or from your own time in the trenches. And there's a whole lot more available that you probably *don't* know about.

If you're looking for ways to drive innovation, improve quality, encourage teamwork, make your company a "learning organization," boost sales or profits, or become a better leader, there's a rich mine of information and advice waiting for you.

Or, to be more accurate, a *minefield*.

For much of what's on offer is less helpful than it's made out to be. Overblown promises and practical application are poles apart. The ideas you fall for may not be all they're made out to be. Applying them might be a lot harder than "the blurb on the box" promises, and they may not do what you expect of them. Much of what you've been led to believe about management is just not so. A lot is pure hokum.

Ignorance of what's known about management is one reason executives are so prone to wild goose chases. Somewhere, just around the next corner, is the insight they need – or so they think. But they'd do well to heed the observation of Walter Kiechel III, a prominent management writer, that "it has sometimes been hard to distinguish between profound insight and hyped-up trivia."[35]

The business arena is awash with empty assurances of superior performance through this recipe or that. In most firms, the air is thick with half-truths, myths and mumbo-jumbo, whose main contribution is to create work, sow mayhem, and get in the way of results.

Companies lay huge bets and take absurd risks on the basis of what's no more than snake oil – concocted by very smart people, to be sure, but snake oil nonetheless. Many popular management ideas are what IT geeks would call "vapourware" – fluff cloaked in hype. Management-speak is strewn with terms that are code for ... *nothing you need to know about.*

Any sensible executive is keen to find better ways to manage. Indeed, every sensible executive should actively seek new ways to manage. So it's natural for them to be alert for new thinking, and to try ideas they've just read about in a business journal or newspaper article or that they've heard from some guru. Occasionally, this works. But much more often, it leads to disappointment, as they discount proven principles and practices to grab onto "breakthrough" ideas that almost certainly will take them nowhere.

Consider, for example, the response to Tom Peters, superstar of all superstars in the firmament of management advice. He has an astonishing ability to notice what companies, executives, and employees are doing, make sense of why it matters, and suggest where future practices will go. Whether it's the "wow!" in products and processes, the need to see work as projects, or the potential for design in virtually everything, he has inspired much thought, debate, and writing. But he is less an inventor of new ideas than a reporter of things he sees happening. Using liberal examples – Walgreens here, John Smith there, "Look what they're doing ... you can too!" – and an evangelical speaking style, he gets his audiences jumping.

But what does he actually give them? He told a *Financial Times* interviewer, "I say to people, 'You got a bad deal, paying money to see me. I have utterly nothing new to say. I am simply going to remind you of what you've known since the age of 22 and in the heat of battle you forgot.'"[36]

Few hawkers of management advice would make such a confession. Theirs is a fashion industry. The managers who pay them want to be told, "Here's a red-hot new idea for you. One you've never heard before." So it's smarter for them to create an illusion of newness than be seen to dredge up more of the "same old same old."

Superficial learning

Judging from the sales of business books, the popularity of non-academic journals such as *Harvard Business Review* and *Strategy+Business*, and of general business magazines like *Fortune* and *Business Week*, and the demand for speakers like Hamel, Collins, and Peters – not to mention Seth Godin, Guy Kawasaki, Jack Welch, A.G. Lafley, and legions of unknowns – managers do want to learn. But most of them pepper their experience with a haphazard sprinkling of deep insights, common sense, fads, myths, and buzzwords.

This is not to say that their sources don't add value; some surely do. What is in doubt is whether or how managers use the information available to them. Do they understand it well enough to be able to apply it well? Do the various ideas they bring into their firms add up to a coherent whole? Do they develop *their own* joined-up theories of management?

From watching top people swerve rapidly from idea to idea, I am sure the answer to all these questions is "No."

While business books sell in huge numbers, most of them are never read. They look impressive on office bookshelves, but whatever wisdom they contain stays between the covers. And it's the same with journals and mainstream business magazines – except that many of them wind up in dustbins.

Those who hear Tom Peters doubtless forget most of what he blasts at them before they go home. But some of it surely sticks. Some of it probably causes them to reframe their views of business, and gives them the language to reframe what they talk about back at the office. This, in turn, may lead to some experimentation, some change. And maybe even some better results.

Peters calls himself a "professional agitator."[37] And he does that better than anyone.

Advice traps

"Modern management theory is no more reliable than tribal medicine," say John Mickelthwaite and Adrian Wooldridge in *The Witch Doctors*, a blistering critique of management gurus. "Witch doctors, after all, often got it right – by luck, by instinct, or by trial and error."[38]

Many others have been equally dismissive of what's dished up as serious knowledge about a serious subject. Their main gripe is that much of the advice on offer is flaky at best, downright nonsense at worst.

In a *Harvard Business Review* article titled "Evidence-Based Management," Jeffrey Pfeffer and Robert Sutton, professors at Stanford Graduate School of Business, report that only about 15 per cent of physicians base their decisions on hard evidence. The rest rely on "obsolete knowledge gained in school, long-standing but never proven traditions, patterns gleaned from experience, the methods they believe in and are most skilled in applying, and information from hordes of vendors with products and services to sell."

No less alarming, say these authors, is that "The same behavior holds true for managers looking to cure their organizational ills."[39] Ideas emerge and are passed along with scant concern as to their merit. Some quickly fall from favour. Others enter the mainstream of management thinking – often despite the fact that there's little serious evidence or thought to underpin them. A few go mainstream, quickly attracting interest and playing a key role in shaping the management debate.

According to Clark Gilbert and Clayton Christensen, experts in management research, a theory is "a statement of what causes what, and why."[40] But having a clear explanation of some phenomenon goes only so far. If any theory is to be of value, it needs to have specific – and demonstrable – relevance to your business. And you need to not only know *how* to use it, but also believe in it strongly enough to do so.

Established theories should be your weapons of choice. If something worked in 100 other companies, there's a better chance it'll do the same for you than if it seemed to work in just one or two. And if those other companies are similar to yours, and operate in similar circumstances, your odds go up.

But there are no guarantees. As Thomas Davenport and Lawrence Prusak warn us in their book *What's the Big Idea*, business ideas may improve business performance, but "there's no empirical evidence that simply adopting new business ideas leads to stronger business performance."[41]

Management theories are what you make of them. Their value always rests in execution.

The high cost of uncertainty

When managers call me, they want help with strategy. Their specific needs vary, but in almost every case, it quickly becomes evident that two things trouble them and must be dealt with.

First, they lack a "theory of success" – a clear point of view about what they must do altogether to succeed.* They struggle to explain in simple terms what they must do to compete and win. And searching for easy answers to their challenges, they tackle this then that, dabble with one idea and then another – and confuse the hell out of themselves and everyone around them.

Second, and making matters worse, all of them have cluttered radar screens which keep becoming more cluttered. They're at the beck and call of everyone, and new problems keep finding them. They cannot focus because they don't allow themselves to focus.

The cost of managing in such a fog of uncertainty is incalculable. When you don't know what you're trying to do and what you must do, every problem is magnified.

The way out is typically to knuckle down, work harder, seek some new tools, and jump-start some new initiatives. These are layered one on top of the other, which creates yet more trouble. Before these fretful executives know it, their efforts have set them firmly on course to failure.

One immediate consequence is that they demotivate their people and trigger dysfunctional behaviour among them. "Each time a company's employees are called on to master yet another gimmick, their alienation grows," says Harvard professor Richard Hamermesh. "Because employment anxiety is high, they go along to get along."[42] In *Fad Surfing in the Boardroom*, Eileen Shapiro warns that many management tools "hold the potential for wreaking organizational havoc and causing tremendous damage, especially when they are seen as panaceas and applied blindly across a business, without attention to where they might be useful, why, with what other techniques they are being combined, and how, if at all, they should be modified to meet the needs of the company."[43]

Unfortunately, managers aren't likely to know this is happening until it's too late. As they announce new ideas, their people nod and smile and appear to be

---

* More on this in Chapter 11.

signing up. In fact, they're just doing what's politically safe. Their true feelings – "Here we go again!" – are well hidden.

Soon, the corporate conversation turns toxic and politics become rife. Truth, teamwork, and trust all crumble. But there's more trouble to come.

When new initiatives are announced, they're invariably *additions* to what's already there, not *substitutes*. So they add work and complexity, force people to keep switching priorities, and divert resources. Soon, progress grinds to a halt.

5

THINK GENERIC, ACT SPECIFIC

If you ask managers why they've adopted one or other management approach or method, they'll trot out confident answers: to deal with some challenge, solve a problem, or improve some aspect of their performance. They may sound convincing, and indeed their explanations may make sense. But it's more likely there are other, more substantive, reasons that they don't recognize and won't admit:

1. **To give *themselves* a sense of being in control.** By announcing and championing a scenario-planning exercise, say, or a move to lean production, they imagine they understand what needs to be done and the best way to do it. The fact that they're using an approach that appeared to work elsewhere gives them courage. And the fact that they *feel* confident may outweigh any flaws in the tool they choose.

2. **To signal to others that they know what they're doing.** A leader needs followers, and followers need to know they're in safe hands. So do other stakeholders. As Davenport and Prusak say, management ideas have two roles in organizations: to improve performance and provide legitimacy. They show that a company and its people are "diligently attempting to improve their business – whether they truly are or not."[1] To declare that a particular tool is what's needed is to offer assurance: "I understand the situation. I have an answer. You can trust me."

3. **To provide a language for talking about things.** Managers may want a slogan to hook things on, some headlines for a meeting agenda, a catchy phrase they can slip into a speech or the annual report, or an acronym they can use to impress journalists, board members, or shareholders. (Six Sigma theory gives you "deviations," "black belts," "root causes," "zero defects." Supply chain management gives you "vendor managed inventory," "order fulfilment rates," "integration." Strategic planning offers "vision," "mission," "values," "objectives," "tactics," "action plans," "stretch targets," "balanced scorecards," "strategy maps,"

and much, much more. And of course, management-speak is replete with acronyms: MBO, TQM, ABC, BPR, BHAG, ERP, MRP, EVA, ROI, CFROI, blah, blah, blah.)

4. **To create a sense of busyness.** Fads can be handy fillers. They give people something to do, and managers can use them to create the impression that something meaningful is going on. Launching a new initiative offers a good reason for meetings, conferences, workshops, training sessions, corporate videos, and so on. Goals can be reset. People may be given new responsibilities. Jobs can be shuffled – or filled with new recruits – and there may be a need to change the business model or redesign the organization. In no time, the word goes out that "Joe is a real kick-ass manager! This place is humming!"

5. **To provide cover for non-delivery somewhere else.** It's never easy for managers to face the fact that a project they introduced is going badly. Nor does it matter whether it is not "fit for purpose" or just poorly executed: it has to be made to disappear. And starting something else may be just the diversion that'll do the trick.

To expect any and every new idea to make a positive difference would be foolish. But the fad business is big business. This is an industry teeming with keen sellers and slavering buyers.

And many managers are indiscriminate impulse shoppers. Like kids in a candy store, they can't get enough of the goodies on offer. They grab whatever comes into sight and readily shell out big bucks for it. Often they don't understand what they're buying or how to use it. Then they apply it poorly or half-heartedly. So while their intention is to raise the bar of performance, their misguided, inept, and feeble efforts ensure that the results they want stay out of reach. And as one initiative after another fails them, they intensify their search for the next silver bullet.

The unintended consequences of this lunacy may go unnoticed for some time. Its precise effect might never be evident or measurable. But these downsides need to be weighed up against the fact that management ideas *are* both necessary and valuable.

Why we need them

Management ideas are essential frames for organizational conversations. We like to say that "what gets measured gets managed," but we forget that it's only what's *talked about* that will be either managed or measured.

Sumantra Ghoshal, one of the most influential management thinkers of recent times, tells us that "a management theory – if it gains sufficient currency – changes the behaviours of managers who start acting in accordance with the theory."[2]

When properly applied, says John Roberts, a professor at the Graduate School of Business at Stanford University, innovations in the way organizations are run "lead to better economic performance, affecting the wellbeing of the people of the world. By changing the way work is done, they change people's lives."[3]

New ideas may be necessary for many reasons: for example, to make the most of new technologies, drive productivity and quality, capture advantages from scale or scope, improve efficiency and effectiveness, provoke innovation, or drive change. If they're well chosen and thoughtfully applied, they may indeed lead to better results.

But the input of "idea practitioners" (the term used by Davenport and Prusak) may bring other benefits too:

1. Merely being *seen* to pursue the latest thinking can do wonders for the reputation of a company and its leaders. It changes *perceptions* about business performance. "Companies that embrace new ideas are likely to have higher stock prices and to appear on 'most admired' lists," say Davenport and Prusak. "Both investment analysts and the press seem to believe that companies that adopt new ideas are better companies than those that don't."[4] (Though positive views will quickly turn negative if results don't follow to match the hype!)

2. An executive's image and impact *within* her organization may equally be enhanced when she's seen to be at the cutting edge of new thinking. ("The Boss gets it. She knows what she's doing.") The very fact that she's familiar with the latest trends, has a clear point of view about what management ideas to apply, and pushes an apparently well-thought-through agenda, can instil confidence in people and inspire and mobilize them.

3. In human affairs, almost *any* message may be better than none. Promoting an idea signals what the priorities are, and focuses attention, energy, and resources. Obviously, it should provide sound guidance and help people make sensible trade-offs, but by triggering action – *any action* – it can open up opportunities not only for learning, but also for luck. ("Whoever does the most stuff has the highest chance of doing well," says Tom Peters.[5])

Having a clear point of view about what works and why – and what you need to do and why – does raise your chances of success. That your management theory hasn't been verified by a bunch of experts may matter less than the fact that you have one at all. When you speak with conviction, and sound as if you've thought carefully about your position, you score points all around. By framing a situation and how best to deal with it, you relieve others of that responsibility, and guide them in their work.

On the other hand, if you don't make your point of view apparent, your lack of certainty leaves people to make up their own minds about what you believe: "If she's not for A, she must be for B" – and B is then whatever they imagine. Operating in an information vacuum, they create their own sense of reality. So the absence of ideas about managing can lead to chaos and inertia.

As a leader, both your decisions and your *non*-decisions send signals. The mere fact of doing something will often make you a whole lot better off than if you do nothing. (There are times when you'll do best by just waiting, reflecting, letting things be.[6]) But doing the *right* things is obviously preferable. The theories you adopt should drive action in a way you want.

It's doubtful that most management ideas bring the results that they promise, but that may not matter. The placebo effect is alive and well in business. A consultant's advice to "take two pills and call me in the morning" may be just the confidence-booster you need.

Consider how that might pay off:

- Listening to a scenario specialist may embolden you to try them yourself. Even if you do it badly, the exercise might yield an insight about the environment or help your team agree on some new priorities.
- Taking advice to think about your core competences might lead to valuable conversations about what you do well, how customers' demands are changing, where you should focus in the marketplace, and how you might need to change. Or it might lead you into a discussion about other competitive issues. So although you don't talk about competences exactly as the theorists intend you to, they provide a starting point for other useful debate.
- Hearing about other firms' success with benchmarking or outsourcing might inspire you to experiment, and perhaps to discover new ways to cut costs and improve your service.

A leader's directives to "cut cycle times," "embrace diversity," or "lock in our customers" create an impression of understanding and even mastery. Taking even a clumsy, half-hearted stab at strategic planning, bottom-of-the-pyramid marketing, or open innovation will get people thinking and could result in some new insight or action. When that happens, you at least have a chance to get lucky. Or, at the very worst, you create opportunities to learn.

Elusive answers

You'd think that by now there'd be widespread agreement on what works in management and what doesn't. After all, a great deal of brainpower has been applied to this matter for a very long time. Vast amounts of money have been spent trying to get to The Truth. But useful answers are extremely hard to dig out.

Here's why:

1. **Management is a fuzzy subject.** It's the key activity in every institution and so lies right at the heart of human affairs; but it's an entangled topic, linked to many other fields of study, and its boundaries are vague.

   Management has roots in economics (choices about the use of resources), sociology (large-group behaviour and institutional structures), anthropology (the evolution of humankind and its societies and customs), and psychology (individual and small-group behaviour).[7] But matters of politics and law, physics, engineering, systems, ecology, technology, art – and even the weather – all come into play one way or another in every manager's average day.

   But unlike those areas, where deep knowledge, expertise, and specialization matter, and there's respect and even reverence for experts, management is something that anyone and everyone feels competent to pronounce on – and does so at the drop of a hat. So we get wads of advice, much of which is uninformed, unfounded, unsound, biased, contradictory, impractical, or just plain absurd.

   Friedrich August von Hayek warned us to be sceptical. In his 1974 Nobel acceptance speech titled "The Pretence of Knowledge," he said:

   > Unlike the position that exists in the physical sciences, in economics and other disciplines that deal with essentially complex phenomena, the aspects of the events to be accounted for about which we can get quantitative data are necessarily limited and may not include the important ones.[8]

2. **Corporate performance is relative.** The fact that a firm's sales have risen by 20 per cent a year for five years sounds impressive, until you learn that its peer group has grown sales by 30 per cent.

   One researcher noted that a ten-year investment in each of the 18 companies profiled in *Built to Last* would have yielded a return of 150 per cent. "That's not too bad," he said, "until you compare it with an S&P 500 index fund, which would have given you a 250 percent return. And if you'd had the foresight to pick up a copy of *Fortune*'s 100 Best Companies to Work For each year over that same period and invested in the public companies, you would have gotten a 600 percent return."[9]

   When you say a firm is "the best" or "doing well," the question you have to answer is, "Compared to what?"

3. **Results are always influenced by the context in which they're produced.** It's much easier to get good results in times of optimism and hope. When the economy is growing rather than in recession. When regulators exercise a light

touch rather than tie things up in red tape. Or when competitors accept that stability in an industry is desirable, rather than try to kill each other.

Growing sales by 20 per cent in any one year could be either an excellent outcome or quite underwhelming. When the tech sector took off in the late 1990s, many firms and their executives rode the wave and looked fantastic. But when the bubble burst, all their flaws were revealed.

Similarly, synchronized global growth from 2001 to 2008 provided a lot of companies with a powerful tailwind. Quite naturally they claimed credit for their success, and hordes of admirers pointed to them as examples of "how to do it." But the sharp economic collapse in late 2008 showed them to not be all that clever. And the management "solutions" promoted since the start of the slump haven't been the same as those that sounded so right in the good years.

4. **Clues are scattered all over the place**. You find them in books, articles, and speeches, and all over the internet. In the comments of employees and the memories of ex-employees, and of customers, suppliers, competitors, and many others. And in the opinions of analysts, academics, and writers.

So deciding what's of value as opposed to what's merely interesting is no easy matter. Which of a multitude of factors affects business performance? In what way? Where's the proof? Are there other possibilities? Might things be different in other circumstances?

Chances are that X (culture, say, or a certain management style or performance-monitoring process) isn't the real cause – or the *only* cause – of Y. Nor is it easy to be sure that good results are a consequence of any *single* initiative such as job enrichment, balanced scorecards, Six Sigma, market disruption, or incentives based on some currently popular financial metric. Instead, a dense web of factors makes the difference.

5. **Cognitive biases**. The answers that researchers arrive at almost always depend on how they framed their initial questions. And framing depends not only on past knowledge and experience, but also on emotions and values. Nobody begins a study with their mind a blank slate.

What you may not easily discern when looking at research is the "confirmation bias" that causes us to hunt for information that supports our narrative, see only what we want to see, and conveniently gloss over anything that hints at other possibilities.

So scholars seek information that proves their hypotheses are right. And if you ask managers why they think their firms are doing especially well, you'll get answers like, "It's the culture." "We have a very flat structure." "We move fast." Or perhaps they'll say, "Our mission is clear to everyone," "Our customer loyalty programme has made a huge difference," or "We know how to develop talent." But are they right? Are the reasons they give the *only* ones? It's hard to tell.

As Donald Hambrick warned in an *Academy of Management Executive* article:

> Beyond the obvious challenge of gaining access to executives and directors, researchers need to be reminded that these people are under extraordinary psychological and social pressure to put a lofty sheen on how they portray their motives, abilities, and behaviours. Namely, they lie a lot. They don't mean to, and they may not even know they are doing it ... So beware.[10]

6. **Cause and correlation are often confused**. A common research problem in every field is that researchers mistake *correlation* (relationships between things) with *causality* (one makes the other happen).

   Students of management seem especially prone to being careless about this. But they "surely head down the road towards bad theory," warn Clayton Christensen and Michael Raynor, "when they impatiently observe a few successful companies, identify some practices or characteristics that these companies seem to have in common, and then conclude that they have seen enough to write an article or book about how all companies can succeed."[11]

   The fact that there's a correlation between companies – that a particular tool or practice is used in 10, 20, or even 200 of them – doesn't mean it's the cause of their performance.

7. **It's hard to know just who or what to believe**. Every business book jacket comes with accolades for the author and the message. Canny authors boast about the thoroughness of their research. Conference promoters trumpet the "take-home value" you'll get from listening to their featured speakers. Getting published in prominent journals such as *Harvard Business Review, Sloan Management Review,* or the Academy of Management's publications gives writers a powerful stamp of approval. Professors from top business schools are assumed to know what they're talking about. But no amount of endorsement or public relations puffery can hide the fact that much management "thought" is of little practical value. What makes a story doesn't necessarily make a difference. Some ideas have been thoroughly tested, subjected to rigorous peer review, and shown to work, but many come unchallenged from their "inventor" to you.

8. **What works in one company won't necessarily work elsewhere**. Since most of the advice we get is based on observation of a sample of firms or managers

– occasionally hundreds of them, but more usually just a handful, and sometimes only one or two – it's always a stretch to conclude that what's gleaned from specific cases has general application.

A host of factors add up to make organizations different from each other. These include their history, stakeholder agendas, investment philosophies, risk appetite, ambitions, resources, strategy, culture, structure, skills and attitudes, past performance, industry circumstances, competitor activity, alliances, processes, and much else.

The impact of a management idea almost always depends more on *who in a firm drives it* and *how they do it* than on the soundness of the idea itself. Powerful advocacy is crucial. The right person may be able to wring results out of even dodgy ideas. However, when executives change jobs, and take ideas that have served them well in one to the next, they may be disappointed by the outcome. Their trusted tool may not work in the new context.

9. **Success and failure aren't equally easy to anticipate or decipher**. A mistake management thinkers make is to think that because failure is often easy to understand, success is too. But this is just not true. A firm's actions may clearly signal trouble ahead, but success is much harder to predict. And even after reports of improved sales or profits are in, to pinpoint what caused them can be like looking for the proverbial needle in a haystack.

For all these reasons, managers' beliefs about their craft are likelier than not to be based on partial truths, flimsy assumptions, and a lot of guesswork. Which makes the management of many firms very much a hit-or-miss affair.

You might be persuaded that your company needs reengineering. Or a balanced scorecard. Or "7S" analysis. But there has to be good reason, because no intervention comes free. There are always direct costs, opportunity costs, and costs of failure.

Would you be right to tell your colleagues that *not* using such tools would hurt your results? And what about not using scenarios, real options, open innovation, or knowledge management? Do you really know if any of these is essential to performance? What proof do you have?

You'd think that by now we'd be able to answer such questions with confidence. That given the vast numbers of smart people studying and practising management, we'd have all the evidence we needed. But listening to executives, and watching the fervour with which they latch on to any idea that sounds new or seems to hold promise, that's obviously not the case.

Choosing tools and interventions for your business is an important matter. "The Truth" can give you a vital competitive advantage. Getting as close to it as possible has to be one of the most important things you do. Being vague must rate as a very serious business risk.

Misleading "evidence"

Researchers typically set out with a hypothesis – "X causes Y" – and then work to prove it. The "proof" may not be all it's cracked up to be, but because managers are busy and under pressure to produce results, they're easy targets for glib answers.

Some commentators study subjects methodically and for a long time before they release their conclusions. Others home in on an issue that interests them or may have popular appeal, cook up a story that suits the times, give it a sexy label, and rush it to market.

The stakes are high in the business of business advice. A good story is worth a fortune. So a common trick is to boast about the thoroughness of a research project: how many years it took, how many people were involved, the huge numbers of companies studied, the hundreds of in-depth interviews conducted, the thousands of documents analysed. Here's overwhelming proof, say the leaders of these efforts, that you should pay attention to our findings (and buy our books, attend our seminars, pay us huge consulting fees, etc.).

More often, though, studies that are held up to explain a new gospel are based on very limited or questionable evidence. Some involve observation of only one company. Some, a mere handful of managers. Samples are picked for analysis on the basis of arbitrary criteria such as growth in market share or profits, innovation, or reputation. Business leaders are asked what made them successful (as if they really know). Employees or competitors may be interviewed. Annual reports and press cuttings are studied. Then – KABOOM! – a "theory" is born.

Good researchers make clear the limitations of their studies: the small sample size; the fact that they only interviewed middle managers, and only in one industry; the lack of a control sample, or whatever. But it suits others to gloss over these details. Intentionally or not, they give the impression that "the truth" they've hit upon is indeed true. And universal.

To be effective in their work, managers have to be both curious and sceptical. They have to confront reality, challenge assumptions, and seek truth by digging deep past glib answers. Yet when it comes to choosing their tools, those disciplines seem not to concern them as much. It's anyone's guess just what the cost of this carelessness might be.

So be careful of copying what seems to work for someone else. What you see may not be the cause of the results you admire. The "lessons" you pick up may not do anything for you.

Be careful, too, about staking your company's future on *one* management idea that seems to have magical powers. There is no such thing. You have to pull a number of levers to get the best results.

Easy answers are beguiling when things are going crazy all around you. So books with titles such as *In Search of Excellence, Good to Great,* or *What Really Works* find a ready audience. Maybe, just maybe, there's something in there that will make a difference!

When "one best way" isn't

The quest for new ways to manage won't end soon. In fact, it must continue because it's necessary. Scholars should keep at their research, consultants do need to keep striving to offer their clients new value through novel insights, and managers do need to be alert to new thinking, learn new methods, and try new things. But at the same time, everyone should be wary of snap solutions and simplistic, one-size-fits-all answers to complex management matters.

Listen to some who know:

- In *Vanguard Management* (1985), James O'Toole tells us there is "no theory X, Y, or Z, no secrets from the Orient, no one-minute quickie, no set of common rules that will permit a corporation to achieve lasting eminence."[12]
- There's a temptation, says Ralph Kilmann, a professor at the University of Pittsburgh's Graduate School of Business, in *Beyond the Quick Fix* (1985), "for both managers and consultants toward the single approach that offers the promise of organizational success."[13] They love the idea of a single hot button, one lever, a silver bullet that will fix everything. This is naive and a reason why both are so often disappointed.
- Says Richard Pascale in *Managing on the Edge* (1990): "The very notion of 'professional management' rests upon the premise that a set of generic concepts underlies management activity anywhere." But "our theories, models, and conventional wisdom combined appear no better at predicting an organization's ability to sustain itself than if we were to rely on random chance."[14]
- "[T]here are no recipes, and no generic strategies, for corporate success," says economist and *Financial Times* columnist John Kay in *Foundations of Corporate Success* (1993). "There cannot be, because if there were their general adoption would eliminate any competitive advantage which might be derived. The foundations of corporate success are unique to each successful company."[15]
- "[T]he very idea that generic techniques can be a source of competitive advantage is illogical," according to Frederick Hilmer and Lex Donaldson, both professors at the Australian Graduate School of Management, in their 1996 book *Management Redeemed*. "In competitive markets, a firm succeeds

because in some key respect it is different from other firms. It may have lower costs, better service, or be easier to deal with or faster to innovate. Firms that do exactly what their competitors do don't earn high returns. If packaged approaches really worked, all competitors would follow the formula and no competitive advantage would be possible."[16]

- Clayton Christensen and Michael Raynor take a slightly different tack in a *Harvard Business Review* article, "Why Hard-Nosed Executives Should Care About Management Theory," which appeared in 2003: "professors and consultants routinely prescribe … generic advice, and managers routinely accept such therapy, in the naive belief that if a particular course of action helped other companies to succeed, it ought to help theirs, too."[17] And in a 2006 article, Christensen says, "Rarely are there one-size-fits-all solutions to a company's problems."[18]

- A five-year study by a team at the MIT Industrial Performance Centre (2005) looked at 500 manufacturing firms around the world, to see if there were common approaches to success. Their conclusion was that "no one model wins all the time."[19]

- "Claiming that one approach can work everywhere, at all times, for all companies, has a simplistic appeal but doesn't do justice to the complexity of business," writes IMD professor Phil Rosenzweig in *The Halo Effect* (2007).[20]

- A paper from the London School of Economics (2007) confirms that "no single dimension provides the key to improved management performance; there is no magic lever for management excellence."[21]

The common theme in these messages is that there's no one best way to manage. There's no quibbling with that. But there's every reason to ask: Are there generic practices that must be applied – but that you can manage in the way you see fit?

Generic management practices

When the legendary Harvard Business School marketing professor Ted Levitt published an article titled "The Globalization of Markets" in *Harvard Business Review* in 1983, it became an immediate hit. His insights came at just the right time. The Reagan and Thatcher revolutions were just taking effect. After years of economic difficulties, recovery was in the air and companies were hungry for growth.

Levitt opened managers' minds to the possibilities beyond their traditional markets. By exploiting customer commonalities, he told them, they could sell the same products or services across countries and cultures and dramatically increase sales. So they should strip their offerings of features and benefits that appealed to customers in specific countries, and provide "generic" value that would have universal appeal.[22]

This set off the rush to "go global," which even today is gathering pace. But Levitt's message was an over-simplification. What firms did not get from it was that to succeed in global markets they should "think global, act local." And that led to some costly stumbles.

Companies like Goodyear, Coca-Cola, Reckitt and Colman, Sony – and countless others – learned fast that to succeed in Cambodia, say, or in Columbia, they had to customize not only their products and services, but also the business models by which they delivered and captured value. And critically, that *the way they managed* – a core aspect of those models – had to change from country to country.

Sony soon coined the term "glocalization." Others latched onto it. Now it's widely accepted that bold ambitions are best met through deep local knowledge and a willingness to do what it takes to fit in. A key change has been that top jobs in foreign markets are increasingly given to locals.

You'd have thought this would arouse interest in country-specific management theories and techniques. But it didn't. One reason, perhaps, is that just as the globalization movement began gathering pace, infatuation with "Japanese management," which started in the early 1970s, was fizzling.

The assumption that Japanese companies were dangerous competitors because of some secret sauce in Japanese culture was never borne out. Tight links between government and business, and the much-admired *keiretsu** system, turned out to be less advantageous than they once had seemed. In reality, both of these factors had downsides. After a remarkable surge from the 1950s to the 1970s, many Japanese firms lost ground to competitors from the US, Europe, China, South Korea, Brazil, and elsewhere – and they continue to do so.

What did make some firms a threat was that they learned American techniques – *which the Americans had failed to embrace* – and applied them with a vengeance. Toyota's leaders visited Ford and GM in the 1930s to study their assembly lines, and lifted the idea of "pull" in materials replenishment from American supermarkets.[23] When Philip Caldwell, CEO of Ford, visited Japan in 1982, Eiji Toyoda said, "There is no secret to how we learned to do what we do, Mr. Caldwell. We learned it at the Rouge."[24] A medal named in honour of W. Edwards Deming, an American quality expert, was awarded annually from 1951 to Japanese firms achieving the best quality. According to historian David Halberstam, "Only an award from the Emperor was more prestigious. But when Japanese productivity

---

* Groups of companies that work closely together.

teams visiting America mentioned Deming to their hosts, few of the Americans knew his name."[25] It wasn't until the lessons the Japanese soaked up from Deming, Drucker, Joseph Juran, Walter Schewart, and others cycled back to America that firms there were able to regain their competitive edge. Supposedly Japanese methods for improving quality and productivity, including quality circles, *kaizen*, *kaikaku, kanban, muda** – all elements of lean production – were actually born in the USA.

In South Africa in the late 1980s, a number of people seized on the mood of transformation in that country, and promoted as a management concept the idea of *ubuntu* – an African belief that "I am nothing without you."[26] But their "theory" could equally have been drawn from the teachings of Christianity, Islam, Judaism, Confucianism, or Taoism. It was no more useful than the Golden Rule to "be unto others as you would have them be unto you." And as had happened with "Japanese management," it conveniently overlooked the reality that companies would be nothing without generally accepted – i.e. mostly American – management practices.

More recently, there's been keen interest in the practices of Chinese, Indian, and Latin American companies. Many of them are now not only national champions but also global giants, and they're held up as proof that emerging markets can produce winners. So it seems sensible to find out how they did it. If they have secrets, these might be useful elsewhere. Or they could help outsiders succeed in the countries where the ideas originated.

But we're yet to hear about any success in identifying management methods invented in those places, distinguished by some national trait, or worth taking elsewhere.[27] The reason is, they don't exist.

Ideas such as "reverse innovation" and "bottom of the pyramid marketing" have recently gained favour because some Asian firms have used them to great effect. But what's new – or specifically *Asian* – about them, except perhaps that they now have labels and are practised more deliberately than they might have been in the past?

Traders have forever had their ears to the ground in foreign markets, and brought ideas back home from them. And they have forever sought ways to attract and satisfy poor customers in remote places. Both of these supposedly novel practices are simply responses to the questions: Who is our customer? What is "value" to them? How can we satisfy them?

Articles in the September 2014 issue of *Harvard Business Review* and summer 2014 issue of *Sloan Management Review* promised to reveal how Chinese

---

* Continuous improvement, radical change, just-in-time, and waste.

management made that country's firms such feared competitors. But readers expecting anything novel would surely have been disappointed. The recipe offered by both journals included: autocratic top-down management, deep knowledge of government and strong relations with key officials, empowerment of business units, projects broken into chunks and assigned to large teams of often less-than-expert people, concurrent activities with tight deadlines, reliance on many outsiders for innovation and resources, and so on. So again, less than you might expect.[28]

What does exist, though, is a set of practices that are truly global. Practices that are both necessary and effective everywhere.

While acknowledging that the effective management of people isn't the only cause of competitive success, Jeffrey Pfeffer, a professor at Stanford Graduate School of Business, reports in his book *The Human Equation* that studies across a range of firms in many industries show that "Substantial gains, on the order of 40 percent or so in most of the studies reviewed, can be obtained by implementing high performance management practices."[29]

According to a five-year study of more than 4,000 mid-sized manufacturers in Europe, the US, and Asia, "firms across the globe that apply accepted management practices will perform significantly better than those that do not." This suggests that improving management practice is one of the surest ways for a firm to outperform its rivals.[30]

Yet the same study found that *"surprisingly few firms have made any attempt to gain an insight into the quality of their management behaviours."*[31] (My italics.) In other words, the people running them seldom, if ever, ask, "Is what we do regarded as 'best practice?' Are we sure it's the reason for superior results in other companies? Is it the best option for us? Is it working the way we expected? Do our various initiatives support each other? What will the long-term effects be? Is it worth the effort?"

There was nothing remarkable about the practices this study focused on. There were just three of them: 1) setting clear long-term targets; 2) rewarding star performers and re-training or moving those who didn't deliver; and 3) monitoring performance to identify opportunities for improvement. All are elements of *growth leadership*, the first critical strategy practice I've highlighted.

In further studies, two of the authors, Nicholas Bloom and John Van Reenen, continued to question the effect of "good management practices." In their 2010 article "Why Do Management Practices Differ Across Firms and Countries?" they confirmed that "Firms with 'better' management practices tend to have better performance on a wide range of dimensions: they are larger, more productive, grow faster, and have higher survival rates."[32] In another article, co-authored with

Raffaella Sadun, in *Harvard Business Review*'s 90th Anniversary issue in November 2012, they reaffirmed the value of sound practices, while noting that "according to our criteria, many organizations throughout the world are very badly managed ... A call for better management may sound prosaic, but given the potential effect on incomes, productivity, and delivery of critically needed services worldwide, it's actually quite radical."[33]

This is ridiculous. We know what works. It's not rocket science. Now we're told that if you just do it, your results are likely to improve and your company will become more competitive. How simple can that be?

But companies *don't* do it. The answers they seek are right under their noses, but they keep hankering after something else.

The practices Van Reenen and his colleagues homed in on are clearly not the only ones firms need. There's obviously more to good management than targets, incentives, and monitoring. These fall under the umbrella practice of growth leadership – which also covers the leadership style, the organizational culture and climate, values, career development, and everything else that leaders do to grow the company and grow the people. But they're so elementary it's hard to know why anyone would ignore them. After all, there's no mileage in making organizational life harder than it need be.

A century of research, plus the practical experience of thousands upon thousands of companies operating across the world, tells us exactly what practices matter altogether. We don't have to guess. There can be no doubt what managers should focus on.

Every manager must deal with these realities:

1. Economic growth is harder and harder to come by;
2. We live in a VUCA environment and the future is impossible to predict;
3. The life-span of business models is eroding fast;
4. Resources are limited;
5. Customers are increasingly knowledgeable, frugal, demanding, and disloyal;
6. Competition is becoming more hostile;
7. Execution is almost always harder than it seems.

There are common challenges – and generic management practices for dealing with them. These practices are critical in all companies, everywhere. They should be the frame for every strategic conversation, the core of every company's culture, and the basis of all training and development programmes. All executives must understand and apply them, or face dire consequences.

The obvious questions, though, are what happens when everyone has the same toolkit? How do firms avoid me-too strategies? And this is where implementation comes into play. Where human factors such as contextual knowledge, experience, insight, imagination, relationships, and spirit make the difference.

Knowing *about* management is no great shakes. Knowing *how* to manage is far harder.

Knowing how to do it across countries and cultures is essential. But knowing how to do it *locally* – wherever that may be – is what separates winners from losers.

It all depends

It's always been necessary for organizations and their managers to organize and conduct themselves in ways that suit their circumstances. But this was a taken-for-granted matter until Paul Lawrence and Jay Lorsch drew explicit attention to it in their 1967 book *Organization and Environment*. Since then, "contingency theory" has been a much-discussed topic.[34]

Clearly, the steel industry faces challenges quite different to those in banking, consumer electronics, or pharmaceuticals. The strategy that brings results in a developed market may not do the same in a developing one. Surviving an economic downturn is an altogether different challenge than managing with the wind at your back. It's one thing dealing with everyday matters, and quite another to drive radical change.

What's more, every company is different and no two days are the same. So management is a dynamic process requiring continual alertness and sensitivity, and constant learning and adaptation.

It should go without saying that managers must know their markets. After all, every place is distinctive, situations change from moment to moment, and strategy is about fitting in. If you're not acutely aware of your surroundings, of their characteristics and their currents – and if you fail to adapt accordingly – you'll always be at their mercy and never perform the way you should.

As an article in *The Economist* reminds us, "The East India Company was able to dominate an entire continent with a few hundred company men because it adapted to local customs, even to the point of co-opting local words such as 'nabob' and 'loot.'"[35]

The biggest lesson companies learn when they arrive in new countries is that life there requires adjustment. The distance between a home market and a foreign market, says Pankaj Ghemawat, is not just a matter of geography, but also of culture, administration, and economics.[36] Fitting in takes time and effort. This is hard enough when you move from one *developed* market to another, but moving to *developing* countries is much harder.

Things there don't work as they do back home. Infrastructure is non-existent or poor. There are skills shortages and mismatches, lousy services, and bureaucratic logjams. Useful information is often hard to come by. Unpredictable politics, rapidly changing regulation, and corruption all present difficulties. In the workplace, attitudes to authority, decision-making processes, time-keeping, and discipline may all be hard to fathom. And in the marketplace, customer needs and behaviours, inadequate distribution channels, and backward payment and promotion methods ensure a stream of challenges.

Most writing on emerging market strategy is about these characteristics and how to get to grips with them. There's little mention of local management theory and practice – and virtually none of *specific* concepts or tools. But why should it be otherwise? Managers everywhere use similar resources, processes and technologies, and services. They must all organize and coordinate work. They must monitor and control activities. And they have to worry about productivity, quality, costs, sales, and profits.

The "basics" of business are the same in every country and company. As Henri Fayol, a French mining engineer, pointed out in 1916, "principles are flexible and capable of adaptation to every need … it is a matter of knowing how to make use of them, which is a difficult art requiring intelligence, experience, decision and proportion."[37]

Alfred Sloan, legendary leader of General Motors from 1923 to 1956, said much the same thing 50 years later. "The task of management," he said, "is not to apply a formula but to decide issues on a case-by-case basis. No fixed, inflexible rule can ever be substituted for the exercise of sound business judgment in the decision-making process."[38] Drucker observed around the same time that many managerial issues are of a routine, generic nature. They crop up over and over again and can be dealt with "through a rule, a principle." But everything else "can only be handled as such and as it comes."[39] And another 30 years on, Lex Donaldson and Frederick Hilmer remind us yet again, in an article in *Organizational Dynamics*, that the essence of management is not technique, but the "disciplined application of a range of ideas to specific situations."[40]

It's knowing what's right for the situation you're in – and being able to do the right thing then and there – that matters.

The rules of engagement change. The critical strategy practices don't.

This should be a huge relief to busy managers. It means you don't have to keep inventing or buying new answers when the ones you already have will serve you perfectly well. There's no point wasting time and money in pursuit of unique solutions when you don't need them.

But it's just as pointless assuming there are general solutions for every problem. You can't clone competitiveness. You do need to apply some common practices. *But you need to do it in the way that suits your specific company.* You also have to understand what is exceptional, and exercise careful judgment in deciding what is or is not a "routine, generic" issue. If you fail to see the difference and appreciate what it implies, you're likely to do the wrong thing.

In our information age, learning about best practices is a doddle. Since there are only a few of them, you don't have too much to get your head around. But the value of any of them lies in how they're used in specific circumstances. *Applying* them is always the problem.[41]

Any time you're asked how to deal with a particular issue, the best answer is "It depends." The same basic management practices might be appropriate everywhere, but the way they're applied must suit local realities. "Think generic, act specific" is the only way to work.

It's probably true most managers understand this and exercise some care in distinguishing between "generic" issues or practices and "exceptions." Yet they often seem much less thoughtful about the management ideas they dump on their firms.

They keep the fad business alive and well. Dilbert has a field day describing their follies.

6

THE THINKERS

You might think that most new ideas about management would come from management scholars generally, and more specifically from those in business schools. In fact, surprisingly few do.

You might also think that of all sources of management ideas, these specialists would be the ones to put your trust in, because rigorous research and the development of new knowledge is such a very big deal for them. But here again, you could be mistaken.

It's worth looking into this in some detail as a precautionary measure, to remind ourselves why the practice of management is so slow to change, why we shouldn't put life on hold while we wait for the next breakthrough, and how difficult it is to know what we're buying.

Academics have long been key players in the advancement of management thought, and their role is crucial. But like everyone else, they're less and less able to deliver ideas that change what firms do. Their collective research efforts yield marginal and diminishing returns; there's an inverse ratio between the volume of their output and its impact on business.

These elite, professional thinkers are encouraged, incentivized, and supported by the institutions they work for. They have access to generous grant funding. They get time to develop new knowledge. There's the prospect of superstar status at top universities and lucrative publishing, speaking, and consulting deals that come with it. Yet most of them continue to churn out material of interest only to themselves and their peers, while adding little to what we already know – and *need* to know – about management.

From 1995 to 2002, only two of the 15 bestselling business books in any one year were written by academics. A review of one survey of management tools showed that only seven out of 25 came from academics, while 18 came from companies, consultants, or a combination of both. Those from universities were used less often and dropped more often.[1]

Of course, this doesn't tell us anything about the practical value of academic output compared to whatever comes from other sources. But it does add to a bigger picture.

Business schools – which have such a central role in management development, and whose very reason for being is the delivery of management knowledge – are disappointing as idea factories. According to Wharton dean Thomas Robertson, perhaps only one in ten business schools has a strong research capability and is intent on developing the insights, concepts, and tools they teach to managers.[2] Distinguished "insiders" have charged that some schools do research primarily to show off their rigour and scientific methods, and thus enhance their prestige.[3] Others say that despite researchers' skills, they apparently are better at recycling ideas than inventing them.[4]

None of this will change while the schools worry about their place in society, their methods, their influence, or their legitimacy. There are three reasons why they'll continue to fret and question themselves.

First, almost all are attached to universities, and bound by university conventions. They may be autonomously administered, and have their own sources of funds, but in their academic practices they toe the party line.

Second, there's the debate about the role and offerings and impact of business schools that began around 2002. It took on new urgency when the global economy melted in 2008, and continues today. They're all grappling with growing competition, a new wave of time-pressed and frugal customers, the boom in online learning, staff shortages, and rising costs, and unsure how to keep their business models in tune with the times.

And third, that debate in turn takes place within a larger debate about the purpose, responsibilities, and practices of business altogether – a matter that's gathering pace and will run and run.

In their early years, write Mie Augier and David Teece in *California Management Review*, business schools in America "were not considered as serious participants in the world of academic scholarship and intellectual pursuit." Lecturers were often experienced executives rather than scholars. They "emphasized practical, not theoretical courses; applied, not basic science; and the contributions of faculty were more often published in practitioner magazines than in academic journals."[5]

But following critical reports in 1959 on the state of American business education by the Ford Foundation and Carnegie Corporation,* business schools changed their focus. They hired more faculty with doctoral degrees, and stuffed their programmes with courses on decision analysis, statistics, and game theory. Rational

---

* Both reports, according to Harold Koontz, were "authored and researched by scholars who were not trained in management." (Harold Koontz, "The Management Theory Jungle Revisited," *Academy of Management Review*, Vol. 5, No. 2, 1980)

thinking was emphasized over intuition and judgment. "Management science" gained credence that Frederick Taylor would only have dreamed of.

"Through the late 1950s and 1960s," says Rakesh Khurana, a Harvard Business School professor and expert on the history of business knowledge, HBS moved away "from what had been a strong clinical training focus and emphasis on 'management as art' in its DBA and MBA programs."[6] Other schools followed.

Even as competition between business schools intensified, schools and their teaching staff became increasingly disconnected from their customers. In a hard-hitting 1971 *Harvard Business Review* article, "The Myth of the Well-Educated Manager," Sterling Livingston, a Harvard professor, warned that "Managers are not taught in formal education programs what they most need to know to build successful careers in management."[7]

Business schools were only partly to blame. Their scholars were their partners in crime, less interested in managers' problems than their own intellectual pursuits. As one business school professor said, at the 1988 Academy of Management annual meeting, "I've been in the real world. It stinks."[8]

Then in May 2005, Warren Bennis and James O'Toole lit a proper firestorm with a *Harvard Business Review* article titled "How Business Schools Lost Their Way." Schools were "institutionalizing their own irrelevance," they said. Some produced excellent research, but "because so little of it is grounded in actual business practices, the focus of graduate business education has become increasingly circumscribed – and less and less relevant to practitioners."[9]

After that, it was open season, and many more leading academics let loose with their own opinions:

- According to Richard Schmalensee, dean of the MIT School of Management, "management school faculty often focus on academic fields such as game theory or econometrics, not on management practice, and their work may have little to do with real business problems. And as business faculty have sought ever more academic status, describing what managers actually do has tended to crowd out prescriptive work on what they should do."[10]
- In her 2005 Presidential Address to the Academy of Management, Denise Rousseau, a professor at Carnegie Mellon University, described her biggest disappointment as being that "research findings don't appear to have transferred well into the workplace ... managers, including those with MBAs, continue to rely largely on personal experience, to the exclusion of more systematic knowledge."

  Less than 1 per cent of human resource managers regularly read the academic literature, she said. But they're not the only ones who steer clear of it.

"Despite the explosion of research on decision making, individual and group performance, business strategy, and other domains directly tied to organizational practices, *few practicing managers access this work*."[11] (My italics.)

- "I'm not aware of any other field in which theory is viewed with such religious fervor," wrote Donald Hambrick, a professor at The Pennsylvania State University, in the *Academy of Management Journal*, "we've gone overboard in our obsession with theory."[12]

- "I think few business schools take the practice of business very seriously," says Pankaj Ghemawat, a professor at Harvard Business School and IESE. "On every topic that CEOs of large companies say they want to learn more about, I have trouble locating academic literature."[13]

- "After 30 years of working in management education," said Murray Steel, a senior lecturer in strategic management at Cranfield School of Management, "I have yet to meet an executive who admits to being influenced by any academic research output. In fact, very few have read any academic journals." He goes on to note that the target for academic research "is not executives or managers but other researchers who will referee their work and recommend it for publication. Consequently, much research is divorced from the reality of management and, hence, from making an impact on its practice."[14]

- According to Freek Vermeulen, an associate professor of strategic and international management at London Business School, "What is being taught in management books and classrooms is usually not based on rigorous research … Management research is not required to be relevant. Consequently much of it is not." But "even relevant research is largely ignored in business education."[15]

- "Business schools tend to operate in bubbles," says Peter Tufano, dean of Oxford University's Said Business School. "These are communities solely focused on business in which business executives with the same values are paraded in front of students. Experiences are socially engineered so that students can spend their entire time without meaningfully interacting with anyone outside business."[16]

- After a 2008 colloquium at Harvard Business School on the future of the MBA, Srikant Datar, David Garvin, and Patrick Cullen, all faculty at the school, noted that there's "little work that synthesizes and translates discipline-based research to make it relevant and accessible to practitioners … Too little attention is given to field-based research that explores real-world management practices and offers insights into how managers actually respond to the contingencies and complexities they face."[17]

- "There has been an incredible race to the bottom by business schools," added

Rakesh Khurana, "... very little general management knowledge has been produced ... we business schools have lost the place where we could be turned to as
a source of basic research and basic knowledge. Very few businesses turn to us.
They turn to other sources of knowledge, such as consulting firms, instead."[18]

These are disturbing observations. Not just because of the credentials of those
making them, but more so because they've been echoed by so many people over
so many years.

Imagine the head of a medical school saying, "Our professors teach medical
science; they aren't interested in teaching doctors to cure patients." Or a dean of
engineering saying, "We're into calculus; explaining how to build bridges and
power plants really isn't our thing." Neither they – nor their institutions – would
be around for long.

But this, by the way, is still the situation in business schools more than 40 years
after Sterling Livingston raised a red flag!

Pursuing irrelevance

In a 1986 article in the *Journal of the American Medical Association*, Drummond
Rennie, professor of medicine at the University of California, San Francisco, said
of scientific research: "There seems to be no study too fragmented, no hypothesis
too trivial, no literature citation too biased or too egotistical, no design too
warped, no methodology too bungled, no presentation of results too inaccurate,
too obscure and too contradictory, no analysis too self-serving, no argument too
circular, no conclusions too trifling or unjustified, and no grammar or syntax too
offensive for a paper to end up in print."[19]

The same can be said about management studies.

Globally, there's a vast pool of serious management researchers and thinkers. But
most spend their time on excruciating analysis of inconsequential issues, then present their findings in a way designed to keep them within the secret society of their
peers. They write for each other, rather than for managers. The result is that even
their best insights fail to get broad attention or gain traction in the marketplace.

A common university practice encourages this. In some countries, academics
gain tenure* by publishing lots of research in "A-level" journals, and not by being
good teachers or helping companies do better. And even where tenure isn't an
issue, establishing a reputation and advancing within "the academy" hinges on
getting into print and being cited by colleagues. "Publish or perish" may push some
to write who otherwise might not, but it also ensures that we get reams of waffle.
And that most of what comes from "the hallowed halls" stays there.

---

* In the US and Europe, though not in Britain.

The way academics present their thoughts seems designed to keep executives in the dark. Obscurity is their friend, so most of their output is impenetrable. They insist on writing as turgidly as possible, using language that no general reader can understand and no busy person will wade through. Unfamiliar words, tortuous sentences, and long paragraphs make their day. Often, they stuff their work with statistics and mathematical formulas. They apparently don't care whether executives learn from their findings, so most of their work never gets to those who are the subject of their studies and should be among their audience. So how are useful ideas "filtering into schools' programmes?" asks Kai Peters, chief executive of Ashridge Business School. "By osmosis?"[20]

According to The Economist, "Even getting papers into a general business publication, such as the Harvard Business Review, rather than an academic journal can damage the career of a promising professor."[21] (Though there's little danger of such damage when, as Rita Gunther McGrath points out, "young scholars are taught not to be concerned with impact," but instead are "counselled to learn how to get articles published in prestigious journals."[22]) What's more, articles from the management publications most likely to be read by managers and to influence them – titles such as Harvard Business Review, Sloan Management Review, California Management Review, Rotman Management, and Business Horizons (all published by top business schools) – are hardly mentioned as references in publications from the Academy of Management.

Academics are in the main not keen on practical answers. If you are able to decipher what they say, and then put on your management hat and apply the "So what?" test to their work, it fails miserably. But this should be expected when they're more concerned with what is than with what should be.[23]

A study published in 1968 sought to learn which behavioural science books or articles were best known to executives, and rated most significant by them. A panel of 45 industrial psychologists nominated 33 contributions, and responses were received from 200 executives. "The most startling and distressing aspect of these executives' replies," said the researchers, was that "only a small portion of them have even heard of many of the articles and books." Even fewer knew specifically what those published works were about, and "only a negligible number" saw them as being of use in "the actual conduct of business." Blame for this was put firmly on authors who stuck with scientific and technical journals, rather than using media that were widely read by executives.[24]

Although far more management books and journals are available to a general audience today than was the case some 50 years ago, the overall situation seems not to have changed. The gap between thinkers and doers is as wide as ever.

Some established professors do publish in both "academic" and popular management journals. They use gobbledygook when they target each other, but switch to plain English in the popular publications that actual managers read. This gets their opinions to a wider audience, and may enhance both their reputations and their earnings. But if they do enrich the management conversation, it's more often by confirming the merit of well-known practices, or weaving new stories around them, than by adding anything new.

"Theory papers succeed if they offer important and original ideas," says an editorial in *Academy of Management Review*. It advises contributors to ask of their work: "What is my big idea?"[25] But if this test were consistently applied, the content of scholarly journals would shrink. Some of what they publish may add something when knowledge for the sake of knowledge is the aim, but an awful lot doesn't. Big ideas are as rare as hen's teeth.

When it comes to *relevance*, the picture is even bleaker. Where are the new findings that might alter what managers are taught, and what do they do? Where's the breakthrough advice everyone is waiting for? "Unfortunately," says Clayton Christensen, "as our understanding of the theory-building process has coalesced, the report card on most of those who research and write about management has been abysmal."[26]

And if past trends are a guide, there's disappointment ahead.

In an editorial in the February 2014 issue of *Academy of Management Journal*, Gerard George, deputy dean of Imperial College, London, says: "Like black cats in coal cellars, published studies are increasingly indistinguishable from previous ones, and the contexts in which these theories are tested or developed tend to fade into irrelevance. Yet, without exception, each article lays claim to a strong theoretical contribution, oftentimes oblivious to the context or the importance of the phenomenon being explained."[27]

But how sound can such research be? Business doesn't function in a vacuum, and theories developed in a vacuum may or may not be valid in other circumstances. You'd have to be delusional or a fool to rely on one of them for a punt on your firm's future.

Or consider another oddity in a field so proud of both its methods and its influence.

Although more than 20,000 journal articles and truckloads of books are produced each year, a great deal of research just criticizes other research.[28] And it typically concludes with the cop-out that "more research in this area is needed," rather than offering a clear point of view or useful advice. The scholars who pump it out not only add nothing of practical value to what we know, they also cast doubt on what we *thought* we knew. And they leave us dangling while we wait for someone to come along with an actual answer.

According to a study by Jean Bartunek and Sara Rynes, only 51 per cent of articles published in five top-tier journals in 1992–1993 and 2003–2007 had "implications for practice." The good news was that there was an increase from 32 per cent in the 1990s to 58 per cent in the 2000s. The bad news: it's unlikely that many of those implications did anything to alter practice. For although the articles providing them "also make prescriptions (i.e., 55% include 'shoulds' or 'musts'), they offer those suggestions tentatively, using language such as 'may' or 'possibly' 74% of the time, and adding contingencies or other qualifications to their recommendations 38% of the time."[29]

Such iffy points of view will either get no attention or too much of the wrong kind. Scholars will rip them apart or use them as stepping stones to further inconclusive research. Managers will disregard them, or assume they offer decent advice and start doing things for which there's no solid evidence.

Another study, by Jone Pearce and Laura Huang, counted the number of "actionable" articles in two of the most prestigious scholarly journals in management from 1960 to 2010. The percentage in *Academy of Management Journal* fell from 43 to 24, and in *Administrative Science Quarterly* from 65 to 19. And although articles on strategy and organizational theory took up more and more space in those 50 years, only one strategy article published in *AOMJ* in 2010 was considered actionable, while 20 were not.[30]

The different results reported in these studies could be due to different criteria for "implications for practice" or "actionable"; to a lack of rigour in deciding which articles met those criteria; to the fact that the studies covered different periods; or because one looked at five journals and the other at just two. But the common message is that a lot of management research is not of much use to managers.

"It cannot be good for any field," observe Pearce and Huang, "to move further and further away from generating new knowledge that those outside ivory towers might use – particularly so for an applied field like management."[31]

But still, the practice continues.

The silo effect

In *How the Mind Works*, the brilliant Harvard neuroscientist Steven Pinker highlights the importance of looking outside a discipline to truly understand it. "Unfortunately for those who think the departments in a university reflect meaningful divisions of knowledge ... psychologists have to look outside psychology if they want to explain what the parts of the mind are for. To understand sight, we have to look to optics and computer vision systems. To understand movement, we have to look to robotics. To understand sexual and familial feelings, we have to look to Mendelian genetics. To understand cooperation and conflict, we have to look to the mathematics of games and modelling."[32]

Management, too, is an integrative endeavour. It hinges, crucially, on pulling together information, ideas and insights from many sources and all directions. "To provide insight into the complex problems that businesses face," write Augier and Teece, "we need to be interdisciplinary because the problems themselves are inter-disciplinary."[33] And indeed, by one account, some two-thirds of management research is based on theories from other disciplines.[34]

But a drive to churn out material for publication, and an obsession with winning peer approval, means ambitious academics must specialize. They tend to "pursue ever-narrower research agendas and to talk primarily to their own discipline," says Harvard Business School professor Geoffrey Jones, co-editor of the *Oxford Handbook of Business History*. This results "in a chronic problem of know-ledge existing in different silos and different disciplines reinventing wheels."[35]

It also means that the more expert scholars become in a particular area, the more their microscopic investigations spur them and their peers to probe, dis-sect, analyse, and describe increasingly esoteric issues.

At the same time, their quest for rigour forces them to put extremely tight "boundary conditions" around what they study. So when they say X works in a specific set of circumstances – time, place, industry, type of firm, or whatever – they potentially exclude all other circumstances.[36]

But to what end? Many of their findings are so far from the interests of managers as to be useless. Or of value only to a limited audience.

And academics don't use them in their classes anyway. The gap keeps widening between what they study and what they teach. Most professors, says Kai Peters, spend their time researching arcane issues, but lean on familiar textbooks to teach "standard practice."[37]

Since finding a profoundly new approach to any aspect of management is now close to being *impossible* – yes, impossible – the pressure to produce new material is bound to lead to bite-sized, incremental advances rather than radical discoveries. After all, it's easier to take a small step forward from existing work, or tease a trivial insight from it, than to take a bold leap into the unknown. And when there's no need to worry that ideas might actually be *tried* by some sucker who's desperate to improve their business results, why stretch?

The history of management research has been punctuated by very few "Eureka!" moments. There is no reason to think this will change. In fact, conditions are in place to ensure that it doesn't.

"Proof" exposed

You'd think that a community in the business of proving things would by now have sound proof of its impact in its field. So you have to worry when a senior vice president at the Association to Advance Collegiate Schools of Business (AACSB), which accredits 687 institutions in 50 countries,* admits that the organization has sometimes pushed research that is narrow, theoretical, and mathematical, *because it's easier to quantify.* "It gives us something to count," he says. "Applied research is more difficult to measure."[38]

You have to worry when a prestigious body like the Erasmus Research Institute of Management in Rotterdam says its measure of managerial relevance is the number of *consultancy requests* and *advisory board memberships* an author gets.[39]

You have to worry when the best measure of scholarly impact is how often a scholar's work is cited by their peers. And when the method one team of researchers uses to assess impact on a "much broader societal level" – assumedly also including managers – turns out to be the "novel approach" of using a Google search to count how many pages on non-educational web domains name those scholars. After all, to assume that being mentioned has any causal link to business outcomes such as productivity, sales, or profits is an astonishing leap of faith.

Starting with a list of 550 members of the Academy of Management, and checking citations from January 1981 to October 2011, these researchers arrived at a final sample size of 384.[40] But cast your eye down that list. Unless you're an insider, "a member of the club," you probably wonder, "Who *are* these people?" And if a few names do ring bells, can you recall how they *changed management*? How many of them were first to identify and describe a critical practice? How many wrote something that stands out as a really Big Idea – and what was it?

According to John Pierce, a professor at the Villanova School of Business in Virginia, "scholarship with real impact on a field of study is rare." He points to a 1998 study which "found that of approximately 33 million articles included in the Science Citation Index from 1945 to 1988, 40 percent were never cited by others, and 56 percent were cited only once. Only 4 percent received two or more citations."[41]

Writing in *Physics World*, Lokman Meho, an expert in library and information science, says, "It is a sobering thought that some 90% of papers that have been published in academic journals are never cited. Indeed, as many as 50% of papers are never read by anyone other than their authors, referees, and journal editors."

Even so, he points out, a huge increase in databases and tools that enable citation searching "shows just how widespread the use and popularity of citation analysis has become." This, in turn, means researchers "need to make it their job to disseminate their work on as many platforms and in as many different ways as possible, such as publishing in open-access and high-impact journals, and posting

---

* As of November 2013.

their work in institutional repositories, personal homepages and e-print servers, if they want their peers to be aware of, use, and ultimately cite their work."[42]

Citations aside, it would be reasonable to expect "new" management theories to be properly tested and validated. But this is seldom the case.

An analysis of 70 articles in the *Academy of Management Journal* and the *Academy of Management Review* showed that while they had been cited over 1,500 times, "the theoretical propositions they offered had rarely been tested in the reviewed work."[43]

Another study found that only *9 per cent* of the theories put forward in the prestigious *Academy of Management Review* were ever tested. Referring to it, Donald Hambrick writes: "Your paper will not meet with a warm reception if you merely claim to be testing a previously proposed line of thought. And reviewers will come right out and laugh at you if you claim to be replicating a prior test of a theory. As a result, the vast majority of published ideas in management are sub-mitted to no tests at all, a handful are subjected to one test, and only a miniscule few are tested over and over in multiple ways."[44]

So there you have it. Theories are developed, published, and then mostly ignored. Even lousy ideas, effectively hyped, may rack up citations – but without ever being properly examined. And if other researchers do refer to them, it's often not to test them, but rather to denounce them or to bolster their own theories. Citations lead to further citations, so a foundation of questionable "findings" props up layers of other equally questionable ones. A willing army of writers, consultants, conference speakers, and other opportunists take them to market. And anxious managers snap them up and try to use them.

The much-vaunted peer-review process, in which articles submitted to a journal are examined and commented on by experts before being accepted for publication, should in theory filter out ideas that don't add value. Editors and referees can be extremely helpful in sharpening an argument. But they can also force changes to the extent that authors hardly recognize what appears in print under their names.[45] And all too often, ossified thinking within the scholarly community ensures that controversial opinions never see the light of day.

These shenanigans occur within a publishing industry that measures its own success by "journal impact factor" – the citation rate of all articles in a journal.* That, however, may have little to do with article quality. Among other reasons, the reputation of authors can affect what editors choose to publish; articles in a

---

* Calculated by counting citations to articles published in a given year to articles published in the past two years, divided by the total number of articles published in the same two years (Meho, 2007).

particular journal tend to cite others in the same journal; long articles tend to be cited more often than short ones; articles usually refer to others in the same language; and American authors mostly refer to other Americans.[46]

"Not only are management researchers involved in practices that restrict the entry of new members into their communities," say Emma Bella and Richard Thorpe in *A Very Short, Fairly Interesting and Reasonably Cheap Book About Management Research*, "journal editors too may intentionally try to manipulate the metrics used to evaluate journal performance, such as impact factors (for example, by insisting authors who submit new research for potential publication must reference articles that have appeared in the journal in the past.")[47]

And this is scholarship!

Talk about an incestuous cycle! Talk about the blind leading the blind! Talk about a house of cards! Talk about a good reason for managers to keep their wits about them when considering new ideas!

But of course, few of them are cautious. Most are more casual about grabbing new concepts than they are about choosing which brand of hot dog or soda to buy for lunch. And whereas a lousy lunch – or *no* lunch – might not matter, the management ideas they choose surely do. Some cost a fortune. Their impact, positive or negative, can be enormous. At stake might be not just improved productivity, sales, or profits, but the very survival of a firm.

If this is the scholarly community's contribution to management thought – to *the future of humankind*, let's not forget! – what about the stuff being dreamed up elsewhere? Imagine what's coming from less disciplined sources. Why should you have more confidence in it?

I make these comments not to denounce research or researchers, but to caution managers about uncritically accepting new ideas. Notice that the people I quote here are *insiders*, talking about their own field of expertise. It's hard to imagine they'd say these things if they didn't feel strongly about them. Yet although they speak up now and then, and their views are published here and there, their indictment of their own community mostly falls on deaf ears. There are just too many reasons to stick with the status quo.

The consultants' edge

In spirited defence of business school scholarship, Leeds University Business School professor Timothy Devinney argues in a *Financial Times* article that it must be "independent of business practice so that we can look at the inconvenient truths ... calling for more 'relevance' potentially removes the great discoveries that may define future practices and approaches that we will not see implemented for a decade or more. None of us are so omnipotent that we could possibly predict what these are going to be as they emerge from thousands of scholars beavering away on topics of no apparent immediate relevance."

He doesn't tell us what those "inconvenient truths" might be or why non-scholars might avoid them. And he goes on to make the astonishing assertion that "Without the nerds doing the nerdy stuff, the gurus would have nothing to entertain you on television or in the airport bookstore."[48]

But academics aren't the only source of new thinking about management. Consultants play an important role too. And across the span of history they may have been even more influential (think Taylor, Drucker, Juran, Henderson, Ansoff, Kenichi Ohmae, and Peters, for example.)

Being an academic provides a patina of credibility and cachet that consultants don't automatically enjoy. And while both groups draw fire for this or that, consultants have long been especially juicy targets for attack. ("They steal your watch, then tell you the time," goes a favourite joke.) Their weaknesses are laid bare in books like *The Witch Doctors*,[49] *Consulting Demons*,[50] and *Dangerous Company* – the last-mentioned's authors warning managers to "always remember that the greatest attribute of the American management consulting industry is its ability to market itself."[51]

Ironically, it's that very need to market themselves that drives consultants to invest heavily in research, produce insights and ideas, and invent solutions for their clients. To be regarded as "thought leaders" can give them a valuable competitive advantage and help them attract business.

Whereas academics tend to work within the confines of their discipline and pursue knowledge for its own sake, consultants thrive by sharing what they learn from assignments with their colleagues and building a body of *useful* knowledge – "intellectual property" – within their firms. The economics of their industry require this. By being able to pluck insights and ideas off the shelf, give them a quick tweak, and sell them to numerous clients, they save time and money, enhance their marketing efforts, and may also generate extra revenues.

When you combine these practices with everyday client interactions about real-world issues, it's little wonder that consultants, rather than academics, have produced many of the most significant ideas about management.

But this doesn't mean you should take every new idea consultants offer at face value. Remember, their "research" methods are often shockingly *un*sound, and they have a blatantly commercial interest in selling their findings. And when intellectual integrity comes up against marketability, guess which wins.

It's worth noting, too, that despite their best efforts, they produce very few ideas that truly advance management thought. Most of their insights are industry- or function-specific – where the energy industry is headed, for example, or how to improve a retail supply chain; or how to make teams effective or use big data to best effect. Breakthrough concepts such as Bruce Henderson's BCG matrix or experience curve are a distant memory (from the 1960s), and chances are remote of anything new that's nearly as impactful.

Executive wisdom

Companies are the breeding ground for management theories. The daily slog of improving results has them constantly trying new approaches to everything they do, from designing and executing strategy to managing people and honing processes.

Ideally, both scholars and consultants would want to be ahead of the game, to be first to explain, "Here's how things should work," or to suggest, "Here's what you should do." But that's seldom the way things pan out. Almost everything they bring us is based on existing knowledge and modified according to what they see or hear – *what is already going on*. In other words, they are more reactive than proactive. Without companies as laboratories and managers as guinea pigs, neither would have much to tell us.

Noticing this, and seeing an opportunity to capitalize on their success, a growing number of executives now tell their own stories. While still in office, or after they've retired, they author books and articles and hit the speaking circuit to share their secrets. They offer little by way of theory, but their experiences and anecdotes are often instructive and motivate others to try new things.

The risk in heeding their advice, though, is that they may not really understand – or wish to *acknowledge* – why they achieved what they did. So they provide an incomplete and inaccurate picture, highlighting aspects of it that show them in the best light.

"Many books by well-known executives and most lectures and courses should be stamped CAUTION: THIS MATERIAL CAN BE HAZARDOUS TO YOUR ORGANIZATIONAL SURVIVAL," says Stanford professor Jeffrey Pfeffer. "That's because leaders touting their own careers as models to be emulated frequently gloss over the power plays they actually use to get to the top ... leaders are great at self-preservation, at telling people what they think others want to hear, and in coming across as noble and good."[52]

Less than it seems

The thoughts of those three groups of players – scholars, consultants, and managers – are decoded, disseminated, reinterpreted, misinterpreted, and mangled by many others. Much of what was originally said is ignored or gets "lost in translation." A lot more is forgotten. But there's still plenty of it out there, just waiting for you to give it a whirl.

When you look critically at all but a handful of management ideas, you'll find that they're based on earlier insights to which they add little or nothing, and are spruced up through a mix of vague impressions, false assumptions, flawed "research," and weak conclusions. And that their popularity rests on ill-informed comment, the advocacy of people who don't know what they're talking about, the efforts of over-zealous publicity machines, or uncritical media hype.

In truth, there's no way to be sure that management ideas from any source will give you the results they promise. You have to treat them all with equal scepticism. Fad-mania can be deadly.

It's obviously sensible to learn from wherever you can – after all, why try to reinvent the wheel? But meaningful lessons aren't as easy to come by as you might imagine. Much of what's touted as truth is far from it. What you think produces positive results in some company may not be the whole picture. What appears to work for them may not work for you. Sometimes it's quite easy to see why a firm is doing well or badly, but mostly it's very difficult.

The management ideas industry is a key actor in world affairs, but looking back at the tools and techniques it has produced so far, it's hard to believe there's better to come. There's every reason for managers to make sure they know what's really needed and what really works – and to do it.

7

STRATEGY STALLED

Questions of strategy – of where and how to compete – have occupied us since the first hominids emerged almost two million years ago in the Cradle of Humankind, just north of Johannesburg, South Africa. At first, they hunted and foraged in that area, but as their numbers grew and when competition for food became too intense, some moved off. Over time, and depending where they found themselves, various groups adapted their diets to meat or shellfish, or roots, grass, fruit, and seeds. They started to specialize.

Later, faced with the same challenges of where and how to compete, early traders set out on foot, ships, camels, or horses to buy and sell salt, silk, spices, and slaves. Like those hominids, they made strategic choices.

The *concept* of strategy dates from the Old Testament and was debated by Homer, Socrates, and Euripides. The ancient Greek term *strategos* meant "the art of the general," "chief magistrate," or "military commander,"[1] and Shakespeare, Tolstoy, Machiavelli, Napoleon, and Hitler all referred to strategy in a military or political context.[2]

To this day, managers rely on ideas about strategy that evolved in battles at Banquan and Trafalgar, and in combat zones from North Africa to South Korea. They've learned about conventional warfare on the plains of Central Europe, and about unconventional methods from special forces operating in the jungles of Vietnam, the slums of Somalia, and the mountains of Afghanistan.

These, then, are the roots of modern business strategy. And the reason that firms selling everything from fast food to high fashion see their competition as war and their rivals as enemies to be attacked and defeated. And why the management advice industry is so taken with military concepts, terms, and analogies.

When the first writers on management and the first business schools in the US got going around the turn of the 19th century, their raw material came from emerging bodies of knowledge on subjects like economics, law, finance, distribution, and industrial organization. But each of these was regarded as distinct, and presented as such.* There was plainly a need for a disciplined way to think about the various challenges facing a firm and integrate its activities. This led Harvard Business School, in 1911, to launch a course in *business policy*[3] to cover "the functions and responsibilities of the senior management in a company, the crucial problems that affect the success of the total enterprise, and the decisions that determine its direction, shape its future, and produce the results desired."[4] And so was "general management" born.

"Strategy," however, was nowhere in sight. In fact, by 1928 it was not yet a required course at any of America's 34 business schools.[5] And for the next 20-odd years, it remained largely unacknowledged and undeveloped as a discipline, even though executives were engaged with it daily.

Taking charge

By the early 1950s, experience gained during World War II in large-scale organization and strategy was being applied in companies. *Business planning* became commonplace. And Drucker was there to codify ideas about it, and guide managers in how they went about it.

Prediction was futile, he told them. The best they could do was take responsibility for "the futurity of present decisions." All results came from outside of organizations, so they should have a deep understanding of what had already occurred in their business environment, and be keenly aware of emerging issues and trends. This knowledge would then aid them in developing detailed objectives and plans.[6]

What he said was not altogether what managers wanted to hear. They wanted certainty. They wanted to be explicit about the outlook for their firms, what resources they would need, and their profitability. And they wanted to be specific about their plans for getting from A to B.

Long-range planning was the answer. Based on the assumption that the future would be pretty much a continuation of the past, it gained early favour at the Ford Motor Company, and was championed during the Vietnam War by US Defense Secretary Robert McNamara, a former Ford CEO. And for a while, it was practised by many other large firms. But when it became clear that the future would be nothing at all like the past, the terminology morphed into *strategic planning*, and then *strategic management*.[7] For this, credit must go largely to Igor Ansoff, Vice President of Planning and Director of Diversification at Lockheed Aircraft Corporation, a pioneering thinker to whose work we'll shortly return.

---

* The Wharton School was founded in 1881, but it was only when Harvard offered the first MBA in 1908 and writers such as Frederick Taylor, Frank and Lillian Gilbreth, and Henry Gantt began publishing, that "management" took hold as a subject.

The naming game wasn't over, though.

In 1963, Bruce Henderson founded the Boston Consulting Group, and to market the firm, began sending notes on *corporate strategy* to potential clients.[8] Like Drucker, he believed that executives needed to manage in as deliberate a way as possible, so as to wield maximum control over the future of their businesses. "Neither experience nor intuition," he said, "is of much help in strategy formulation even if both are vital to implementation. *Systematic analysis of competitive equilibrium is the only technique that works.*"[9] (My italics.)

His opinions found a receptive audience in major companies, and his insights about experience curves[10] and the classification of firms as "stars," "dogs," "question marks," or "cash cows"* became fixtures in the business lexicon.

This reinforced the prevailing belief that strategy was a data-driven, systematic, and logical process that would play out over many years. But with increasing turbulence in the environment, intensifying competition, and accelerating change, managers began to fret about planning too far ahead. Soon, "long-range" came to mean "only" five or ten years.

But a new threat loomed which was to cause a rethink. In the following decade, Western firms came under attack by Japanese companies whose visions stretched 50 or 100 years out. (In fact, Konosuke Matsushita announced a *250*-year plan when he launched Matsushita Electrical in 1932!)[11] So American and European managers started peering further into the future, and extending their time horizons. Strategic planning departments grew larger and more powerful. Strategy documents got thicker.

Meanwhile, there was no let-up in the production of yet more ideas, many of them in response to new challenges that were coming thick and fast. So into the mix from the mid-1970s through the millennium went scenarios, core competence, coopetition, dynamic capabilities, agility, resilience, strategic intent, real options, strategic democracy, and much else. And today, while there's as much emphasis on planning as ever, firms everywhere do it in shorter cycles, and with ever-tighter deadlines.

The result is that we now have a sort-of-discipline called *strategic ... what*?

As long as there's uncertainty about this, there's sure to be confusion within companies. As long as managers wrestle with questions about what labels to use and *how* to deal with strategy, they'll be distracted from actually *doing* it. And as long as they confound themselves with concepts, theories, and the next "new thing," they shouldn't expect greatness.

What they need to know about strategy is simpler than they think. And they need to think about that.

---

* These were used in the BCG Matrix, to determine a firm's *portfolio strategy*.

Three questions

The latest ideas about strategy all rest on a question posed by Peter Drucker in 1954: "What is our business and what should it be?" This is the basic strategy question. Answering it, he advised, began with three further questions: 1) Who is the customer? 2) What is value to the customer? 3) How can he be reached?[12]

Three years after Drucker set down his questions, Igor Ansoff wrote "Strategies for Diversification," an article on growth opportunities which appeared in *Harvard Business Review*. "There are four basic alternatives open to a business," he said. "It can grow through increased market penetration, through market development, through product development, or through diversification."[13] He illustrated these using a four-cell matrix (Figure 7.1), a visual device that was to become part of every consultant's toolkit in coming years.

Figure 7.1

The Ansoff "product/market matrix" quickly won devotees, and has assisted generations of executives in thinking about the shape of their present and future businesses. Along the way it got a useful push from marketing experts such as Philip Kotler,[14] and it's still a staple of marketing and strategy courses in MBA programmes.

But Drucker was there first.

When you add his three questions to the Ansoff matrix, it's clear that they underpin Ansoff's work. And when you look further, it's also clear that they underpin the work of Michael Porter. And of Porter's Harvard colleague, Clayton Christensen, who has made a mega hit with his ideas about "disruptive strategy." And, in fact, of everyone else of consequence in this field, from Derek Abell[15] and Constantinos Markides,[16] to Jay Barney,[17] Richard Rumelt,[18] and Cynthia Montgomery[19] (Figure 7.2).

You can't escape Drucker's basic who, what, how questions. There's nothing to replace them. And whatever advice tomorrow's most brilliant thinkers come up with, you can be sure these will be its foundations.

Figure 7.2

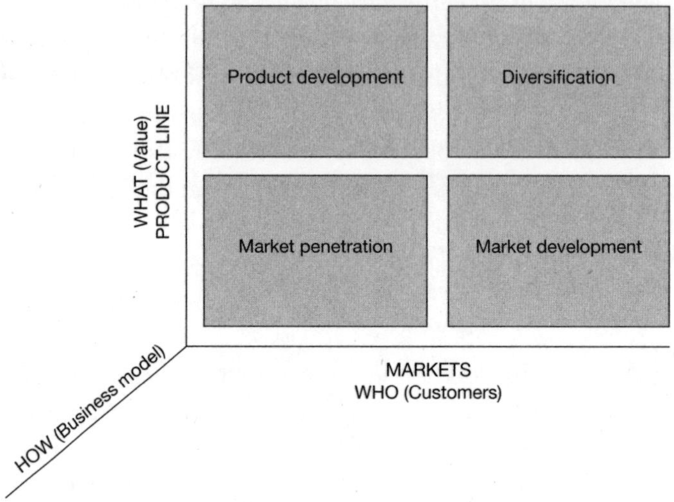

An economist's logic

If there's one management thinker who drew special attention to strategy, and gave managers more of the certainty about it that they craved, it's Michael Porter of the Harvard Business School. Over a period of some 35 years, he more than anyone else made strategic thinking systematic. Using meticulous research, he explained the competitiveness of firms and nations with unprecedented assurance, and produced frameworks and checklists for competitor analysis and the development of strategy which leave little to chance. He is unquestionably the most influential strategy guru of all time, and his ideas are taught in most business schools and widely used in organizations.

As a young industrial economist, Porter saw an opportunity to bring new rigour to strategy. He launched himself onto the strategy scene in 1979 with his "five forces" model, in a *Harvard Business Review* article on "How Competitive Forces Shape Strategy."[20] This framework, along with what he called "generic strategies," became the basis of his 1980 book *Competitive Strategy*.[21] Next, in 1985, came *Competitive Advantage*, in which he introduced the "value chain."[22] And in a 1996 *HBR* article, "What Is Strategy?" he added yet another analytical step by describing the unique configuration of things a company does to deliver value as its "activity system," and stressing the need for "fit" between the elements of that system.[23]

Porter's big contribution was to bring a level of logic and thoroughness – along with what some would say is an utterly excruciating degree of analysis – to strategy. But even more significant than the tools he's provided is the central message that underpins them: that positioning determines profitability, so managers must make hard choices and trade-offs in their choice of customers and ways to reach them. And that even as the goal of "sustainable competitive advantage" becomes more elusive, firms should stick with their strategies over the long haul rather than constantly chop and change.[24]

But sound though his views may be, they're altogether less of a leap than has been made out. His five forces help answer Drucker's question, "Who is the customer?" The value chain and the activity system help decide, "How can he be reached?" But as to "What is value to the customer?" Porter doesn't offer much beyond advising businesses to find the right balance between price and performance.

And this brings us to a serious weakness in his approach: the heavy emphasis on picking things apart. For as Henry Mintzberg has long averred – and this sets him at odds with Drucker and Henderson – strategy is to a great extent an intuitive process. So it's only partly a matter of *analysis*, and mostly one of *synthesis*.[25]

Structural links between your company and its suppliers and customers enable the creation and delivery of value. Deciding those links is, on the surface at least, a matter of analysis and logic. But behind such practicalities is the much bigger issue of what really makes your company different. For it's how you see possible connections and make connections – between insights, ideas, and actions – that enables you to find a competitive edge and then adjust your strategy when things change. It's how you sense and make sense of things that sets you apart. In the absence of instinct and imagination, the "mechanics" of a business will never give you the advantage you seek.

Porter's five-forces framework was developed in an industrial era, so it's moot how useful it is in the information age, when new forces are at work. It also assumes that competition occurs *within* industries, rather than *across* them, as is now so often the case. His insistence that companies have to choose between cost leadership or differentiation was long ago defied by Japanese companies, and then by others; in many sectors today, the only way to compete is through low cost *and* differentiation. And his continued emphasis on analysis in strategy, while downplaying the role of people, has been little short of astonishing.*

It took him a long time to give more than passing attention to the need for

---

* For example, see his analysis of how Southwest Airlines competes, in his June 1996 *HBR* article "What Is Strategy?"

firms to be fast and flexible in order to survive in white water. And although he does agree that strategy needs to evolve over time, he has been slow to admit that *temporary* advantage may be the best a company can hope for, and that rapid innovation and improvement may be the way to win.[26]

As Porter sees it – and before him, Drucker, Ansoff, and others – strategy is best designed from the *outside-in*. And yes, an external perspective does make sense, given the influence of context on a firm's performance. But it's equally important to have an *inside-out* view, so you're clear about what you can and should do especially well, what resources and capabilities you have and need, and how your internal strengths might enable you to exploit opportunities in the marketplace.

Seeing the gap

You'd have thought that Drucker's Big Question – "what is our business and what should it be?" – would forever give managers sleepless nights. But apparently not. So while they *weren't* worrying about it, Ted Levitt spun it into "Marketing Myopia," an article that won him the 1960 McKinsey Award and went on to be one of the most reprinted *HBR* articles ever. His version of that question was: "What business are you *really* in?"[27] (My italics.)

This subtlety was unwarranted. The answer to whichever question managers went with lay not in what a firm did, but in what its customers sought. But Levitt addressed the issue in a particularly memorable way by suggesting that railroads might not have declined if they'd seen themselves as being in the transport industry, rather than just as train operators. That by looking beyond the edges of their industry, they might have seen other profitable opportunities.

Twenty years later, he produced another *HBR* article, "Marketing Success Through Differentiation – of Anything," in which he said that managers should look continuously "for gaps in market coverage that the company can fill … at new ways of influencing buyers to choose one's product instead of a competitor's."[28]

Fast-forward another 11 years, to 1991, when Gary Hamel and C.K. Prahalad observed that a "way to fire corporate imagination is to get managers to explore the white spaces that lie between existing business units." Those white spaces, they said encouragingly, "represent new competitive territory."[29]

Then, in 1994, Jeffrey Rayport and John Sviokla announced that "the traditional marketing mix no longer applies." Thinking about the market *place*, they said, was so yesterday. In a new world, you had to think about market *space*. "Quite simply, in an information-defined transaction space, customers learn about products differently, buy them differently, and have them delivered differently."[30]

In 1999, two INSEAD professors, W. Chan Kim and Renèe Mauborgne, produced yet another "new" way for companies to break away from their competitors.

"Creating new market space requires a different pattern of strategic thinking," they declared. "Instead of looking within the accepted boundaries that define how we compete, managers can look systematically across them. By doing so, they can find unoccupied territory that represents a real breakthrough in value."[31]

The examples these two authors used included a sandwich chain (Pret a Manger), a circus (Cirque du Soleil), a movie-house chain (Kinepolis), a cement company (Cemex), and an aircraft-leasing business (Netjets) – none of which had captured unoccupied space by becoming an e-business. However, in a 2001 book called *Place to Space*, Peter Weill and Michael Vitale dealt specifically with how companies might migrate from their traditional business models to e-business models that combined place and space.[32] So whether real or virtual, the concept of market space was taking hold.

Another apparent advance came in 2004, when Kim and Mauborgne reported that after a five-year study they'd found that high-growth firms approached strategy in very different ways than their less successful competitors. The winners "sought to make their competitors irrelevant through a strategic logic we call value innovation."[33] The laggards concentrated on outcompeting each other.

The following year, they cleverly branded unoccupied territory a "blue ocean" – in contrast to a hotly contested "red ocean" – in a book called *Blue Ocean Strategy*.[34] This was apparently such a valuable insight that INSEAD was prompted to launch a "Blue Ocean Strategy Institute" in a chateau just outside Fontainebleau. The book quickly became a bestseller, and by December 2013 had been published in 43 languages, with 3.5 million copies sold.[35] (An updated and expanded version with more examples was published in early 2015.)

All of these ideas were manna to executives anxious about new competition, particularly from Japan, and enthralled by the possibilities of the internet. But what did they add to what we already knew?

Unpick the commentary and separate *what's* being said from the *way* it's said, and you're left with this: head-on battles against competitors with identical offerings are suicidal; the way to win is to seek market gaps where they aren't playing, and to deliver unique value to your customers. Precisely the advice Drucker gave when he told managers to pay attention not just to their customers, but also to "non-customers."[36]

What customers want

Kenichi Ohmae, a famous Japanese management consultant who for a time was head of the McKinsey office in Tokyo, observed in his 1982 book *The Mind of the Strategist* that "when the company's investments aimed at better satisfying users' current objectives reach a point of diminishing returns, the strategic thinker will explore other user values and search for strategic degrees of freedom to satisfy them by means of technology, service, and the like."[37]

And in "Getting Back to Strategy," a November–December 1988 *HBR* article, he wrote of the need for firms to "*avoid* competition whenever and wherever possible. As the great Sun Tzu observed 500 years before Christ, the smartest strategy in war is the one that allows you to achieve your objectives without having to fight."[38]

The same ideas crop up yet again in Clayton Christensen's recently influential work on "disruptive strategy."[39] When he tells managers to think about "good enough" offerings and "the job customers want done" – phrases now parroted by anyone with anything to say about marketing – he's suggesting that the first step to avoiding head-on clashes is to walk in the customer's shoes and understand what they really need and want. In this, he's just echoing Ohmae, who asks, "What is the user's objective function?"[40] And he's borrowing even more directly from Ted Levitt – who in turn was quoting one Leo McGinneva – when he wrote that "people don't buy things but buy solutions to problems"; they "don't want quarter-inch drill bits. They want quarter-inch holes."[41]

Yet possibly unaware of all this, and definitely undeterred by the fact that once again they were reinventing the wheel, managers overnight stopped talking about which *industry* they competed in, and began talking instead about "the *space* we're in." This might have made them feel very cool and "with it," but I struggle to understand how the switch in language helps most strategy discussions. The core questions haven't changed (Figure 7.3). And even assuming that you do find new customers in that "white space," "market space," or "blue ocean," you still have to answer the what and the how.

Figure 7.3

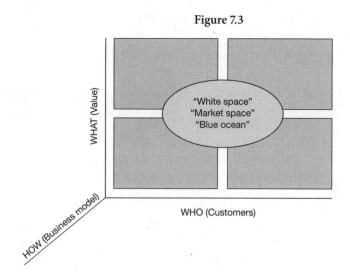

Good at something

The rock-star strategy concept of recent times is surely "core competence." But what is it? To find out, I spent a week at London Business School in the early 1990s with Gary Hamel, who'd teamed up with C.K. Prahalad to popularize the term.

Their 1990 article "The Core Competence of the Corporation" was to become one of the most reprinted *HBR* articles in history.[42] Yet the concept, says Walter Kiechel III in *The Lords of Strategy*, would "muzzy up more corporate conversations about strategy than it would clarify."[43]

The answer I was looking for turned out to be disappointingly *un*-profound: core competencies, I learned, are bundles of knowledge and skills that let you do valuable stuff exceptionally well. To give a firm a durable advantage, they should be rare, hard to "decode," hard to copy, and make a difference that customers will pay for.

The underlying idea of being excellent in something that would distinguish a company from its competitors had been around from time immemorial. Drucker raised the issue in *Concept of the Corporation*, his 1946 opus on General Motors,[44] and gave a short chapter to it – "Knowledge Is the Business" – in *Managing for Results* in 1964.[45] Philip Selznick talked "distinctive competence" in his 1957 book *Leadership in Administration*,[46] and Harvard Business School professors Roland Christensen and Kenneth Andrews began talking about "distinctive competencies" in the early 1960s.[47] Edith Penrose wrote at length about the merits of a "resource-based view of the firm" (RBV)* in *The Theory of the Growth of the Firm* in 1959.[48] In 1965, Igor Ansoff urged managers to understand their firms' "competence profile."[49] In 1984, Birger Wernerfelt published a seminal article on this topic that cemented it firmly in management literature.[50]

And that's where it lurked. Until 1987, when Hiroyuki Itami, a professor at Hitotsubashi University, published *Mobilizing Invisible Assets* – in my view, one of the best business books of all time.

Itami began by confirming the importance of internal strengths – specifically, information-based resources. But he then went a step further, arguing that coupling those resources with "unreasonable" ambitions could enable firms to overcome external constraints and acquire a competitive edge. A firm must "transcend its current level of invisible assets," he wrote. "A dynamic imbalance of strategy, resources, and organization is necessary for a long-term strategy." [51]

The work of all these authors gave Hamel and Prahalad their springboard. Their "competence" article was followed in 1993 by "Strategy as Stretch and Leverage"[52]

---

* This term is now used interchangeably with core competence or core capabilities.

– the "dynamic imbalances" Itami spoke of. And then by another *HBR* article and a book, both titled "Competing for the Future," in 1994.[53]

The two business school professors explained things in an engaging, metaphor-laden way, and both of them became huge drawcards on the speaking circuit and as consultants. But what gave real traction to their take on RBV theory was not so much that they offered a radically new approach to strategy, but rather that they were in tune with the *zeitgeist*.*

In the 1980s and early '90s there was global infatuation with "Japanese management." How was it, executives and policy makers desperately wanted to know, that such a small island nation, which only 40 years earlier was on its knees, could punch so powerfully above its weight?

Itami's work, though not widely known, provided answers. Hamel and Prahalad added colour – and a great deal of practical advice – through numerous examples of how Japanese firms configured and leveraged their resources and capabilities to take on the world. They yanked RBV out of obscurity and polished it up. The strategy community leapt onto the bandwagon, and in no time there was a spate of books, articles, and conferences on the subject.

Until this time, strategic thought had evolved quite smoothly. But suddenly there was a divide – an inside-out camp vs. the outside-in crowd. And when thinking people lose perspective about a complex matter like strategy, and start talking about it in stark black-or-white terms and believing that there's one right way to deal with it, common sense flies out of the window.

Michael Porter was well versed in the need for "distinctive capabilities" from his days of writing and teaching business policy with Roland Christensen and Kenneth Andrews in the early 1980s. His thoughts on value chain analysis and activity systems dealt in detail with these. Yet he was initially derisive about core competence, and though he came to refer to it later, he always put it firmly in its place.

"The resource-based view just cannot stand on its own," he said in a 2002 interview. "Yet there are elements of real insight there. If you could hook the resource based view to the value chain, to strategic choices, and ultimately to profit, then you could build a more robust role for resource/capability thinking."[54]

And again in 2011 he showed his bias for outside-in thinking and his conviction that positioning was paramount. "I am not a big fan of the concept that a company has only one, or a few, core capabilities," he said. A firm needs many related capabilities. A narrow, inward focus distracts managers from thinking about the unique position of their companies, and how they can leverage it. There's also the risk of over-estimating a company's strengths.[55]

---

* The spirit of the times.

Bain's 2013 *Tools Survey* ranks strategic planning in first place, with core competence sixth. But what are we to read into this? The difference is no doubt due to the survey listing a number of tools and asking respondents which they use. Those who tick the strategic planning box don't all tick the core competence box too. Some managers will no doubt take this to mean that a) strategic planning and core competence are separate issues, and b) planning is possible without considering competence, or c) if you give competence enough attention, planning isn't necessary.

Of course, none of these is true. Strategic planning is a valuable process. But if it doesn't include thinking hard about what's inside your firm, and how you can combine, strengthen, or exploit what's there, it'll never get you to a significant competitive advantage.

Not so disruptive

Every decade has its big ideas, and tech-mania at the turn of the 20th century shot "disruption" into the stratosphere, from where it now casts its blinding light well beyond the management universe.

Like core competence, though, it's less of a revelation than it's made out to be. Both ideas have shaken up thinking in a lot of companies, but managers could have achieved exactly the same results using yesterday's knowledge. And like any idea, both of these may have the perverse effect of *impeding* rather than facilitating strategic thinking when they're misunderstood.

Disruption as a concept grew out of a study by Joseph Bower and Clayton Christensen, both professors at Harvard Business School, which saw light in a 1995 *HBR* article titled "Disruptive Technologies: Catching the Wave."[56] Their findings were subsequently moulded into a theory by Christensen, making him a household name in management circles (an article in *The New Yorker* called him "the most influential business thinker on earth")[57] and spawning many books and articles by him and others. Thanks to determined promotion and the bandwagon effect, disruption is now a term you hear in almost every management discussion – though it's seldom used in exactly the way Christensen proposes. For example, at the World Economic Forum's annual meeting in Davos, Switzerland, in January 2014, an entire televised session was given to disruption; yet the comments of the high-powered panel gave no hint that any of them had ever heard of Christensen or his theory.

The gospel according to the Harvard professor goes like this:

In their quest for the most profitable customers, companies innovate and improve aggressively – and give customers more than they need or will pay for. And the more intently they listen to their customers, the more they up their game and sustain that gap.

While they focus on the next-generation performance needs of the most attractive customers, guerrilla competitors sneak in under their price umbrella and target less attractive customers who're being overlooked or under-served. The upstarts ask, "Who is not getting attention?" and "What is value to those customers?"

The customers they aim at have basic needs. They're not in the market for state-of-the-art products. So these firms can ditch the bells and whistles and keep costs and prices low.

Initially, the leading firms don't see a threat. The challengers' offerings are of no appeal to their best customers, and they aren't chasing them anyway. The customers they lure are ones who want low prices, will be satisfied with "good enough" offerings, and won't be missed.

But this is just a lull before the storm. Quite soon, more mainstream customers are tempted by the no-frills competitors. They need to forego some of the "value" they've grown used to, but what they get does the job – plus it's easier to use, more convenient, and more affordable.

Many established players have been hurt this way – think clothing, airlines, steel, medical devices, consumer electronics, autos, and so on. But then they make things worse for themselves.

In an effort to counter competitors who won't play by their rules, they typically race even faster up the value path. They up their quality, invest even more in innovation, jazz up their design, and pile on features and benefits. But in their increasingly desperate efforts to stay ahead of their enemies, they also stay ahead of their customers – and the cost of their overkill forces them to keep hiking their prices.

Some customers stick with them because they don't mind paying more for products that they perceive to be at the bleeding edge. In fact, high prices might fit perfectly with their self-image. But as the number of defectors grows, the pool of such buyers gets smaller. And the harder firms try to hang on to their traditional business, the more they lock themselves into their "superior" strategy – and the worse things get for them.

The irony that Christensen points to is that by doing precisely what seems to make sense, and what conventional management wisdom advocates, companies undermine themselves and engineer their own demise.

But what makes this "theory" disruptive? What step change does it bring to strategy? What did we know before we were told, "Here's a new way of competing – it's called disruption – and here's how disruptive competition works?"

"The job to be done"

Following Christensen's thinking over the years, it's hard to avoid a sense of *déjà vu*. Even a quick glance back into the history of management thought reveals that much of his theory is to be found in Marketing 101 and Strategy 101. And that as a management innovation, it's no great shakes.

Start with the notion of disruption.

Surely it has been the goal of every strategist in history? Didn't they all want to interrupt things and cause upheavals in the competitive landscape? Didn't they all want to nullify their competitors' strategies and seduce customers with novel offerings? Didn't they all strive to throw their competitors off-balance by turning their strengths into weaknesses? Didn't they all want to replace old paradigms with new ones and change the rules of the game?

Of course they did. So while strategy has always been about the creation of advantage, it's also about "the creative destruction of an opponent's advantage," says Richard D'Aveni in his 1994 book *Hypercompetition*. And the goal of strategy "is to disrupt the status quo."[58]

Now consider two notions that are apparently fundamental to disruptive strategy, and sure to crop up whenever disruption is mentioned.

First, there's "the job to be done." As in: what problem is your customer actually trying to fix? Or what "value" does your customer actually seek?

Far from being a fresh insight, this is one of the oldest ideas in the marketing playbook. So old, in fact, that it's impossible to pin down its origin.

The earliest hucksters knew that what turned customers on was not so much the *features* of a product as its *benefits* – what it did for them. "My favorite headlines focus on benefits," said John Caples, who began his copywriting career at the Ruthrauff & Ryan mail-order company in 1926, and went on to become a giant in advertising lore. "When people consider new products or services, they want to know how their lives will improve. Don't keep them guessing, throw that benefit straight into the headline."[59] This principle led Elmer Wheeler, a famous American sales trainer in the 1930s, to coin the phrase, "Don't sell the steak – sell the sizzle." And generations of marketing folk have had this basic belief drummed into them.

It goes without saying that Drucker was one of the first management experts to grasp the importance of marketing as opposed to selling, and to write authoritatively about it. "The customer never buys a product," he said in 1954. "By definition the customer buys the satisfaction of a want.... What the manufacturer considers quality may, therefore, be irrelevant and nothing but waste and useless expense."[60] Forty-five years later he was still banging the same drum. "What is value to the customer," he said in *Management Challenges for the 21st Century*, "is almost always something quite different from what is value or quality to the supplier."[61]

But if there are clear links between Drucker's views and what Christensen says, Ted Levitt had a way of explaining things that blurred the lines even more. "People do not buy gasoline," he said in 1960. "They cannot see it, taste it, feel it, appreciate it, or really test it. What they buy is the right to continue driving their cars." (Their "job to be done.")[62] And in his 1983 book, *The Marketing Imagination*, he wrote: "people don't buy things but buy solutions."[63]

Another marketing guru, Philip Kotler, had said the same thing in 1980 in *Marketing Management: Analysis, Planning and Control*, which continues to be a standard textbook in marketing courses.[64] And Kenichi Ohmae repeated it in a 1998 *HBR* article, "Getting Back to Strategy," where he wrote that strategy "means working hard to understand a customer's inherent needs and then rethinking what a category of product is all about ... if your objective is to serve the customer better, then shouldn't you understand why that customer drinks coffee in the first place? ... Why do people take pictures in the first place?" Getting back to strategy begins with "the simple-sounding questions about what products are about."[65]

The second key theme in Christensen's thinking is "good enough" – as in products or services that satisfy customers' most basic needs, but no more. But again, we've heard this before.

In *The Marketing Imagination*, Levitt warned against overshooting customer needs and wants, telling over-eager marketers: "The customer may actually want and expect *less*."[66] (My italics.) But then he went even further. Within months of his book appearing, he published an article in *HBR* titled "The Globalization of Markets,"* which provided as good a blueprint for disruption as you could hope for.

By stripping away the features and benefits that made products particularly appropriate for particular markets, he argued, firms could sell them to many more customers across the world. Many Japanese companies had discovered "the one great thing all markets have in common – an overwhelming desire for dependable, world-standard modernity in all things, at aggressively low prices. In response, they deliver irresistible value everywhere, attracting people with products that market-research technocrats described with superficial certainty as being unsuitable and uncompetitive."[67]

As many firms have learned to their cost, however, being "good enough" doesn't bestow a permanent advantage. At best, it's a starting point for a new phase of competition. For as soon as it's evident that there's a sizeable market for simple,

---

* An idea Drucker had touched on 15 years earlier when he said, "The whole world ... has become one economy in its expectations, in its responses, and in its behavior." (Peter F. Drucker, *The Age of Discontinuity*, New York: Harper & Row, 1968)

cheap, and convenient products, competitors will quickly pile in. It may be possible for a brief moment to hold some at bay by cutting prices further, but that simply speeds up commoditization.

This is doubtless what lies ahead for most companies that follow Christensen's recipe for disruption. And the only way off that slippery slope is by *adding* value. So round and round they go.

Early in 1990, I spent much of a day with Levitt in his office at Harvard Business School. We talked about his globalization article, and I showed him my own focus-value-cost model (Figure 12.3). "That's exactly right," he said. "It's the only way to compete. Everything begins with who your customer is, and the job they want done. And every company has to keep offering new value to those customers, even while driving costs down so prices will stay low."

And what about Christensen's observation that the more closely firms listen to their best customers, and the harder they work to deliver what those customers say they'd like, the greater their chances of offering too much?

Of course, this is possible. Customers are demanding, and their expectations keep rising. If you give them an inch, they'll take a mile. But to *not* listen because you fear they'll mislead you is daft. To do that is to shift responsibility for your future from your hands to theirs.

So the real problem is different than Christensen sees it.

It's how to balance listening to customers and learning from them with making up your own mind about how to serve them. It's how to use their opinions to inform your insights about potential new value and new competitive advantages – while also cooking up ideas they can't imagine, which will change their lives.

Faith in "the voice of the customer" gripped managers during the 1980s, but as Steve Jobs demonstrated, and many marketing and advertising experts have testified, customers are often clueless about what "value" they might buy in the future. Until they see a product or try a service, they may have no idea it's possible, let alone that they'll like it, want it, or be willing to pay for it. Until you take the risk of launching your offering into the marketplace, you cannot know whether it will succeed or fail.

In the mid-1980s, Coca-Cola ran taste tests between its original brand, a "new Coke," and Pepsi-Cola. After consumers voted for the new product by a 2-1 margin, the 100-year-old company did the unthinkable, and with huge fanfare made it their new "mother brand." But within months, angry customers forced a retreat: "old Coke," which had been labelled "Coke Classic" as a mark of respect and to keep it around, was hastily relaunched and the new product was quietly dropped.

"Some people say, 'Give the customer what they want,'" said Jobs. "But that's not my approach. Our job is to figure out what they're going to want before they do. I think Henry Ford once said, 'If I'd asked people what they wanted, they would have told me, 'A faster horse!'"[68]

As experience shows, there is no way to be sure what customers will buy tomorrow. But there's no point in closing off any opportunity to minimize that risk by learning as much as you can, as fast as you can, from wherever.

OK, so what about Christensen's advice that to compete with disruptors, the leader should spin off a totally separate business unit?

Nothing new here, either.

More and more companies have learned that "it is futile to expect the truly new to come out of the existing product divisions within the company," wrote Drucker in 1968. "The new needs a 'separate development' division which is responsible for it until it is no longer 'new' but an established going, successful business."[69]

Scholars, executives, consultants, analysts, and journalists have long been aware that getting into the low end of almost any market is most likely to succeed with an "ultra-lite" business model, and a cost-conscious team intent on winning with bare-bones offerings. Which often means a totally separate business unit.

Time and again we've seen companies come a cropper when they tried to launch "fighting brands" from operations designed to offer premium products. High overheads and complex organizational arrangements make it impossible to play that game. As Porter keeps reminding us, firms have to make hard trade-offs and sacrifices; they can't be half-pregnant. If they wish to compete on price, they have to compete on costs.

This means having to address factors like their staffing, structure, and value chains. But there's also the matter of mindsets. As Levitt told me: "You've mastered what you know, and suddenly you're asked to master something you don't know. So there are a lot of deep human resistances. And they're understandable."[70]

A corporate culture suited to the top end of a market can't easily embrace the bottom end too. Teams that have played with big innovation budgets and mastered the development and marketing of cutting-edge offerings are unlikely to get excited about turning their attention to ones that are more affordable and less sophisticated. This isn't the challenge they seek. Different people are required. And they must be managed in different ways.

The fact is that much of what Christensen says is yesterday's news. It has been reported and advocated, written about and spoken about, for decades. You don't have to probe too deeply to find the precedents.

So in three, five, or 25 years from now, will we look back on the Christensen era as a disruptive one *in the annals of strategic thought,* or one in which we gave due recognition to what we knew before he came along? And will his version of disruption continue to hold the high ground, or will it become watered down, lose momentum, and fall from grace as so many other management ideas do?

My bet is that disruption *à la* Christensen will soon be seen for what it is: an interesting take on the focus-value-cost principles. For one thing, all strategy should be disruptive, and those principles apply to every company in every market. Secondly, customer expectations change. They want more and more for less and less – and in this time of hyper-competition they know they can get it. So even if your low-priced disruption attracts them today, you'll struggle to hold onto them when competitors undercut you even as they add superior functionality, design, and convenience. And that is bound to happen.

If there's one important thing all the chatter about disruption has achieved, it's to focus managers' attention on the three basic strategy questions: who is your customer, what is value to them, and how will you deliver it? (Though you have to ask what *else* those well-paid people might have been thinking about!)

The fact that disruption, as Christensen describes it, has become such a fetish, could be seen as a sad indictment of academic thought and management practice. But a more reasonable view is that it simply reflects reality.

"Unless you already believe in disruption," writes Harvard history professor Jill Lepore, in a harsh critique of Christensen and his theory in *The New Yorker*, "many of the successes that have been labeled disruptive innovation look like something else, and many of the failures that are often seen to have resulted from failing to embrace disruptive innovation look like bad management."[71] An incensed Christensen accused her in a *Businessweek* interview of "a criminal act of dishonesty – at Harvard of all places,"[72] for her interpretation of his work. The flurry of comment sparked by this spat highlighted just how commonly his ideas are misconstrued and how loosely the term is used.

Discovering or developing new ways to manage is no easy task. To fall for every so-called breakthrough idea that comes your way makes no sense. But nor does it make sense to overlook what has been so painstakingly learned over so many years.

As Levitt said, "Man lives not by bread alone, but mostly by catchwords." So it's important to pick those catchwords with care, and to be clear about what they mean and how they might be applied.

From intentions to action

Although strategy has constantly had new labels attached to it, little has changed in practice. Managers still have to do what they've always had to do.

But it should concern us that while a range of tools has been created to help them pull things together into a holistic approach, arriving at "the way we work here" remains a challenge. There's one stream of advice about how to figure out a strategy and another about how to execute it.

Executives have always seen strategy as a way to shape the direction and results of their organizations. And they've always approached it on the basis of three false assumptions: 1) that strategy is a plan, 2) that they understand the future better than they possibly can, and 3) that by precisely mapping out how their instructions will be turned into action, things will turn out as they wish.

Following World War II, these assumptions became ever more firmly entrenched. A new era of business growth saw firms rapidly expand and become more complex. Consumerism took off and competition became more intense. So strategy became an ever more disciplined activity. This led academics and consultants to develop new methods of forecasting and analysis, new techniques for making strategic choices, and increasingly convoluted diagrams describing the strategy process. And it led many firms to set up departments of strategic planning, and tie strategy more tightly to budgeting.

All this had many *un*planned effects. Strategy chewed up more and more executive time. Paperwork piled up. Organizational rigidity set in. People at the top accepted bigger workloads, people at lower levels learned not to think or show initiative, and risk became a filthy word.

More than half a century later, executives are still captivated by the illusion that they can control events with precision. They've fallen in love with SWOT analyses, scenarios, Michael Porter's concepts of "generic strategy," "five forces," and "value chains," and with "key performance indicators" (KPIs), "core competences," and "outcomes." Budgeting has become a ritual and familiar old return on investment (ROI – which has been around since 1929!) has been shunted aside in favour of newfangled measures like "total return to shareholders" (TRS), "economic value added" (EVA™), and "cash flow return on investment" (CFROI).* And to hook everything together into a cohesive system, there are now "balanced scorecards" and "strategy maps."

This is what managers are taught in business school. This is what they read about. This is the grab bag they reach into for enlightenment. This is their "best practice."

But is this the best way to go?

When strategy meets reality

Much of what we're told about strategy suggests that it's all about analysis and decisions, and if you get these right, success is virtually assured. But we're reminded every day of the unpredictability of the world and the yawning gap between inten-

---

* For more on these concepts, see my book, *Value Management* (Cape Town: Zebra Books, 2004).

tions and action. And when you look back through many decades of thinking about strategy, one thing stands out: *the failure of the smartest minds in the field to offer a unified view of how to craft a winning strategy and turn it into action.*

Strategy design and execution embrace almost every managerial activity. Yet what we have is a hard-wired view that these are altogether different kinds of work and need to be addressed *separately*, by different people and at different times. So there's one set of ideas about making strategy and another about making it happen.

And to add even more complexity to executives' lives, there's also a welter of stuff on matters such as innovation, culture, structure, operational effectiveness, quality, and so on – all of which are important – which is dished up in a piecemeal way rather than as an integrated whole.[73]

The advisors companies call on don't help matters. There are specialists in every aspect of management; generalists are few and far between. Topics crucial to strategy, and so interlinked that it's not only difficult but also senseless to separate them, are addressed one at a time. Some people specialize in scenarios, others in lean processes, and still others in human capital or project management. There are experts in performance management, and quality, and … everything else. One consulting firm is known for its work in strategy development, another for turning strategy into action. Academics pump out ever-narrower studies on one of these or the other. Popular management journals feature articles that reinforce the paradigm of strategy then action.

Design experts have produced more than enough ideas about how to analyse a market, or position a firm or its products. They know how to ferret out information about customers and competitors, and cobble it into a point of view. "Here's your situation," they'll tell you. "These are your options. This is how you should compete."

Experts in execution – usually quite different people – have cooked up long lists of ways to set goals, define actions, gather resources, motivate people to do the right things, monitor and measure results, and the rest. So we have two distinct kinds of work – with a chasm between them.

But strategy design and execution are messy, iterative, interconnected processes. They don't occur in isolation or in a neat sequence or to order. When you meet with your team to plan your company's future, strategy may be the central issue, but it's by no means the only one. You have to take into account a host of other contextual and managerial matters. All affect your strategy in one way or another – and your strategy affects them. Design spills into execution, and execution spills into design.

An easy way to visualize the situation is simply to draw a line down the middle

131

of a blank page, and write DESIGN in the left-hand column and EXECUTION on the right. Then, list the managerial activities involved in each. After only a few lines, you'll see that the words you need to use – change, innovation, culture, leadership, goal-setting, communication, and so on – apply to both columns. So how might you deal with these overlaps?

The usual way is to clutter a firm with interventions, priorities, and projects. To create masses of work that doesn't connect. But that's obviously not smart.

More than 50 years after Ansoff's first book, advice about how to compete and win is still offered in bits and pieces, much like a jigsaw puzzle. And analysis still trumps synthesis – so strategy concepts tend to be helpful in picking things apart and understanding a firm's situation rather than pulling them together. It's left to managers to see the complete picture and work out how to link the pieces.

To deal with this challenge, Kaplan and Norton attempted in the Centennial issue of *Harvard Business Review* to describe a complete "management system." Here's the idea:

> The loop comprises five stages, beginning with strategy development, which involves applying tools, processes, and concepts such as mission, vision, and value statements; SWOT analysis; shareholder value management; competitive positioning; and core competencies to formulate a strategy statement. That statement is then translated into specific objectives and initiatives, using other tools and processes, including strategy maps and balanced scorecards. Strategy implementation, in turn, links strategy to operations with a third set of tools and processes, including quality and process management, reengineering, process dashboards, rolling forecasts, activity-based costing, resource capacity planning, and dynamic budgeting. As implementation progresses, managers continually review internal operational data and external data on competitors and the business environment. Finally, managers periodically assess the strategy, updating it when they learn that the assumptions underlying it are obsolete or faulty, which starts another loop around the system.[74]

The magazine's editor at the time, Tom Stewart, told readers they were getting "a magisterial article about how to build a management system that works." He then added, "(Only half-joking, around the office we've called it the only management article you'll ever need.)"[75]

Or might it be the *last* management article you'd ever *want* to read? Big businesses are complex and there's lots to coordinate and do, but this "system" takes things to extremes. Is it what you need for your company? Would you be able to apply it? Have you got time – and is this the best way to use your time?

The Kaplan and Norton "management system" is another step towards precision and control in business. It probably depicts more or less what happens in many large firms. But it reflects a school of thought about strategy that sits uneasily in today's VUCA environment.

What Ansoff understood

Ansoff is best remembered for only part of his message – for providing a systematic, analytical approach to making decisions and plans for the long term. But there's more for which he gets little credit. Ahead of many others, he understood that strategy is designed and executed in conditions of turbulence and surprise, and must enable firms to deal with them. So human attitudes, beliefs, and behaviour are major factors in winning rather than losing.

- His pioneering 1965 book, *Corporate Strategy*, a managerial classic, has been slated for its emphasis on analysis. But by the end of only the second chapter he describes an "adaptive search method for strategy formulation."[76] (Does this sound like Henry Mintzberg's 1987 insights about "emergent strategy": "Managers who craft strategy ... are responsive to their materials, learning about their organizations and industries through personal touch"?)[77]
- In a 1968 article, Ansoff wrote: "Since the early 1950s, confronted with the growing variability and unpredictability of the business environment, business managers have become increasingly concerned with finding rational and foresightful ways of adjusting to and exploiting environmental change."[78]
- In *Implanting Strategic Management*, published in 1984, he said that "during the first seventy years of the 20th century systems evolved in response to two challenges: the increasing discontinuity, complexity, and novelty of challenges on the one hand, and the decreasing visibility of the future on the other." Managers he talked to expected "frequent discontinuities, changes which will be faster than the firm's response, events which will be only partially predictable before they impact on the firm."[79]
- In the Preface to *The New Corporate Strategy*, a 1988 update of his first book, he said: "The past thirty years of experience have shown that strategic planning works poorly, if it works at all, when it is confined to analytic decision-making, without recognition of the enormous influence which the firm's *leadership, power structure, and organizational dynamics* exert on both decisions and implementations."[80] (My italics.)

Midway through the 30-year timespan of Ansoff's writings, strategy was in trouble. According to Joseph Bower, a professor at Harvard Business School, corporate strategy had become "a common rubric covering a wide range of activities from planning, to budgeting, to blue sky ruminating about the state of the world."[81]

A strong opinion had formed by then that planning was a waste of time. You couldn't see the future, so it was pointless trying to anticipate how it would pan out. Entrepreneurship, innovation, fast learning, and agility were getting a lot of press. The role of people in strategy was gaining attention. The volume of success recipes was exploding.

And managers were less clear than ever about how to compete and win.

They'd slogged their way through the analysis-choices-action jungle, and hadn't found what they wanted. They'd tried every framework and questionnaire in the book, but with mixed results. And while they sliced and diced, probed and analysed, they also made many critical decisions on the fly – while driving their cars, taking a shower, or in brief chats with various people – relying on their gut feelings and doing things that weren't in their formal plans. Sometimes, this worked out, and sometimes it was disastrous.

Their strategy for strategy was a mess. Yet still, little has changed.

"Over the past 20 years," write Michael Mol and Julian Birkinshaw, researchers at the Management Innovation Lab at London Business School, in their 2008 book *Giant Steps*, "strategic planning has fallen into disrepute for a number of reasons."[82] Obvious ones are that it's impossible to know the future, constant change and surprise are a reality, there's growing complexity, and execution is extremely difficult. Less obvious is the fact that strategy is but one element of a much larger picture. Crafting it at any specific moment in time is one thing; orchestrating it over time is another matter altogether.

Ironically, Igor Ansoff himself was sceptical about strategy. It's "an elusive and somewhat abstract concept," he said. "Its formulation typically produces no immediate concrete productive action in the firm. Above all, it is an expensive process both in terms of actual dollars and managerial time. Since management is a pragmatic, result-oriented activity, a question needs to be asked: whether an abstract concept, such as strategy, can usefully contribute to the firm's performance."[83]

Managers obviously think it can. Those who make money advising them are unlikely to go with Ansoff. Any hint of a challenge suggests opportunities. Because so much has already been said about management, it's inevitable that their offerings will become more and more complex, and their promises more extravagant.

Still searching

While it is true that some recent authors have offered useful insights about how to find the most favourable market position, it's important that we put these into historical context and don't get over-excited about them. The underlying concepts that have been so successfully retrieved and "leveraged" are well known.

You don't have to scratch far below the surface of many "new" ideas to see that in essence they're not new at all. What gives them fresh appeal is 1) snappy branding that makes them memorable and easy to talk about; 2) a sprinkling of up-to-date examples of who's using them and how they might be used elsewhere; and 3) handy checklists to help managers apply them.

But Drucker's questions are still the ones to start with. The Ansoff matrix and its stepchildren will be useful 50 years from now – and even after that. Ignore what these gurus have given us, and you'll be unlikely ever to achieve your competitive potential. Apply it, and you'll almost certainly raise your game. You'll not only gain crucial insights into your current situation and future possibilities, but also steal a march on your competitors. For you can bet that many of them aren't thinking through things as carefully as they should.

According to one study, only 15 per cent of managers use the Ansoff matrix, and it's one of the tools – along with Porter's generic strategy model – that they most often drop.[84] So what do they look for in a tool if they don't fancy this one? How do the majority of executives make their most fundamental business decisions if they're not thinking through the issues highlighted by this simple matrix? What drives the quest for something else, when we already have what we need?

So beware of overlooking the "basics" while you struggle to make sense of your new landscape. The starting point for strategic thinking today is no different than it was in the distant past.

When all is said and done, every company always had to do the same essential things – and must do them today:

1. Identify their "right" customer;
2. Understand that customer's needs;
3. Develop a business model to satisfy customers better than competitors;
4. Get the necessary resources, and continually strengthen them;
5. Focus all efforts on specific results;
6. Unleash the imagination and spirit of people;
7. Keep learning, innovating, and improving.

The eight critical strategy practices make it happen.

The age of intuition

It's widely assumed that once upon a time the world was a more stable and predictable place, which meant that managers could operate largely in logical, rational, and deliberate "left brain" mode. Then, seemingly overnight, they were faced with the need to decode weak signals, make sense of complex patterns, pull together fragments of information from many sources, and create breakthrough ideas. So "right brain" skills such as intuition, insight, and imagination became the new competitive weapons.* Relational, integrative thinking became essential. It's a critical management skill, says Roger Martin, formerly dean of Toronto's Rotman Business School, because it "produces possibilities, solutions, and new ideas."[85]

In reality, history has been punctuated by both stability and change. Strategists have always had to embrace them simultaneously. Analysis and planning have always coexisted with gut feel and instinct. Responsiveness has always been a crucial survival mechanism.

However, it is true that today's executives do have more to cope with than those of yesteryear. Making sense of things is harder than ever. Nor has the method been invented that will predict with certainty what's ahead, interpret exactly what it means, or advise what to do about it. New technologies and new algorithms will certainly help in future. But even as they evolve, the mysterious processes of the human mind will be no less critical.

- As Henry Mintzberg tells us, "the key managerial processes are enormously complex and mysterious ... drawing on the vaguest of information and using the least articulated of mental processes. These processes seem to be more relational and holistic than ordered and sequential, and more intuitive than intellectual." When he studied how managers made 25 important strategic decisions, one of his biggest surprises was how few of them reported using explicit analysis. Mostly, he says, they relied on judgment.[86]
- "When applied to business – where judgments are made with messy, incomplete data – statistical and methodological wizardry can blind rather than illuminate," say Warren Bennis and James O'Toole.[87]
- According to Russell Ackoff, professor of management science at the Wharton School, "the best planning ... requires at least as much art as it does science."[88]
- "To this day," says former world chess champion Gary Kasparov, "I do not look for a mathematical solution when I play chess. I'm always trying to find something unconventional, even poetic – something more than just analytics."[89]
- In his absorbing biography of Steve Jobs, Walter Isaacson writes: "Indeed, he was a genius. His imaginative leaps were instinctive, unexpected, and at times magical. He was, indeed, an example of ... someone whose insights come out of the blue and require intuition more than mere mental processing power. Like a pathfinder, he could absorb information, sniff the winds, and sense what lay ahead."[90]

---

* The notion of split-brain thinking was developed by Roger Sperry in 1977. It has since been shown to be wrong.

Warriors from Sun Tzu to Clausewitz, Von Molthke, Jomini, and the US Navy's Seal Team Six have grasped the importance of thinking on your feet and going with the flow of a battle. Learning "in the moment" has always been key to being able to fight.

The best executives have always been "whole brain thinkers," adept in juggling logic and magic. But the need for this has become more pressing. There's now more awareness of how decisions actually get made, and a growing understanding of the iterative nature of crafting and conducting strategic conversation.

In what is probably the first real management textbook, *The Practice of Management*, published in 1954, Peter Drucker predicted that "the days of the 'intuitive' managers are numbered," and went on to promise that "the manager can improve his performance in all areas of management, including the managing of a business, through the systematic study of principles, the acquisition of organized knowledge and the systematic analysis of his own performance in all areas of his work and job and on all levels of management."[91]

But this prognosis about the future of the intuitive manager was wrong. In fact, the age of the intuitive manager is just beginning.

From battlefield to boardroom

In the scheme of things, business strategy is a new craft. Our understanding of it comes from many disciplines. There's screeds of information and advice about it, and millions of people have had some experience of it. Yet even as warfare changes and military strategists abandon yesterday's methods and invent new ways to fight, managers persist in working in much the way they always have.

The past few years have seen a swing from big battles involving tens of thousands of troops supported by tanks and aircraft, to attacks by small teams of highly trained soldiers who rely on information, speed, stealth, and high technology to take out enemies.[92] At a state level, there's also growing emphasis on "soft power" – the use of information, persuasion, and diplomacy – in addition to, and sometimes as a substitute for, "hard" power battles.[93]

Modern fighting forces place great emphasis on intuition and judgment in executing their plans. Their troops have to make split-second decisions in the heat of battle. They have to size up their situations and plot and coordinate their actions when all hell is breaking loose. Every person counts. Initiative and teamwork are life-or-death matters.[94]

These forces are meticulous in their planning and preparation. They train and retrain their people, subjecting them to tougher and tougher challenges so they develop not just the skills they need, but also what Alvin and Heidi Toffler in their book *War and Anti-War* have called "the intangibles of combat" – personal qualities of motivation, confidence, emotional commitment, morale, and resourcefulness.[95] Troops are fanatical about selecting, testing, and maintaining their gear, and it's constantly upgraded. They gather copious amounts of intelligence about their targets ahead of any battle. They rehearse attacks down to the last detail.

Then, immediately after each enemy encounter, they engage in "after-action reviews" (AARs) to dissect what happened and to learn what worked and what didn't. In structured reflection sessions, they deal with four questions:

1. What results did we aim for?
2. What results did we get?
3. What caused those results?
4. What must we keep doing or improve?

The result is that conflict by conflict, clash by clash, they sharpen their fighting capabilities. They learn not just "what to do," write Marilyn Darling, Charles Parry, and Joseph Moore in "Learning in the Thick of It," an *HBR* article, "but also, more important, about how to think ... in a fast changing environment, the capacity to learn lessons is more valuable than any individual lesson learned."[96]

Given business strategy's military heritage, you'd think managers would pay more attention to all this and lift some of these practices. But firms are mostly still stuck in planning mode, and neglect other factors that affect their fighting ability. Many of them don't know nearly enough about their true situation or their context. They're not serious about developing and equipping their people. They don't practise or reflect on their moves.

And as to intuition and judgment – well, those are for the leaders, not the rest. All of which is potentially fatal.

8

PEOPLE FIRST

At the very time that Porter's teachings were becoming gospel, managers were waking up to the fact that their world was changing faster than they were – and certainly faster than their organizations were able to. Every day brought surprises. The competitive landscape was transformed as the forces of privatization, deregulation, and globalization – along with a flood of new capital and a surge in entrepreneurship – swept aside old structures, conventions, and constraints. The relentless advance of computer technology and software innovation changed conceptions of work, entertainment, and play. Demographic and social shifts redefined markets and led to new customer behaviours. The rapid spread of democracy caused old flags to come down and dictatorships to collapse, and nations to rethink their policies and realign their interests. Then, when the Berlin Wall fell in 1989 and China came back into the mainstream of world affairs two years later, everything accelerated. The world was on steroids.

As its "clock speed" suddenly gained pace,[1] and as competition became white hot in every market sector, companies engaged in a race to the future. The sales of laggards vaporized as their customers were snatched away, and they found themselves stuck in desperate catch-up mode. No one could afford to sit on the sidelines while others tore ahead.

Speed became a key competitive weapon.[2] Executives who'd learned their trade in more benign circumstances had to learn to sense and respond fast to changes around them. They had to work harder at continuous improvement, while also striving to be more innovative and agile. They had to embrace advanced technologies that were making yesterday's processes obsolete and enabling firms to work in radically new ways. And they had to shift to lean processes which eliminated chunks of time and masses of waste in offices and factories.[3]

But as John Naisbitt had foreseen in his 1982 bestseller *Megatrends*, people were at the same time becoming more important than ever. "The more high technology around us," he said, "the more the need for human touch. That is why the human potential movement that advocates both discipline and responsibility is such a critical part of the high-tech/high-touch equation."[4]

And as John Seely Brown and Paul Duguid point out in *The Social Life of Information*, "by overlooking both the social aspects of work and the frailty of technology, design that attempts to replace the conventional work systems may often merely displace the burdens of work ... design needs to attend not simply to the frailty of technological systems and the robustness of social systems, but to the ways in which social systems often play a key part in making even frail technology robust."[5]

Much ado about precious little

Compare what doctors knew about infection control during the Anglo-Boer War with what they know today, or an engineer's approach to bridge-building then and now, and the difference is huge. But compare what was known about management then with what we know today, and you can barely spot the difference.

Remarkably, in the one area of human affairs that affects almost all others, we're stuck in deep sand. In both theory and practice the wheels keep spinning.

Henri Fayol told us in 1916 that management had five aspects: forecasting and planning, organizing, commanding, coordinating, and controlling. His ideas held sway from when he published an article that year titled "Administration Industrielle et Générale – Prévoyance, Organisation, Commandement, Coordination, Contrôle" in the *Bulletin de la Société de l'Industrie Minérale*, until it appeared in English in 1949 as the book *General and Industrial Management*.[6]

Fast forward a couple of decades. The fundamental work of managers was still much the same. According to Drucker, it comprised five basic tasks: 1) setting objectives, 2) organizing, 3) motivating and communicating, 4) measuring, and 5) developing people.[7]

Fast forward again, to Henry Mintzberg in 2009, explaining the roles of managers as: 1) communicating, 2) controlling, 3) leading, 4) linking, 5) doing, and 6) dealing.[8]

And then, in 2010, Michael Porter and Nitin Nohria suggested that a CEO's many activities fit these categories: 1) direction, 2) organization, 3) selection, 4) motivation, and 5) systems and processes for implementation.[9]

The context in which executives operate evolves constantly, of course, but the core tasks don't. Maybe you'd want to tone down or take out the "command" part, and drop in "coaching" or "mentoring" – such contemporary ideas! – but the other activities are as valid today as they were 90 years ago. All of them have to do with the same critical job: *getting results through people.*

Now look at the *practice* of management – in other words, *how* those things get done. Here, too, it's more of the same.

It's sobering to note, for example, that General Motors introduced a bonus plan for managers as far back as 1918. According to Alfred Sloan, this "had an important effect in creating an identity of interest between management and shareholders." But he understood – as many of today's managers seem not to – that there was more to motivation than money. After a colleague wrote to him, saying, "The potential rewards of the Bonus Plan to ego satisfaction generate a tremendous driving force within the Corporation," Sloan commented that this was reinforced by "*a fairly general practice of having each recipient's supervisor deliver the bonus notification letter.*" (My italics.)

Sloan was concerned about his other employees too. In the 1920s the car giant provided not only first-rate medical services, fine cafeterias, locker rooms, showers, and parking for employees, but also group life insurance, a savings and investment plan, recreational facilities, payments for suggestions, training, and opportunities for handicapped workers.[10] All thoroughly modern practices.

It's equally sobering to recall that 50 years ago Hewlett-Packard introduced management by objectives (MBO), "management by walking around" (MBWA), company picnics, employee share ownership, small divisions, and many other managerial innovations now regarded as state of the art in "progressive" workplaces.[11]

Or consider the astonishing lack of headway in growing leaders for tomorrow. Executives complain about a dearth of skills, and know their future hinges on building their "leadership pipeline."[12] So this is no trivial matter. But few of them do much about it. And those that make an effort go about it in much the same ways as it's always been done.

"Internal development was the norm back in the 1950s," writes Wharton School professor Peter Capelli in a recent *Harvard Business Review* article, "and every management practice that seems novel today was commonplace in those years – from executive coaching to 360-degree feedback to job rotation to high-potential programs."[13]

Similar examples are to be found in every other area of people management. There's plenty of bragging about thought leadership in this area, but scant evidence of it. There are constant exhortations to do things differently, but little hint of what that might mean and hardly any new action to speak of.

So don't get too excited about apparent breakthroughs. They're few and far between. When they do come along, they usually don't get widely adopted – or only after a long delay. And besides, the value of most of them may not be clear-cut.

The slow pace of organizational change

"Every generation believes itself to be at the forefront of a new managerial frontier," say Robert Eccles and Nitin Nohria, "and posits the coming of a new organization that will revolutionize the way people live and work."[14]

So yes, we have flattened organizations, hired more temporary workers, encouraged people to work away from the office, and outsourced many functions – and not just because technology makes it possible and sensible. It's better for a firm to excel at a few things than be mediocre at everything, and keeping costs down is imperative. Also, employment costs are rocketing, commuting is time-consuming and usually creates pollution, and career women struggle to balance their home and office responsibilities.

Yes, there is a general trend towards involving people more in decision-making and giving them responsibility for their own work – because new social mores demand it, new organizational realities make it hard to control them, we need to tap into their insights and knowledge and unleash their imagination and spirit, and we need to accommodate the ambitions of "Millennials."

Yes, there is now plenty of diversity at all levels – because of the spread of democratic values, a shortage of skilled white males, an explosion in the number of educated women, agitation by a powerful feminist movement, new demographics in which minorities play an ever-greater role, and an ageing workforce.

And yes, new technologies do make it possible to work in ways that were inconceivable only a short time ago.

In a 2006 special report on "The New Organisation," *The Economist* contrasted the working conditions of yesterday's "organisation man" and today's "networked person." But, "despite the dramatic changes in the way people work," it said, "the organizations in which they carry out that work have changed much less than might be expected ... In other words, 21st-century organisations are not fit for 21st-century workers."[15]

Eight years later, the manifesto of the Management Innovation eXchange (MIX), an open innovation project launched by Gary Hamel, provided this promising update:

> The Internet has spawned a Cambrian explosion of new organizational life forms – including Wikipedia, Intrade, Digg, Facebook, Innocentive, Topcoder, Twitter and more than 160,000 open innovation projects. The fast-evolving social technologies of the Web – blogs, mash-ups, online forums, crowdsourcing, folksonomies and wikis – are extending the range of human creativity and collaboration in ways that would have been unimaginable a decade ago.
>
> On the Web, we observe amazing feats of management that require little or no management oversight. We finds (sic) complex organizations that thrive with little or no organizational structure. This raises the hope that, with a little imagination, it may finally be possible to overcome the troublesome trade-offs

that have bedeviled management theorists and practitioners since the pyramids were built.[16]

It may indeed be possible. But when you get past admiring tales of groundbreaking organizational designs and processes, and look for examples of successful firms that are configured or function in radically new ways, there's in fact little to see. Sure, there are some outliers, but they tend to be clustered in the high-tech sector and enjoying the first flush of youth. Innovators are the exception rather than the rule, and there's little uptake of their practices across a swathe of companies. Whatever changes there might be in the broader ecosystem of organizations have been tentative and experimental rather than quantum leaps, and maturity almost always brings conformity. Google's management practices might be widely admired, but are hardly what you'd call mainstream.

Maybe we should remind ourselves that, way back in 1974, Peter Drucker wrote that "the typical businesses of today are multiproduct, multitechnology, and multimarket." Their central problem was "the organization of complexity and diversity." So "liberation and mobilization of human energies – rather than symmetry, harmony, or consistency – are the purpose of organization."[17]

Maybe we should remind ourselves that in 1987, John Sculley, then president and CEO of Apple Computer, observed: "Third-wave companies are the emerging form, not only for high-tech companies, but for all institutions."* Whereas second-wave firms, by his definition, were characterized by hierarchy, structure, stability, tradition, and dogma, these new ones were flexible networks in which individuals and values mattered, and information was the critical resource.[18]

Maybe we should remind ourselves that, in 1988, *Fortune* predicted that in the 1990s companies would have to speed up product development and decision-making and be able to adapt their structures quickly to new business conditions. "More than being helped by computers, companies will live by them, shaping strategy and structure to fit new information technology. They will engage in even more joint ventures, gaining access to techniques and markets they might not have developed on their own. And they will have to cope with a work force made more demanding by a scarcity of labor."[19]

We should perhaps remind ourselves too that, in 1989, Harvard professor Rosabeth Moss Kanter observed that managers were "watching hierarchy fade away and the clear distinctions of title, task, department, even corporation, blur."[20]

These sentiments are repeated *ad nauseam*. There's no shortage of crusaders to warn us that our fuddy-duddy organizations have no place in a hyper-fast,

---

* He fired Steve Jobs!

technology-powered world with a super-smart workforce. Yet while business and its environment have undergone seismic shifts, organizational architectures and management theories have not. And no amount of fading and blurring, and no amount of rah-rah, hides the fact that top-down management and ever-tighter controls are a persistent reality (think back to Kaplan and Norton's management system, mentioned in Chapter 7).

So bring back Chester Barnard, Carl Rogers, Edith Penrose, or Douglas McGregor; dress them in jeans, T-shirts, and sneakers; adorn them with tattoos and skewer rings through their ears and noses; and let them loose on your managers. Or call in veterans like Edgar Schein or Karl Weick. What they said way back is just what you hear from today's most progressive thinkers – while all around you, winning firms forge ahead under the firm hand of their autocratic bosses.

Why is this so? Probably because it's what works for most firms and their managers. Not as well as it should, maybe, but better than the alternatives.

Why else would companies shift from hierarchical to matrix structures – with all the attendant hassle and cost – then swing back again? Why would they make a big fuss about decentralizing, then claw back responsibilities, tighten controls, introduce new rules and systems, and re-centralize power? Why would they allow people to work from home for a while, but then change their minds and insist that they come to the office? Why would they order fewer, smaller, shorter, more informal meetings, but then do an about-face and demand *more* meetings with tighter agendas and detailed outputs? Why the growing appeal of performance management systems that do little to encourage performance and much to impede it, and that promise fairness and transparency yet lead to rigged evaluations, politicking, and pissed-off people?

This is remarkable, given the sheer scale of the global management laboratory and how eager executives are to find new theories, tools, and techniques. But what's even more remarkable is how blind we are to the fact that some of the ideas we're so keen to replace actually are quite useful, and will be for a long time to come.

New work, new workers

A century ago, managers were largely ambivalent about the value of their people, viewing them as a necessary expense rather than an invaluable resource. "Best practice" didn't include gushy notions about working conditions. Training and development programmes and succession plans were of little concern in most companies. Values statements had yet to replace policy manuals.

Today, most management thinkers deride "Taylorism" or "Fordism" and call for a more humanistic approach to management. Firms talk empowerment and engagement and employee value propositions. But as with strategy, they have little grasp of historical facts and they're not breaking new ground.

Frederick Taylor made a name for himself before World War I by studying steelworkers and promoting what he learned about work processes as "scientific management." Every job, he said, should be unpacked into its various parts, and people should be given strict instruction on how to do each part so they could work with maximum efficiency. His ideas, says historian Anson Rabinbach, had more impact than any others in the history of industrial organization.[21]

Around the same time, Henry Ford lamented: "Why is it that when I ask for a pair of hands, a brain comes attached?"[22] – a damned nuisance, at odds with the demands of mass production! And executives, not paying attention to what *else* Taylor and Ford said about work and workers, by and large fell into the habit of under-rating and over-managing people.

But things were not quite as they seemed or as they've been recounted over the years. Folklore and facts got badly entangled. A simplistic and badly skewed view of management took hold.

Peter Drucker, who obviously read Taylor more carefully than most, offered a fuller and more balanced view of what scientific management involved. Taylor's motivation was neither efficiency nor profit, he said, but rather "the creation of a society in which owners and workers, capitalists and proletarians had a common interest in productivity and could build a relationship of harmony on the application of knowledge to work."[23] Drucker also points out that Taylor was way ahead of the game in calling for the demise of "the boss" and advocating what much later was celebrated as "servant leadership."[24]

As for Ford, he obviously knew more about managing people than he gets credit for:

> Undoubtedly the employing class possesses facts which the employed ought to have in order to construct sound opinions and pass fair judgments …
>
> The health of every organization depends on every member – whatever his place – feeling that everything that happens to come to his notice relating to the welfare of the business is his own job …
>
> It is particularly easy for any man who never knows it all to go forward to a higher position with us.… The spirit of crowding forces the man who has the qualities for a higher place eventually to get it …
>
> If the factory system which brought mediocrity up to a higher standard operated also to keep ability down to a lower standard – it would be a very bad system, a very bad system indeed.
>
> A system, even a perfect one, must have able individuals to operate it.

No system operates itself. And the modern operation needs more brains for its operation than did the old. More brains are needed today than ever before, Although perhaps they are not needed in the same place as they once were.[25]

"The Ford Motor Company," says historian Allan Nevins, "which in 1911 had no labor policy at all, possessed three years later the most advanced policy in the world." An employment department set up by John Lee developed an integrated approach with four components: 1) principles of scientific management, 2) industrial welfare, 3) centralized employment, and 4) a formal process for employee voice and dispute resolution.[26]

By no stretch of the imagination or the facts were "Fordism" or "Taylorism" all sweetness and light in either philosophy or practice. No amount of gloss can hide their dark side. But it's unfortunate that critics have had the upper hand in shaping their legacy.

A narrow and biased grasp of what both men were about did lead to major workplace changes with hugely positive results. But it also ensured that firms in the following decades would fail to unlock their own potential – *thanks to their own managers*. An emphasis on systems, process, discipline, and measurement – on squeezing maximum performance out of every worker, regardless of their wellbeing – came to dominate management thinking. People were and still are given short shrift in too many organizations.

Based on what Taylor and Ford were *thought* to have said, and on social norms that prevailed until around the 1960s, managers have clung to their command-and-control ways. And even though the social milieu has radically changed, technology has transformed work, and the human resources movement has sweated hard to overturn authoritarian behaviour in organizations, the battle is far from being won.

The workers at Bethlehem Steel, where Taylor developed his ideas, and in Ford's plants, were mostly uneducated and had little experience of working in large companies. Mass production was a new idea, and factory systems, technologies, tools, and techniques were still being developed. Close supervision was essential.

Much of today's workforce, on the other hand, is highly educated, ambitious, and restless – and averse to being bossed around. The new challenges companies face make it imperative for them to utilize their people in new ways, and give them more responsibility and freedom.

Many managers, it's true, have become less strict and more democratic. Many more talk the talk. But fine words are a poor match for hierarchical structures, policy manuals, job descriptions, decision rights, budgets, governance and reporting requirements, health and safety regulations, performance measurement and reviews, reward systems, and similar realities. And there's no escaping the fact that much managerial conduct rests even today on the view that people are dolts, can't be relied on, need bosses to think for them, and should be firmly directed and kept on a short leash.

Competing management styles

The notion of leaders and followers, thinkers and doers, has been around forever. Wherever there are organizations – in politics, society, warfare, sport, or business – some people are charged with giving instructions, and others with taking them. After all, work must be organized. Resources must be focused. Actions must be coordinated. "Social living," says Harvard professor Ronald Heifetz, in his 1998 book *Leadership Without Easy Answers*, "depends on authority.... Our systems of authority serve vital social functions. Without comprehending these functions, one can no more exercise leadership than Boeing Aircraft can design airplanes and ignore gravity."[27]

Following the military example, a command-and-control style of management was readily adopted during the Industrial Revolution. Taylor legitimized it. Two world wars disgorged millions of servicemen and women into the civilian work-force who had been brainwashed into following orders without question. And in a strange irony, the approach became even more entrenched in the "Swinging Sixties" – an age of liberation when the pill, drugs, and the Beatles symbolized an "anything goes," freewheeling lifestyle.

Strangely too, the era that saw most new thinking about *strategy* – 1960 to 1980 – also saw the emergence of new ideas about *people* and how to manage them. The process had actually begun in the 1940s, at the Tavistock Institute of Human Research in the UK. But it only gained momentum in the 1960s, largely through the efforts of the Esalen Institute in Big Sur, California, and the Human Potential Movement which was founded by Maslow, Carl Rogers, and Rollo May. Then came organizational development, stream analysis, T-groups, sensitivity training, participative management, quality circles, organizational learning, diversity management, servant leadership – and much else. All of which encouraged senior executives to "let go" and enlist not just the hands, but also the heads and the hearts of their people.

That was a time of great change, and the dawn of the information age. True to form, Drucker marked it by coining the term "knowledge worker." (Since he was an economist by training, it's possible he derived the notion from Beatrice Webb, the British economist and social activist who talked in 1898 about "brain workers."[28] Or he may have got it from Taylor.[29] He does credit the Austrian-born economist Fritz Machlup for the term "knowledge industries," which Machlup used in his 1962 book, *The Production and Distribution of Knowledge in the United States*.[30])

In his 1968 book, *The Age of Discontinuity*, Drucker observed: "In the last twenty years the base of our economy shifted from manual to knowledge work, and the centre of gravity of our social expenditure from goods to knowledge."[31] As a result, many jobs were changing. They required a new breed of people who could think for themselves. Managing these scarce and valuable individuals required a new approach, and new skills.

This left us with two management paradigms, clearly at odds with each other: on the one hand, command-and-control – faith in *systems*; on the other, a touchy-feely approach – faith in *humanity*.

Executives tend to naturally favour one or the other. But they oscillate between them, depending on circumstances, and practise bits of both. They do exactly what "contingency theory" says they should, but with little thought to the unintended consequences of their behaviour. And those consequences are entirely predictable.

Amid the waffle about trust, openness, and shared responsibility, many managers operate on the basis that "being in charge" means they can and should tell others exactly what to do, and how to do it. So in one moment, they bark orders, demand compliance, and measure things to death, while in the very next they proclaim: "We're one team." "We're all equals around here." "You know what needs to be done ... and I respect your ability to do it." And best of all, "I know you'll make the right decision."

When managers act schizophrenically they drive their people crazy. When they fail to reflect on how they come across to others, they complicate their own lives and everyone else's. Instead of providing certainty and clarity, they foster confusion and complexity. Instead of eliminating unnecessary work, they add to it. And instead of creating a climate in which high performance is likely, they stir conflict and foster negative attitudes and dysfunctional behaviours.

Achieving the right balance between systems and people has always been a challenge, and will be no easier in the future. How to do it should be right at the top of the research agenda (though it's hard to imagine that after all this time any dramatically new insights will come). Working at it must be right at the top of the executive agenda.

Semantic fantasies

As the message sank in that "people matter," it was only a matter of time before someone would come up with a new way of showing their 110 per cent commitment to it. So it's trendy now, in this age of political correctness and inane bullshit, for staff or employees to be called "human capital," "talent," "colleagues," or "associates," or by some moniker based on local language and culture. For firms to dish out titles like "VP of People and Culture," "Transformation Leader," or "Creative Genius," and make lofty statements about "talent enhancement." And for bosses to profess their belief in "empowerment," "authenticity," "managing by values," "the wisdom of crowds,"[32] and "managing the whole person." (And following advice from Tom Peters, for individuals to think of themselves as brands, and package their own specialness as "Brand-me.")[33]

Much of the verbiage that wafts around organizations is laughable, and does no one favours. Instead of hiring people, they now "onboard" or "land" them.[*] Cutting costs by slashing jobs is "downsizing," "rightsizing," or "resizing." Firing is now "de-hiring," "redeployment," "delayering" – or even more ludicrous – "enhancing career opportunities." Old-fashioned hygiene factors such as pay, medical and pension benefits, seating, parking, and vacation time have been loosely bundled with almost anything else that affects employees' comfort, health, safety, and security, and rebranded as "wellness."

But why do firms assign titles and use terms so obviously out of touch with reality? And why, you have to ask, do managers keep grasping at verbal straws when plain talk would serve them far better?

"Human capital" has a serious ring about it, suggesting as it does that people warrant as much care and concern as other types of capital. But of course, there's a useful ambiguity to it. When times are good, people are wooed and coddled. But when there's a slump (and bosses' jobs and bonuses are at risk), they're treated as coldly as balance sheet items and shunted out the door in appalling numbers. In a crunch, "our most important asset" turns out to be as disposable as a paper clip.

But wait. There's no end to this inventiveness.

"We should not confuse human beings with human capital at all," argued Tom Stewart,[†] in a 1998 *Fortune* article. "It's more helpful – and more useful – to think of employees in a new way: not as assets but as investors. Shareholders invest money in our companies; employees invest time, energy, and intelligence. Shareholders pay an opportunity cost.… Employees, likewise, when they hitch their wagon to one star, forgo the chance to ride with another."[34] (Stewart made a good point, but his suggestion never caught on. Maybe "human capital" has a more appealing ring to it than "human investors!")

Or take the daffy notion of "talent management" – now even sexier than human capital. If talent in most fields is a rare thing,[‡] how is it apparently something that *everyone* in business brings to the party?

---

[*] They also "land" projects or programmes, rather than execute, implement, complete, or otherwise just do them.

[†] A senior editor at *Fortune* at that time, he later became the editor of *Harvard Business Review*.

[‡] The *Concise Oxford Dictionary* describes "talent" as a special aptitude or faculty – not widespread in most workplaces!

Can it be true that there are no dull, mediocre, ungifted plodders around? Why are HR executives expected to "unleash talent" when they don't manage the people who are supposedly blessed with it? And what makes them think they can do it?

Another term now in vogue, thanks largely to the efforts of consulting firms such as Gallup, and to "best company to work for" contests, is "engagement." Having displaced "communication" in common discourse, and "organizational climate" in business terms, "engagement" pervades almost every book and article on management. We don't talk to people any more – we "engage" them. We used to measure employee satisfaction, but now we track their "engagement."

Oddly, since Kurt Lewin pioneered organizational climate studies in the 1930s,[35] there's been surprisingly little mention of climate in the management literature. An index search of the thousand-plus management books in my own library comes close to drawing a blank. Climate appears in the title of just one[36] and the index of a few others, and gets passing comment here and there.[37] It's the same with journals. Meanwhile *measuring* climate remains a widespread practice, and human resource executives still refer to climate studies when talking about the health of their firms.

But how has dumping climate in favour of engagement benefited management practice? The answer: it hasn't, except for focusing renewed attention on how people feel at work – though maybe that alone is something to cheer! Meanwhile, playing fast and loose with language has caused needless confusion.

According to my *Oxford English Dictionary*, climate is a noun describing weather conditions. Engage is a verb meaning to occupy, attract, or involve. So logically, a firm's climate – or "weather" – determines how people feel at work, and thus how engaged they'll be in it. Climate surveys and engagement studies are both used to assess this.

Climate is the product of 1) *hygiene factors*, such as working arrangements, policies, role clarity, decision rights, and rewards; and 2) *behavioural factors*, such as involvement, challenges, communication, respect, trust, recognition, support, and opportunities for growth. All of which management can influence.

Engagement, in turn, is a consequence of a firm's climate, a response to the environment. It's a reflection of people's interest, involvement, and commitment to their work; their willingness to go the extra mile; and perhaps – at a stretch – their loyalty to their employer.*

This distinction may seem like semantic hair-splitting. But it matters. *You can*

---

* As diagnostic tools, climate, engagement, and employee attitude or satisfaction surveys all measure the same things; so I'll use the terms chosen by my sources to comment on the effects of climate factors on workplace attitudes.

only change employee engagement levels by changing the climate. (The same applies, as we shall see, to changing culture.) So uncool though climate may be, it will continue to be a vital lever for change. In fact, as I'll show in Chapter 12, growth leadership (Critical Strategy Practice #1) is impossible without specific attention to climate.

The high cost of low morale

Many years ago, I was interviewed in New York for a senior job in a multinational company. One of the executives who vetted me was the firm's president emeritus, a wise old man with decades of experience. When we chatted about what I'd need to do to make an impact in the business, he said, "You'll have to make a lot of changes, and the big challenge will be to take your people with you. Strategy alone won't get you the results you want."

Ninety-nine out of 100 leaders would doubtless endorse what he said without a second thought. They'd all agree that getting results through others is what their jobs are about. But doing it remains the most vexing challenge for most of them and their organizations.

For all their assurances of their deep belief in people, those they're supposedly so concerned about don't buy it. Employee surveys continue to reflect high levels of dissatisfaction. And the problem rests firmly with managers themselves.

Many of them continue to think they can wring results from disgruntled employees while not working hard enough to create an environment in which people will shine. They use new language and say all the right things, but keep acting in the same old ways – ways that often turn people off, not on. This is apparent from exit interviews which commonly point to *management behaviour* as a key reason people resign. The cost to companies, if you could quantify it, is surely horrifying.

A Gallup study showed that from 2000 to 2008, employees saw little improvement in the way they were managed.[38] A 2004 study by Towers Perrin, a global recruitment firm,* showed that only 12 per cent of the UK workforce was "highly engaged."[39] A Gallup survey in the US in 2006 put the number at 27 per cent, with an alarming 14 percent of the others "actively disengaged" and 59 per cent "not engaged."[40] Another Towers Perrin survey, in 2007, of close to 90,000 respondents in 18 countries, showed that 21 per cent were "fully engaged," 41 per cent were "partly engaged," 30 per cent were "partly disengaged," and 8 per cent were "fully disengaged."[41]

McKinsey reported in 2009 that "employee motivation is sagging throughout the world – morale has fallen at almost half of all companies ... at a time when

---

* Now named Towers Watson.

businesses need engaged leaders and other employees willing to go above and beyond expectations."[42] By the end of 2012, another Gallup study concluded that only 30 per cent of American workers were "engaged, or involved in, or enthusiastic about, and committed to their workplace." Of the 70 per cent "not showing up to work committed or delivering their best performance," 52 per cent were "not engaged" and 18 per cent were "actively disengaged."[43] A study of German workers produced a similarly bleak picture.[44]

Such low levels of engagement imply that most of your people are at work physically but not mentally. That around *two-thirds of the people in almost any team are not working at anywhere near their potential*. So while you might have plenty of "warm bodies," you're missing their imagination and spirit. They're sort of paying attention, sort of applying their minds to their jobs, sort of making an effort.

Imagine the cost of their half-hearted "contribution"!

Those slouches need space, furniture, equipment, IT backup, pay, medical and pension support, sick leave, and so on. They use their time to play political games (or computer games), trawl the internet, hook up with friends on social media, obstruct key change efforts, and otherwise foul up the works. And worst of all – because this is the biggest cost and a major constraint on any company's performance – they soak up management time and attention. So instead of going after opportunities, senior executives are distracted by trying to get results from people who have no interest in producing them.[45]

You can be sure, however, that most of the firms where all this happens have enthusiastic HR functions and state-of-the-art policies, and that managers make all the right noises about people. Enlightenment, clearly, is doing little to prevent managers from failing in their most important task.

Happiness pills

Human motivation has been studied for centuries. Ford, Taylor, and Sloan all saw the need to create workplace conditions that would improve performance. Researchers have produced a flood of opinion about the effect of context on employee perceptions, emotions, motivation, and behaviour. By now, there should be no doubt that feelings affect performance – or that positive feelings bring positive results. Nor should there be any need for yet another new way to promote feelings that will bring out the best in people.

To perk employees up and get them on side, firms typically turn to "satisfaction" programmes. Get people to feel more satisfied with their work, the thinking goes, and they'll work harder and smarter. So organizations everywhere are racing to provide the best offices, canteens, child-care, recreational facilities, and much else. "Be happy!" they tell their staff. "Have fun!"

So happiness has become the next new thing in management, perfectly timed amid the gloomy mood that settled across much of the world after the 2008 financial crash, and thanks also to interest by economists and others in finding better measures than GDP of national wellbeing. We all love to be happy and everyone has views on what it takes, so there are plenty of evangelists spreading the gospel.[46] Here's the ultimate management "tool," they assure us. And there's more than enough evidence that a happy workplace is likely to be a productive workplace.[47]

"Taking steps to help employees start the day off on the right foot is something more organizations might want to consider," suggests Wharton professor Nancy Rothbard, following a large study on the impact of happiness. "To enhance performance, it is critical to both acknowledge and reset the negative mood that employees bring with them to work."[48]

And so it is. But there's more to doing that than balloons, jokes, and pandering to people's every whim.

- According to Rensis Likert, a 1955 study by the Institute for Social Research at the University of Michigan showed clearly that managers with "a favourable *attitude toward men*" achieve significantly better performance than those managers who don't score as well.[49]

    Likert's own observations revealed the effect of four different "management systems" – approaches ranging from autocratic to democratic – on productivity. Some "low-producing" managers, he said, saw the need to move towards "System 4" (democratic), but only *after high levels of productivity had been achieved*. But they had things back to front: the productivity they sought was unlikely until *after they had changed to System 4*.[50] (My italics.)

- Abraham Maslow, perhaps best known for his notion of "self-actualization," was another who gave a lot of thought to workplace psychology. His notes on management got to a very limited audience of scholars when they were published in 1962 under the title *Eupsychian Management*, and it wasn't until they were republished in 1998 as *Maslow on Management* that his influence widened. He doesn't mention climate in these works, but he does emphasize the importance of how people feel at work, and how "enlightened management" ... "can improve them and improve the world and in this sense be a utopian or revolutionary technique."[51]

- It was the same, too, in *The Farther Reaches of Human Nature*, published in 1971, where he writes: "man has a higher nature which includes the need for meaningful work, for responsibility, for creativeness, for being fair and just, for doing what is worthwhile and for preferring to do it well."[52]

- In a 2001 *HBR* article titled "Primal Leadership," Daniel Goleman, Richard

Boyatzis, and Annie McKee tell us: "The leader's mood and behaviors drive the moods and behaviors of everyone else ... the leader's mood is literally quite contagious, spreading quickly and inexorably throughout the business ... a leader's premier task – we would even say his primal task – is emotional leadership."[53]

- More recently, there's research by Teresa Amabile, head of the Entrepreneurial Management Unit at Harvard Business School, which shows a strong link between feelings and creativity. Joy and love are positively associated, while anger, fear, and anxiety are negative. When there's conflict in a group, creativity goes down, as it does when people compete instead of collaborate. When people are happy one day, creativity goes up the next. When they do work they love, and engage deeply in it, creativity takes off.[54]

- Another Harvard professor, Rosabeth Moss Kanter, says in her book *Confidence*, "A positive emotional climate of high expectations reinforces self-confidence. Winners' behaviours and attitudes – including abundant communication, thorough preparation using detailed metrics, mutual respect and deep knowledge of one another's strengths, the desire to work together and help one another succeed, and an empowering environment of shared leadership – reinforce confidence in one another."[55]

So there you have it. Create a nourishing climate and you gain in multiple ways: productivity rises; people become fulfilled, more creative, and confident; and financial returns improve.

As an article in *Strategy+Business* tells us, "Annual investment in the publicly held 'Best Companies' would have yielded, from 1994 to 2006, a return of more than 600 percent. By comparison, an investment in the Standard and Poor's 500 would have yielded 250 percent, and the 18 companies lauded in *Built To Last*, the 1994 bestseller written by Jerry Porras and Jim Collins, would have yielded only 150 percent."[56]

There's so much evidence of the benefits from improving a firm's climate that only a fool would ignore it. Of all the ways in which you might improve your results, this is one of the most practical and powerful. If you don't use it, most of your other efforts will be less effective than they otherwise might.

The magic of work

A little known but critical fact is that *the cause-effect link between job satisfaction and performance works two ways.*[57] Satisfaction leads to improved performance, and performance drives satisfaction. Positive feelings influence results, and results induce positive feelings. "HR managers probably say we want to keep our employees happy because that leads to high performance," says Phil Rosenzweig, author of *The Halo Effect.* "And it probably does, but the opposite causality is probably even stronger. High-performing companies tend to have satisfied employees."[58]

This single insight demolishes what has become conventional wisdom in many change-management efforts. It tells managers that replacing deeply ingrained beliefs and habits with new ones is most likely through a two-pronged process involving both *persuasion* and *practice.* People need to be persuaded that change is a good idea.[59] And they need to practise new behaviours to learn that change is possible and the results it brings are desirable.[60]

When a firm does well, its reputation is enhanced and it can reward people better,[61] so they feel proud, secure, cared for, and valued. At the same time – and perhaps even more important – being part of a winning team gives them a sense of *achievement.*

Frederick Herzberg told us in 1959 in *The Motivation to Work,* a book co-authored with Bernard Mausner and Barbara Snyderman, that "Five factors stand out as strong determiners of job satisfaction – *achievement, recognition, work itself, responsibility,* and *advancement* – the last three being of greater importance for lasting change of attitudes."[62]

Years of research by Mikael Csikszentmihalyi, professor of psychology and education at the University of Chicago, add weight to this view. It is "flow," rather than happiness, that makes for "excellence in life," he says. This state is one we feel in our best moments, when we are totally focused on a clear challenge and completely absorbed by it, and get immediate feedback on our performance. "There is no space in consciousness for distracting thoughts, irrelevant feelings…. The sense of time is distorted: hours seem to pass by in minutes. When a person's entire being is stretched in the full functioning of body and mind, whatever one does becomes worth doing for its own sake; living becomes its own justification."[63]

According to this explanation, Csikszentmihalyi's "flow" is just another term for "engagement." The process he describes fits perfectly with the findings of Likert and others.

It's apparent that there's not just a straight-line progression *from management practices to climate to performance,* but rather a cyclical process linking them continuously together. So almost any work is not just about producing results, but also – and perhaps even more important – about preparing people to produce even better results in future.

Attention, please!

Another apparently little-known but equally critical fact is that while money is an important motivator, and gets huge attention, *meaning* – or purpose, as it's commonly termed – is far more powerful, yet gets virtually none.

People need to pay their bills, but they're inspired by the belief that they matter, they can make a difference, others respect them, and they can learn and grow. This is what gives them a reason for being.

Involvement in important conversations and important work gives them purpose. It focuses their efforts and ignites their spirit. So if you craft and conduct those conversations well, anything becomes possible; but get them wrong, and bad things will surely follow.

- The famous Hawthorne experiment, which was conducted from 1924 to 1932, broke new ground in ostensibly showing that people respond positively to attention from management.[64] That study has its critics, but there's now more than enough evidence from others that the general conclusions were right.
- The great quality expert, W. Edwards Deming, hammered away at the same ideas during the 1940s and '50s.[65]
- McGregor highlights these ideas in his landmark book *The Human Side of Enterprise,** coining the terms "Theory X and Theory Y" to explain how managers' assumptions about people affect the way they treat them, which in turn affects the way those people behave. What you expect, he said, is what you get.[66] (He, in turn, was building on the work of Maslow and Argyris.)[67]
- The Towers Perrin report I cited earlier tells us that the single most important driver of employee engagement is "senior management's sincere interest in employee well-being."[68]
- Countless others – from Peters and Waterman (*In Search of Excellence*), to Linda Gratton (*Glow*) – have dished up the same advice.

Attention on its own is unlikely to change people's behaviour. But attention *while giving feedback* is. A sense of progress is a key element of a sense of self.

This is the conclusion of "What Really Motivates Workers," a report on a multi-year study of 600 managers and "hundreds of knowledge workers in a wide variety of settings," in *Harvard Business Review* in January–February 2010.[69] But long before that, it was recognized by Alfred Sloan when he talked about the effect of his supervisors personally delivering bonus notification letters. It was a central theme of David McClelland's 1961 book *The Achieving Society*.[70] And of Frederick Herzberg's 1968 *HBR* classic, "One More Time, How Do You Motivate Employees?"[71] In *The Age of Discontinuity*, Drucker wrote: "What the knowledge worker needs to be positively motivated is achievement. He needs a challenge. He needs to know that he contributes."[72] And let's not forget Ken Blanchard and Spencer Johnson's *The One Minute Manager*, first published in 1982, in which

---

* In 2001 the Academy of Management voted it the fourth most influential book of the 20th century.

they advised: "Catch people doing something right and give them a one-minute praising."[73]

A business is not a social club. Managers should never forget that their job is to produce results, not to create a cushy environment in which people can just have a good time. They should do whatever is reasonably possible to make life in their firms enjoyable, but as a means to an end and not an end in itself.

Every manager, and certainly every HR person, should know all this. Yet pervasive as performance management systems are, an astonishing number of people still get little or no feedback on how they're doing. For years I've asked participants in my business school classes, "How many of you have had open, accurate, honest, useful feedback on your performance in, say, the past six months?" Across companies – most of which have state-of-the-art performance management systems – about 10 per cent of people raise their hands. Sometimes, *no* hands go up. Jack and Suzy Welch report the same dismal response from their audiences.[74]

"Best practices" are, almost without exception, not common practice. Almost every executive can tell you how to manage people. They know all the buzzwords, all the coolest ideas. But they'll also tell you that the very practices they advocate are missing in their own workplaces.

"Commitment, far from being something that has to be created in employees, is a natural, psychological need of every person," wrote Douglas Sherwin in a 1972 *HBR* article. "But we in management frustrate it at the source by assumptions and practices that we apply in the organizing process."[75]

This is inevitable, as there's little or no understanding of climate, whether as a concept or as a lever for improving performance, or of its impact on performance. Prescriptions for "fixing it," dispensed by HR, usually focus on things *they* can do – information sessions, workshops, training, complex performance management systems – rather than on what *managers* must do.

Culture, on the other hand, gets plenty of attention – though often for the wrong reason and in the wrong way.

Getting to grips with culture

In Search of Excellence broke new ground in not just highlighting the importance of corporate culture, but elevating it to cult status. "If the strategy revolution was forcing companies to look outward more than they ever had before," writes Duff McDonald in *The Firm*, his biography of McKinsey, "what *Excellence* did was force that gaze right back inside again."[76]

The study that led to the book was a McKinsey initiative to deepen its expertise in organizational behaviour. Peters and Waterman were strongly influenced by Douglas McGregor's "Theory X" and "Theory Y" views from the early 1960s. They would also doubtless have been influenced by the work of Richard Beckhard, a pioneer in the field of organizational development, who wrote in 1969: "A significant aspect of the theme of the seventies – *'the active and continuing search for excellence'* – will be an organization climate in which people can grow and develop, in which creative capacity can be unleashed, and in which people's personal needs for moving towards their own potential can be significantly achieved in the work setting."[77] (My italics.)

Others joined the choir and added layers of mystique.* Changing culture became big business for consultants. An infestation of "change management" projects spread across the globe, with culture their target of choice. Managers en masse came to believe that "getting the right culture" was Step One in getting new results. They were also persuaded that with the help of a savant, a few motivational speeches, some rah-rah workshops and funky T-shirts, doing that would be as easy as snapping their fingers.

But whereas changing a firm's structure or switching to a new computer system are one-off projects with a clear start and finish, shifting culture is an altogether different matter. As Michael Beer, Russell Eisenstadt, and Bert Spector tell us in *The Critical Path to Corporate Renewal*, "Change efforts that begin by creating corporate programs to alter the culture or the management of people in the firm are inherently flawed, even when supported by top management."[78]

There are plenty of complex, time-consuming, and costly approaches to changing culture and a seemingly limitless market for them. But in time, I suspect, the notion of culture change will be seen for what it is: one of the most hyped, least understood, and most disappointing fads ever.

It has bogged firms down in pointless work, and its impact has been decidedly patchy. Organizational change of almost any kind is notoriously difficult, and most attempts at it fail to deliver the expected results. Culture is an especially thorny matter. Yet firms try again and again, with or without new leadership, to "fix" it.

Executives who champion culture-change efforts are likely to give them the thumbs-up – for obvious reasons. People on the receiving end are often derisive.

Cause and consequence

There's no disputing that culture *is* a powerful influencer of behaviour – not a soft side issue that can be safely ignored. It affects everything firms do and the way

---

* It was predictable, amid a bunfight in a marketplace eager to learn what culture could do, that the term itself would get a makeover. And along came … "organizational DNA!" That sounds cool, but what the hell does it mean? strategy&, which sells it as a management tool, says it's "a metaphor for the underlying factors that together define an organization's 'personality' and help explain its performance." (In other words, a metaphor for culture.)

they do everything. There's truth in that old saw that culture trumps strategy, so it must be aligned with strategy and support it, or it'll suck the life out of even the best of intentions.

Adapting culture to an ever-changing context is essential in meeting strategic goals. This is one of the most important aspects of managerial work. To do it well, managers need to understand what culture is, why it exists, and what causes it to change.

Talk about culture at a societal level tends to be about what's easy to notice in individuals and groups: their language and customs, how they dress and behave, and what they eat. Talk about a *firm's* culture tends to be about its leadership style, work practices, teamwork, quality and service, the appearance of its facilities, promotional materials, and other visible factors. Mention may also be made of the kinds of people that are employed and how they're promoted and rewarded, innovation practices and results, where investment is directed, and policies regarding health and safety or the environment, and so on.

But this is a superficial and unhelpful grasp of what culture is and what shapes it – and why it's so difficult to change.

According to Edgar Schein, professor emeritus at MIT, and one of the most insightful authorities on this topic, culture is deeply rooted in our assumptions, beliefs, values, artefacts, and symbols, and we conduct ourselves in certain ways because we've learned that they work and we can survive by practising them.[79]

Because culture is finally a behavioural matter, it's an outcome of factors that shape behaviour. Managers' assumptions about the people around them are communicated in many ways. For example, says Schein, "McGregor's big insight ... was that if a structure implies a certain assumption about human nature, people may begin to adapt to that structure by behaving in a manner they are 'expected' to behave ... the structure of an organization serves important functions and thereby becomes a key element of the culture."[80] Similarly, offering incentives for innovation, praising people for taking risks (or punishing those who do), or investing heavily in new technologies, all send compelling signals about how management thinks and the behaviours that are valued.

A simple analogy helps explain culture and what's needed to change it.

What happens is this: our brains record our lives, capturing sights, sounds, smells, tastes, touches, and other experiences and merging them into a point of view about what will enable us to survive.* Then, whenever we face a new challenge, we scan those memories to check for anything that might help us deal with what's ahead. So our past informs our future. Whether we realize it or not, we're effectively prisoners of our experiences, both guided and constrained by "what we know."

---

* Also known as a mindset, world view, paradigm, or mental model.

This is as true for individuals as it is for groups (though with groups we're talking about a *collective* record of the past). Our life story frames what we see and how we make sense of it.[81]

Culture is a product of memory, and memory is a product of experience. Thus culture is both a cause and a consequence. It shapes the way we act, and in turn is shaped by that action.

Because it's not easy to wipe either personal or organizational memories away, and it takes time for new ones to take hold, culture is extremely "sticky." It's as subject to "path dependence" as any other resource, and the resulting "lock-in"* kills agility by making it much easier to keep doing what we've always done rather than change course.

If employees are to consistently bust a gut for customers, they need some reason to think that great service makes sense. As they act on this assumption, they accumulate memories of how they delivered it and the effect that had – which reinforces their beliefs, strengthens their commitment, and leads to more of the same. Through a process of practice and reflection, a service culture gradually takes hold.

The same applies where, for example, cost control, quality, innovation, or excellent execution are key goals in a company. Visible and vocal leadership gets things going, but *the only way to shift culture is to encourage and enable people to do new things so they learn their way into a new mindset.* This is an ongoing task, not one you can pull off in a few workshops or even in a few months. And it's definitely not one that can be left to some consultant or to HR. It has to be right at the top of the leader's agenda.

As you express your point of view to the people around you, they develop an understanding of your assumptions, values, and beliefs. But they won't necessarily share them. That will only happen after they test them as operating rules and try new behaviours – whether as a result of persuasion or the use of influence or power – thus changing "the way we do things around here."

As Schein told me in an interview, "You change people's behavior, and you may eventually influence their beliefs. If you define culture as a common learned response, then it changes with success. Change comes from success, not from somebody imposing something new. When people ask me to diagnose or change culture, my first question always is, 'Why?' And, 'What problem are you facing that makes you want to change anything?' You need to force them to be clear about the business problem or organizational problem that's motivating any change. And then the culture comes in."[82]

Until firms do things, they have no idea what they *can* do. "Possibility think-

---

* More on these concepts on page 200.

ing" is a wonderful notion, but it's no more than that if it doesn't inspire someone to do something new – to let go of what's familiar, and to explore and experiment. As Goleman, Boyatzis, and McKee tell us, lasting change comes through practice. "It takes doing and doing, over and over to break old habits. A leader must rehearse a new behavior until it becomes automatic – that is, until he's mastered it at the level of implicit learning. Only then will the new wiring replace the old."[83] The same applies to everyone else.

Culture is an integral part of strategy-making. If you accept that people are critically important to strategy today, and will become even more so in the future, you have to involve them in the actions that will enrich your firm's culture. Only by being passionate about this will you be able to deal with the changes in your environment and fight your way to competitive advantage.

Slow down and get real

There's been no shortage of smart people trying to upend what we know about managing people and replace it with something better. But get past statements of noble intent, filter out the noise, and strip away the jargon, and you're left with precious little.

The fact is, yesterday's knowledge and practices are alive and well – and for good reasons. They may be cunningly camouflaged by hip language, quirky names, crafty metaphors, and fancy wrapping, but the assumptions on which they're based, the core ideas, the basic elements, remain unchanged.

It's hard to find a company today that doesn't aspire to being "the best company to work for." Everyone knows that people, not technology or systems, make things happen. Everyone knows that there's a war for talent and that keeping your employees happy is not a nice-to-do. So if everybody knows these things, why has it taken us so long to wake up, and why do most managers not practise what they preach?

The vast majority of companies stick to "conventional" HR practices, and many do extremely well by toeing the line. Only a handful hire, manage, develop, or reward people in out-of-the-ordinary ways. Some of these firms may perform well, though it's hard to be sure that novel practices are the reason.

So before you fall for the idea that a revolutionary approach to managing people is necessary – or available – just count to ten and think about what you're thinking about. Do you really need to do this? Is that glitzy new idea really new? Does it make sense? And if you think it's necessary, can you *do* it?

Making a big leap will be costly, risky, and hard. Plugging in proven methods will be much simpler. And you don't have to wonder whether they're worth it or not.

As with strategy, I'm not advising you to shut your mind to the possibility of innovative ideas about people management. What I am suggesting is that you reflect carefully on your intentions and the ways you might achieve them. That you have a clear grasp of the practices that are known to produce results. And that you put common sense ahead of blind faith.

Research tells us that the chances are not good of *any* change effort being successful. Unintended consequences always lurk. It's easy to get distracted and derail what's already in place and working for you. So surely it would be best to start with ideas that clearly matter and are known to work, rather than trying to invent a new management approach yourself.

Bold leaps are thrilling, but baby steps often make much more sense.

9

LEADERSHIP LOST

Around the world today, there's growing criticism of leaders and anxiety about an apparent absence of leadership in many fields, amid a rising clamour for "good leadership." It's probably no exaggeration to say that anyone on earth over about the age of six has a view on the matter.

Yet of all the factors that affect the performance of organizations, this one is perhaps the least well understood and the most shrouded in mystery. It shows up at critical moments to "save the day," but is often absent when it's most needed. It plays out in public and we equate it with vision, boldness, courage, decisiveness, morality, and integrity – but it's ultimately an expression of deeply private thoughts and feelings. We know it when we see it, but until we see it we have no idea it's there.

In 1978, James McGregor Burns, one of the most influential modern writers on leadership, noted that "A recent study turned up 130 definitions of the word."[1] Just 27 years later, Warren Bennis and Burt Nanus put the number at 350, while commenting: "Never have so many labored so long to say so little."[2] And another 27 years on, Barbara Kellerman, of the John F. Kennedy School of Government at Harvard University, had it at 1,500, along with some 40 different theories of leadership.[3] However, given that comment about leadership is often buried within books, articles, speeches, and elsewhere, with no precise view on what it is, any estimate is bound to be wide of the mark.

"The scores of books, papers and speeches on leadership of the business enterprise that come out each year have little to say on the subject that was not already old when the Prophets spoke and Aeschylus wrote," said Peter Drucker. "[T]hree thousand years of study, exhortation, injunction and advice do not seem to have increased the supply of leaders to any appreciable extent nor enabled people to learn how to become leaders."[4]

Unanswered questions

Definitions trouble us. But even more concerning is that there are still more questions than answers about this crucial topic, which plays such a large part and is so evident in every aspect of our lives. While there's no shortage of observations and advice that may be helpful in one way or another, *we don't know much for sure.* Most disconcertingly, we aren't sure how to *do* this thing that we agree is called leadership.

Harvard Business School professor Rakesh Khurana reports in his book *Searching for a Corporate Savior* that after decades of scholarly work, leadership "remains without either a widely accepted theoretical framework or a cumulative empirical understanding leading to a usable body of knowledge."

Alarmingly, too, he says, "There is no conclusive evidence linking leadership to organizational performance.... While the CEO does indeed affect firm performance in particular situations, even then the overall CEO effect is swamped by contextual factors such as industry and macroeconomic conditions."[5]

In a thorough review of leadership literature, published in 2009, Bruce Aviolo, Fred Walumba, and Todd Weber paint a depressing picture of the state of leadership research.[6] And Porter and Nohria report that, "Despite the fascination with CEOs, the only in-depth scholarly study of the CEO's job was conducted more than thirty years ago (Mintzberg, 1973). The only other in-depth studies of the CEO's job of which we were aware were conducted by the Conference Board (Stieglitz 1969, 1985) and in a McKinsey & Company study (McLean et al, 1991) ... it has been several decades since there has been a study of the nature and challenges of the CEO's role, and the determinants of CEO effectiveness."[7]

Says Kellerman:

> I offer an assessment of academia, of where we are now in the evolution of Leadership Studies as an area of intellectual inquiry: I would say fair to middling, at best ... it is not as if no good work has been done, as if there are no people or programs that meet the highest standards of leadership scholarship. Rather it is that after four decades or so, progress has been, to put it politely, slow. The effect has been particularly deleterious on leadership training and development, in part because ... what exactly such training should consist of remains vague or, if you prefer, a question on which there is no appreciable agreement. One reason is that we have too many choices: too many competing experts offering too many competing pedagogies, most of which are based neither on empirical evidence nor on a well-established theoretical tradition. Moreover, we do not know which particular pedagogy suits which particular circumstance; nor have we reached consensus on what could be considered a core leadership curriculum.[8]

Reflecting on this, you have to wonder what leadership researchers have been up to all this time, and when they might come up with some actual answers. This is an important subject, after all. But as with the rest of what we need to know about managing organizations for results, the omens for progress are not good.

Some of the questions that continue to intrigue us and vex researchers are these: Do we need leaders? What is the job of a leader? When and how might leaders make a difference? What are the traits of the best leaders? What skills do they need? What is best practice for those who occupy leadership roles? How are leaders developed?

We don't know whether it's best to be humble or heroic. When to switch from "transactional" to "transformational" mode. How to deal with people who play political games. How to manage within a matrix structure or in circumstances which make face-to-face contact impossible.

Autocratic leadership is essential in some circumstances, whereas a democratic approach works best in others. Charisma, servant leadership, and authenticity – all of which are common themes in corporate corridors today – are by no means guarantees of success.

There are strong opinions on every aspect of leadership, and untold thousands of studies behind them. Anecdotes and examples – and even mythology – also have their roles. History is replete with accounts of leaders and leadership. There are insights too, in biographies and autobiographies; novels and essays; popular movies ranging from *Lincoln* to *The Lion King*; interviews and documentaries; and everyday media. And role models range from Hannibal and Jesus to Winston Churchill and Nelson Mandela.

American presidents commonly turn to the experience of their predecessors when they face a crisis. Military leaders study how past battles were won or lost. Harvard Business School has hired Sir Alex Ferguson, the legendary Manchester United football coach, "to share his remarkable leadership journey" and help executive education participants "make a profound difference in the world."[9] Leadership courses are taught not only in business schools and universities, but also by a host of other providers. No corporate training programme is complete without a major focus on leadership. There are leadership "experts" everywhere (most of whom have never led anything).

Few people would dispute that companies need leaders. *Strong* leaders. We're quick to point to a Thomas Watson, Jack Welch, or Steve Jobs to prove the point. And indeed, the very first of the critical strategy practices is what I have termed *growth leadership*.

As is the case with the other practices, the search for new knowledge about leadership will continue. But it is extremely unlikely that there will be any major revelations – and not for lack of trying.

Leaders or managers?

In 1973, Peter Drucker wrote in *Management Tasks, Responsibilities, Practices* that "management, that is, the organ of leadership, direction, and decision in our social institutions, and especially in business enterprise, is a generic function which faces the same basic tasks in every country and, essentially, in every society.... It has to think through the institution's mission, has to set its objectives, and has to organize resources for the results the institution has to contribute." But later in the same book came a strange semantic swerve. Having told us that management is the means by which leadership and direction are provided and decisions get made, Drucker suddenly announced that it was "inappropriate to speak of managers as leaders. They are 'members of the leadership group.'"[10]

But what could this mean? Might it take a *clutch* of managers to provide leadership – and if so, where would that put individual leaders? Is there a role for them? Are they all part of the "leadership group," or are some above it ("supra-leaders" who lead the manager-leaders)? One can only speculate on Drucker's intentions, but his equivocation was a sign of things to come.

In a 1977 *HBR* article titled "Managers and Leaders, Are They Different?" Harvard professor Abraham Zaleznik argued that indeed they are.[11] When a colleague of his, John Kotter, published a book called *Power in Management* in 1979, there was no mention of leadership in the index. But Kotter soon began to stamp his own authority on what was to become a raging leadership-vs-management debate in management and academic circles. Managers deal with complexity, he wrote in a 1990 *HBR* article. Leaders deal with change.[12] And the same year he published another book, *A Force for Change*, with the subtitle, *How Leadership Differs from Management*.[13] Meanwhile, others were latching onto the idea and adding their own wrinkles to it. According to Stephen Covey, for example, "Management is a bottom line focus: How can I best accomplish certain things? Leadership deals with the top line: What are the things I want to accomplish?"[14] Such conviction was contagious. The message spread – clearly with little thought to its flawed logic. So leading and managing came to be generally understood to be different types of work, performed by different types of people.

This is unquestionably one of the most damaging paradigms in organizations today. However, by 1995, even Kotter had begun to temper his rigid opinion. "Success in managerial jobs increasingly requires leadership, not just good management," he said. "Even at lower levels in firms, the inability to lead is hurting both corporate performance and individual careers. Organizations that stifle leadership from employees are no longer winning."[15]

Henry Mintzberg, one of the finest and most thoughtful management scholars around, puts it like this: "How would you like to be managed by someone who doesn't lead? That can be awfully dispiriting. Well, then, why would you want to be led by someone who doesn't manage? That can be terribly disengaging: how are such 'leaders' to know what is going on?"[16]

Those definitions "create a false dichotomy," says Harvard professor Jay Lorsch. "[T]he most effective leaders turn out to be very good managers as well ... if the only way to be a leader is to be bringing about change, there are an awful lot of us who think we are leading others when according to this dichotomy we are not."[17]

There's no point at all in further debate about non-existent or insignificant differences between management and leadership. There's nothing to be gained – and much to be lost – by continuing to moan that organizations are over-managed and under-led. Nor are we helped by the many books and articles that bang on about this divide, the gurus who make a big thing of it, or the widespread emphasis on it in business schools.

The belief that managers and leaders are different species, of quite different stature, and with different roles and responsibilities is sharply at odds with the notion that they're at one in crafting and conducting a single, seamless conversation. It also jars with the trend towards greater empowerment, which in theory lets people loose to make decisions and makes them accountable for the outcomes. And, worst of all, labelling people sends strong messages to them and everyone else, which almost certainly affect their self-esteem and motivation, as well as other people's opinions and expectations of them. In this, leaders will always come out on top. If management is regarded as a stepping-stone to leadership, it will be clear who has the most power, who should get the biggest pay, and who should enjoy the most freedom.

The only possible excuse for clinging to this "false dichotomy" is that it makes life simple for anyone who deals with organizational design, pay scales, performance management, or training and development. Put people in one box, and they get treated one way. Put them in the other, and the goodies are different.

Firms do need structure and clear reporting lines. Everyone cannot have the same authority to make decisions. But surely, if people are to perform as well as they can, they should be treated accordingly. Surely, if they're expected to reach their full potential and be all that they can be, every possible impediment should be shunted out of their way and every possible enabler put in place. It's ridiculous to talk about human capital and talent, about wanting people to show initiative and be entrepreneurial and collaborative, and about expecting them to "fail fast," "seize the moment," or "just do it," while at the same time inferring or imposing a class divide.

I see leadership as *creating a desirable future by getting results through others.* This is a practical definition, as it focuses attention on three tasks:

1. Deciding what a "desirable future" might be;
2. Deciding what results are needed to get there, and how to achieve them;
3. Gaining the support of a range of stakeholders to make it happen.

This is the work of anyone who goes by the title of either manager or leader. It requires them to inspire a sense of purpose, encourage people to volunteer their imagination and spirit and push their own limits, and ensure that necessary activities are properly carried out.

The fact that some people have to spend much of their time determining where next to expand, dealing with external stakeholders, or negotiating M&A deals, while others focus more on functional matters, does not justify creating a divide through arbitrary and ill-founded designations. Both groups are simultaneously leaders *and* managers.

As Drucker said, "it is the test of an organization that it make ordinary human beings perform better than they are capable of, that it bring out whatever strength there is in its members and use it to make all the other members perform more and better. It is the test of an organization that it neutralize the weaknesses of its members."[18]

The problems of the new century will only be solved, and its promise realized, if organizations pass these tests. And that will only be possible if they make "leaders at every level" a reality rather than an empty catchphrase.

From self to situation

The December 2001 *Harvard Business Review* was a special issue given to "Breakthrough Leadership." Now, that was cause for excitement! Here we were bound to learn something new.

But along with that banner, the cover also announced: "It's personal." And "Why knowing yourself is the best strategy now." And a feature article by Daniel Goleman, Richard Boyatzis, and Annie McKee began with the comment that their research "showed an incontrovertible link between an executive's emotional maturity, exemplified by such capabilities as *self-awareness* and *empathy*, and his or her financial performance."[19] (My italics.)

This, remember, in the first year of the new millennium. A couple of thousand years after the Bible admonished us to "Know thyself"; after ancient Greeks inscribed those words in the forecourt of the Temple of Apollo; and after they were used by Plato. And more than 400 years after Shakespeare had Polonius tell his son Laertes, "This above all: to thine own self be true."

And let's not forget Ralph Waldo Emerson's 1841 admonition:

Insist on yourself; never imitate. Your own gift you can present every moment with the cumulative force of a whole life's cultivation; but of the adopted talent of another you have only an extemporaneous, half possession. No man yet knows what it is, nor can, till that person has exhibited it. Where is the master who could have taught Shakspeare [sic]? Where is the master who could have instructed Franklin, or Washington, or Bacon, or Newton? Every great man is an unique.[20]

More recently, the same idea has been served up in pop-psychologist Wayne Dwyer's 1976 bestseller, *Your Erroneous Zones*.[21] And in Stephen Covey's 1989 blockbuster, *The 7 Habits of Highly Effective People*, which was based on his review of centuries of advice on success for his PhD thesis.[22] And in just about everything written or said about success after Covey.

Empathy, which is the second aspect of emotional maturity according to Goleman, Boyatzis, and McKee, is part and parcel of the social skill of tuning in to other people and adjusting your behaviour to theirs. But again, this is not news.

In the 1940s psychologists began studying the effect of an organization's situation on leaders and followers. One of them, Fred Fiedler of the University of Washington, came to the view that a group's performance depended on both its situation and its leadership style, and in 1967 put forward a "contingency model" of leadership effectiveness.[23] (Lawrence and Lorsch used the same term at exactly the same time. But whereas Fiedler focused on *leadership*, they referred to the broader need for *organizations to adapt in their totality* to their environment.)[24]

Meanwhile, Robert Blake and Jane Mouton had exploited the same line of thought in their 1964 book *The Managerial Grid*. They introduced a matrix on which executives could plot whether they were more inclined to focus on production or on people. This would help them surface their underlying assumptions about management and be aware of their most comfortable style, decide what most suited a particular situation, and if necessary adjust their approach.

The grid did not offer "a mechanical explanation of managerial behavior," Blake and Mouton averred. "As in any applied setting, the answer regarding what is best can only be given in the light of existing realities."[25]

The appeal of the device, however, lay precisely in its paint-by-numbers nature. And although it soon went the way of the dodo, there were variations to come on its central thesis.

One refinement was the social-styles model, which had executives reflect on whether they were more comfortable dealing with a task or with people, and if they preferred asking or telling when communicating. According to their choices, they'd be labelled "Driver," "Analytical," "Amiable," or "Expressive." And by recognizing which of these styles was preferred by other people, they could adapt their own style.[26]

Then Paul Hersey and Kenneth Blanchard published an article on the "Life Cycle Theory of Leadership" in *Training and Development Journal* in 1969, followed by numerous other articles and books – several of them bestsellers – on what they called "situational leadership."[27] Consulting and training firms pounced, and mashed these ideas together and commercialized them. And as a result, the terms "contingent" and "situational" – which as originally used mean quite different things – became conveniently jumbled.*

The core message, though, is simply "different strokes for different folks" and "a time and a place for everything." Not a rocking revelation when you think of all the effort that went into producing it. And not a huge advance from what Dale Carnegie advocated in his famous book *How to Win Friends and Influence People*, which was published in 1936.[28]

But give management thinkers their due: they certainly have a knack for seeing what should be apparent to anyone, and turning it into gold. The two ideas I've mentioned here – be yourself and adapt your behaviour to your context – are hardly earth-shattering. Nor did we stumble across them yesterday. But just look at the hype that's been created around them! Look at the spin-offs! Imagine what might come next!

Self-awareness – which has recently been given new life as *authenticity* – is widely regarded as *the* standout leadership quality today. But look at its pedigree. Its origins are clear, the basic idea is unchanged, and only a few semantic tweaks hint at an attempt to keep up with the times. Now, look forward. Try to imagine when it won't matter that we understand ourselves and act consistent with the reality of who we are. Or what flash of scholarly inspiration might one day enable us to ratchet up our authenticity. Or what such enlightenment, if it were to come, would cause us to *do* differently – and how that would lead to better results.

Just as self-awareness is enjoying new-found status, so is adaptability. Ronald Heifetz explains one aspect of it – the need for leaders to alternate between standing back from work to gain perspective, and plunging into the thick of it – as leading from "the balcony" or "the dance floor."[29] Jim Collins uses the metaphor of "mirrors and windows" to emphasize the need for leaders to adapt their communication to whatever situation they're in.[30] And of course, the same

---

* Contingency theory deals with the relationship between the environment, the organization, and its purpose and performance criteria; situational leadership focuses on the relationship between leaders and followers.

theme features strongly in books, articles, and training courses on emotional intelligence.

But like self-awareness, the need to be adaptable – or, in current parlance, *resilient* – is not new. Neither will it go away. Even so, decades from now, most of us will still be creatures of habit. The best we can hope for is that someone will come along with a clever new way to remind us – yet again – that we need to be flexible when dealing with other people. The *how* will always be a stumbling block.

Emotional intelligence seems to be the answer. But maybe it's not all it's held to be. Maybe it's another example of hype trampling facts and common sense.

Its origins lie in "social intelligence," a concept developed by American psychologist John Dewey back in 1909. Eighty years later, Peter Salovey of Yale University and John D. Mayer of the University of New Hampshire coined the term "emotional intelligence."[31] Then, in 1995, Goleman, a psychologist and at the time a science writer for the *New York Times*, brought it to public attention in *Emotional Intelligence*,[32] a book that has subsequently sold more than five million copies, been translated into 40 languages, created an industry of consultants and speakers, and turned a concept into a buzz-phrase and an HR fetish.

Despite wildly successful marketing and wide adoption, though, there's evidence that it counts for little more in organizations than personality traits or cognitive ability. In fact, after analysing hundreds of studies of thousands of employees in 191 different jobs, Dana Joseph of the University of Central Florida and Daniel Newman of the University of Illinois concluded that it accounted for *less than 1 per cent* of job performance.[33] And after reviewing research on leadership, HEC professor John Antonakis concluded that "claims made by EI proponents regarding the apparent necessity of EI for leadership or organisational performance are unsubstantiated, exaggerated, misrepresented or simply false."[34]

This is something of a surprise, given that organizations are social institutions, and human behaviour drives their performance. But any firm seeing emotional intelligence as a silver bullet would do well to first consider all available facts about it. To glibly accept the assurances of its fans, and incur another cost and distraction, is not a smart move.

The competitive advantage of tomorrow

Leading any organization requires a high degree of intelligence. Mostly what's meant by this is high *cognitive IQ* – the ability to figure things out, solve problems, make decisions, and so on – which is the best predictor of performance. But much more than that is necessary. Firms today need people at all levels with high *strategic IQ* and its close ally, *contextual IQ*, as well. Such individuals are not only able to process information according to well-established norms, but also have specific strategic thinking skills and are acutely attuned to the world in which they operate.

Since strategy is largely an intellectual activity, you'd think that strategic IQ would be an obvious concept deserving of serious attention by both management thinkers and managers. But it's not one that gets much comment, and there's a dearth of books or articles about it. I've never heard a single CEO or HR executive talk of strategic IQ or the need to build it. Harvard Business School began offering a short course in the subject in mid-2012, but I'm not aware of other schools following suit.

Professor John Wells, presenter of the course and author of the book *Strategic IQ*, says that when hiring people with leadership potential, firms should seek curious individuals with "practical intelligence" – rational, creative, emotional, and social intelligence – and a strong commitment to learning. These are obviously personal traits. Surprisingly, though, he explains strategic IQ as an *organizational* ability to steer a firm "purposefully in a winning direction,"[35] or "the capacity to adapt to changing circumstances."[36] A combination of "smart strategy," "smart structure," and "smart minds," he says, leads to "high strategic IQ."[37]

Following this tack, Wells' book and the course both cover almost everything a firm does to overcome inertia and be nimble and adaptive. So they offer a very general – and very useful – overview of strategy altogether. But strategic IQ deserves more focus. Bundling it with issues of strategy and structure is bound to detract from its personal nature and pivotal role. It's not just *an* essential factor in any company's competitiveness, it's *the* essential factor.

In my view, strategic IQ is specifically "the ability to *think strategically*," which in turn leads to the ability to *act strategically*.[38] This is firstly an *individual* capability, which must be sought and deliberately developed. Only then can it become an *organizational* capability – and it must.

To survive and thrive in a rapidly changing world, you need people who can see the big picture, make sense of what's happening around them, and make rapid and sound decisions about how to respond – not efficient drones who're oblivious to their environment, mindlessly take orders, and just do as they're told. The need is even greater with an educated, mobile workforce, unable to constantly turn to Head Office for instructions, and expected to make decisions on the fly. But while much has been said about the importance of teams, empowerment, virtual organizations, organizational learning, emergent strategy, the wisdom of crowds, innovation, and so on, one key point is glossed over: without a particular set of intelligences, no one will ever be worthy of the label "strategist." And which company do you know where there is a deliberate, systematic effort to develop strategic thinking capabilities *outside* of the executive ranks?

You need to bother about this because, as I wrote in my 1988 book *The New Age Strategist*, "while the 'strategist' might be one person, or even a small team ... strategy formulation is not the strict preserve of that person or group – and certainly not of top management. The fact is, because so many of a firm's people might set off a response to environmental changes, strategic management is a task almost everyone must be involved in."[39]

Then, in a 1998 article titled "Questions of Strategy," I said, "Business strategy, like every journey through life, is a learning process. The ... goal of every organisation should be to raise its 'strategic IQ' – the ability of every person to participate to the best of their ability in scanning the environment, providing new insights, applying their imagination, and exploring the bounds of what's possible."[40]

But this led to two questions: 1) what capabilities does an individual need in order to participate in that way; and 2) how to develop them?

For answers, I dug into books and journals on management, psychology, and education; talked to leaders about their growth experiences; and watched people making decisions at work. And the more I read, saw, and heard, and the more deeply I reflected on it, the more convinced I became that what we needed to know was, in fact, both clear and simple – and staring us in the face.

Multiple intelligences

Strategic IQ is yet to gain the attention of scientists and management gurus, but you might think about it like this: Assume you're about to hire a consultant to help you with your strategy. You obviously want the best strategy you can get. What mental skills would you expect of the person you're about to rely on?

Surely they'd be these:

- **Foresight** – the ability to see into the future and anticipate what lies ahead, what's likely to happen, and how things are likely to unfold;
- **Insight** – the ability to cut through clutter and complexity and to understand things incisively and in a new way;
- **Analysis** – the ability to collect information, decipher and make sense of it, and make it useful;
- **Imagination** – the ability to see what others have not seen, and to think "what could be" where others are content with what is;
- **Synthesis** – the ability to connect disparate snippets of information, different sensations and perceptions, and unrelated ideas, to give them new meaning;
- **Judgment** – the ability to weigh up situations, facts, feelings, opinions, and so on, and to make choices about what must be done in a way that best balances risk and reward and leads to the most desirable outcomes possible (Figure 9.1).

Figure 9.1

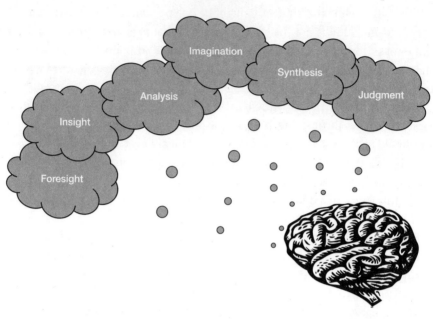

Now, if these are the traits you'd want in a consultant, what about the people on your own team? What should you seek in them? What should you strive to develop in them? What do they need to fulfil their purpose in a VUCA world?

Answer: *exactly the same capabilities.*

But what happened to *creative* IQ, you might wonder? And the answer is, it's a product of all the six elements in my model. Creativity involves a complex thought process. The celebrated advertising man, David Ogilvy, looked for "a richly furnished mind" when he interviewed potential recruits, because he knew that creating great ads was about synthesis – about pulling together images, sounds, and other impressions, and linking them into something new. And that could only happen if the people he considered had a lot of raw material – or "stuff" – in their heads.[41]

And *rational* IQ? Same thing: if the term refers to the ability to confront and deal with reality, to keep a cool head under pressure, and to make well-reasoned decisions, all of those come from the capabilities in my model.

It's clear from this description that strategic thinking skills are quite different from social (or emotional) skills. But they are equally a product of both nature and nurture. So while it's safe to assume that most people have them to some level or other, it's not smart to leave their development to chance.

As I pointed out in my 2001 book *Making Sense of Strategy*, "The 'strategic IQ' of your firm is, literally, a life and death factor," for this is the one skill that makes everything happen. And the best way to ensure it is through strategic conversation. I went on to say:

Most valuable human development takes place in the school of hard knocks, not in the classroom. Most people's growth and inspiration results from their day-to-day activities and interactions. The conversations they're involved in shape their attitudes and aspirations, and impact on their capabilities. Yet, common practices ensure that too many individuals are constrained rather than liberated, and that only a few are able to think and act strategically.

In effect, people are forced to short-change their companies, because their companies cut them out of the conversational loop and limit what they can do and what they can become.

While the "heavies" engage in a "big conversation" about the firm's context, its challenges, its strategy, and so on, the majority of employees are allowed to take part only in a "small conversation" which focuses narrowly on their jobs, their specific tasks, the methods they use, and the results they must get. The very people who most need practice in strategy are least likely to be given the opportunity to do it.

The strategic IQ of most firms is pathetically low – not because of the tools they use to make strategy, but because of the process. But you can change that fast, by immediately involving as many people as possible in your company's "big conversation." This single step will do more than anything else to align and motivate your team, and to empower them to conquer tomorrow.[42]

One tool. Nothing complicated about it. Yet more powerful than anything else.

Nothing better than this

What we need to know about leadership – what leaders must do and what they must bring to the job – is brilliantly captured in two books that are worth dusting off and putting right on top of the pile on your desk.

The first of these is *Leaders* by Warren Bennis, whose reputation as an expert in this field was unmatched, and Burt Nanus, which was published in 1985. "No clear and unequivocal understanding exists as to what distinguishes leaders from non-leaders," they write, "and perhaps more important, what distinguishes *effective* leaders from *ineffective* leaders and *effective* organizations from *ineffective* organizations."

But from a two-year study of 60 successful CEOs and 30 outstanding public-sector leaders, Bennis and Nanus concluded that "leadership is something that can be learned by anyone, taught to everyone, denied to no one." All the leaders they chose displayed four specific skills – what the authors called "managements":

1. **Attention** – the ability to focus people on what matters;
2. **Meaning** – the ability to turn challenges into opportunities for growth and significance;
3. **Trust** – the ability to instil confidence by consistently walking their talk;
4. **Self** – the ability to inspire themselves through their self-talk.[43]

The work of leaders is complicated, so it's easy to dismiss an explanation of it that comes down to four words. But not so fast. Pithy though this recipe may be, it encapsulates the essence of what leaders must do. Through their words and actions, they frame the world for those around them. This means they must continually ask themselves: What must our people *know* so they can do what they need to do, and how should they *feel* so they will do what they need to do? And what must I do to make it happen?

Now, let's consider the characteristics that define effective leaders.

Leadership is a quality, a process, a practice – and above all, an art. It involves leaders, followers, and their context, so it's situation-specific and dynamic, and has to be made up on the run.

There is only so much about it that can be taught, and the rest is up to genes and experience. The subtlety and nuance that can turn crises into victories and problems into opportunities may be impossible to explain in a book, a classroom, or even a one-on-one coaching session. The wisdom that leaders require comes only through action and reflection. Time on the job counts for a lot.

Without doubt, though, some people are more suited to leadership than others. Whether because of attitude or aptitude, they have what it takes. They're emotionally secure and socially adept. They're future-focused, smart, and able to make a respectable ratio of good vs bad decisions. Their skills include communication, relationship-building, motivation, and negotiation. Every firm should obviously aim to have as many of these individuals as possible – at all levels.

This brings me to the second book, *On Leadership*, by John Gardner, a former US Secretary of Health, Education, and Welfare, and an advisor to three US presidents. Published in 1990, it draws on other scholars who have "reviewed the extensive body of research in the field," and suggests 14 attributes of effective leaders. They're not present in every leader, and their importance varies with the situation. There are plenty of similar checklists around, but I can think of none that beats this one:

1. Physical vitality and stamina;
2. Intelligence and judgment in action;
3. Willingness (eagerness) to accept responsibilities;
4. Task competence;
5. Understanding of followers/constituents and their needs;
6. Skill in dealing with people;
7. Need to achieve;
8. Capacity to motivate;
9. Courage, resolution, steadiness;
10. Capacity to win and hold trust;
11. Capacity to manage, decide, set priorities;
12. Confidence;
13. Ascendance, dominance, assertiveness;
14. Adaptability, flexibility of approach.[44]

Some people are born with some of these traits. Few have all of them in equal measure. But fortunately, as with the skills advocated by Bennis and Nanus, most of them can be learned and developed with practice. And the best opportunity for that lies in work itself.

The search for better answers will go on. Anxiety about knowing who has what it takes to be a leader, what they must do, and the best way to do it will see to that. But pause for a moment. Consider what we've learned in the past five, ten, 50 years. Think about whatever interesting insight or piece of advice about leading has just crossed your desk. What does it suggest you do differently than you did before it arrived?

What has it taught you that wasn't available years ago?

Leadership research has not taught us much so far, and there's no reason why it should make tomorrow's leaders better off. It surely is not going to reveal new ways of shaping and communicating a vision, managing and motivating people, encouraging innovation, or bringing about change. Nor will it make values more meaningful, or raise the bar in terms of integrity, morality, or ethics.

Brain scientists are making great progress in understanding how the human mind works. Psychologists, too, are pushing into new territory. But will further discoveries in these areas fundamentally change the way we lead organizations? Not likely. What will make a difference, though, is learning more about our context, becoming more aware of the human condition, and being at all times sensitive to the culture, values, and needs of the people around us. The ability to function effectively within a changing world is what will enable some people to stand out and make their mark.

All we've got

With due respect to Khurana's reservations, leaders do make a difference. They are essential. The results they get are indeed moderated by their context, but it is they who craft and conduct the strategic conversations that are key to a firm's performance, and without which organizations degenerate into some version of George Orwell's animal farm. This is work for which some people are better suited than others. Everyone can no more captain an Airbus 380 or lead a football team to victory than successfully head even a medium-sized company.

Everyone can, however, contribute to fostering a nourishing workplace rather than a toxic one. Everyone can make a direct impact on those around them – their colleagues, their subordinates, and their bosses. This matters, because individuals who are fulfilled by their work are most likely to volunteer their imagination and spirit to it. They'll go the extra mile because they enjoy what they're doing, and achievement adds to their satisfaction. And the more people there are who actively work at this in an organization, the better off all will be.

But we need to be absolutely clear about what leads to positive feelings, because an organization's climate is a lot more than happy talk.

First come sound organizational arrangements (role clarity, decision rights, working conditions, resources, support, SHE and HR policies, rewards, etc.). These are the bedrock – which is why they're called hygiene factors. They're also an easy target for action by HR, who can directly influence changes in them. In the scheme of things, however, their positive impact may be much less than the *dissatisfaction* that arises when they're not attended to.

The bigger issue is people's perceptions and feelings. How they perceive their working environment, but more importantly, how they perceive *themselves.*

Both HR and the executives they support need to constantly remind themselves of that adage, "Nothing succeeds like success." They need to ensure that they do whatever it takes to keep satisfaction levels high, *and* to put the same effort into the practical measures that enable high performance.

Fortunately, says education expert Malcolm Knowles, "An organization provides an environment for adult education, an environment that either facilitates or inhibits learning."[45] Companies are classrooms. They're where people learn most of their business skills. Yet few managers get this. They miss out on the very best opportunity for developing their people – and *at no extra cost.*

They give them time off for training, but often in skills that don't quite fit. They assume that what's learned outside will be automatically turned into action inside. And they do little to groom people for the jobs of tomorrow through the work of today.

Yet simply by changing the way they involve their employees, and treat them, they could grow them more effectively than by any other means.

Simply by changing their workplace conversations; by seeing themselves and their experienced colleagues as teachers and guides, and every interaction as an opportunity for teaching and learning; and by investing time and effort in sharing their knowledge, they would see an improvement in both skills and motivation.

So here we are, after decades of T-groups, sensitivity training, servant leadership, emotional intelligence – and any number of other notions and nostrums regarding people and performance – with this simple guide to creating a high-performance workplace:

1. Treat people fairly, respectfully, and consistently;
2. Give them important work, big challenges, clear goals, authority to make meaningful decisions, and responsibility for results;
3. Communicate openly and honestly with them, and shower them with more information than they need;
4. Listen to their suggestions, opinions, and concerns, and above all, to their *feelings*;
5. Provide the facilities, resources, and support that enable them to excel;
6. Involve them in "big conversations" and treat their inputs seriously;
7. Give them fast, honest, and helpful feedback on their performance;
8. Celebrate their wins and help them grow through failure;
9. Link rewards to performance, and show that there are consequences for non-performance or behaviours at odds with organizational expectations;
10. Think of the workplace as a classroom, and do whatever it takes to give people the richest possible learning opportunity in it.

Given how much money there is to make from breakthrough concepts, you can be sure that plenty of people will try to pull better rabbits out of the hat than these. But this formula has always applied – even if firms have been slow to apply it. And it will still be the one you need in 2020 … 2050 … and beyond.

There's no point in wrestling over the semantics of these matters. Nor is there any point in continually questioning whether leaders make a difference, what they must do to be effective, or what kinds of people they should be. The jury is in and the verdict is clear.

Leadership is not an airy-fairy concept. It all comes down to the way you frame the space in which people work, and how you help them frame the world. It has always been this way, and always will. And we know exactly how to do both things.

10

SO FAR, SO *BLAH!*

Individuals have always had to adjust their behaviour to survive and thrive as conditions around them changed. So have organizations and societies. Changes in management thinking have almost all come in response to external circumstances rather than in anticipation of them. And future management practice is just as likely to be reactive rather than proactive, evolutionary rather than revolutionary.

In any era, what grabs managers is mostly new *themes* – customer service, emerging markets, cost-cutting, the war for talent – and a new *agenda* for business, rather than new *theories* of management. Only occasionally do management ideas make major waves.

The context of business affects results as much as the way a business is managed – and in many cases even more. Politics, new technologies, economic cycles, competitor moves, social changes, labour relations, regulation, supply disruptions, natural disasters, and many other external factors require firms to shift their focus and shuffle their priorities. Favourable conditions can give them a helpful tailwind; unfavourable ones create a headwind. Managers whose companies do well in fair weather don't necessarily perform in the eye of a storm.

While historians and other commentators like to label various periods in history – the Stone Age, the Renaissance, the Industrial Revolution, the Information Age, and so on – many of their categorizations are purely arbitrary, a matter of opinion and expediency rather than of fact. So while Toffler, for example, talks of three "waves of change that have occurred over the past two centuries" – the Agricultural Wave, the Industrial Wave, and the Information Wave[1] – someone else might describe things differently. Similarly, there are many ways to group and describe the concerns and practices of managers in different eras.

In 1988, Peter Drucker stated that since the turn of the century, there had been two big shifts in thinking about organizations: the separation of ownership from management, and the introduction of command-and-control mechanisms.[2] (Not much progress in 88 years!)

Stanford professor Harold Leavitt saw things differently, and in a 2003 *HBR* article suggested that there had been *three* major management innovations in the past 50 years. First, he said, there was the human-relations movement, which began shortly after World War II. Then came "analytic management (or management by the numbers)." And third was what he and Jean Lipman-Blumen called "hot groups" – cross-functional teams put together to work on projects, then disbanded when they were done.

As with Toffler's three waves, these management trends broke over each other but nothing washed away. "The three approaches were simply piled – often not very coherently – onto whatever was already in place," said Leavitt. "Yet, like many odd combinations, the unlikely mix of organizational practices has proved to be both popular and surprisingly nourishing for the companies concerned."[3]

In fact, the field of management has seen more changes than either Drucker or Leavitt claimed, but these have indeed piled up incoherently. At the start of the 20th century, there was no body of knowledge about management. Developing one has been a work in progress ever since. Along the way, we learned about mass production, marketing, strategy, systems thinking, lean production, automation and information, innovation, motivation, teamwork, big data, and much else. And over time, we've paid more attention to people, realized that an organization's agility was probably more important than its planning ability, and rediscovered the value of deep connections with customers. Some of what we've learned has been useful, and endures. Much of it enjoyed fad status for a brief moment, then fell from favour.

The point is that at different times, managers and management scholars have focused on different issues, concepts, or practices because they happened to make sense just then. What's fashionable in one era falls out of favour in another. And one era's fad is often resuscitated many years or even decades after it dropped off the radar screen, because it seems right.

In the 1970s, Japanese management was a big deal. In the 1980s, it was excellence and reengineering. In the 1990s, core competence, globalization, Six Sigma, balanced scorecards. And the first decade of this century brought us disruption, blue ocean strategy, human capital, design thinking, big data, bottom-of-the-pyramid marketing, open innovation, sustainability, and so forth.

All of these were products of their time. So what will be the products of the times ahead?

A call to action

For all of the industrial era, every business has faced one common challenge: innovation. How to keep reinventing itself and its offerings for a changing world. Along the way, and almost unnoticed, a strange thing happened: the "innovation" label was attached more often to products and services than to new management practices that might deliver them.

Some two decades after Drucker's and Peters' comments, Gary Hamel, one of the most influential strategy thinkers around, sought to change this. "In most industries," he wrote in "Bringing Silicon Valley Inside," a *Harvard Business Review* article that won the 1999 McKinsey Award, "newcomers are creating much of the new wealth.... If you want your company to join the pantheon of wealth-creating superstars, you have to shift the balance of effort from stewardship to entrepreneurship in your organization ... you're going to have to figure out how to set up and sustain dynamic internal markets for ideas, capital, and talent."[4]

Four years later, he added more meat to the idea. New markets and new wealth, he said, could only be created through new business concepts that changed how firms created, delivered, and extracted value. The way to do this was "to unleash ideas, passion, and commitment across the company ... to move from innovations as exceptions; move beyond innovation as a specific role or structure, beyond innovation as a once-in-a-while project, to thinking about innovation as a deep capability."[5]

That set him off on a new mission. A *Harvard Business Review* article titled "The Why, What, and How of Management Innovation" was followed by the establishment at London Business School of the Management Innovation Lab, and publication of a new book, *The Future of Management*. In it Hamel wrote: "I dream of organizations that are capable of spontaneous renewal, where the drama of change is unaccompanied by the wrenching trauma of a turnaround. I dream of businesses where an electric current of innovation pulses through every activity, where the renegades always trump the reactionaries. I dream of companies that actually deserve the passion and creativity of the folks who work there, and naturally elicit the very best that people have to give." And he promised that "management innovation possesses a unique capacity to create difficult-to-duplicate advantages."[6]

"Modern management practice," Hamel wrote in another *HBR* article, "is based on a set of principles whose origins date back a century or more: specialization, standardization, planning and control, hierarchy, and the primacy of extrinsic rewards."[7] There, and in a subsequent interview with *The McKinsey Quarterly*, he kicked up a lot of dust about "orthodox" management practices, organizational designs, and ways of managing people, warning that they wouldn't save firms from failure or painful restructuring.[8]

To identify management practices in need of innovation, Hamel and a "renegade brigade" of 34 academics, CEOs, consultants, entrepreneurs, and venture capitalists got together in California for a two-day conference in 2008 to address two questions: "What needs to be done to create organizations that are truly fit for the future? What should be the critical priorities for tomorrow's management pioneers?" The results were published in a *Harvard Business Review* article, "Moonshots for Management," in February 2009 (Figure 10.1).[9]

Figure 10.1

The "moonshots for management"

1. Ensure that the work of management serves a higher purpose
2. Fully embed the ideas of community and citizenship in management systems
3. Reconstruct management's philosophical foundations
4. Eliminate the pathologies of formal hierarchy
5. Reduce fear and increase trust
6. Reinvent the means of control
7. Redefine the work of leadership
8. Expand and exploit diversity
9. Reinvent strategy making as an emergent process
10. De-structure and disaggregate the organization
11. Dramatically reduce the pull of the past
12. Share the work of setting direction
13. Develop holistic performance measures
14. Stretch executive time frames and perspectives
15. Create a democracy of information
16. Empower the renegades and disarm the reactionaries
17. Expand the scope of employee autonomy
18. Create internal markets for ideas, talent, and resources
19. Depoliticize decision making
20. Better optimize trade-offs
21. Further unleash human imagination
22. Enable communities of passion
23. Retool management for an open world
24. Humanize the language and practice of business
25. Retrain managerial minds

Adapted from Gary Hamel, "Moonshots for Management," *Harvard Business Review*, February 2009

Yet for all the intellectual firepower brought to that conversation, the "grand challenges" this group identified are disappointingly stale. There's no questioning their importance, but to say, "We've heard it all before" is no exaggeration. A few examples from the past half-century or so prove the point:

- In his 1946 classic *Concept of the Corporation*, Peter Drucker wrote: "Faced with an ever growing need for executives and engaged in a technological and efficiency competition which is becoming fiercer all the time, the corporation simply cannot afford to deprive itself of the intelligence, imagination, and initiative of 90 per cent of the people who work for it, that is, the workers."[10]

- In his famous 1960 book *The Human Side of Enterprise*, Douglas McGregor advised: "It is important to note the distinction between making people *feel* important and *making* people important."[11]

- In 1961, John Gardner wrote in *Self-Renewal: The Individual and the Innovative Society*: "What may be in most need of innovation is the corporation itself. Perhaps what every corporation (and every other organization) needs is a Department of Continuous Renewal that could view the whole organization as a system in need of continuous innovation."[12]

- In his 1970 blockbuster *Future Shock*,[13] and in a 1972 report to the telecommunications giant AT&T, later published as *The Adaptive Corporation*, futurist Alvin Toffler described many of the changes confronting organizations, anticipated others, and proposed ways to deal with them.[14] "We are, in fact, witnessing the arrival of a new organizational system that will increasingly challenge and ultimately supplant bureaucracy," he said. "This is the organization of the future. I call it 'Ad-hocracy.'"[15] He expanded this argument in his 1980 book *The Third Wave*, noting that "second wave" (Industrial Age) companies operated according to six principles: "standardization, specialization, synchronization, concentration, maximization, and centralization," and concluding that "every one of the fundamental principles is under attack by the forces of the Third Wave" (the Information Age).[16] A decade later, in *PowerShift*, he said, "Today we are living through the next power shift in the workplace ... a new kind of autonomous employee is emerging who, in fact, does own the means of production. The new means of production, however, are not to be found in the artisan's toolbox or in the massive machinery of the smokestack age. They are, instead, crackling inside the employee's cranium – where society will find the single most important source of future wealth and power."[17]

- In the early 1980s, the Tarrytown conference centre just north of New York City became a hot spot for management thinkers. Robert Schwartz, a former New York bureau chief for *Time* magazine, and chairman of the centre, was a true believer in management innovation. "The world hungers for a new type of organization," he wrote in the November 1983 issue of *The Tarrytown Letter*, "in which the individual is no longer a blind servant conforming to a dictated purpose. What people don't yet recognize is that the business community has created an environment in which workers can grow to new levels of competence – and can transform themselves into a more sophisticated future staff." And he went on to say that what "we *must* do now" is explore "nothing less than a total intellectual and pragmatic renaissance in American Management."[18]

- William Ouchi, whose 1981 bestseller, *Theory Z*, was based on the notion that "involved workers are the key to increased productivity," reminded managers that "Theory Z culture assumes that any worker's life is a whole, not a Jekyll-Hyde personality, half machine from nine to five and half human in the hours preceding and following."[19]

- Trend-watchers John Naisbitt and Patricia Aburdene reported in their 1985 book *Reinventing the Corporation*: "One of the most fundamental shifts, of course, is the movement away from the authoritarian hierarchy – where everyone has a superior and everyone has an inferior – to the new lateral structures, lattices, networks, and small teams where people manage themselves."[20]

- In two articles in the *California Management Review* in 1990 and 1991, Tom Peters admonished managers to "Get Innovative or Get Dead." He provided dozens of examples of companies doing out-of-the-ordinary things to foster what he called the "renegade atmosphere" in order to drive product and service innovation and dominate their markets.[21]

- In a 1996 interview, Michael Hammer, famed for bringing "reengineering" to the management lexicon, put it like this: "What we need is a very different mode of operating. We need ways of operating in which decisions are made by those much closer to the work.... We need a model in which people on the front lines, armed with a basic strategy decided by senior management of the company, are given a lot of autonomy and responsibility for deciding things on their own. A model where management exists, not to direct and control or to supervise, but rather to facilitate and enable."[22]

However, while executives everywhere have been enthralled by such revolutionary rhetoric, they have mostly been reluctant to act on it. They echo its themes in meetings, speeches, annual reports, and conferences, yet stick resolutely to their old practices. Now and then they might experiment with something new, but by and large they are careful not to stick their necks out too far. And at the first hint of trouble they are quick to snap back into controlling mode.

In 1988, James O'Toole, editor of *New Management*, an excellent magazine published by the University of South California, which came and went in just a few years, lamented that "the New Management philosophy that, in 1983, we were so confident would sweep the country, has alas, lost steam in most large corporations (and fizzled out entirely in others)."[23]

When *Fortune*'s mammoth 472-page 70th Anniversary issue hit the stands in March 2000, the internet boom was in full swing. Everywhere you looked, someone was turning conventional wisdom on its head. The rules of the business game were being reinvented by a new generation of entrepreneurs. Nerds in college dorms were challenging corporate giants. They were dismissive of tradition, ignorant of business practices that had been developed over generations, and intent only on delivering the next new thing. Skateboards, pets, and pizza became as common in the workplace as hoodies, sneakers, and body-piercing. A new language emerged of "network effects," "scaleability," "footprints," "eyeballs," and "hits." That ugly word "profit" was at last getting its comeuppance: "Don't worry about it," said the new millennium's pioneers, "just get momentum and everything will be OK." And piles of mainstream money flowed their way as investors scrambled for a piece of this action.

It was timely, then, for *Fortune* to celebrate "The Amazing Future of Business." But the magazine's editorial director, Geoffrey Colvin, penned a sobering note:

> The big issues managers are wrestling with now – what really attracts and motivates the best knowledge workers, the value of teams, organizing by projects, using infotech wisely, the flattening of hierarchies – those were seen quite clearly by the best management thinkers decades ago (yes, decades). Yet for all we read about bold companies managing in new ways, most enterprises continue to noodle with functionally organized, many-tiered hierarchies, the mechanistic model of a century ago. And in truth, if you talk to employees candidly, you'll find that many still feel they're treated like oxen.[24]

Hamel's basic message is to involve more people in decision-making, treat them better, and allow them freedom to be inventive. "Decision-making will be more peer based; the tools of creativity will be widely distributed in organizations," he says. "Ideas will compete on an equal footing. Strategies will be built from the bottom up. Power will be a function of competence rather than of position."[25]

Yet as I've shown, he's far from being the first to propose such changes in organizational behaviour. Frederick Taylor pointed to that need in his 1912 Testimony to the US Congress. "In essence," he said, "scientific management involves a complete mental revolution on the part of working men – and on the part of those on the management side, the foremen, the superintendent, the owner of the business, the Board of directors – as to their duties towards their fellow workers in the management, towards their workmen and toward all of their problems."[26]

The same advice was offered by Robert Townsend in his 1970 bestseller *Up the Organization* (a book "for those who have the courage, the humor, and the energy to make a non-monster company, or a non-monster piece of a monster company, operate as if people were human").[27] And it was offered by Jeanne

Liedtka and John Rosenblum in a *California Management Review* article in 1996.[28] And by Ronald Purser and Steven Cabana in their 1998 book *The Self Managing Organization.*[29] And in scores of other books and thousands – no, make that *tens* of thousands – of articles. (And, in fact, in my own previous ten books, written since 1987.)

Hamel excitedly points to the management practices of Ricardo Semler, CEO of Semco, a Brazilian firm, as an example of what might be done. But Semler's views have been widely known since Tom Peters raved about them in *A Passion for Excellence,* written with Nancy Austin in 1985,[30] and in *Liberation Management* in 1992[31] – not to mention in countless speeches. Semler himself wrote about them in *Harvard Business Review* in 1989,[32] in his hugely popular 1993 book *Maverick,*[33] and again in *The Seven-Day Weekend* in 2004.[34] And he, too, is a sell-out conference speaker. Yet while managers swoon when they hear his message, he has few imitators.

It's hard to see what conceptual advances either Hamel or Semler have made over many others who said similar things a long time ago. ("The elements of Semler's approach were hardly revolutionary," observe Hilmer and Donaldson. He made it work "because of consistent application and experimentation over a number of years."[35])

Very little of what we're being fed today is new. Not the advice to rethink management or the need to humanize the workplace. And given the huge investment in time and effort that has gone into dreaming up new answers, it's hard not to be disillusioned when you look at the results.

We've heard it all before – in many guises – over and over again. And we keep hearing it, from successive generations of dedicated researchers and commentators. They poke into organizations, conduct exhaustive statistical analyses, slice and dice data, conduct "meta-analyses" of previous research, and try desperately to wring sense out of the shards of information they gather. Yet after all that, the best they can do is dish up familiar advice – predictably dressed up as "a paradigm shift," "extraordinary insights," "a long-awaited breakthrough," "an intellectual tour de force," or "a welcome breath of fresh air."[36] They ignore the fact that many companies and executives have tried their potions in one guise or another, and abandoned them. So if innovation is turning new ideas into action, there's little of it here.

One common refrain is that although the Industrial Age symbolically gave way to the Information Age around 1956, when for the first time in the US more people were employed in services than in manufacturing, we're still stuck with Sloan's industrial model.[37] But so what? Should everything from the Industrial Age be tossed aside? Of course not. In fact, given the extreme complexity in modern firms – especially in manufacturing – coordination is more difficult than ever, and is impossible without far tighter controls than those needed in Sloan's day.

In 2006, Hamel and a colleague, Julian Birkinshaw, a professor at London Business School, invented the Management Innovation Lab, a collaborative venture between LBS and the Woodside Institute (also founded by Hamel) in California. "As a starting point," said Alan Matcham, the "MLab's" first executive director, "the Management Innovation Lab takes the core tasks of management – controlling, planning, developing people, motivating and goal setting – and examines the deep-seated beliefs or 'truisms' underpinning each task. Reframing those truisms to address today's challenges is our essential aim" (Figure 10.2).[38]

Figure 10.2

Hierarchy of control	Division of labour	Planned outcomes	Standardization	Monetary motivation
• Direction-setting, power, and control belong at the top, so that's where the smartest people should be	• Tasks should be divided and focused for maximum efficiency	• The future is reasonably predictable, so a firm can "plan its work and work its plan"	• "One best way" solutions will lead to consistency, stability, and harmony	• People respond to incentives, and money is the most powerful motivator

Adapted from Tom Brown, "Innovation Station," *Business Strategy Review*, Summer 2007, Vol. 18, Issue 2

However, those truisms had already been reframed. "At least until recently," wrote Henry Mintzberg and Alexandra McHugh in 1985, "the underlying assumptions of organizational design have been that organizations require articulated objectives, sharp divisions of labor; clearly defined tasks, well-developed hierarchies, and formalized systems of control." At the time, these authors noted, strategy-making was largely about planning – but this was "inconsistent with more contemporary forms of structure and sometimes with the conventional forms as well."[39]

MLab was initially located at LBS, but by 2009 had moved to Silicon Valley. In October 2009, Birkinshaw published an article in the organization's newsletter (it also appeared on the LBS website) saying:

I don't believe we need to completely reinvent management. Yes, there are changes afoot, made possible in part by the emergence of Web 2.0 technologies. But a lot of these putative changes – towards empowered, flat, emergent, and virtual structures – have been promised for decades. Rather than reinventing management in toto, we need at least to rethink the choices we make about how we manage. Every organisation has an implicit management model – a set of choices about how direction is set, how workers are motivated, how decisions are made, and how activities are coordinated. Sometimes the traditional top-down approach works fine, sometimes a more organic, community-based model is more appropriate. The best managed companies – the ones that can potentially derive competitive advantage from their management model – will in the future be the ones that make conscious choices that suit their circumstances, rather than falling back on the default model invented by Frederick Taylor and Alfred P Sloan in the 1920s and 1930s.[40]

Say *what*?

We don't need to "completely reinvent management" after all? Sometimes "the traditional top-down approach works fine" … the best companies will be "the ones that make conscious choices that suit their circumstances"?

What was all the to-do about? Was there *ever* any point in trying to encourage management innovation? Is management innovation possible or necessary? Should it be left to academics and consultants, or is it something managers themselves should pursue?

The hype has thus far had little effect. One review of *The Future of Management* questioned "whether we don't already have too many management principles, more than a few of them contradictory, and whether the real problem is determining how to employ them in very different contexts – contexts that often place significant constraints on management action."[41] Such scepticism is well founded. The last blog post on MLab's website, "Employee Centred Management," by Birkinshaw, appeared on 26 October 2011.[42]

When Harvard Business School asked in 2011, "What will be the single most promising area of research or study in the next 10 years?" the answers were predictable: "management of information technology, leadership, governance, innovation management, the networking of organizations, and social responsibility." Nitin Nohria, dean of the school, suggested that research was needed into "applying management principles to addressing complex social problems."[43]

Hamel remains convinced that big changes lie ahead. In a March 2012 *Financial Times* interview titled "Still on the Cusp of a Revolution," he says that "we are going to see a greater revolution in how companies are run and managed over the next decade than we've seen over the last 100 years."[44]

We shall see.

Help wanted

If there's one initiative that should inspire new thinking about management, it's Hamel's latest project, The Management Innovation eXchange (MIX). Taking a leaf out of his own book, and according to the project website, this is "an open innovation project aimed at reinventing management for the 21st century" by eliciting, provoking, and sharing new ideas.[45] Partner firms include London Business School, McKinsey, Gartner, and Australia National Bank.

In April 2013, MIX announced "The Leaders Everywhere Challenge," with Hamel and Polly Labarre asking:

What are some of the ways an organization might broaden its internal leadership franchise? Several leverage points come to mind. A company could ...

- Break big units into smaller units, thereby creating more opportunities for individuals to become full-fledged business leaders.
- Support the formation of informal teams and "self-organizing" communities where "natural leaders" get the chance to shine.
- Push down P&L responsibility and give lower level employees a lot more decision-making autonomy.
- Syndicate the work of executive leadership by opening up the strategic planning and budgeting processes to everyone in the organization.
- Use peer-based review and compensation systems to identify and reward leadership wherever it occurs.
- Systematically de-emphasize the formal hierarchy in favor of more fluid, project-based structures.
- Work to legitimize the notion of "bottom-up" leadership through communication and recognition systems.
- Distribute the work of critical staff functions by giving associates at all levels the opportunity to help reengineer core management systems and processes.
- Hold leaders responsible for increasing the stock of "leadership capital" within their organizations through coaching and delegation.
- And perhaps most importantly, systematically train individuals in the art and science of "leading without power."[46]

But all this came to mind ages ago. In fact, to lots of minds. So is it really a call to action, a step towards a new kind of management for the times we're in?

Crusaders like Hamel have changed the world. His dogged efforts must be applauded. The organizational changes that he calls for are badly needed. Maybe he will have more influence in bringing them about than others have done.

But while we wait for nirvana, be sure you do what you have to do.

Is anybody listening?

It's ironic that at the very time Hamel and others call for a shift to a more human-istic approach – Leavitt's half-century-old "first wave" – we see many aspects of management *practice* heading the other way.

Control tools like balanced scorecards and computerized "dashboards" are increasingly popular; KRAs (key result areas), KPAs (key performance areas), performance agreements, and service-level agreements are everywhere. Firms use a widening array of financial measures such as ROI, ROE, EBITDA, CFROI, and EVA™. While there's much talk about "flat structures," "matrix organizations," "social networks,"[47] "differentiated networks,"[48] "clusters,"[49] "lattices," "shamrock organizations" (Charles Handy's charming metaphor[50]), and "spaghetti organizations,"[51] hierarchies remain the design of choice.[52] And while we're told that top-down management is giving way to bottom-up management, and that we should think of strategy as design, work as projects, and temporary cross-functional teams as the way to accelerate innovation, none of these is normal.

We swoon when we hear about what happens inside Google, IDEO, or Whole Foods Market. We pay big bucks to listen to big-name gurus like Hamel or to rebel executives like Richard Branson. And we snap up books and articles that offer the promise of revolutionary management ideas. Yet in the majority of firms, little or nothing changes.

Is it possible that the majority of managers just don't get it? Can it be that untold millions of them, in firms across the world, faced with extraordinary challenges and under awful pressure to produce results, are so set in their ways that they keep doing the same old things for no good reason?

In some cases, yes. Even when there's a compelling case for change, managers may be unaware of alternatives or not sold on them, or comfortable with their management style, or just busy with other things. They may be happy with their current tools and techniques, which are familiar and seem to work, and there's not enough pressure on them to try something different.

In some cases, "If it ain't broke, don't fix it" might be prudent. But there's a fine line between complacency and thoughtfully staying with the status quo.

If there are better ways to manage, you owe it to yourself and your company to find them and try them. Maybe – just *maybe* – a "management innovation" will be the elixir that you need to succeed. But while you're hunting for one or waiting for it to come along, conventional wisdom may be the medicine you actually need.

However unfashionable it may be to admit this, many familiar practices actu-ally make sense. For example, hierarchies, while much maligned, offer significant benefits.[53] At times, autocratic leadership – "Do it my way, and do it now!" – is essential. Zero-based budgeting forces you to start with a clean slate rather than put a red line through items you're paying for now. Meetings provide a far richer quality of communication and interaction than even the best video-conferencing. People with goals usually outperform those who have none.

As more gurus jump on the bandwagon of management innovation, it's sure to become a focal issue in companies everywhere. Managers who are slow to get religion will be tagged as Luddites.

With so much changing all around us, it's hard to imagine that management practices will be unchanged in 50 or 100 years from now. But it's equally hard to imagine just what real changes might come about.

Tomorrow's winners in business will be those with a clear grasp of theory and practice, and a sober approach to both.

The promise of technology

If there was one factor making management innovation not just desirable, but absolutely imperative, it would be technology. Already, it has radically changed the way firms work. And as it continues to advance ever faster, its influence will grow.

More and more tasks will be automated in offices and on factory floors, and fewer, smarter people will be needed for many functions. More tasks will be out-sourced – not just to suppliers, but also to customers. New levels of complexity will become manageable, enabling companies to lower their costs and also offer new value. Workers in all functions will be empowered by easier access to more useful information. Many of them will be more mobile, and spend more time working away from the office. Decision-making and risk management will be improved through the availability of more and more information, along with the ability to dissect, explore, and learn from it – big data. Organizations will be more transparent, and areas of strength and weakness will be instantly apparent.

All of these developments have been predicted for decades. As they arrive, they're sure to change the way companies recruit, train and develop, manage, and reward their staff. But does this point to a revolution in what we know about management, and to a great leap forward in the practice of management?

The answer is no. The fundamental tasks of management will remain the funda-mentals. And the critical management practices will remain critical. Innovations may bring new effectiveness to these, but won't lessen their importance or take their place.

Knowing and doing are different

The message we're getting is a seductive one: *innovation in the way you manage will lead to innovation in products and services and the way you produce and deliver them, which in turn will lead to better profits.*

Management innovation → Value innovation → Profit improvement

Reality, however, is not this straightforward. Cause and effect are not as predictable as we might be tempted to believe. Innovations in management do not automatically lead to either new value or improved profits. The linkages are tenuous, at best.

The advice of gurus who talk about management innovation spans everything from idea markets and the wisdom of crowds to biotech breakthroughs and shrinking memory chips. One pushes real options in strategy, or the application of neuroscience in leadership or marketing; another goes on about the need to cut energy use in factories, improve security for online customers, or streamline delivery systems. Countless others agitate for breakthrough products and services that "take value to a new level," "disrupt the marketspace," and "create new wealth."

As a result, managers who get the management innovation bug don't know where to start. They're torn between experimenting with a way of managing that might only pay off years down the line, or coming up with new offerings that promise a quicker payoff. Chances are that most will go with the latter, as it's by far the easier way out. And anyway, without a changing value proposition, no firm can hope to be competitive for long.

The future of management obviously demands a lot of thought, which may yield some innovations. But are such innovations necessary? Should they be *your* priority?

If you believe that business performance cannot improve much with more of the same, then the answer is clearly yes. But before you go there, consider what "the same" might be. Is it what we *know* about management, or what you currently *do* in your company? In many cases, there's a world of difference.

If firms under-perform, it's almost certainly because they slip up in the critical practices, not because they lack new practices. So before you get carried away in a hunt for different answers than the ones we already have, start with what we've got. Concentrate on mastering those. Work at them for the next 30, 60, 90 days, and you'll almost certainly make changes and improvements that will serve you well in the future.

PART TWO

THE WAY FORWARD

11

ESSENTIAL PRINCIPLES

Well, you've been warned. With the keen help of the management advice industry, you run the risk of baffling yourself, complicating your management approach, and burdening your organization with theories and tools that won't help you get the results you want. There's a very real possibility that your ideas about strategy, and the way you make strategy in your firm, hurt rather than help your performance.

There are many ways to think about strategy. Most centre on how to make smart decisions while sidestepping the fact that it's human beings – with all their foibles and fallibilities – who make and execute those decisions. A plethora of tools assist with the analysis of markets, customers, competitors, and value chains. Others provide systematic ways to tackle issues that range from organizational design and innovation to productivity and quality. Their technical flavour is reassuring in a messy world, and they promise a safe and easy path to success.

But don't be duped. Aside from other weaknesses, their very purpose is to simplify things. And what they omit can be far more important than what they include.*

Crafting a strategy is nowhere near as straightforward as following a recipe to make a chicken pie (and even with the same recipe, two cooks won't necessarily get the same results). Successfully executing strategy involves insights, emotions, power, politics, attitudes, aspirations, relationships, judgment, skill, and many other human factors. It always requires learning and adaptation. Context always plays an overriding role.

Simplicity is imperative in organizational matters. But it's only a hop and a skip from there to being dangerously *simplistic* – to relying on naive and one-dimensional thinking that disregards the realities of working in a dynamic system

---

* My own models, which feature in this book, do the same. Hence my constant emphasis of contextual sensitivity in thinking about strategy, and of the human factors that take decisions in one way or another.

with tangled feedback loops that multiply as you work. So even as you strip away complexity, you need to accept it and embrace it. Only when analysis meets synthesis is it possible to come out on top in a VUCA environment.

Crafting and conducting a strategic conversation is not a straight-line, box-ticking exercise that can be wrapped up in a prescribed time, or that comes to a definite ending. It's a convoluted, iterative process that happens in boardrooms and retreats, at office coffee machines and in the gym. It involves one-line comments, brief chats and long meetings, and teleconferences and PowerPoint presentations. It moves along in fits and starts, doubles back, and twists and turns in unexpected directions. Decisions born from much agonizing in a workshop may be overturned before you get back to the office. Months of data gathering and analysis may be no match for gut feel or lucky breaks. A single customer visit can have more impact on your future direction than a costly consultant's report. An accidental insight or serendipitous encounter can change the course of history. Grand plans that emerge from the C-suite may fizzle in light of remarks by someone in an executive's family.

However, no company can do well for long by bumbling along and dabbling in this and that, and just waiting to see what happens. There has to be some clarity about its purpose and intentions, and certainty and coherence in what it does. This requires hard choices, which have to be made deliberately rather than by default.

But there also has to be openness to new information and ideas, and a willingness to take them on board and change direction in a heartbeat.

Striking this balance is never easy. Your best hope lies in a management approach based on sound principles and the eight critical strategy practices, and that combines patience with decisiveness.

Imagine this

You've just been appointed CEO of your company. As an outsider from another industry, you know little about your new organization or its challenges, even though you learned something about them during your interview process. Now, you're getting ready for your first session with the top team – all of them strangers to you.

Your intention today is to kick off a journey to better results than the firm has been delivering. This occasion also offers you a once-off opportunity to show off your grasp of business in general and *this* business in particular, explain what you stand for, and spell out your priorities and what you expect from the team. It won't necessarily be a make-or-break encounter, but your credibility is on the line. It's a big event!

What you say will set the tone for the future. So you'll do well to think long and hard about what your audience needs to know from you, and you from them. What will your key messages be?

I've sat through lots of these meetings, and it amazes me how ill-prepared many executives are for their all-important first moment in the spotlight.

Should you sound tough, knowledgeable, in charge, and clear about what needs to be done? Or should you try to come across as pleasant, folksy, humble, ready to listen and learn, keen to involve everyone in designing the future? Do you talk about yesterday's failures or tomorrow's possibilities? Should you spell out your goals this early? What should your key themes be? What *unspoken* impression should you aim for?

At moments like this, everyone's watching. A new leader always causes tremors. Some people are jumpy, because everyone knows about "new brooms." Some are thinking, "Here we go again." Bullshit detectors are finely tuned. Every word and gesture will be picked apart, interpreted, and recorded. One slip can have a lasting effect. Anything that sounds like a commitment or a deep personal belief will be filed away for later use, so to deviate or go back on your word will ring alarm bells as it'll show that you didn't mean what you said. This is where trust is established ... or destroyed.

There are as many ways to handle such meetings as there are to skin a cat. You might be tempted to go in with complete answers to every possible question, but that may be unwise. You might be better off using this first opportunity to spell out your point of view specifically enough to leave no doubt that you know what you're doing and that there's reason for confidence in you, but also broadly enough to leave some wiggle room – some space for discovery and invention. And for the input of others who've been around longer than you.

Many of the same challenges await if you're already in place as a leader. Maybe you want to announce a major acquisition. Or new growth targets. Or maybe your firm is in trouble and you have to turn it around. Or you have to deal with a competitor who's eating your lunch. In every case, you have to inspire confidence in yourself and the strategy you propose, and get people to back you. This can be a daunting task, and the stakes are high. So you need to give yourself the best possible shot at success, and not set yourself up to fail.

Here are some critical lessons I've learned – *principles*, in fact – that will help you. I've written about many of them for a long time. As with the eight critical strategy practices, they apply to every company, everywhere.

Lesson One: The Ten-Buck Test

All strategy involves the commitment of resources for a future you can't see.

Like you and me, companies have limited resources and many possibilities for using them. So managers have to make difficult choices and trade-offs, and whenever possible, apply resources to opportunities, not problems. They have to say yes to some things, but no to even more. Doing everything isn't an option. Trying to do too much is a key cause of failure. When you lose focus and lapse into "spray and pray" mode, you court trouble. Instead of being outstanding in one important thing, you inevitably become mediocre or hopeless at it – as well as at others that don't matter as much, if at all.[1]

Think about this as making bets for tomorrow, "ten bucks" at a time. And then subject every business decision – about products, markets, people, technologies, structures, systems, processes, projects, contracts, or whatever – to what I call "The Ten-Buck Test." Simply ask, "Is this the best way to use our ten bucks?" If it's not, you probably shouldn't do it.

Every bet is a risk. But every bet is also a *learning opportunity*: whether they turn out well or badly, they teach you something. Making them is the only way to move your firm forward, and to build the physical and mental muscle you need to compete. The faster you do this, the better, especially when you and your competitors are all doing more or less the same things.

This brings us to two concepts that can either make or break a business.

Strategic bets come with different levels of risk and reward. What they all share is that once made, they become "sunk costs." Some are easily reversible, while others offer no escape.

Ideally, as they add up, they make your firm stronger and give you a *rational* reason to keep going – and to commit even more to the same course. But if things go awry, *emotion* may stifle common sense and keep you moving in the wrong direction. "We've come this far and invested so much, that we can't quit now," you tell yourself. "Just another few steps, and the big payoff will come."

But the payoff you seek may never come.

On the contrary, the further you continue down the same path, the more vulnerable you can make your firm. Your bets lead to what economists call "path dependence," with successive commitments locking you ever more tightly into a particular course of action – and thus making it more difficult to *change* direction.[2] The very doggedness that's so essential to success can ensure your downfall.

Deep and valuable knowledge about an industry, markets, and customers can't be plucked off a shelf. Figuring out how to compete and designing and fine-tuning a business model seldom happens overnight. It takes time and hard work to develop resources, capabilities, infrastructure, and relationships, and when these are combined they can give you a competitive advantage that can't be easily or quickly copied. So while sunk costs and path dependence may lead to outcomes you don't want, you can't live without them. But best you think about them early, and try to anticipate their effects and mitigate whatever risks may come with them.

Strategy provides a context for your bets and helps you weigh them up before you make them. But the strategy must be clear and specific to do this. If, like many of the executives I meet, you fail to show 100 per cent commitment to a purpose, or keep changing your mind about where you want to take your firm and how you'll get there, you'll squander energy and effort. Necessary as "thinking out of the box" may be, it becomes the enemy of results when it gets more airtime than "Focus! Focus! Focus!"

Lesson Two: It's All About Framing

Peter Drucker effectively defined strategy when he counselled executives to think through "what is our business, and what should it be?" and "who is our customer, what is value to them, and how can we deliver it?"

Strategy is as much about choosing an advantageous market position as it is about choosing and executing the activities that deliver on the promise of that position. So it all comes down to sense-making – the creation and communication of *a point of view about where and how a firm will compete*.[3]

The common factor in all this is people.

As Chester Barnard observed in his 1938 book, *The Functions of the Executive*, companies are social organizations, and "the first executive function is to develop and maintain a system of communication."[4]

Such a system requires common language, clear messages, and an effective process. Providing these is the work of leaders – of strategists. Their effectiveness depends on how they frame and re-frame what their organization is about: its *situation*, the *challenge* it must deal with, its *theory of success*, and the *activities* in which it must excel.[5]

By crafting and conducting their strategic conversation around these four issues, with constant reference to the eight critical practices, they determine what gets talked about, and thus what gets attention and what gets done (Figure 11.1).

1. **The situation.** In crafting your strategy, nothing is more important than understanding the current state of your organization and its environment, and what stands between you and success.

To sensibly decide where you want to take your company, and how best to do it – and to manage the risks you'll surely encounter – you need to know as much as possible about conditions in and around your organization, what's changing, and what may lie ahead.

This knowledge won't guarantee success, but it does give you a sound basis on

Figure 11.1

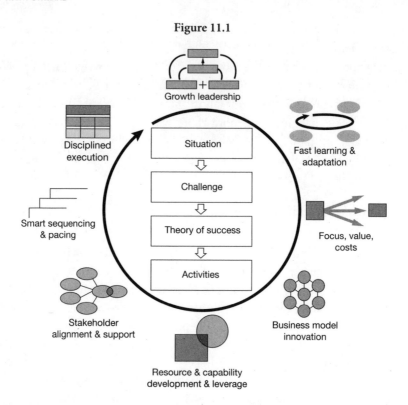

which to define your strategic challenge, set realistic goals, decide which activities you must excel in, and pinpoint your priorities. Uncertainty, on the other hand, will lead to a lack of focus and so to unnecessary costs, waste, and inefficiencies. And the less you know, the more likely it is that things will go wrong.

But the way you frame your firm's situation does more than inform decisions. It also sets a *tone* within your organization.

You could, for example, portray things as either promising or dire. Or you could speak of new regulation, a technology trend, or a shift in buyer behaviour as either problems or opportunities. Whether you're upbeat or downbeat will influence how people feel, which in turn will affect their behaviour, so you have to be mindful of how you come across. Initial impressions are sticky, and you may not be able to easily erase them. Actions do speak louder than words, and framing is about far more than just making a speech. Everything you do and the way you do everything sends signals, and the people around you watch like hawks to understand what you really mean.

A host of factors affect the way you see your situation. First, there's the mass of facts, impressions, opinions, and insights that you glean from social interactions, the news, reading, seminars, presentations, social media, debates with colleagues, customer visits, and innumerable other sources. This is your raw material, and you need lots of it. Then there are your cognitive capabilities – your mental processing power. And finally, there are filters such as your natural optimism or pessimism, and your mental models, values, prejudices, preferences, and experience.

These not only shape your perceptions of your current reality, but also your assumptions about the future, and thus how you define your strategic challenge. So this is where you can distinguish yourself from your competitors.

Even though you and your competitors may both have access to the same information, it's what you do with it that makes the difference. Cognitive capability and filters cause the same raw material to mean different things to different people. Faced with the same objective circumstances, you and your competitors are likely to arrive at different views of "the truth." The version you choose defines your strategy and powerfully influences the actions that follow.

This brings us to a paradox that every leader must embrace.

Napoleon is reputed to have said, "A leader is a dealer in hope" – his point being that you need to promise better times ahead, or no one will follow you. But Jack Welch, in typically blunt fashion, admonished leaders to "look the future in the eye, and see the reality that is, not the one you want to see."

Both statements are valid, and you have to keep them both in mind when you discuss your strategy. Crafting and conducting a strategic conversation demands facts, but it's your *attitude*, the way you project your message – and above all, your *actions* – that determine how those facts are perceived, and hence how they influence behaviour.

Some firms are able to break all records in terrible conditions, while others go out of business. The difference might lie in strategy, but the way their leaders choose to frame their situation invariably plays a part.

This is not to say that you should try to put a gloss on all bad news, or pretend that all's well when everyone can see that it's not. Honesty and straight talk can't be optional extras in strategic conversation. Without them, it's impossible to do the right things. You need them for effective decisions, and even more for effective execution of those decisions. If you refuse to confront reality, or massage facts, you'll create risks and destroy trust. And you'll soon be found out.

A clear understanding of your situation might be exactly what you need to light a fire under your team and spur them to action. But you need to avoid dwelling on the difficulties you face, and rather focus on what you and your team can do about them. So talk less about the past than the future. Use the way things are as a means to get to what they could be.

In an old joke that Ronald Reagan used to tell, a farmer finds his little boy digging through a pile of manure in the barn on Christmas Day. "What are you doing," he asks. And the kid answers, "If there's manure around here, there's got to be a pony!"

Strategy is about finding that pony.

2. The challenge. The first question in strategy is, "What is the question?" If you don't start here, and spend time coming to a precise answer, you and your team are bound to run around aimlessly.

Maybe there's a spectacular opportunity ahead. Maybe there are signs the economy is about to improve, and a surge in sales is likely. Maybe you're poised to enter a foreign market, take advantage of a new technology or distribution channel, strike up a new partnership, or merge with another firm. All of these call for particular actions. But you can't do everything, so you need to narrow down the possibilities.

But what if you're swamped by problems? Or even just one problem? What if a competitor has suddenly become more aggressive, and is cutting prices, opening new branches, and targeting your best customers? Or your offerings have passed their shelf life, and your business model has become obsolete? Or customers are deserting you, your sales are vaporizing, and your firm's survival is at stake? Again, in every case, you need to be clear about what the core challenge is, so you can craft your strategy accordingly.

3. A theory of success. Strategy is an *intention*, not a fact. Until you act it out, you have no idea whether or how well it'll work. But if you don't have an opinion on which activities and actions will lead to which results, you'll have no basis for designing your business model or planning your way forward. You won't know what to focus on, so you'll blow resources on needless work.

Your theory of success is a hypothesis which says, "If we do A, B, and C, the result will be D."[6] You might already have one, but chances are it's *implicit* rather than *explicit*, and fuzzy rather than precise – none of which is helpful. For only if you're totally aware of the logic of your recipe, and can spell it out to people who need to know it, will it be a useful tool.

This means, once again, that simplicity and clarity are paramount. So forget about writing a multi-page essay. Get to the point. "Given this situation, and facing this challenge, this is what we must do, and why, and how."

This is not rocket science. But don't take anything for granted. This is where the eight critical practices come into play, and each of them holds game-changing possibilities.

You might not be able to pare down your ideas to "one moving part" (to borrow from Drucker), but the closer you can get to that, the better.

4. Activities. The analysis and thought you put into your strategy has one goal: to ascertain the activities on which you should focus your ten bucks and the actions that will turn them into strengths and bring the results you want. This is where the rubber meets the road, and where winners emerge. Get this right, and you get off to a good start – instead of continuing to worry about *what* to do, you can forge ahead with *doing*. But get it wrong, and you'll fritter away your ten bucks.

The activities you choose must each have a specific purpose. They must also enhance each other, and they must function as a whole. So they must be chosen, designed, and configured individually, but with the *complete system* in mind. The same applies to your actions. Only through such symbiosis will you get the most bang for your ten bucks.

Porter's concept of an "activity system" provides a useful way of thinking about how a company can create unique value. But it doesn't tell the whole story. In focusing on *processes*, it ignores other factors that tell you which actions you must focus on, and that provide an enabling context for those actions, affect their execution, and may in fact be every bit as important as any of them.[*]

If your point of view about where and how to compete is to be of any worth, it has to be based on facts and logic. You have to be able to explain it fast. And insofar as possible, your audience needs to understand it – and feel as confident about it – as you do.

In contrast to this simple, sound, and practical approach, traditional ways of packaging and presenting strategy, whether in a document or a slide deck, are shockingly poor ways of framing it. Instead of simplicity, they bring complexity. Instead of clarity, they bring confusion. Instead of cutting to the chase and telling people, "Here's what we must do, and how, and by when," they leave them wondering, "Where are we going? Does it make sense? Can we do it?" And, most concerning, "So what am *I* supposed to do?"

I'm firmly convinced, by overwhelming evidence from myriad sources – and especially from my own interactions with thousands of managers and even more people in other roles – that this insanity is the reason so many firms cannot compete. They're crippled and often killed by their own conversations.

Framing is the one management tool every leader needs to be acutely conscious of, and to deliberately apply at every opportunity. It is, after all, what communication is all about, and what makes society and its institutions – including companies – what they are.

---

[*] See my 7Ps framework for business models on page 235.

Lesson Three: Clear, Concise, Coherent Purpose

Every business, like every human being, needs a reason to exist – a "hill" to aim for. This gives them context, direction, and an overarching goal, to both guide and inspire them.

Vision and mission statements are meant to do the job. Some firms have swung to "strategic intent," a term which has been around since Hamel and Prahalad invented it in 1989.[7] "Purpose" is also gaining favour.[8] So we have four notions that capture the essence of what a firm is up to, and it's not unusual for managers to use them all, depending on what pops into their minds.

Even when firms are consistent, few of them use any of these "tools" well. Managers lose sight of why they're necessary. Instead of being specific about where they want to go, and what they will and will not do, they waste their time on flowery prose that says nothing. Their first and possibly most crucial decisions fail to inform the goals and activities that follow. Without a compass, their people flail about and do their own thing, regardless of the greater good. And as it becomes increasingly impossible to align them, controls have to be tightened and even the smallest decisions have to be delegated upwards.

When CEOs brief me ahead of a strategy project, they almost always tell me, "We need to revisit our vision and mission." But more often than not, they can't remember what these say – and when I talk to their colleagues, it turns out that none of them can either. It's the same in my business school classes, where 20 or 30 senior people from a range of large firms have no idea of what's in their own statements. (And these are the very people who so diligently crafted that guff!)

You have only to suffer through one or two strategy sessions where senior people argue about the precise wording in vision or mission statements, to understand just how hard it is to create shared meaning. "Excellent," "the leader," and "world class," can be interpreted in countless ways. Companies inevitably fall back on the same words – service, innovation, integrity, responsibility, accountability, professionalism … yakkety-yak – for added gravity and excitement, but these also mean different things to different people, and are forgotten before the ink dries.

Deciding whether to declare that shareholders rank above customers, or the other way around, can waste a ridiculous amount of time. Even worse are tortuous debates about whether to insert a comma in a sentence, or a full stop; or to call your employees "associates" or "colleagues"; or to include an instruction to "Have fun!"

To help clients deal with this muddle, I remind them why they need any statement at all, and I suggest that they stick with purpose. It is, after all, what vision, mission or strategic intent are about. But I warn them that what they wind up with will only be useful if they ruthlessly edit their thoughts, and capture them in language that people will understand.

There are four questions to consider:

1. **Who do you serve?** Who is your "right" customer? What other stakeholders must you consider? How do you rank them, and what trade-offs are you willing to make between their various demands?
2. **What value do you deliver?** What do customers get from a relationship with you? What is your "difference"? What do you do for other stakeholders?
3. **Why does your company matter?** Why is the world better off for having you around? Why should anyone support you? What would it mean if you disappeared?
4. **What is your ambition?** What do you want to achieve, and by when?[9]

When you draft your company's purpose, you might be tempted – or pushed – to say more than you need to. But it won't help you to cobble together every thought you have about products, markets, people, and saving the planet. Nor will it help to proclaim your aim to be No. 1 or the leader or the most admired in your industry, without good reason or an explanation of what that means or how you'll know if you get there. Or to boast about your passion, ethics, and integrity, or your commitment to customers, brands, community, equality, or diversity. Oh, and by the way, that you will make superior profits too!

While such beliefs, aspirations, and qualities might be laudable, and you might indeed mean to work at several of them, they can't all be the reason your firm exists. Besides, the more bloated your purpose becomes, the harder it will be for you to remember and communicate, and the less likely it will be to guide or inspire anyone.

Your business purpose must be clear, concise, and coherent. It must signal immediately what you're about. And it must lead logically to the goals and activities that will bring it to life.

It serves a real and vital purpose. But only if you frame it tightly and don't get carried away as a wordsmith.

Lesson Four: Profit First

Organizations exist to create value for a range of stakeholders – all of whom think they should be first in the pecking order. However, it's impossible to treat them equally. If you suggest to your people that you should do that, they'll be all over the place – and you know what'll happen to your ten bucks!

In the good old days, few people would argue that the business of business was to make money for investors. But times have changed, and companies have had to become attuned to the demands of other stakeholders. Issues such as climate change and inequality are making news, and themes such as customer service, people management, and diversity have risen up management agendas.

The purpose of business as a social institution is a touchy one. The problems of the world will ensure it becomes the subject of even hotter debate in future. But there's no getting away from the reality that businesses exist to make a profit – and this won't change. They're money machines. They may have many goals, but producing more money than they use is No. 1. And the simple reason is that if they fail at this they cannot fund their future. They cannot replenish or upgrade their resources, improve their capabilities, or invest in innovation or marketing. Nor can they expand their operations or reward their people appropriately. Investors will abandon them. They immobilize themselves.

Whatever else they set out to do – uplifting communities, aiding charities, sponsoring education or medical services, caring for the environment, assisting suppliers, developing products and services for bottom-of-the-pyramid customers – they do for their own advantage. There may be an element of altruism, of course. But when you get past the PR spin, money is always the prime motivator. With few exceptions, shareholder interests trump noble intentions.

So managers' careers and earnings depend on their ability to produce superior and sustainable profits. Financial metrics have a firm hold on the top spot as measures of performance. Doing good is an increasingly necessary aspect of managers' jobs, but first they must make money for themselves and their investors.[10] No amount of public or political pressure will change this reality. Nor will it help to fudge definitions of sustainability or attempt to erase profit from them.

In 1970, Nobel Prize-winning economist Milton Friedman sent ripples of excitement across the corporate landscape with a provocative article in *The New York Times* titled "The Social Responsibility of Business is to Increase its Profits." Pulling no punches, he wrote: "In a free enterprise, private-property system, a corporate executive is an employee of the owners of the business. He has direct responsibility to his employers. That responsibility is to conduct the business in accordance with their desires, which generally will be to make as much money as possible while conforming to the basic rules of society."[11]

Friedman's view sends shudders down the spines of many people. The excesses of Wall Street are largely his fault, they say. As are many failures of corporate governance, the ethical missteps of managers, environmental damage, rocketing executive pay and depressed wages, brutal corporate restructuring and job cuts – and global poverty and inequality.

When Jack Welch was being considered for the top job at General Electric in 1980, he was asked by the then chairman, Reginald Jones, to spell out his views on running the giant firm. "What we have to sell as an enterprise to the equity investor," he wrote in a long letter, "is consistent, above-average earnings growth throughout the economic cycle.... The discipline to balance both short and long term is the absolute of such a strategy."[12] As a result of a speech he gave a year later, "Growing Fast in a Slow-Growth Economy," he has been credited with launching the shareholder-value-maximization movement.[13]

But even as managers joined it in droves, and even as investor influence has shot up, an increasingly outspoken and empowered citizenry and intense media scrutiny have scared the hell out of business. Powerful activists and movements like Greenpeace and Occupy Wall Street can't be ignored. Political pressures and regulation force firms to override their selfish interests and behave differently than they might otherwise do. Corporate social responsibility has become a major concern – not least among a new generation of employees. Business leaders have no choice but to proclaim their commitment to "doing well by doing good."

In his 20-year tenure as chairman of GE, Welch's aggressive attitude to growth won him the title of "Neutron Jack," and his ability to ride economic cycles and deliver strong earnings year after year was legendary. According to a *Business Week* article in 1997, "he often was asked: 'How much more can be squeezed from the lemon?' His standard reply was that there is 'unlimited juice' to be had by gaining greater operating efficiencies."[14] Yet in a 2009 *Financial Times* interview, he made an astonishing about-turn. "On the face of it," he said, "shareholder value is the dumbest idea in the world. Shareholder value is a result, not a strategy ... Your main constituencies are your employees, your customers and your products."[15]

If that shook managers, Michael Porter offers comfort. An economist himself, who has always pushed the primacy of profit, he has subtly adjusted his message. In a 2006 *Harvard Business Review* article, "Strategy and Society," he and Mark Kramer advocate "a new way to look at the relationship between business and society that does not treat corporate success as a zero-sum game."[16] And in a follow-up in 2011, they argue: "Businesses acting as businesses, not as charitable donors, are the most powerful forces for addressing the pressing issues we face.... The purpose of the corporation must be redefined as creating shared value, not just profit per se."[17]

On the face of it, these shifts are game-changers. But they're not all they seem to be.

Peter Drucker always saw profit as a result, not a goal, and wrote at length about the social responsibility of business. GE has always been mindful of its social impact, and even on Welch's watch, when it drew fire for various "social misdemeanors," such as refusing to clean up the Hudson River, it spent heavily on doing good elsewhere. Balanced scorecards are popular because they depict profit as just one measure among equals.

However, from careful reading of the articles by Porter and Kramer, it's clear that none of the firms they cite was prepared to forego profit, or put anyone but shareholders first, in producing "shared value." Whether they cleaned up their processes, served poor people, enabled entrepreneurs, or assisted communities nearby their operations, it was because *there are opportunities to make money doing these things.* Or at least, because it helped them polish their marbles so they could continue making money from doing business as usual in all other respects.

The need to create shared value isn't a new one. But today it's more important than ever for everyone – and will become even more so. Not for some fanciful reason, and not just because business is a social citizen and does have social obligations, but because growth opportunities in traditional markets are dwindling, and this is the only way to connect with previously unserved or underserved markets. Paradoxically, this means that making profits demands *more* attention, not less.

If the now popular term, "inclusive strategy," is taken to mean that all a firm's stakeholders will gain equally by its existence, or that profit is anything but essential, business will be imperiled. If, on the other hand, it goads managers into asking, *"How can we serve all our stakeholders to make bigger profits?"* we'll all be better off.

As I said in the first few pages of this book, companies are the engines of society, and humankind depends on management performance. But the needs of the world are outstripping the ability of business to play the role it should. This makes it all the more urgent that managers clarify for themselves what role they intend their firms to play, then get back to basics and do what makes sense and what works.

Why is this matter of the purpose of business important to you? Because if you're unclear about what you intend for *your* business – why it exists – your uncertainty will infuse everything you do. The pressures you face to be everything to everybody will have you bouncing from one stakeholder agenda to another, and you'll satisfy no one.

You may be deeply uncomfortable with the notion of shareholder primacy. You may sincerely believe that business has a larger purpose, and that your company is there for the "greater good." You might be convinced that you should put your people or your customers first, or that innovation should be your clarion call. But think about it. Think about the logic and the implications of whatever you decide. Ask: will it get you *all* the results you seek? Will it get you the support you need? And will it apply through the inevitable business cycles that affect every firm?

Agreeing with Friedman, another Nobel economics laureate, Robert Solow says, "It's not the business of the individual manager to say, 'What would be good for the health of the economy?' It's primarily the business of the individual manager to increase efficiency and profitability."[18]

The choice is yours. For me, it's clear that profit comes first, though with due attention to the range of other factors that contribute to it. This should not be something to fudge or deny.

Lesson Five: Balance the Basics with "Searing Insights"

If there's one question that bedevils strategic thinking and gets strategists' knickers in a twist, it's this: *Should you start with where you are or with where you'd like to be?*

The answer is, you have to do bits of both. Strategists have to manage the present and the future at the same time. They have to run their current businesses as well as possible, but with a long-term purpose so they have direction and don't zigzag all over the place. This requires that they excel in the basics, while at the same time seeking breakthroughs that will lead to future success. And that they know what they will do to get from here to there (Figure 11.2).[19]

Figure 11.2

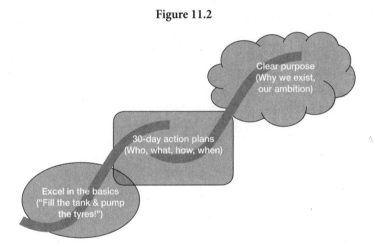

When CEOs call me to talk strategy, they almost always have radical change in mind. They want innovation rather than "mere" improvement. Yet often, when I learn more about their firms, it becomes clear that a "moonshot" is not the first thing they should aim for.

What they should do instead is get their basics right – or, as I tell them, *"Fill the tank and pump the tyres!"*

Finding novel ways to do business is no easy matter. It requires resources and concerted effort. It seldom happens overnight. Besides, any organizational change brings stress, and extreme changes are usually systemic and traumatic. If a firm's foundations aren't sound, reinventing its strategy can throw everything out of whack.

Managers who can't get their current business to work properly are unlikely to do better trying to invent and run something totally new. If they're unable to make the most of what they've got, there's no reason to back them when they gamble on the unknown.

This is not to say they should forego radical changes that might be necessary for their future growth and survival. A major revamp of their businesses might well be the only thing that'll save them. But this shouldn't be a distraction from fixing what's broken or not working, and wringing every last drop of sales and profit from the current business. Often, there are huge untapped opportunities right under managers' noses. Yet they blithely leave money on the table while they chase after "a better way."

Whether managers like to acknowledge it or not, every business is bound by the rules of whatever game it plays. For all the noise about traditional industry definitions having given way to new notions of "market space," and despite the hullabaloo about "strategic degrees of freedom," "blue oceans," and "thinking out of the box," most companies have less freedom than they imagine to change those rules.

In times past, industry boundaries might have been obvious and stable – seemingly cast in stone. Today, they may be blurred and shift constantly. But as fast as one innovator redefines them, others follow. As markets mature, a "dominant logic," is figured out, tested, and settled on by many players. New rules are established. Soon, competitors all do roughly the same things in roughly the same ways, and their offerings converge.

But bucking the system can be fatal.

When Lou Gerstner took on the challenge of turning IBM around in the early 1990s, he came under intense pressure to break "Big Blue" up, and change direction. But he refused, saying,

> It is extremely difficult to develop a unique strategy for a company; and if the strategy is truly different from what others in the industry are doing, it is probably highly risky. The reason for this is that industries are defined and bounded by economic models, explicit customer expectations, and competitive structures that are known to all and impossible to change in a short period of time.[20]

This is why banks behave in many ways like other banks, steel companies like steel companies, and oil companies like oil companies. One fast-food chain might sell chicken while another sells burgers, but their underlying operations are much the same. A manufacturer of jam doesn't have infinite choices about what ingredients to use, how to make the product, or how to distribute it. Nor can it act like a business selling motorbikes or insurance. Sure, there may be lessons to learn from other industries, but there are "boundaries" too. And the jam maker's competitors are equally constrained by them.

Sameness is imposed by regulation, and facilitated and accelerated by the rapid adoption of common management practices, the global diffusion of information and technology, and the ready availability of services and finance. All of these cause firms to act like each other, leaching away any differences in their offerings and leading to a proliferation of me-too products and services.

In big, evolving markets this may not matter immediately; there's room for everyone – at least for a while. But as competitors race down the same path, they start falling over each other. Before they know it, customers can't tell them apart and bruising price wars erupt.[21]

And things get more complicated. Many firms operate within complex webs of stakeholders, all hustling for influence. Companies that compete head-to-head with similar offerings face the threat of complementary and substitute products and services that change the way value is perceived and delivered. Factors such as information, rising consumer power, global supply chains, outsourcing of virtually every function, and competition from non-traditional players all muddy the waters.

The notion of "key factors of success" has been around for decades. And although innovation junkies treat it with scorn, and you hear about it less often than in the past, it's as relevant today as ever. You and your team might have a lot of fun if you throw caution to the wind and begin your strategic conversation with visioning and "backcasting,"* but you can't wish current reality away. You are where you are and the sector you compete in is what it is. So get the basics right, and you'll put yourself in the best possible state for success.

What are "the basics" in your business?

Systematic analysis is essential in thinking about a firm's rules of the game. But on its own, it won't lead to lasting advantage. Without an element of magic, all the logic in the world isn't worth much.

In a comment on his book *Giants of Enterprise*, a study of seven famous busi-

---

* Thinking back from the future.

ness leaders, Harvard historian Richard Tedlow observes that they "all stood for something in their company, in their industry, and in society. In addition, they all had a *searing insight* they were able to communicate clearly and concisely to others – like Henry Ford's observation at the beginning of the 20th century that what people in the country needed was an inexpensive automobile."[22] (My italics.)

Do you have a "searing insight" about your business? What is it? Put yourself in the shoes of your people, customers, competitors, or others, and imagine what it sounds like – and means – to them. What actions will it lead to? What behaviours will it drive?

> ## What's your "searing insight?"

All this presents you with a difficult balancing act. Managing the present and the future at the same time requires masterful orchestration of your strategic conversation. People must be kept mindful of the constraints they face in a particular market, and working at the basics, even while they're encouraged to break loose and explore new possibilities. And resources – *that darned Ten-Buck Test again!* – must be allocated in ways that make possible results in both the present and the future.

Lesson Six: Choices for Action

To emphasize their bold, overarching, and long-term intentions, nations and armies have a long tradition of packaging them as "grand strategy." This is stirring stuff, so management thinkers were bound to follow suit. In an early definition of corporate strategy, Harvard Business School professor Kenneth Andrews said this:

> Corporate strategy is the pattern of decisions in a company that determines and reveals its objectives, purposes, or goals, produces the principal policies and plans for achieving those goals, and defines the range of businesses the company is to pursue, the kind of economic and human organization it is or intends to be, and the nature of the economic or noneconomic contribution it intends to make to its shareholders, employees, customers, and communities.

Business strategy, he said – or what would now be termed *competitive* strategy – was "less comprehensive and defines the choice of product or service and market of individual businesses within the firm."[23]

Andrews and his HBS cohort taught legions of managers to think of strategy as a high-level view of how a firm should go about its business. Their students happily accepted this, given the virtually universal belief at the time in top-down control. They were more than content to wallow in platitudes and vagueness while giving short shrift to *activities* and *action*. If they were ultimately responsible for tough decisions, the laborious analysis that underpinned them was for lesser mortals. Micro-management was a pejorative term, and being branded a micro-manager plainly marked you as not being a leader.

The "vision, mission, values" gang continues in this tradition, as sure as ever that lofty notions and fine intentions will bring the results they want amid the scrum of hypercompetition. But this ignores two costly disconnects between strategic intentions and results:

Disconnect #1. Messages are lost in translation between the C-suite and the front line. Strategists decide one thing, and people who're supposed to make it happen choose to do something else. Or they follow instructions, but do it badly. Or they fail to adapt what they must do as circumstances change.

Mixed messages are a fact of organizational life. It's normal for high-level strategy to be ignored, misinterpreted, or side-stepped at other levels – sometimes deliberately and sometimes because nothing is clear. And managers themselves either cause or worsen both problems.

They overestimate their ability to make themselves understood, and underestimate how much ongoing time and effort it takes. They assume that saying something once is enough. And that what they say arrives in other people's heads exactly the way they said it, and means exactly what they intended. And they kid themselves that when they speak, they're *believed*.

Communication is without question the biggest challenge in any company. Just because we all do it every day is no reason to think it's easy or that we're good at it. More than anything else, it makes the difference between success and failure.

Disconnect #2. The future is highly unlikely to turn out as the masterminds upstairs assume it will. Despite their best efforts to stay in tune and in touch, they only become aware of many changes long after they've emerged – and certainly long after people anywhere near the action can sense them. By the time they snap into action, and get around to redesigning their strategy and issuing new orders, it's too late. If, like so many, they stick to a one-, three-, or five-year planning cycle, there's no chance that they can stay in sync with their context. A divide between what they do and what they should do is assured. And the gap keeps getting wider.

These disconnects are so normal and so evident, and their impact so serious, that you'd think there would be more alarm about them. But managers keep getting predictable surprises on both counts. Things seldom work out as they expect. Their scintillating schemes are constantly upset by human nature, the internal machinations of their organizations, and the unpredictability of the outside world. Good intentions turn out to be no match for harsh reality.

Most firms continue in this futile mode. But as it has become increasingly apparent that strategy is only as sound as the activities that underpin it, and that turning strategy into action is finally what counts and is always a challenge, smart managers have come to realize two things.

First, no amount of analysing and scheming will on their own bring success. The only thing that will do that is being better at a selected set of activities than rivals are. Since deciding what not to do is every bit as important as deciding what to do, every component of a company's business model must be carefully chosen. They must all mesh with each other, and the effect of each must be amplified through meticulous execution. The whole must be greater than the sum of the parts.

And second, strategy is a learning process. Commitments must be made, but they're for a future you can't quite see. So the best you can do is face up to that risk and then learn and adjust as fast as possible.

The past three decades have thus seen a distinct shift in thinking about strategy – at least by some people. Whereas once it was considered to be an intellectual undertaking, all about decisions and quite separate from the messy business of doing actual work, now the line is blurred. Whereas once it was assumed that the future would be much like the past, and that strategy could and should be designed to unfold in a predictable way over multiple years, today even the shrewdest strategy can unravel in days or weeks. So if ever there was merit in fussing about the difference between strategy and tactics, or about the relative importance of strategy and operational excellence, that time is long gone. Such hoary debates slow things down just when they need to be speeded up.

Strategy is not a desk job. Strategic thinking guides action, but learning through action is the only way to keep strategy relevant and effective.

The famous Tom Peters battle cry to "Try lots of stuff" is just what many companies need to hear. "Ready, fire, aim" goes down a treat in management conferences, and Nike's "Just Do It" has been filched by any number of managers keen to show their mojo. But just being busy won't make any company competitive. Action without reason is likelier to bring costs and risks than positive results. Action that doesn't lead to useful learning is wasteful.

Studies by McKinsey Global Institute have shown that in the same industry across countries there are "almost always dramatic differences in either labor productivity or total factor productivity." These differences, says Robert Solow, who has long served as academic advisor to MGI, were to be explained not by differences in technology or investment, but rather by "organizational differences, to the way tasks were allocated within a firm or division – essentially to failures in management decisions."[24]

For strategy to be effective, it must be specific, not only about high-level aims, but also about the actions that will occupy low-level people. Anything less is just hot air.

- Fred Gluck, founder of McKinsey's strategy practice, made a point of this in a 1979 paper that he drafted for the consulting firm's staff, in which he advised that strategic planning should result in an "integrated set of actions designed to create a sustainable advantage over competitors."[25]
- According to UCLA professor Richard Rumelt, "Strategy is a way through a difficulty, an approach to overcoming an obstacle, a response to a challenge." The cleverest strategies, "the ones we study down through the years, begin with very few strategic resources, obtaining their results through the adroit coordination of actions in time and across functions."[26]
- Michael Porter writes, "The essence of strategy is choosing to perform activities differently than rivals do."[27] The primary purpose of a strategy is "to inform each of the thousands of things that get done every day, and to ensure that those things are all aligned in the same direction."[28]
- And Eric Van den Steen, a member of the HBS Strategy Unit, provides the best definition of strategy that I know of, saying it's "the smallest set of choices and decisions sufficient to guide all other choices and decisions."[29]

All of these experts make it plain that strategy is not an end in itself, but rather a means to *getting the right things done*. This has led to another shift: in the way managers understand their roles and how best to drive performance.

Struggling to wring results from strategies that too often ape those of their competitors, they've relied increasingly on execution to differentiate themselves. This has brought a sharp rise in the number of books, articles, courses, and conferences on execution, many pointing to the need for intense, hands-on involvement in operational matters. So management by vague decree has given way to managing by getting down and dirty in the trenches with the troops. Micro-management is alive and well – though practised under the cloak of empowerment, "leaderless teams," "self-organization," and other fashionable notions.

There's a lot to be said for the "loose-tight" approach identified by Peters and Waterman in *In Search of Excellence*.[30] Managers have everything to gain from being more overt about it, and everything to lose by pretending that loose is good and tight is bad.

The dilemma, as with so much else, is how to strike the balance.

Lesson Seven: Strategy Is Change Management

Strategy doesn't have a neat beginning and end. Creating and executing strategy can't be cleanly separated. Insights, action, and results are bound together in an intricate process. Change is always the intention – and it must be the outcome of every strategy intervention.[31]

When I wrote my first book, *Communicating for Change*, in 1987, I examined many change-management models, and concluded that all of them were based on four essential steps:

1. Create dissatisfaction with the status quo;
2. Debate possible futures;
3. Act to learn;
4. Review and revise (Figure 11.3).[32]

The same process applies to strategy (more on this on page 229). And because both strategy and change management are about getting a firm to a different place, separating them is illogical. But that's typically what happens.

Making things worse, efforts to bring about change usually begin and end with trying to change people's minds so they will change. That seldom works.

Figure 11.3

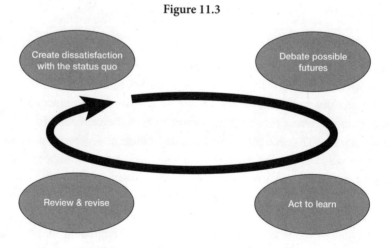

Leaders often have clear opinions about what needs to change in their firms. But as my simple model shows, and as Edgar Schein confirms, there's a lot to gain from involving other people early in coming to a view on what must change, and why and how. Sharing power this way means you don't have to sell the need for change or try to convince them that you're right. Having summed up a situation themselves, they'll be more inclined to consider different possibilities, and to act on them. And when they then reflect on the results, they're almost certain to say, "So far so good, but there's more to do" – so the cycle becomes self-perpetuating.

The emphasis from the start and throughout is on action. On enabling people to practise new behaviours, and on learning by doing. On taking advantage of success to build confidence and encourage further progress. And as we'll see, these are all key to making a firm fast and flexible.

I can't remember when last I walked into a firm where there was no change-management project under way. This is astonishing, given that they're costly and distracting and have a terrible record, with study after study showing that around three quarters of them don't deliver the expected results. Hiring consultants to help with them seems smart, but often is due to managers dodging the work themselves. Instead of seeing change management as an integral aspect of strategy and thus of everyday work, they treat it as an oddity – an add-on and a nuisance, that they can safely hand off to someone else.

The four-step process that I've outlined applies as much to wrenching, company-wide "strategic" change as it does to lesser problems such as moving office, shifting to flexitime, bringing in new technology, or introducing a new procurement system. And it applies equally to any effort to improve innovation, quality, or productivity.

Change may demand new organizational arrangements such as HR policies, promotions, pay, and incentives. It may be helped along by an internal communications or training programme, the upgrading of equipment or offices, or a new corporate identity or advertising campaign. But what really triggers and sustains it is a new conversation.

Change management always was, and always will be, the work of leaders. They craft and conduct the strategic conversation that cycles through these steps. Consultants and HR executives can help the process along, but change is not their job. It's the job of anyone who is responsible for the performance of other people. Only they can bring it about and make it a way of life.

Lesson Eight: A Single, Seamless Conversation

Most people see leadership, strategy, and change management as discrete tasks to be worked at separately, at different times, and probably by different people (Figure 11.4).[33] But this is a flawed paradigm, which leads to unnecessary work and costs, destroys agility, and is no doubt a significant cause of poor performance.

Figure 11.4

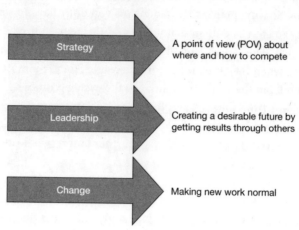

From the moment you start thinking about where and how to compete – or maybe even before that – you should also be thinking about how you'll turn your intentions into action. And since executing strategy almost always requires your people to change what they do and how they do it, it's a change-management challenge.

Even as you start working your plan, you should be thinking about how you'll change it when you need to. Strategy cannot be cast in stone. Your environment changes constantly, and you have to adjust to it.

The change cycle makes it glaringly obvious that leadership, strategy, and change management are in fact integrated in one seamless, continuous process (Figure 11.5). Each affects the others. It makes no sense to deal with any of them in isolation.[34] Doing so is sure to get in the way of performance.

Figure 11.5

Leaders must be both strategists and change managers. Strategists need leadership and change-management skills to get results. And change management begins when you make strategy, and is dependent on leadership.

Each of those functions depends on one and the same tool – strategic conversation.

Lesson Nine: Everyone Needs Strategic IQ

Shortly after a senior executive once introduced me to a colleague, he said, "He wants to be a strategist; what's the best way to do that?"

This should be a concern to every company. Every organizational activity relates to strategy in some way or other. But because strategy is seen as a specific function, it occurs to few business leaders that there's value in building strategic capabilities across a wide swathe of their people. So achieving this is seldom an explicit goal, and little effort is made to provide opportunities for it to happen.

Strategy is a learned skill. It's a slog. It requires knowledge, perspective, wisdom, and courage that no amount of formal training can provide. Without having lived, and soaking up information and experience – and without actually "doing" strategy – you cannot become a strategist. Strategic IQ doesn't come from the pages of a book.

Sure, some people may have a feel for numbers, an innate ability to quickly see what matters in a sea of information, or a way with words. But that's only a start. Becoming a strategist is a matter of long practice rather than a birthright.

Exposure to many situations is a prerequisite. It's one thing to read accounts of clever strategies or debate case histories, but nothing beats having to shoulder responsibility in a crisis or make life-or-death decisions. As one study suggests, it's especially useful for executives to defend their firms against a takeover – a real war toughens them up and teaches them things they wouldn't learn otherwise.[35] But not everyone will live through such an extreme event. Everyday battles must suffice.

Just as you can't learn about soldiering from watching war movies, you can't learn about business strategy from the sidelines. You have to do it to "get it."

Companies that deliberately facilitate the learning process will have a huge advantage over those that don't. The opportunity lies in using everyday work as the route to growth.

Social and emotional skills are the subject of diagnosis and development. Strategic-thinking skills warrant the same attention. So formal training in futures and systems thinking, analysis, and decision-making should reach more people than it does. But *informal* development – real-world practice in making strategy – is equally vital. "Presence of mind requires constant practice," says William

Duggan, associate professor of management at Columbia Business School, in his book *Strategic Intuition*, "so you expect the unexpected every waking moment."[36] Only by involving people in your most important strategy debates will they learn as much as they need to, and become as valuable as you expect them to be.

By now, you've probably heard about ice hockey ace Wayne Gretzky's famous saying, "You have to skate to where the puck is." You have to anticipate where it will be. How can you do that? Is it guesswork? Can you analyse the speed and direction in which the puck is travelling, compute your own speed and direction and the position of other players, decide on a new move, and – *almost in the same instant* – change direction? No doubt some of that just happens in the frenzy of a game. But more likely, your unconscious takes over, and instinct sets your course.

Studies of chess masters, and of exceptional performers in other fields, show that it takes about ten years of intense study and practice to become expert. This has led to the notion of "the ten-year rule."[37]

- When Gary Player was a young man, he modelled himself on Ben Hogan, one of the greatest golfers of all time, who was famous for practising relentlessly to develop his "muscle memory." Player spent ten hours a day on the practice tee, hitting 1,000 balls each session. Later, when he was one of golf's "Big Three," and someone suggested that he owed his success to luck, he snapped back, "Yes, and the more I practise, the luckier I get."

- Seven minutes from the end of the 1995 World Cup rugby match final between South Africa and New Zealand at Ellis Park, Springbok Joel Stransky caught the ball, spun around, and booted it straight between the goalposts to win the match. It happened so fast, he had no time to think.

  At that critical moment, Stransky didn't need to think. At least not consciously. Years of training, practice, and game experience clicked together and told his muscles what to do.

- In a wonderful little book called *Zen in the Art of Archery*, published in 1953, Eugen Herrigel, a German philosopher, tells how he learns archery in Japan as a means to understand Zen. The first year is devoted to learning to draw the bow "spiritually." Then follow months of practice in releasing the arrow. And then more months and years of work, until after one shot, the Master exclaims, "Just then 'It' shot!"[38]

  "It" shot itself. Herrigel had spent five years learning how to get out of his own way.

- Steven Spear, a senior lecturer at MIT and an expert on auto manufacturing, describes how a fictional young engineer with two master's degrees starts work at Toyota. For the first six weeks he watches workers on the production line, looking for ways to help them improve. This is followed by another six weeks watching machines operate, and thinking about how he and his team can increase their uptime. Then comes ten days in a Toyota factory and supplier plants in Japan, watching and learning some more.

At the start of each week, the engineer meets with his boss to talk about the work ahead. They meet again at the end of each week to discuss what's happened. Along the way, the new recruit discovers the value in observation, and learns the importance of allowing his work teams to find their own solutions to problems. Only after this immersion is he given real responsibility. And that's the start of a continuous learning process.[39]

Companies send people on strategy courses, but ask them why and they'll tell you, "Peter needs to catch up with the latest concepts," or "It'll be good for Maia to do a refresher." But while this might be helpful, it doesn't turn people into strategists.

Courses, reading, and exposure to experts are all helpful, but ultimately the only way to develop real competence is through deep immersion in strategy-making in the hurly-burly of the workplace.

It strains credibility to imagine that *everyone* can become a brilliant strategist. And most employees will probably never be directly involved in "strategy" roles in their firms. But if they're given the chance and the encouragement to learn as much as possible about strategy, they will undoubtedly be more effective in whatever work they actually do. They'll be better equipped to handle new challenges and assignments, and their firms will be better equipped to compete.

12

THE CRITICAL PRACTICES

Companies that do exceptionally well in the future will be those that are most intensely focused on the possibilities of tomorrow. They will be curious and adventurous, and driven to do more, better, faster – at ever-lower cost. They will bring us astonishing new products and services, delivered in ways we cannot yet imagine. And they will change the way we see the world, think of ourselves, and go about our lives.

These firms will work in a way that is informed by history, grounded in reality, and known to bring the best results. They will have a clear view on what it takes to compete and win, and will pursue bold goals through the imagination and spirit of their people. The eight critical strategy practices will be the core of their approach, and they will apply them resolutely and with discipline that borders on the fanatical.

Now, let's look more closely at those practices.

You might wish for long explanations about them, along with a full set of instructions for implementing them. But if I spell things out, you won't need to figure them out. And that's not the best start if you're to make ideas your own.

So I'm staying with my own mantra that less is more, and simpler is better.

I'll tell you why you need each practice, and how they add up logically to a powerful approach to management. And I'll suggest some of the issues and questions you need to consider in order to compete today and in the testing times that lie ahead. But the rest is up to you.

You'll get the most from the practices by reflecting on what you read here, thinking about them and talking about them with your team, and then deciding for yourselves how to apply them. Learning by doing is the essence of the Harvard case-study method, the Toyota Production System, and every successful approach to change management. As the adage says: "Give a man a fish, and you feed him for a day; show him how to fish, and you feed him for a lifetime."

Just as you don't need to keep scrabbling for new ideas in what Drucker so aptly called the "'management gadget bag,' of techniques for the efficiency expert,"[1] neither do you need as much guidance as you might imagine to implement any of these practices. There are no deep secrets here, only common sense. Having worked on all of the practices, with countless companies, I can assure you that they're easy to understand and introduce without extensive handholding. Excelling in them will take hard work, but if you keep reminding yourself why you need them, and persist in using them, you'll get what you want from them.

Let's be clear about the real purpose of all concepts, tools, or techniques:

Every management idea is a framing device – and no more than that. All of them are based on particular assumptions about what leads to success. All that any of them does is promote and explain a particular approach to dealing with one issue or another, and encourage a certain way of talking about it. This, in turn, influences decisions and actions.

On their own, management ideas do nothing. Until they provoke and shape conversations, they're worthless. For until that happens, they have no effect at all on behaviour – or results.

Balanced scorecards get managers talking about the range of performance measures most important to them. Porter gets them talking about whether to pursue a "generic" strategy or one aimed at "differentiation," and how best to structure their "value chains" or "activity systems." Disruption theory invokes discussion about "sustaining" and "disrupting" innovation, "the job to be done," and "good enough" offerings. And the language of lean processes draws attention to doing things "right first time," and the elimination of costs and waste.

The eight practices define what you and your colleagues must talk about, and hence what you'll pay attention to and where and how you'll apply your resources. Together, they're based on the assumption – which is borne out by abundant research – that to be competitive, every company must:

- Be led by people who are driven to grow their business, and to do it by growing their people;
- Learn what's happening in its world, and adapt, faster than rivals;
- Focus on making a difference that matters to specific customers, and continually deliver new and better value to them while also lowering costs;
- Design and create a sound business model – and change it when necessary;
- Get whatever resources and capabilities it needs, continually strengthen them, and use them to best effect;
- Develop and maintain sound relationships with stakeholders;
- Do things at the right time and speed;
- Be highly effective at execution.

Excellence in all of these requires that you talk about them – and not now and then, but constantly. Only by doing that will they ever become habits, and add up to an unassailable advantage.

Along with the principles I described in the previous chapter, what follows will enable you to craft and conduct the strategic conversation you need now and in the future.

#1: Growth leadership

The first imperative for success is leaders at all levels with an unswerving commitment to growth, who live the tenet: "*Grow the business by growing the people*" (Figure 12.1).

Figure 12.1

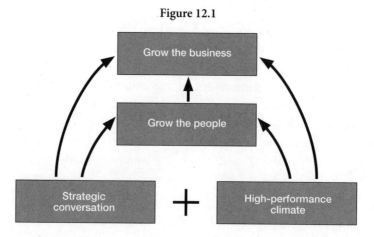

Growth – in sales and profits, as well as resources and capabilities – enables a company to survive in a hostile world, fund its future, and play a positive social role. If a firm doesn't get stronger, it will become weaker in relation to its competitors and less appealing to customers and investors; and other stakeholders may either shun it or take advantage of it.

So you may choose how much to grow, or how fast, but "grow or die" is a binary choice.

But make no mistake: business growth is neither natural nor normal. It doesn't come just because you turn up or make rousing speeches about it. It's an *aberration* – an out-of-the-ordinary product of ambition, risk-taking, investment, innovation, and action; and also, perhaps, of luck. It often involves many setbacks and a great deal of discomfort.

Growth is born from the imagination and spirit of people, and results from both the fierce implementation of bold decisions and excellence in the small stuff. The single most valuable contribution of leaders is that they shape the conditions that foster it. So they must *want* it, and be driven to seek the market and organizational opportunities that will make it possible. They must have a clear "theory of success" to provide direction and guide choices about strategies, programmes, business model design, activities, and resources. And they must enable and inspire their people to perform at their best, to continually improve themselves, and always to push the bounds of possibility.

They do all this by crafting and conducting the conversations that are the seed-bed of growth.

Of course, much else must be put in place, and we'll come to that shortly. But all depends on people. Nothing happens without them. Only if they volunteer insights and ideas, cooperation and effort, will a firm perform anywhere near its potential. They are either a limiting factor, or an engine of opportunity.

We all know this. There are no surprises here. Except, perhaps, why so many companies persist in acting as if it were not true!

It's not unusual for senior executives to be ambivalent about growth. Or to express bold ambitions while failing to table strategies or build organizations that have any hope of achieving them. But their most common mistake is to not put their people front and centre of their strategies.

So the first and most important management practice – the one that affects all others – has to be a focus on people. On hiring well and managing them in a positive and constructive way, while at the same time growing them so they become more capable and confident.

Achieving both of these goals depends essentially on two levers. The first is strategic conversation, because that crystallizes a firm's theory of success, and determines what gets attention and the actions that follow – and thus what people experience and learn. Second is a high-performance climate, as that determines how people are able to work, and how they feel about doing it – which affects their motivation and facilitates exceptional endeavour and achievement. Only by coupling an effective strategic conversation with a high-performance climate can you get the results you want.

That climate is shaped partly by the bundle of organizational arrangements that enable results – structure, working environment, policies, pay, and so on – but perhaps even more, by the kinds of people who are hired and how they're managed. So matters like management style, skills, culture, communication, decision rights, training and development, and coordination and control, all come into play.

The social aspect of strategy is so important that short-changing it is bound to hurt results. Yet in too many firms "people issues" are treated as an afterthought – a hassle that HR can deal with. This is foolish and short-sighted. The HR function is critical, but *only managers can manage their people*. It is they who craft and conduct the strategic conversation, and they who create the climate in which people work by coaching and mentoring, guiding and inspiring, and providing rapid feedback and frequent praise.

"Growth leadership" is not a catchphrase. It's not a fad, an optional extra, or an on-off project or intervention that can be applied here or there or sometimes. It must be an everyday practice, and be evident everywhere. So it must be a core philosophy in your company that is embraced by everyone – but most especially by anyone with any responsibility at all for the performance of others.

#2: Fast learning and adaptation

We live in a world of constant, rapid, and often unpredictable change – a VUCA environment. The pace of change and its magnitude vary from industry to industry, but all firms sooner or later have to face the reality of turbulence, surprise, and disruption. All executives have to make decisions for a future they can't see. They have to keep making those ten-buck bets, and the stakes are high.

No method exists to provide perfect foresight. No amount of scenario-planning, SWOT exercises, or big data crunching will do it. Predictions are big business, but fortune tellers and other futurists have an abysmal record.[2]

Shell has used scenarios for more than 30 years, and is their most famous champion. But even so, the company missed three of the most significant changes of the early 21st century: China's sudden emergence as an economic power, the anti-globalization movement, and the spread of global terrorism.[3]

Nate Silver has a formidable reputation as a statistician, and might have been remarkably accurate in forecasting the outcome of the 2008 US presidential elections, but he can no more see the future than anyone else.[4] His predictions for the 2015 UK general election were as hopelessly wrong as those of most other pollsters.[5]

The "black swans" that Nassim Taleb warns about are everywhere. "Almost everything in social life is produced by rare but consequential shocks and jumps," he says, "almost everything studied about social life focuses on the 'normal,' particularly with 'bell curve' methods of inference that tell you close to nothing."[6] Yet shortly after his book *The Black Swan* hit the shelves in April 2007, and then flew off to become a bestseller and make "black swans" an everyday term, the Great Crash caught all but a few economy watchers off guard. Then came the Arab Spring, the rise of Isis, the collapse in the oil price, Russia's invasion of Crimea, and so on – with none of us any the wiser about what's next.

"We are blinder than we think," says the bestselling economics writer Tim Harford.[7] And that includes all of us.

But there's little pity for managers who use this as an excuse for poor performance. Through thick and thin, they're expected to deliver. They have to produce results, even in the "fog of war."

The only way they can keep their firms relevant – and *alive* – in an ever-changing context, is by being hyper-alert to what's going on, and speedily adapting their strategies and operational activities to new circumstances. There's obviously a role for systematic forecasting techniques, but it's even more vital to develop four specific organizational capabilities that will make this everybody's work:

1. *Sensing* change early and *making sense of it*;
2. *Imagining* possibilities;
3. *Doing* something about them;
4. *Reflecting* on what's happened in order to learn and exploit experience, build new strengths, and maybe adjust course.

These capabilities are linked in a continuous cycle. They frame what you and your colleagues need to talk about as you deal with the challenges of the day. So they're the golden thread of your strategic conversation and thus the essence of the strategy process (Figure 12.2). And since they're also a natural outcome of that conversation, the surest way to develop them is simply to keep referring to them and reminding people of their importance.

Figure 12.2

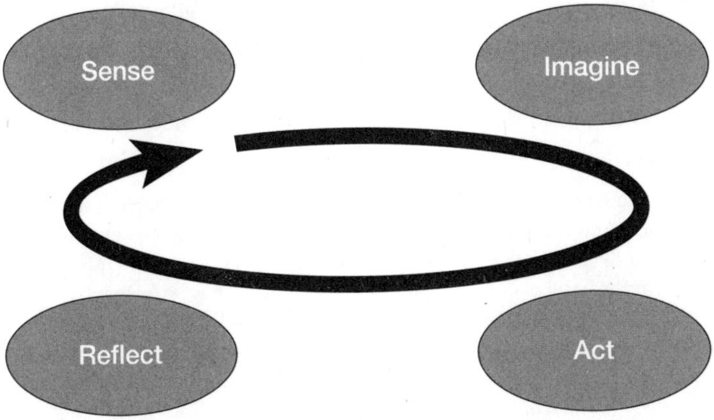

Because even insignificant human interactions are essential enablers of fast-cycle learning and adaptation, almost all of them provide opportunities to make your company more alert and more agile. There are three ways to make sure that they work for you:

1. Make a big thing about the four capabilities. Post a picture of the cycle on your walls. Encourage people to ask, before any speech, any meeting, any decision, or any change: Which of the four skills is this about? How can we make the most of it in what we're about to do?

2. Since you can't know who among your employees will offer the next insight or idea that could change your business, go with "the wisdom of crowds." Make information widely available. Encourage people to read, watch the news, and debate current affairs. Open up lines of communication. Tell people that you value their views, and encourage *all* of them to speak up. Ensure that they're heard – and that they know it. Ask probing questions. Ask for insights, ideas, and advice. Dish out praise at every opportunity. And perhaps offer incentives for the really good stuff.

3. Assign small teams to concurrent activities and lots of low-cost experiments. Break down tasks so they can be shared among individuals and groups, with tight timelines for results. Make rapid feedback normal. And as the aim of this process is learning and adaptation, and not perfection, go out of your way to applaud both success and failure.

In the race to the future, what I call "fast-cycle strategy" provides valuable advantages, so it has to be a way of life in every part of every organization.[8] It applies to strategy altogether, but also to every function, and every activity.*

Sensing, imagining, doing, and reflecting affect everything your company does and the way it does everything. So constant effort must be made to entrench and strengthen these capabilities – and to moving through these steps faster than your competitors.

You will no doubt have noticed that this cycle not only explains the strategy

---

* Similar cycles underpin the advice of pioneers of the quality movement (remember the Plan-Do-Check-Adjust method advocated by Deming and Shewart), and of the latest thinking in that field (Jeffrey K. Liker, *The Toyota Way*, New York: McGraw-Hill, 2004). They also form the basis of current military practice. And they've been implicitly or explicitly suggested by authorities on learning, leadership, and strategy, such as Chris Argyris (*Knowledge for Action*, San Francisco: Jossey-Bass, 1993); Noel Tichy (*The Cycle of Leadership*, New York: HarperBusiness, 2002); Karl Weick and Kathleen M. Sutcliffe (*Managing the Unexpected*, New York: John Wiley & Sons, 2007); Donald Sull (*The Upside of Turbulence*, New York: HarperCollins, 2009); Willie Pietersen (*Strategic Learning*, New York: John Wiley & Sons, 2010); Peter J. Williamson and Eden Yin ("Accelerated Innovation: The New Challenge from China," *Sloan Management Review*, Summer 2014); and Eric Ries (*The Lean Startup*, New York: Crown Business, 2011)

process, but also *precisely maps the change-management process*. The very actions that ensure your company's survival, and are key to its growth, are the same as those that are essential in driving change – and thus in leadership, quality improvement, continuous improvement, and innovation:

- **Sensing** change almost always triggers **dissatisfaction with the status quo**;
- **Imagining possibilities** is most likely when you **debate possible futures**;
- **Doing** things means action, and it's by acting that you **learn**;
- **Reflecting** is a vital aspect of **reviewing** progress, and of knowing what to revise.

By enlisting all your people as your firm's eyes and ears, and involving them deeply in important conversations whenever you can, you gain in multiple ways. For one thing, they'll become aware that change is a crucial aspect of competitiveness – and that *they* have an important role in strategy. Second, they'll alert you early to what's changing in and around your organization, and what might need attention, and they'll bring you suggestions for dealing with it. Third, they'll be motivated to act when called on to do so. And fourth – and here's a huge bonus – they'll learn about strategy and develop their own strategic IQ.

All this is free.

So simply by staying alert and deliberately talking about what's going on, conditions are created for change. And your firm becomes more fleet of foot and more agile.

These discussions should happen not just in strategy meetings, but in other meetings too. They should also happen at the water cooler or over a sandwich at lunch – in fact, almost any time people get together. This keeps the need for change top-of-mind, and makes them less inclined to resist it. And it not only triggers "what if" thinking, but also entrenches it in your company culture.

For conversations to have value, they must be about the real issues – both positive and negative – that affect organizations. And since we live in an unsettled world, and bad news is so prevalent, bad news is likely to get a lot of airtime. This may raise fears, which can immobilize people. But it also presents an opportunity, as it can increase their dissatisfaction with the status quo, and spur them into action. So you need to be sensitive to what's being said, and to the tone and the mood, and balance reality and hope in your strategic conversation.

#3: Focus, value, costs

"Concentration of forces" – i.e. *resources* – is one of the oldest principles in strategy. The Ten-Buck Test has to be applied to everything you do, and the way you do everything. You have to focus your resources on the "right" customer and not get into spray and pray mode in an attempt to satisfy everyone. You have to clarify your "difference" and why it matters, and put in place a way to deliver it.

Drucker's *who, what,* and *how* questions demand hard choices. But no matter how astute the initial decisions may be, they alone won't enable a firm to sustain its competitiveness for long.

Follow the logic:

1. Different customers seek different value. By and large, they all want to get as much as possible, and pay as little as possible. But they range along a spectrum, with those who want maximum performance at whatever price at one end, and those who'll be satisfied with much less – but at the lowest possible price – at the other.
2. By setting clear criteria for which of them you should chase and who to ignore, you narrow your target market and improve your chances of success. You define your *right* customer – the customer who's best for you – by considering factors such as their profit potential, their expectations, how easy it will be to reach and attract them, your after-sales obligations to them, what they'll do for your reputation, what you'll learn from them, how they pay, and what competitors offer them. You then weigh up your choice of customer against your *real* ability to capture and keep them. And you're ruthless about scratching from your prospect list anyone who doesn't meet your criteria.
3. Once you know where you're going to focus, you ask: What is our difference, and why does it matter to that customer? And using your knowledge of them, and of your competitors, you create a compelling value proposition.
4. Finally, you think about what it'll take to deliver on your promise, and you design a business model to do it.

This, according to much of what's said about strategy, will give you a unique advantage. A *sustainable* competitive advantage.

But beware of jumping the gun and assuming you're set to compete and win.

In theory, you could do this thinking on your own, or perhaps with a small team. Or you could leave it to a strategy department or consulting firm, and simply endorse whatever they come up with. In reality, however, logical, rational decisions provide no more than a starting point from which to pursue competitiveness. They'll get you only so far.

The overall context is in turmoil. Customers are a moving target, with changing needs, wants, and buying behaviours. Competitors innovate and improve relentlessly, make new promises, and drive down prices. Whatever value you offer today will have a short shelf life. So just to keep up, let alone get ahead and stay there, requires you to constantly drive customers' perceptions of value *up*, while simultaneously driving your own costs *down*. There's no other way to win (Figure 12.3).

And this is a *social* challenge. One that requires the imagination, initiative, enthusiasm, energy, collaboration, and hard work of people across your organization, and of other business partners too. You can't impose these, and no amount of planning will unleash them. Nor will all the technology or systems in the world help. Quite simply, key stakeholders must *volunteer* themselves to this task, or you're stuck.

Figure 12.3

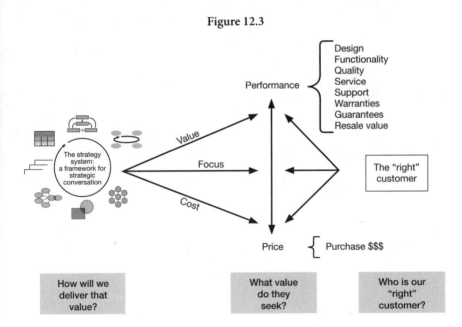

If you watch competition unfolding in almost any sector today, this is what you see happening. So to cling to the notion that you can plan a perfect strategy around the who, what, how questions, and then sit back and watch the money roll in, is to ignore reality. Strategy is a living process, and competitiveness is a moving target. Both rely as much, and maybe even more, on rapid improvement and innovation, flexibility, and adaptation. These have to be integral aspects of strategy, and not optional extras. *All the critical strategy practices must kick in and support your focus-value-cost intention.*

#4: Business model innovation

A company is a value-delivery machine. Its business model is its operating blueprint – a description of how it creates and delivers value for its various stakeholders – so it frames key choices and decisions that managers must make, and depicts them as a system. And whether explicit or implicit, every company has one.

Because business conditions change constantly, and companies must keep offering new value, business models can become obsolete while you're thinking about other things. What works in one period can be a recipe for failure in another. So the race to the future is essentially a race for business model innovation.

Ideally, your theory of success should guide the design of your business model. But what actually happens is often different. A firm's concept of how it should function typically takes shape over time, and not altogether deliberately, as it works out how to survive. Changes also occur here and there in the organization. Interest in yesterday's practices wanes. New practices creep in, some of them unseen. The theory of success – if ever it existed – becomes something else.

Managers in upstart, internet-centric firms appear to give a lot of attention to their business models, but few others do the same. Managers talk about specifics such as strategy, product offerings, organizational structure, or processes, but rarely address their value-delivery system in a holistic way. They seldom ask: "How can we reframe our business to produce different results?" This makes them vulnerable in the short term, and doubtless hurts their profits. It also lessens their chances of finding better ways to compete in a different future. And every commitment they make to their current model – those ten-buck investments – makes inertia more likely.

One excuse for not thinking about your business model is that "What we're doing works." Another is that other matters seem more urgent. But the most common reason is that managers simply lack a way to address the issue. Although the term is bandied about by analysts and business journalists, it appears far less often in business books or serious journals, or is buried amid other matters. It's hardly ever highlighted as being critical, and it doesn't feature prominently in business agendas.

In fact, there's nothing mysterious about business model design. As my "7Ps" framework shows (Figure 12.4), the focus should be on a set of key factors which add up to a view of how you compete. Thinking through them separately and in combination will help you evaluate your present competitive strength, identify your weaknesses, and hopefully see new possibilities. It should also foster conversation about the *linkages* between the elements. Like a system of gears, the components obviously have to fit snugly together and turn smoothly.

Figure 12.4

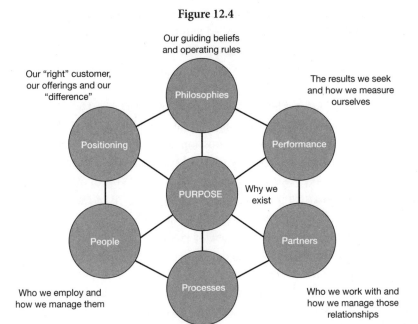

I developed this framework after Harvard Business School professor Christopher Bartlett and Sumantra Ghoshal, a professor at London Business School, published a series of three articles in *Harvard Business Review* in 1994–95, based on a five-year study of 20 successful global firms.* "Senior managers of today's large enterprises must move beyond strategy, structure, and systems," they argued, "to a framework built on *purpose, process,* and *people.*" This was necessary because "The great power – and fatal flaw – of the strategy-structure-systems framework lay in its objective: to create a management system that could minimize the idiosyncrasies of human behavior."[9] (My italics.)

That was a lightbulb moment for me. I'd published an article of my own, just before the Bartlett-Ghoshal series, in which I outlined a model for strategic thinking based on 7Ps.[10] I had always been convinced that the role of people in strategy was underplayed, and I'd been thinking for a long time about how to elevate it. The 7S framework developed by Peters and Waterman went some way towards this, but fell short as an aid to designing business models. But now I immediately saw the potential for creating a new framework for business model design, that would

---

* Their findings were later published in their excellent book, *The Individualized Corporation,* HarperBusiness, New York: 1997.

capitalize on those troublesome "idiosyncrasies of human behavior." And after interviewing Bartlett by phone,[11] I added four more elements than he and Ghoshal had highlighted, to create such a framework – the 7Ps.*

When you design your business model – or redesign it – think about this:

Purpose – every business leader must ask and answer two of Drucker's favourite questions: "What is the business?" and "What should it become?" He was probably the first to describe these as its mission and vision. But as I pointed out in Chapter 11, these terms are so badly misused and abused that there's a strong case for simply asking, "What is your business purpose?" Why, in other words, does your company exist? Chances are, you'll be able to say it in fewer words – and more clearly – than if you went the mission-vision route.

A compelling purpose obviously helps you align efforts and apply resources in an integrated way. But more than that, it frees you from the urge to use strategy to prescribe every move far into the future. Telling your team, "We're going for Hill X, not Hill Y or Z," is a first step towards empowering people to contribute their own ideas about how to get there. And it's essential if they're to be trusted to make appropriate decisions in the heat of battle, perhaps far from home, without having to keep referring back to a strategy document or a boss.

Philosophies – these are the guiding beliefs and operating rules that affect every area of a business, from its Purpose to its market Positioning, from its Performance criteria to its People, and from the way it engages with the Partners in its ecosystem to its Processes (the other six Ps).

Examples of questions to ask: Should we go for top-end customers, or chase those for whom price is everything? Should we make or buy what we sell? Should we encourage open innovation or pursue it in-house? What kinds of people should we hire and how should we treat them? How will we balance our responsibilities to various stakeholders? How should we handle difficult customers, or customer complaints and service issues? Should we be diligent about maintenance, or get to it only when there's an accident or a breakdown? How far should we go in caring for the environment? How serious should we be about good governance, and what measures will we put in place to ensure it?

One firm's philosophy will be to invest in bleeding-edge technologies; another will invest more cautiously. One will have a hearty risk appetite, while another

---

* The version here is the product of 20 years of trial and error, using this framework with numerous companies; yet despite extensive use with clients, it differs from the original only in that Products has been replaced by Performance.

will be happier with smaller bets. One will try to keep a mature business alive at all costs, while another will deliberately eat its own lunch.

By proactively thinking through the assumptions that underpin your theory of success, you avoid having to do so when you're under pressure or somehow caught off guard. You also ensure that your Ps are aligned, and that people won't make on-the-hoof decisions about one of them that clash with those about the others. By making your philosophies known, everyone knows where they stand, and what's acceptable or not. So like purpose, they're a means to empowerment.

Positioning – this is where you decide: Who is our "right" customer? What value (products or services) do we provide to them, with what features and benefits? And what is our "difference"? To make wise choices, you need as rich an understanding as possible of your customers and your competitors, of the dynamics at play in the marketplace, and of the trends or forces that might disrupt them.

It's one thing to choose a position, and quite another to defend it against aggressive competitors. Is this *possible*? For how long? What will you need to do to hold on to it? What will cause its value to erode? What will make it *im*possible? Who might threaten you, and how? What might cause your customers to change their relationships with you, or leave?

Positioning can be a powerful source of competitive advantage, and should be the backdrop to every strategic conversation. But in most industries, it's becoming less easy to sustain whatever advantages it confers, so its ally – *execution* – is accordingly becoming more critical. Unexplored markets are few and far between, and once-attractive niches are being carved up. More analysis and slicing-and-dicing will bring diminishing returns. Nor are branding and customer loyalty programmes any assurance of future sales or profits. You may out-think your enemies for a while, and you should try; but you should also aim to out-run them, by doing what you do better and faster than they can. It's the only way to win.

Performance – Every company needs to excel in a range of activities, so it has to set goals and measure its performance using a variety of metrics. But in their efforts to be thorough, and to control as much as they can, most of them try to be too precise about too much – often even putting numbers to things that can't be measured. They keep adding to their to-do lists, and in no time everyone has too many goals or key performance indicators (KPIs). This is not only massively time-consuming, but also gums up the review process, pins people down, and wreaks havoc with the empowerment that firms so fervently espouse.

In fact, there's no need to know everything about everything. A simple set of metrics will serve most firms – and certainly most people – perfectly well. So you need to decide what matters to you, what you have to know, and how the information will be accessed, presented, or used. And your high-level targets must link clearly to those at a functional and personal level, and to the actions that will follow.

People – This covers everything from who you hire, to your company climate, culture, and management approach; and from your organization's structure and HR arrangements, to training and development. This is where Growth Leadership comes into play.

Customers aside, there's no aspect of business where good intentions are less evident than in these matters. In almost every strategy assignment I've ever worked on, people have featured surprisingly low on the agenda. Assertions about people being "our most important asset," or ambitions to be "a great place to work," are mostly hollow. Yet without people, an organization is nothing. No other lever has the same impact on results.

Every firm needs people with the right mix of skills, attitude, and experience. Some know exactly what they have and where the gaps are, and have excellent recruitment and development programmes. But many are uncertain about who's there and who they need – or who they should let go. They're slack about replenishing their pipeline, their retention efforts are misguided, and development is an afterthought.

Very few decisions about people can be made on a purely rational basis. Here, perhaps more than in any of the other elements of your business model, your core beliefs – your philosophies – can and should override all else. So you need to be especially aware of them, and take them into account. If you ignore them, you might strike it lucky with some of your choices, but it's far likelier that you'll make lots of costly mistakes.

Partners – Even small firms today have more stakeholders than in the past. A swarm of players influence their ability to function, and their competitiveness (see Critical Practice #6), so building sound relationships with them has to be high on any strategist's agenda. This is especially the case with those stakeholders you can describe as business partners.

Investors, suppliers, your people, and their labour unions naturally fall into this category. But you need to look outside of your organization too. Work is increasingly outsourced or given to temporary workers. Supply chains are becoming more complex, and suppliers and distributors play a growing role in value-adding processes. So do *customers*, who are becoming "prosumers." And research scientists, financiers, and advertising agencies all contribute directly to your success.

You might have established relationships with many of these today. But are you getting all you need from them? Are there other ways you might collaborate with them? Are there more that you should be working with?

Processes – Companies create, deliver, and capture value through a set of processes, which in turn comprise various activities. Strategy determines what's needed, but competence and performance in various activities make any strategy feasible and worthwhile – or not.

Many processes and their component activities are internal, and under your control. But many occur externally, and coordination and control can be onerous. Your ability to do this can be a key source of either strength or weakness.

Every function, from R&D and administration to manufacturing and marketing, involves numerous processes. Some of these are routine, so can be solidly embedded into your organization. Some only come into play from time to time, so there has to be a way to bring them in and get them up and running – often very quickly – when you need them, and to let them go when they've done their thing.

Processes are just one element of your business model, and most are elements in a *system of processes*. So they have to not only fit and enhance your overall business model, but also fit together and enhance each other. Only when they do both, will you be able to drive value up and costs down. If they don't, you'll destroy value and add costs.

Before you settle on any process, be clear about what you expect it to do, and ask: Will it bring the results you want? How will it affect whatever else you do? Will it enable you to scale up your business? And look ahead and consider how you might make it more valuable in the future, and when and how you might need to improve or replace it, or do something else altogether. What will your options be then? What will *their* impact be? What else will you have to change?

Remember, that from the moment you adopt a new process, and especially when it comes with big costs, path dependence kicks in. So you need to be as sure as possible that what you begin will take you where you intend going, and that you'll be able to make it more and more of a strength over time, rather than being thwarted by it.

The 7Ps framework is a diagnostic tool that encompasses both the hard and the soft issues that contribute to your competitiveness. It helps you systematically unpack your organization, poke into its innards, and engage your team in new conversations. This obviously should be done with some regularity – perhaps as part of your normal planning process. But it will have even more value to you if you reflect on it continuously.

Every aspect of your business model is in constant flux. Every one of the Ps offers opportunities to make your firm more competitive. Only by thinking about them one at a time, all the time – and all together as well – will you exhaust all your possibilities.

Until then, don't assume that you've run out of ways to improve your performance. Until you've taken your business model apart and thought about each element of it, and considered how they interact with each other, you're probably foregoing opportunities for profit and growth.

#5: Resource and capability development and leverage

A company's resources (the inputs it requires to create value) and capabilities (the skills and processes that enable it to turn those resources into value) are vital assets (Figure 12.5). These define both the game a company can play and how it can do it. Competitiveness originates in the way they're combined.[12*] Since their value erodes as circumstances change, they need to be constantly enhanced or replaced.

Some resources are "hard": they're "things" or "stuff" which are generally visible and include cash, buildings, plant and equipment, raw materials, and components. Others are "soft": they're knowledge-based, and include data, brands, reputation, patents, and relationships.

Figure 12.5

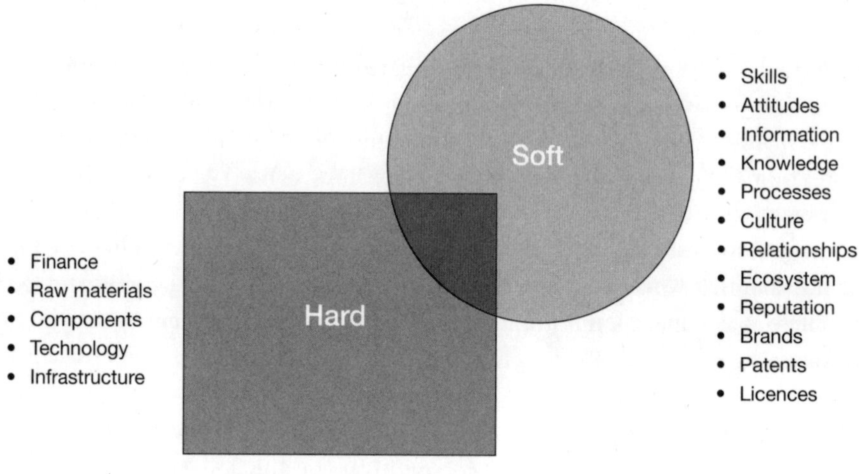

- Skills
- Attitudes
- Information
- Knowledge
- Processes
- Culture
- Relationships
- Ecosystem
- Reputation
- Brands
- Patents
- Licences

- Finance
- Raw materials
- Components
- Technology
- Infrastructure

Soft

Hard

---

* The resource-based view of the firm, core competence, and dynamic capabilities all rest on such combinations and mean essentially the same thing: what enables you to compete.

Some resources may be quickly, readily, and even cheaply available. Some are rare, costly, and hard to get or develop, maintain, and keep. With few exceptions, though, they're available to anyone who wants them and is prepared to pay for them. So for many firms, they're no longer the competitive advantage they once were – unless they are used in new ways.

Capabilities are a different matter altogether. They enable you to find new ways to use resources, and to apply them. They're always soft, so you can't buy them off the shelf. For example, it can take years to build a brand or a reputation or learn how to miniaturize an electronics product, build a "green" car, or operate in a foreign market. Even if you hire skilled people, it takes time for them to fit into your organization and for their knowledge to diffuse through your team. And a packaged training programme only shows its value when what it teaches becomes a way of life – which doesn't happen overnight.

If you don't have a reasonably clear view of where you intend taking your company, your approach to developing resources and capabilities will be haphazard. You'll face constant dilemmas over where to spend your ten bucks. Instead of methodically and holistically bolstering your strengths, you'll waste money and effort on a stab here and a stab there. Nothing will ever gel as it should.

Since path dependence is an inevitable consequence of developing resources and capabilities, the very strengths that you develop in your business can lock it into a strategy that becomes inappropriate.[13] Changing direction may become extremely difficult and time-consuming – or impossible. So in making any commitment, you should keep flexibility firmly in mind. Measures such as outsourcing work, employing temps, leasing equipment on short-term contracts, or entering into partnerships with clear exit terms can greatly enhance your adaptability.[14]

When you assess the worth of your resources and capabilities, beware of seeing value that's not there. Merely performing some or other activity doesn't make it a core competence or distinctive capability. If customers don't care about what your combination of resources and capabilities does for them, they won't buy from you. If those resources and capabilities don't enable you to do something special for them, they won't pay your price. And if your resources and capabilities don't enable you to earn superior profits, there's not much point in them.[15]

Owning a fleet of trucks is of little benefit if competitors keep their costs lower than yours through leasing. Massive server farms and sexy algorithms won't give you an edge for long if others are able to copy you. Mastering the use of laser technology in your factory won't help you if the products you make don't offer customers unique and meaningful benefits.

An inside-out approach to strategy will never get you to the best combination of resources and capabilities. You have to take an outside-in view too. And you have to keep revisiting your conclusions, and adjusting your bundle of assets.

#6: Stakeholder alignment and support

Most companies today have a growing array of stakeholders who have some or other interest in them, and can effectively "vote" for or against their success. These might be individuals, groups, or organizations. Some will be more aligned with your goals than others. Their power varies too, and they exercise it in different ways.

Some, such as shareholders, staff, suppliers, distributors, and customers, are keen for you to succeed, are very directly involved with your business, and require constant attention. Others are less "in-your-face," less influential, and less demanding. Competitors mostly want to make life hard for you, or are intent on seeing you fail.* Regulators can allow you to have a shot at success or *ensure* that you fail. The media, lobbyists, and other activists hold powerful sway over your reputation and your ability to conduct your business (Figure 12.6). The shape of this ecosystem and the power dynamics within it are sure to change as players come and go and change their minds.

Figure 12.6

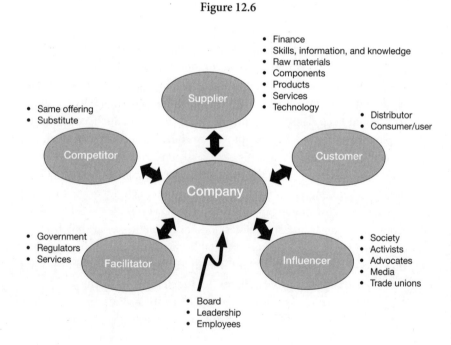

---

* In some instances, "good competition" is in everyone's interests. The existence of a number of competitors may keep regulators off their backs, and some level of industry stability is good for profits. Competitors may also play other valuable roles, for example, as suppliers or distributors.

Insofar as possible, these players must be persuaded to act in support of your firm's goals. To help rather than hinder you. To line up in total support of your efforts to build win-win relationships with customers (Figure 12.7).

Figure 12.7

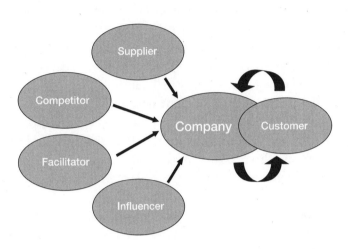

Stakeholder management is a never-ending communications challenge. To deal with it, you need to be clear about who your stakeholders are, and how they influence your business. You need to understand their agendas, and what they can do to affect your fate. And you need to develop deliberate strategies for managing your relationships with them,* and assign specific people to doing it.

Because all firms have many stakeholders, and interact with them in many ways – face to face; through various media; and via intermediaries, contracts, employee relations, logistical arrangements, services, structures, and an almost infinite number of others – this is not "a job" that can be left to a communications department. It has to be everybody's business.

That's one more reason for your strategy to be clear, and for all your people to understand your intentions.

#7: Smart sequencing and pacing

Strategic planning is a taken-for-granted activity in most firms, even though it has a dodgy reputation. It clings doggedly to top spot among management tools,

---

* The need for stakeholder management applies similarly to "value ecosystems," open innovation, and crowd-sourcing, all of which are being increasingly adopted as ways to accelerate innovation, cut costs, and lock-in customers.

despite mounting evidence of its weaknesses. If ever there was an example of hope upstaging common sense, this is it.

In theory, plans – whether strategic, tactical, or operational – should be detailed and precise. In the real world, however, this often proves to be pointless. Any plan is only as sound as the assumptions it's based on, and these are often hopelessly flawed; but even if they're not, the environment keeps changing in surprising ways, and what makes perfect sense one day makes none the next.

Meanwhile, new issues suddenly become priorities, critical projects hit potholes and delays, and costs run wild. Enthusiasm fizzles, and day by day, wonderful plans unravel and become increasingly irrelevant.

But this doesn't mean that you don't need plans, or that you should give up on planning. What it does confirm is that you need to be realistic about what's feasible and what you should aim to achieve. That while you need to be as specific as you can, you also need to allow yourself the space to change your mind. And that *crafting and conducting your strategic conversation is always a work in progress.*

To achieve what you intend for your company, you should have a roadmap of sorts, and some idea of how you'll get where you want to go. Resources are limited, and you can't do everything – and certainly not all at once. And as you advance, you have to coordinate a multiplicity of actions. So although you'll have to make many decisions on the fly, the process can't be altogether haphazard, nor can you leave everything to the winds of chance or the whims of the moment.

Some issues demand immediate attention, and you have to respond fast. But do they affect the fundamental thrusts of your strategy, or make its key themes redundant? Probably not. But if there's a hint that they might, you need to pause for breath, put them into perspective, and think about what that might mean altogether.

A single issue can throw a strategy out of whack. But strategy is about more than one unexpected problem or opportunity. Having done your thinking and made your choices, there are some things that you have to keep doing, in spite of the noise around them.

These larger decisions should be made, and acted on, in the order and at the time and speed that make most sense. Some must come before others because they're building blocks for what follows, and without a solid foundation you'll run into trouble later. Some must be swift, in order to seize an opportunity or steal a march on competitors – or just because it's possible. Always, you should try to move at the speed that suits you, rather than what's *apparently* dictated by some external force. And you need to be resolute about this, because more often than not you'll have more time than you're led to believe. Someone else's "urgent" doesn't have to be yours.

Being first to market can be an advantage. Getting in early lets you establish a base, grab the choicest customers, sign up the most powerful business partners, and possibly define the rules of the game; and it gives you time to tweak your strategy. On occasion, though, it will be wiser to advance in a more measured way – to "sniff the wind," learn from the experience of others, and make your moves when you have a clearer sense of what it'll take to play and win.[16]

Penetrating any new market can take far longer and be more difficult than you think. It's the same with launching a new product into an *existing* market, or changing some aspect of your strategy. There's always something to learn, and you have to put resources and capabilities in place. You might think you can move faster by skipping a few steps, but it might be impossible. Or you'll pay for it later. Moving too fast can be every bit as perilous as moving too slowly.

Stretch goals are a powerful way to unleash energy in a firm, but they need to be carefully balanced with "baby steps." Asking people to achieve things that are clearly out of the question is pointless and dispiriting. At best, they might get marginally further than they otherwise would have, but there's a risk that any sense of achievement will be dampened by the reality of failure.

Project managers know that the best way to complete an assignment is to break it down into pieces, with tight but reasonable delivery dates for each of them, and to tackle first things first. They understand that success in one task motivates performance in the next. Yet other executives tend to be careless about these matters, and often rush headlong into trouble as a result.

A useful way to map your path to the future is to draw what McKinsey refers to as a "strategy staircase" (later termed "horizons to growth"), which shows what you'll do in Year One, Year Two, and so on (Figure 12.8).[17] Seen like this, it's apparent that you have to learn to walk before you can run; that some things simply cannot be done before others, no matter how badly you might want them to; and that all commitments have consequences.

When you have a sense of the big picture, and a reasonably long view, you're more likely to do more or less the right things, at the right times, and to put tomorrow's resources and capabilities in place where and when you need them. But no firm advances exactly as its managers intend, and certainly not for long. Nor does any firm get to the future in a straight line. Things *will* go wrong, and your best-laid plans will crumble or blow up in your face. So you have to keep rethinking and adjusting your course and your activities, and the sequence and speed of your actions.

Figure 12.8

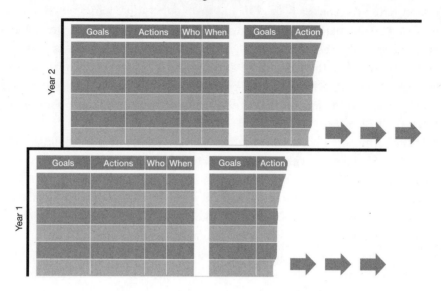

#8: Disciplined execution

Planning a way forward is one thing; making it happen is another challenge entirely. Designing strategy is invariably much easier than turning it into action. In fact, there's abundant evidence that poor execution, rather than deficient strategy, is the biggest impediment to growth in companies worldwide, and that corporate leaders see operational excellence as their number-one challenge.[18]

There are many reasons for this. But the root cause lies in our common perception of how to fix the problem. The usual formula goes like this:

1. Communicate the strategy to everyone who'll be involved in any way;
2. Make their goals and roles clear, and give them the resources and support that they need;
3. Track their progress;
4. Hold them accountable for results.

This sounds logical and straightforward, and is a good outline. But it leaves out a lot. So it reinforces a mistaken view of what execution really entails, and ensures that firms will keep getting it wrong.

For one thing, it suggests that execution is a mechanical process that comes *after* strategy, and is largely about telling people what they must do and then checking how they fare. It also assumes that there will be no surprises, that the strategy that's announced is as good as it gets, and that there's no need to encourage fresh thinking. And it makes things sound much simpler than they almost always are, by

implying that if a strategy is explained, it is understood; that people will sponta-
neously align themselves behind it; and that cooperation across functions will
occur as a matter of course.

None of which is true.

Forces are at work in almost every organization that can tear it apart and
derail its strategy, and the purpose of management is to hold things together and
enable firms to predictably and consistently produce desirable results. But they
will only achieve the *best* results if they are able to balance focus and conformity
with freedom to dissent and experiment.

To do this, they need to understand execution in two ways.

First, execution is *project management*.[19] Getting the results you want is too
important to be left to chance, or to the whim of individuals. Some people may
naturally "get things done," and whenever possible they should be assigned to the
most important activities. But no firm can rely on only the rare few with this
ability. Nor can commitment or teamwork be taken for granted.

In the absence of discipline, things quickly go awry. Once a sense is created that
there's no direction, or roadmap, or any urgency about key actions; that ignoring
commitments and missing deadlines is OK; and that excuses will be tolerated, a
pervasive rot quickly sets in. The climate turns toxic. Complacency takes over, and
a lack of progress leads to further slackness. Non-delivery becomes a habit and an
underlying cultural assumption – "This is the way we do things around here."

So there needs to be a systematic way to get things done, and everyone must
understand it and stick to it.

The challenge, however, is not just to get X or Y done, but *how to get Jacob or
Jane – human beings with their own agendas, values, inclinations, and abilities –
to do it*. And to do it within a context of politics, pressure, resource constraints,
constant interruptions, missteps, conflicts, and glitches.

The challenge, also, is to get Jacob and Jane to go above and beyond the call of
duty, and contribute even more than the strategy requires of them. And to ensure
that when things change around them, they'll respond with insights and ideas
that the planners hadn't thought of.

This brings us to the second aspect of execution: the fact that it is, in effect,
change management. Turning strategy into action always requires some kind of
change, so beneath its technical guise it is fundamentally a social process. It hinges
far more on the emotions and attitudes of individuals than on organizational
structures, systems, or rules.

People need to understand a firm's purpose, its situation, and the challenge it
faces. They need to know what its goals are, and how they might be achieved, and
who should do what by when to produce them. And, most crucially, they need to
know how they personally fit into the picture.

But merely *telling* them all this – no matter how well you do it – won't suffice. You cannot ever safely assume that what you say is what people hear and understand, or that what you ask them to do is what they will do. You always have to worry about the two costly disconnects that I described in the previous chapter.

The simple rule is: Keep telling them, over and over again. At every opportunity, and in every way you can. *Communicate! Communicate! Communicate!*

Because strategy is a process and not an event, and because it's dynamic and complex and reliant on people, the only sensible time to start thinking about how to execute it is *when you begin crafting your strategic conversation*. That's when you need to motivate people to let go of the past and accept the need for change, and when you need to ready them to do different things, and do things differently. That's also when you need to make decisions about the critical practices that will affect and facilitate ongoing change. And it's when you start *conducting* the conversation that will inspire and guide new action.

One vital yet underestimated forum for that conversation is the meetings in which you review progress. These can either be viewed as a nuisance that takes you away from "real" work, or as an opportunity for learning and growth. To waste them is a crime against your company – but that's exactly what many managers do.

Their reviews are tedious affairs, with packed agendas and vague goals. People pitch up reluctantly, and ill-prepared, and rely on flaky assumptions, weak excuses, and obfuscation to avoid hard decisions and accountability. Discussions meander off course when something interesting comes up, and go on for too long.

If a strategic conversation is to be effective, it must be rigorous and robust – and always respectful. Performance reviews must be the same.

Strict deadlines are always necessary, and keeping them short creates a sense of urgency. But some projects and activities will take many months or even years, so there has to be a way to sustain progress towards them. Many firms like the notion of 100-day goals, because that seems sensibly assertive.[20] But I go further, and push clients to break all tasks into 30-day chunks, with no-holds-barred reviews at the end of each phase. This achieves five things:

1. It makes work doable, because people can get their arms around one small piece at a time;
2. It puts huge pressure into the system, thus reducing the possibility of wheel-spin (which is one of the big enemies of change);
3. It lets you – and everyone else – quickly see who is performing, and who's not, so you can either dish out kudos or take remedial action before things get out of hand;
4. It lets you see *what* is working and what's not, in real-time, so you don't need to wait for many months to discover that you need to adjust your strategy;
5. It speeds up learning.

This approach shines a harsh light on performance, so it can make people extremely uncomfortable. Some managers quickly come to dislike it, because they have to conduct the reviews on schedule every month – and they have to be uncompromising about them. They have to exercise a firm hand, and people must be held accountable for results. If they let anyone off the hook for non-delivery, things will rapidly come unstuck.

Every review is an occasion not only to look back to learn, but also to look ahead and decide what's next. Each one sets things up for the 30 days ahead. So again, the tone of your conversation matters as much as the content. If people arrive expecting to be berated and insulted, they'll be unlikely to give of their best. If, on the other hand, they find themselves in a demanding yet positive environment, they'll be more constructive. They'll soon realize that these sessions are necessary and useful to the organization, and help them personally too.

Disciplined execution is the eighth critical strategy practice, but this doesn't infer it's last in a strict chain of activities, or should be the last one to get attention. For although it does depend on each of the others, they also depend on it. So like culture, it is both a consequence and a catalyst.

Fast-cycle strategy brings clear advantages. *Fast-cycle execution* is an essential component of them.

Figure 12.9

Our purpose	
Our situation	
The results we want	
How we'll deliver them	
1-Year goals	

Goals	Actions	Who	When

A way of working

These practices may sound too obvious. Doesn't *everybody* know all this? Doesn't *every* company do it?

On both counts, the answer is a resounding no.

If someone asked you to explain your firm's management approach, would you immediately talk about the eight critical practices? Would you be able to say that you apply them all, and that you do it well? Not likely. And this, despite the massive amount of evidence that confirms their necessity and their value.

But nor would most other CEOs have a better story to tell. And that's why, as I said in the Introduction, the way is open for you to gain the advantage you want more easily than you think.

The eight practices help you frame your point of view about how to compete and win. They comprise an integrated set of actions, a way of working, that will get you the results you want. But you need to commit to all of the practices and to this complete approach, then stick with it and make it a way of life in your firm. And whatever else you do, it must fit with these practices, complement them, and support them. If you don't take this seriously, your people won't either.

When you get going, don't let your initial enthusiasm fade and die. Remind yourself that when you introduce any new management idea, your people are alert for any sign that you're not convinced about it, or committed to it for the long haul. If you falter, you'll put your credibility at risk. You'll raise the level of distrust and cynicism, and reinforce the "BOHICA effect" ("Bend over, here it comes again!") that lurks in every organization.

Of course, all firms have many other things to do. As Russell Ackoff famously said: "Managers don't solve simple, isolated problems; they manage messes."[21] A host of issues clutter their agendas, weigh them down, and distract them, so these eight practices won't always be top-of-mind for them.

Some firms will apparently prefer other recipes, yet still succeed. Not every company will apply all of these practices in precisely the way I describe, or apply them all well. And if you asked managers in winning companies about the secrets of their success, it's quite likely that few of them would immediately cite these practices. However, if you dug deeper, you'd find this is exactly what the best performers do. So if they do this *implicitly*, imagine how much better they might do if they were *explicit* about it.

Of course, even if you do go with the tried and true, you may not get the results you want. Many factors affect business performance. With the best will in the world, things won't always go your way. So echoing Tom Peters, when he commented on the eight principles in *In Search of Excellence*, I offer no guarantee that if you apply these eight practices you'll make your company a winner.[22]

But here's the difference. Whereas you might have some latitude with the *Excellence* prescriptions, you have none with these. Whereas you may get away with being less than 100 per cent committed to any of those, you don't have the same liberty here.

But what if every firm *were* to apply these practices? What if you and your competitors all did the same things – one by one, and in combination? Wouldn't that level the playing field and kill anyone's competitive advantage?

To some extent, it would – and it's likely to happen because there are few secrets in business today. And now there's this book. But there's almost no possibility that everyone would do everything *in the same way, and equally well*. The bigger risk is that you slow your own progress and blunt your own edge through your *inattention* to these basics, while competitors excel in them. That you keep searching for silver bullets, when you already have what you need.

I'd like to have found sexier titles for these practices, for that's the way management writers seem to hook their readers. But there was no need. The practices are what they are.

Where to from here?

By now, you must be wondering: should you bother looking for new ways to manage?

My answer: an unequivocal *yes!*

Innovation in management is as worthy a goal as innovation in processes, products, or services. If you can find a new and unique way to run your business, you may just turbocharge your competitiveness. So stay alert to other ideas, learn all you can about them, and evaluate them alongside the eight critical strategy practices. But if ever you think there's a case to experiment with them, be cautious about dumping one of these for one of those.

As a rule of thumb, begin with what is known to produce results, and aim to do it brilliantly. Chances are you'll make a bigger difference faster by getting the basics right than by trying to reach the moon with a sputtering organization. Not getting the basics right will ensure you don't get far.

Before you disrupt the way you work with new ideas – and you will disrupt it – be clear about what you expect to achieve. Why the need? Why now? Are you perhaps already applying "best practices," but just not getting what you should from them? (And are they really *best* practices, or just fads of the moment?) Might you be better off starting from scratch and trying to discover or develop some completely new approach? And if you did do something new, what else might you sensibly *stop* doing?

Maybe you do need to radically change the way you do business. But if your firm is like so many others, that radical change may be less about experimenting with the latest ideas about management than about actually *using* familiar ones.

Slow down, act fast

A lot of clever people have been trying hard for a very long time to make their firms more competitive. This is a never-ending quest, and for reasons I've explained, most find it both daunting and frustrating. They almost always underestimate just how hard it is and how long it takes to change their ways.

As Frederick Taylor pointed out, "If anyone expects large results in six months or a year in a large works he is looking for the impossible."[23] Eiji Toyoda, scion of the family that founded Toyota, and his production head, Taiichi Ohno, took 20 years to fully apply the ideas that became the Toyota Production System. They arrived at most of the principles of lean production by the early 1960s, and the firm has been relentlessly using them and fine-tuning them ever since – for 50-some years.[24] The renowned leadership skills of General Electric have been honed over more than a century. Apple, Nestlé, SABMiller, and Boeing have been decades in the making.

Some of the changes you want to make will doubtless take a long time. Others can be made in next to no time. So it makes sense to *slow down* in thinking things through and deciding what to do, and then to *act fast*.

None of what I've suggested needs to be chewed to death. Nor should you see complexity in it that doesn't exist. The eight critical strategy practices make playing to win as simple as it can be. But when all is said and done, their value lies entirely in how you use them to talk your way through the challenges to come.

And that you can start doing right now.

Choose your commitments with care

My many years of experience as a consultant have taught me that managers are highly unlikely to stick with what they say in strategy meetings. No matter how definite they seem at the time, they'll soon be busy with something else.

This happens because things change and they have to adapt. But it also happens because they simply change their minds.

Many of their "commitments" – whether to a strategy, an action, or a practice – turn out to be hot air. They say what sounds right for a particular moment, but haven't really thought it through, and may not really mean it either. Then, real-world events overtake them, making even their best intentions inappropriate.

Another reality is that they don't clear the decks for new initiatives. Instead, they just load their latest ideas onto work already in the system. This clogs the corporate arteries and confuses everyone.

And, as if they need more reasons to fail, they also flit from one management idea to another, often trying to use concepts they don't understand and don't know how to apply.

A lack of commitment and staying power is normal, not an aberration. It shows up in many ways.

You see it when managers talk in their vision statements about being "world class," but then won't do what it takes to get there. When they proclaim the need to be a "low-cost supplier," but won't make the hard decisions required to get their costs down. When they say, "Customer service is our competitive advantage," but then stay as far away from customers as they can. When they say, "People are our most valuable resource," but then act in ways that show they don't really mean it. When they boast about being "disruptors," but won't invest in innovation or risk destroying their current business. Or when they insist on planning in great detail for the next five or ten years, but then quickly get knocked off course by unexpected events, or second-guess themselves for no good reason.

Incentives muddy the waters too. Managers make a hoo-hah about one process, but track and reward different performance. They say, "We have to be passionate about customers," but then dish out bonuses based solely on profit growth. Or they trumpet the need for innovation, but celebrate and reward cost-cutting. And their actions blot out their words.

Commitment – whether to a strategy, a practice, a project, or a set of values – is critical to business success. But staying committed is extremely hard. No two days are the same. There are many distractions. There's always something more interesting or urgent to do. And sudden winds blow companies this way and that.

In summary

1. **Don't allow your search for new ways to manage to distract you from attending to the basics of your business.** You may get bored doing this, but fight the feeling. If you err on the fundamentals, no amount of management novelty will save your bacon.

2. **Don't confuse a *style* of management with fundamental *ideas about* management.** The way you manage, and the theories you use, are related but different.

3. **Don't dump proven practices too quickly.** It is very tempting to keep trying new ideas. Some may have immense value. But changing almost anything is more disruptive, distracting, difficult, and time-consuming than anyone expects. There are always hidden costs and unintended consequences. And in any case, we have a pretty good idea of what works, so perhaps you should simply start doing it. Or maybe intensify your efforts.

4. **Before you adopt any new management idea, check its soundness.** Who produced it? What assumptions is it based on? What evidence supports it? Where else and under what circumstances has it worked? Why might it be good for you – and can you make it work? If you don't do your homework, you're looking for trouble.

5. **Think through how you'll make the switch from one management practice to another.** You may believe that introducing new ideas will make you look like a visionary, and give your business a lift. And maybe it will. But beware of throwing the baby out with the bathwater. New ideas are inherently risky – and, as we have seen, in short supply – so best you introduce them cautiously, and test them carefully.

6. **Consider how you'll integrate your new approach into your current business model.** It's easy to foul up the works. To assume that any new idea will "plug and play" is to play with fire; most don't. Because an organization is a complex system, a seemingly minor change can have ripple effects that cause trouble in unexpected places. Some of your people will resist what you do, or be unable to adapt to new ways. New processes may not sit well with old ones, and information systems might not talk to each other. Customers and suppliers may baulk if you suddenly expect them to act differently. For these reasons, and others, it's important to a) take a holistic view of things before you start tweaking, and b) think hard about *how* you'll make changes.

7. **Allow for change to be harder than you think, and to take longer and cost more.** Most change efforts fail. Delivery dates are missed. Budgets are overshot. Outcomes are off-beam. You might imagine that you can do things differently, but don't bank on it. Be ambitious, by all means, but be realistic too. Stretch goals and tight deadlines are essential in getting things done, but unreasonable expectations can set your team up to fail.

And above all,

8. **Travel light and don't keep adding to your already heavy workload.** Keep things simple and make the eight critical strategy practices a way of life. They are the critical core.

13

IMPLICATIONS FOR
BUSINESS SCHOOLS

It's not clear which is the best route into business. Even as formal education became more important as an entry ticket, it remained a joke that the only way to get to the top of a company was to start at the bottom. For most people, progress up the ladder was slow. While they might have been given various assignments to prepare them for high office, there was little additional effort to develop them. Things changed with the advent of the human resources era, which brought in a more balanced approach, combining quicker career moves with odd breaks for additional training.

Today, however, with costs under pressure, there's a tendency for firms to recruit people who can hit the ground running – and an acceptance that they'll want to move up, and be likely to move on, quite fast.

For many executives, business school is where they get to know about "the basics," and the Master of Business Administration degree has come to symbolize what these institutions are about. The number of new MBA graduates in the US went from 26,000 in 1970 to 67,000 in 1985, and it's estimated that around 500,000 MBAs or their foreign equivalents were awarded worldwide in 2011.[1] "India now has around 2,000 business schools," says *The Economist*, "more than any other country. China has fewer, but their numbers are growing quickly. It has an estimated 250 MBA programs, graduating around 30,000 students each year. This is less than half the number it will need over the next decade."[2]

The Great Recession took a heavy toll on business school admissions. And although there are signs of improvement, "Demand for MBAs remains soft," says a January 2014 report in *The Economist*. "Some schools, particularly lower down the pecking-order, may find their new state-of-the-art classrooms sparsely populated."[3] Tuition fees are up, the starting salaries of graduates are down, and many schools have shifted from two-year to one-year programmes to make their offerings more cost-effective and cut the time students have to spend away from work.

But this is about more than economics. The first years of this century have seen a growing debate about the value of not only the MBA, but also of business schools themselves – a debate that's mostly fuelled by business school professors and deans. In questioning the relevance of what they do, they've put management ideas under the microscope. They're not only rethinking their teaching methods, but also asking if management can actually be *taught*.[4]

"Strip away the hype surrounding the MBA," writes Della Bradshaw in the *Financial Times*, "and it is difficult to come up with hard evidence to prove that 100 years of management education, and the MBA degree in particular, have been beneficial to business or society. Indeed, even among its proponents, many are questioning whether business schools teach the right things, in the right way, to the right people." She quotes one recent graduate who says an MBA can give "a sheen of knowledge – it's a bullshitter's paradise."[5]

As industries evolve, the players within them work out the rules of the game, and competitors settle on a "dominant design" which has them all acting like each other. And that's exactly what happened to business schools – despite their theoretical knowledge of strategy, and despite the fact that they preached the importance of differentiation, innovation, adaptation, and so on.

"It is a rare profession where failure to obey its own rules is practically a condition of entry," says *The Economist*. "The most fashionable phrase today is 'disruptive innovation': professors solemnly warn people that entire industries face powerful new forces and that comfortable incumbents are at the mercy of swift-footed challengers. But when it comes to their own affairs, business schools flout their own rules and ignore their own warnings."[6]

In the opinion of Stanford professor Jeffrey Pfeffer, an outspoken critic of business schools, "A degree has value only if the degree is scarce, and the MBA is completely unscarce." The only MBA worth getting, he says, is one from an elite school.[7]

The No. 1 promise schools make to prospective students is, "With our MBA, you'll make more money." So they're all hustling to lure applicants who expect to make an impact – and earn fortunes – soon after they graduate. This is leading them to reinvent their offerings and become increasingly smart and aggressive about promoting themselves. Yet when business school graduates were asked in one survey about the most important benefits they gained from their time doing an MBA, this is how they responded:

- 38% – skills and knowledge;
- 31% – a network of contacts;
- 28% – the brand value of the school they attended.[8]

Think about that. Apparently, almost *two-thirds* of the value they derived from their costly and arduous business education had nothing to do with what they learned about managing – or, for that matter, about the world around them. The payoff was mostly about meeting people and being able to hang the right certificate on their walls, both key to getting good jobs, promotions, and pay. Echoing this, the *Financial Times* reports that in a survey of 2009 MBA graduates, 47 per cent said they'd had job offers through their alumni network, 32 per cent had hired someone through such contacts, and three out of four believed their contacts would open doors for them in the future.[9]

There is some evidence that firms run by CEOs with MBAs do no better than those run without graduate degrees. And that executives with graduate degrees in fields other than business or law do "significantly better in terms of risk-adjusted performance."[10] These findings may or may not affect hiring trends or business school curricula, but filling classrooms could well prove to be a harder sell in future.

A 2007 survey of 500 CEOs of S&P companies in the US by Spencer Stuart, a global executive search firm, showed that 97 per cent had a bachelor's degree and 67 per cent had some kind of advanced degree (MBA, master's, or doctorate). But in the "Top 100" firms, the number of CEOs with an MBA fell from 37 per cent in 2006 to 32 per cent in 2007.[11] A 2012 study by *US News & World Report* showed that Fortune 500 CEOs with both college and graduate degrees held 200 MBAs and 140 other advanced degrees.[12] A 2013 follow-up by the magazine found that 61 CEOs of the top 100 companies on the Fortune 500 list had no MBA.[13] According to the *Financial Times*, 29 per cent of the world's largest 500 listed firms are headed by an MBA graduate – two-thirds of them with a degree from a school in the top 100 in the *FT* Global MBA Ranking 2014. But that leaves 71 per cent of CEOs who don't have an MBA.[14]

Growing numbers of youngsters with business ambitions now study liberal arts subjects, engineering, or science rather than business; and for many employers they are the most prized hires. In a Gallup-Lumina Foundation study which asked 623 US business leaders to rank the importance of four factors on hiring, 84 per cent put candidates' knowledge of their field first, followed by their skills (79 per cent), their college major (28 per cent), and where they got their degree (9 per cent). Conclusion: "Getting a job and achieving long-term success in one's career may increasingly depend on demonstrating real value to employers through experience and targeted learning – and increasingly less on degrees, even if they are from prestigious universities."[15] Only half of McKinsey's new recruits have MBAs, while the others have PhDs or degrees in areas ranging from medicine to law.[16] The executive MBA course at Cheung Kong Graduate School of Business, the first private business school in mainland China, includes classes on philosophy, Eastern and Western religion, global history, and literature.[17]

"For the past few years," says Said Business School's Peter Tufano, "I've asked chief executive officers and other business leaders: 'What forces will transform business in 25 years?' My experience is that they quickly converge on a set of topics that business schools don't teach: demographic change; natural resource constraints; technological trends like big data; and such considerations as equity and justice that will all alter the rules of the game under which business operates."[18]

Learning about management is evidently coming to be seen as less important than learning about the world and learning to *think*.

From concepts to context

In "Managing Our Way to Economic Decline," which was published in 1980 and overnight became one of the most influential *HBR* articles ever, Robert Hayes and William Abernathy warned that "during the past two decades American managers have increasingly relied on principles that prize analytical detachment and methodological elegance over insight, based on experience, into the subtleties and complexities of strategic decisions." A key reason, they suggested, was the increase since the mid-1950s in the number of business leaders with backgrounds in finance and law rather than production. This resulted in a focus on financial engineering, cost-cutting, and mergers and acquisitions, at the expense of long-term attention to R&D, innovation, and process excellence.[19]

For all the attention this article attracted, and despite the alarm it caused, companies kept working ever harder at doing precisely what Hayes and Abernathy warned about. And even as the profit motive and shareholder greed came under fire, and even as matters such as social responsibility, "inclusive strategy," "bottom-of-the-pyramid" marketing, governance, and sustainability rose up the corporate agenda, accountants and lawyers kept their hold on plum jobs – thanks to the tech meltdown in 2000–2001 and the global financial crunch which came in 2008. And business schools continued to emphasize their traditional offerings, which underpinned the management behaviours that Hayes and Abernathy blamed for America's economic slide.

The inertia that's so normal in other organizations affects business schools too. Many are university departments and must function within the constraints and conventions of their university parents. Accreditation bodies influence what they must teach, and economic pressures may lead to over-emphasis on long, costly courses which boost their revenues. And a collegial culture and entrenched teaching staff make it hard to change.

But none of this will wash in the future.

With competition rising, schools will have to become more market-oriented. They'll have to redesign and reconfigure their programmes, or they'll become irrelevant. They'll have no choice but to switch from their current focus on *concepts* to a new emphasis on *context* (Figure 13.1). On equipping managers with a toolkit of just a few critical practices, exposing them to the richest possible understanding of their world, and inspiring them to be perpetually curious and alert.

Figure 13.1

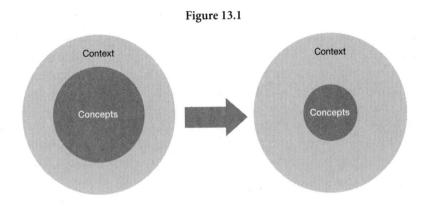

As Hayes and Abernathy pointed out, managerial skill is about more than analysing markets, crunching numbers, doing deals, organizing work, and motivating people. Those are all aspects of it, and very important too. But equally necessary is sensitivity to the *zeitgeist* – a grasp of business trends and global affairs, and a greater sense of social responsibility than was demanded in the past. And the future will require executives to be even more in touch with their context, even more mindful of their impact, and even more intuitive, creative, and adaptive.

People at low levels in organizations must necessarily deal with *internal* matters, so they must be equipped with functional skills. The higher they go, however, the more they need to be attuned to what's going on *outside* of their business – in politics, economics, the environment, technology, and society, and with customers and competitors. Their skills must include interpreting what they see, anticipating possibilities, building relationships, working with others, persuasion, communication, negotiation, and conflict resolution. Above all, they must develop the *nous* and the courage to make high-risk decisions in conditions of extreme uncertainty.

Four years after the Hayes and Abernathy article appeared, a special report in the January–February 1984 issue of *Harvard Business Review* began: "In the assessments of the part U.S. managers have played in our reduced industrial competitiveness, one theme emerges – that business schools are part of the problem." Its authors then went on to list a new set of goals for business schools.

Unsurprisingly, these included helping students develop self-awareness and a commitment to lifelong learning, along with skills in communication, negotiation, problem-solving, and people management. But even more emphasis was given to their awareness and understanding of the *zeitgeist* – of a rapidly changing and increasingly complex context; of their industries, the environment, and different cultures; and of the "sweep of history" and the "development of science and the diffusion of technology."[20]

Astonishingly, these recommendations have only recently featured in the review by many business schools of their offerings. But they're more relevant today than they were 30 years ago, and there's now a real urgency about pursuing them.

The conversation is being helped along by the fact that criticism of business schools and their faculty in shaping the business agenda and business practices has tended to be mostly about *contextual* issues and how firms should respond to them. High on the list have been the role of business in society, the mitigation of climate change, and governance. So leadership is right up there, with calls being made for more attention to the character, ethics, and integrity of leaders, and to the provocative matter of executive compensation.

Sumantra Ghoshal warned in an article published in *Academy of Management Learning & Education* in 2005, that "bad management theories are destroying good management practices."[21] And when the world was hit by the financial crisis, fingers were quickly pointed at Harvard alumni like Stanley O'Neal and John Thain (former CEOs of Merrill Lynch), Christopher Cox (former chairman of the US Securities Exchange), Rick Wagoner (former chairman of General Motors), Hank Paulson (former US Treasury Secretary), and naturally, at former US president George W. Bush, all of whom were key figures in the debacle.

Inevitably, business schools also took hits. What had they *taught* these people? Had they encouraged and spread a culture of greed? Why had they been so intent on pushing the gospel about shareholder capitalism? Why hadn't they done a better job of teaching ethics[22] or risk management?

These are all good questions, and they have prompted a range of answers.

Professor Anita McGahan, associate dean for research at the Rotman School of Business at the University of Toronto, suggests that the culture of business can be changed "by teaching differently: a lot less financial engineering and a lot more hard work to get people focused on building innovative, creative, value-creating institutions."[23]

Taking a more radical view, Harvard professors Rakesh Khurana and Nitin Nohria suggested in a 2008 *HBR* article that it was "time to make management a true profession."[24] The notion of an "MBA oath" – a voluntary pledge by MBAs to "create value responsibly and ethically" – was proposed by a group of 2009 Harvard MBA graduates, and the project is now supported by students and teachers at more than 250 schools around the world, and by the Aspen Institute and the World Economic Forum.[25]

The effect of such initiatives is yet to be seen. But it's hard to imagine that business schools will survive if they stray too far from their traditional role. As another Harvard professor, Robert Simon, argues, "business school curriculums have increasingly emphasized doing-well-by-doing-good at the expense of competitive advantage." They're distracting students from the core need to compete to win.[26]

The research agenda

As an enterprise, academic research on management is a let-down. True, there are exceptions, but overall the impact can only be described as wanting.

This failure puts an unwelcome focus on business schools. Criticisms of their contribution to management thinking will almost certainly escalate. But re-establishing their relevance won't be quick or easy. They need to change in three related ways.

First, they need to apply their minds to their raw material – insights and ideas. What's needed, says Richard Schmalensee, is that "business schools' research agendas must become primarily driven by real-life management problems. But in order for this change to happen, problem-driven research must become recognized and honoured as a great way to advance, not jeopardize an academic career."[27]

Second, they must make sure they have enough staff and that their teachers are up to the job. This will be easier said than done. Economic constraints will continue to be an issue. The demand for skills that's hurting companies everywhere is affecting business schools too. They're scrambling for staff. Says Judy Olian, dean of the UCLA Anderson School of Management, "We have a very large number of pending retirements of baby-boomer faculty members, exploding student enrolments, and a huge increase in the number of business schools around the world."[28] At the same time, laments Harvard Business School dean Nitin Nohria, "For many bright business students, the differential between what an MBA can earn in business, versus in academics, is just too great to justify a career in teaching."[29]

Caught between a shortage of teachers and an audience that wants real-world insights and advice, schools are bringing in more executives as guest lecturers and hiring more of them onto their faculty. Perhaps over time this will lead to more research into practical issues, and give us more useful advice about management. But for a long time to come, the pressures and conventions of academia will conflict with the demands of the marketplace.

Managers, unfortunately, will pay heavily for this. They'll be the ham in the sandwich – under pressure to perform, yet overloaded with unhelpful theories, and confused about how to use them.

This brings us to the third area where change is needed – what and how schools teach.

The online threat ... and the opportunity

Rising demand for management education is causing more and more schools to open for business, so competition among them is fierce. Until very recently, they've got along with a 100-year-old business model. But like so many other businesses, they suddenly face a new threat – in their case, massive open online courses (MOOCs).

The arrival of these disruptors should have been foreseen, but wasn't. Their impact is yet to be fully understood and felt. Thanks to them, education has in the most literal sense gone viral. Their explosive growth is forcing business schools to review everything from their economics to their offerings. They and their teachers are learning how to package and deliver online course material. Distribution channels like Coursera, edX*, and Udacity will become more effective, and will be joined by others. And organizations like Udemy and Fedora let teachers produce their own ebooks or sell their lectures at low cost and independently of their universities.

Right now, many online courses are available for free, with fees due only if students wish to write exams and get certificates or degrees. The dropout rate of these courses is high, and it's unclear just how effective they are.[30] But they're gaining traction and undoubtedly threaten business schools' traditional offerings.

Research from Open Education Europa shows that the number of MOOCs worldwide shot up from 962 in September 2013 to more than 2,500 by June 2014; in Europe they went from 277 to 600.[31] Already they're democratizing education in poor countries far from top-tier universities. Students in places like India and Brazil are "signing up in droves" for free courses from Stanford, MIT, and Harvard.[32] Some business schools use online programmes to provide introductory courses which prepare students for classroom participation. Internet access is a problem but is improving fast, and videos that are now streamed live will soon be downloadable. Language presents another challenge, as most courses are still in English; but partnerships between online platforms and institutions that teach French, Spanish, and other popular languages will quickly expand the market.

Whether MOOCs "replace, reinforce or undermine the traditional university model," says a *Financial Times* commentator, "the real test of their success will be

---

* A $60 billion collaborative venture between Harvard University and Massachusetts Institute of Technology, which is intended to reach one billion students. (Antonio Regalado, "The Most Important Education Technology in 200 Years," *MIT Technology Review*, 2 November, 2012)

whether the sophisticated and high-tech learning content can be transferred into credible accreditations for employers."[33] But this won't be an issue for long. As big-name institutions pour into the field, as student numbers soar, and as it becomes evident that their online studies do enable them to bring value to employers, doubts will give way to a new acceptance all around.

If accredited universities are to benefit from this, they will need to challenge their conventions and rethink what they do and how they do it. But the threat to their business models is not the only one they'll face. Perhaps even more dangerous will be the invasion of non-traditional providers into their territory. A new ecosystem is in the making, of venture capitalists, freelancing lecturers, corporate universities, upstart challengers, technology providers, and organizations whose business is knowledge.

The World Economic Forum has announced a "Forum Academy" in partnership with edX, designed to bring "a Davos-level curriculum on global, regional, and industry topics to a global audience."[34] It will present the thinking of global leaders online, for ongoing and certified professional development, and can either be seen as a clear threat to business schools or a useful complement to their course menu. Either way, it'll change what they do. And you can bet that in no time, other organizations – think World Bank, International Monetary Fund, Organization of Economic Cooperation and Development, International Labour Organization, think tanks, consultancies like McKinsey and Deloittes, news publishers – and a swarm of others, will join the rush to share what they know.

"Online learning is a disruptive innovation to what we do," says Clayton Christensen. "It will get better and better and I see people every day saying 'I won't go to campus but will take courses online' ... The technology will ultimately be good enough that we don't need people like Clay, or everyone will hear from Clay on the internet."[35]

The economic leverage of MOOCs providers is astonishing. According to Anant Agarwal, the CEO of edX, a three-person team of a professor and two assistants teaching analogue-circuit design to 400 MIT students can instruct 10,000 online, and could deal with 100 times that number.[36]

To deal with the new competition, many business schools, including six of the top ten schools with full-time MBA programmes in the *FT* rankings, already offer their own MOOCs.[37] This is making their own business arena more crowded, and they're eating their own lunch. So more innovation will be essential – and the pace of innovation will doubtless increase.

One challenge is for lecturers to learn how to present their material in ten-minute video bites. This isn't as easy as it seems. There's no time for lengthy anecdotes, jokes, or other fillers. The message has to be simple, clear, and complete.

Students hunched over their computers or mobile devices – maybe on the far side of the world – must immediately grasp it without the to-and-fro of a classroom, and be able to use it. Discussion forums enable them to share and debate ideas, but the experience is altogether different from being in a classroom, and must be crafted accordingly. Some schools assign mentors to work alongside students. A "flipped-classroom" model which blends online learning with classroom debate will become more prevalent.

In these tough times, there's a huge need for people with practical rather than theoretical knowledge. Graduate education offers job seekers less of an advantage than in the past, and for many people the opportunity cost makes no sense. On current trends, the future will see ever more people choosing to get the knowledge they need as fast as possible and not pay for a piece of paper to hang on their walls.

The clear implication is that business schools will have no choice but to teach *less*, teach it rapidly – and charge less. They'll have to focus on "the basics" that enable their customers to find work and show that they can make a difference right away.

Less study, more action

By no stretch of the imagination should it take a year or two for managers to learn the theories of management they really need. A few weeks should do the trick.*

If you doubt this, consider that Accenture teaches essential consulting skills to new recruits in three weeks. McKinsey recruits who don't have MBAs get a six-week business course and are then deemed "fit for service."[38]

Or consider the "advanced" executive programmes that have become important money-spinners for many business schools. These typically last from three to 12 weeks, and cover a comprehensive gamut of subjects. And while it's true that some may be "top-up" or refresher courses, it's also true that most providers pad their theoretical offerings with lengthy case-study discussions, class exercises, field visits, inputs from guest lecturers, and so on. The value of all this is largely a matter of perception, so when push comes to shove, some of it is sure to be dumped in favour of tighter focus on the core curriculum.

While MBA students might expect to get a lot of theory, executives who sign up for these courses want stuff they can use immediately.[39] To attract them, schools are racing to redesign their products to provide real "take-home value" – ideas and information that participants can take straight back to work. In future, what-

---

* I'm talking here about strategy, leadership, and change management, and not technical subjects such as accounting, finance, statistics, or economics.

ever the duration of courses they offer, they'll need to find new ways to package and deliver "how to" advice, while also making more of contextual matters.

Building blocks in disarray

You'd think that business schools would ensure that various parts of their programmes hang together in a way that makes them useful to those studying them. And that subjects, theories, concepts, exercises, and challenges stack neatly onto one another like Lego blocks. But there's no consensus among schools about what should be covered, how it should be taught, or in what order. And the links between ideas are often not made clear. So each school – and often each lecturer – provides a different bundle of information. Topics that should be dealt with early come too late. And the same issues and themes crop up in one module after another.[40]

"Today, it's not even clear what an MBA consists of anymore," says Harvard's Khurana. "The challenge we face is how do we re-legitimate ourselves as a source of foundational knowledge."[41]

The University of Chicago, for example, has only one obligatory MBA course with an almost infinite number of options around it. Yale School of Management offers an "integrated curriculum" in which themes like "Competitor," "Investor," "Employee," "The global macroeconomy," "State and society," "Customer," "Sourcing and managing funds," "Operations engine," and "Innovator" are addressed by teams of teachers.[42] Other schools package things in a variety of different ways.

One of the challenges they all face in designing their programmes is to decide where the boundaries should be for a particular subject. When teaching strategy, say, how far into leadership, organizational behaviour, or operational issues should they wander?

A study of how the best college teachers teach found that most of them ventured outside the traditional definitions of courses. The authors of the study concluded that "success in helping students learn even some core material benefits from the teacher's willingness to recognize that human learning is a complex process." This made it necessary to "apply a sweeping sense of educational worth that stemmed not only from any one discipline but rather from a broad educational tradition that values the liberal arts (including the natural sciences), critical thinking, problem solving, creativity, curiosity, concern with ethical issues, and both a breadth and depth of specific knowledge of the various methodologies and standards of evidence used to create that knowledge."[43]

This brings us to the question: what must managers know about *management* in order to manage better?

Answer: much less than we imagine. As Pfeffer and Sutton tell us, "practicing evidence-based management often entails being a master of the mundane."[44] If a handful of core ideas were well known, understood, and practised, most firms would be better off. But as long as there's uncertainty about the basics, attention to other issues will be less than productive. Burdening executives with a lot of interesting management theories may help them in an oblique way – but is far more likely to confuse them hopelessly.

In the real world

Learning *about* management may be quite easy, but learning *how to do it* is arduous and messy. It takes hard work and a lot of thought to develop a personal theory of success – a point of view about what must be done, why, and how. And it takes years of practice to learn about *managing*.

In addition to an understanding of the principles of management, executives also need more than a passing knowledge of economics, politics, society, technology, psychology, and many other subjects. And they need not just theoretical knowledge, but deep immersion in those topics in order to grasp their practical implications.

Above all, they need to learn to think and learn.

Formal education or reading provides essential building blocks. But most of what executives need to know can only be soaked up over time. "The future of management education is not the future of the MBA," says David Schmittlein, dean of MIT Sloan. While he wants the school to retain its focus on research and "recapture the intellectual high ground," he also aims to focus more attention on the practical application of ideas.[45]

"You cannot create a manager in a classroom," says Henry Mintzberg.[46] You can only learn it by *doing it*. You have to manage to become a manager. Research by Pfeffer and Sutton shows that "knowledge *that is actually implemented* is much more likely to be acquired from learning by doing than from learning by reading, listening, or even thinking."[47] (My italics.)

Case-study teaching is popular for just this reason. Action learning, which has coaches working closely with teams of students on projects agreed with client firms, is also common. And many schools send students on field trips, not only to study a range of organizations, but also apply their newfound skills or maybe act as consultants to them. But if their teaching staff are unable to credibly bridge the gap between the classroom and the real world, the payoff from such efforts will be limited.

Business schools will not be able to deliver real value if they simply provide chunks of knowledge, then wave goodbye to the people they teach. Their alumni programmes as they are won't be enough. Nor will intermittent contact with the organizations that send them delegates or hire their graduates.

To play a meaningful role in the different world that lies ahead, they will need to develop new levels of involvement with their students, with companies, and with other players in their environment. This will require them to ask: How do we become lifelong partners of those we teach, inspiring their intellectual journey and their ongoing personal and career development? How do we build on and enrich the on-the-job experience that companies provide? How do we bring to firms the cutting-edge knowledge that will make them more innovative and effective than their competitors? Who must provide what knowledge? How will we afford it?

Like the firms they serve, business schools are in a race to make their value propositions more attractive. One way some of them do this is by wrapping their teaching in foreign travel, outward bound-type activities, cook-offs, drumming, theatre visits, and much else. They may not admit it, but they evidently see their business as "edutainment." This is a lot of fun and the stuff of pleasant memories. It may also open students' eyes, give them fresh perspectives, and help them develop useful contacts. But does it make them better managers? Now, that's a matter for serious research!

A portfolio of possibilities

Business schools today, as never before, face the need to rapidly progress from delivering a basic, undifferentiated offering to one that will significantly impact on lives and careers. A few are already some way towards achieving this; they need to move even faster. The rest need to wake up, because their customers are shopping around, and they're in danger of becoming irrelevant.

In *The Marketing Imagination*, Ted Levitt shows how firms can stay ahead of the game by adding layers of value to their offerings. *Generic* value is the basic product or service – the "ticket to the game." *Expected* value is what buyers seek. *Augmented* value takes satisfaction up a notch through the addition of features and benefits. And *potential* value is the best that any vendor can possibly do.[48]

Whether they recognize it or not, the product of most business schools today comprises a generic core of management skills, wrapped first in ever-deeper contextual understanding, and then in a variety of experiences that may in some way prove to be life-changing. It provides a set of tools and some understanding of the world in which they'll be used. And it goes some way to helping participants learn about themselves and how to deal with the people around them, widen their horizons, and discover new possibilities.

But the schools of tomorrow will need to rethink both the content of this offering and the delivery process.

They will need to see the generic core as the least they must do to attract customers, and also an opportunity to differentiate themselves quickly and at low cost.

This assertion is sure to draw flak. The very fact of the core being "generic" implies that there's limited scope for teaching it differently. So the two outer layers seem obviously to be where schools must seek opportunities to carve out a new and even more vital place for themselves in career development.

But think again. The generic core is target No. 1 for challengers. If it gets eroded, the *raison d'être* of business schools will be lost. Weakness here would be the kiss of death.

There's no shortage of customers willing to pay to understand the critical practices. There will be tens of millions more in future, as workers in emerging markets seek managerial skills as quickly and cheaply as possible, and the digital revolution enables learning far from a physical campus.

Consider, for example, the opportunity for The African Management Initiative,[49] which aims to develop one million managers by 2023. One possibility is to provide teaching in a wide array of subjects, and hope students take away enough practical knowledge to make a difference. A second is to pare down the course menu, and quickly equip them with what they must know. Surely, in a continent desperate for upliftment and chronically short of management skills, the second option makes most sense.

In a *Financial Times* article entitled "Caught between a rock and a hard place," Vasan Dhar, a professor and director of the Center for Business Analytics at NYU Stern School of Business, says: "Over the decades many refinements have gone into what constitutes a 'good bundle' of courses. But the internet, by virtue of being global, instantaneous, mobile, social and free, has unleashed a dizzying array of learning modalities that were not previously possible and essentially disrupt this model."[50]

For some schools, this presents an opportunity. Others will make themselves dizzy by trying to create their own unique bundles of courses, and in the process, losing sight of their customers' needs.

Real strength in the generic core will always be vital. There's research to be done to find new and better ways of dealing with each of the critical practices – and work to be done in marketing and teaching them.

By equipping customers quickly, cheaply, and easily with the knowledge they need about the critical strategy practices, schools will be able to give more time and attention to contextual matters, charge for them, and generate annuity income from them. A small but potent core is the nucleus of a virtually unlimited portfolio of more lucrative offerings.

Clayton Christensen and Harry Erring suggest in their book *The Innovative*

University that "learning occurs best when it involves a blend of online and face-to-face learning, with the latter providing essential intangibles best obtained on a traditional college campus." These intangibles are *discovery, memory,* and *mentoring.* Discovery involves the development of knowledge. Memory enables university scholars to "help learners gain their footing in the flood of information that might otherwise overwhelm them." Mentoring gives those learners the benefit of ongoing, supportive relationships with their teachers.[51]

These three "extra-economic goals" are vital components of a business school's potential offering. But unless schools excel in the core, they will fail to equip their customers with the basic knowledge and skills they really need. And *until they shrink their core offering,* they will not have the resources or the time for what will increasingly matter to those customers.

The outer layer of value – a life-changing experience – may be triggered by new information, but by definition it cannot be *delivered.* It must be *lived.* So while chat rooms, webinars, videoconferencing, group work, and the like might lead to some new insights, their effect is limited. There's no substitute for live one-to-one contact with professors and other mentors, travel that takes individuals out of their comfort zones, or direct interactions with people of other cultures. And this is where business schools can retain a distinct edge.

The proviso, of course, is that they find ways to demonstrate the relevance of such activities. For there will be little tolerance for imaginary lessons as the pressures on managers increase.

Improving management development is an urgent matter for all of us. It must begin with a common-sense view of what we know about management, what we need to know, and the abysmal payoff from management fads and high-blown theories.

Business schools have for the past century played an increasingly important role in improving the performance of both business and non-profit organizations. There's a lot riding on what they do next.

APPENDIX

WHAT POPULAR STUDIES TELL US

Producing checklists for success is the stock-in-trade of management experts. Here are some famous examples – seven books and two articles. Each offers its own take on management, and there's merit in all of them. Not surprisingly, for reasons I've spelled out, there's little here that's particularly remarkable or innovative, and there are many similarities and some overlap.

Unfortunately, none of this guarantees anything.

BOOKS

In Search of Excellence by Thomas J. Peters and Robert H. Waterman (New York: Harper & Row, 1982)
1. A bias for action
2. Close to the customer
3. Autonomy and entrepreneurship
4. Productivity through people
5. Hands-on, value-driven
6. Stick to the knitting
7. Simple form, lean staff
8. Simultaneous loose-tight properties

Built to Last by James C. Collins and Jerry I. Porras (New York: HarperBusiness, 1994)
1. Clock building, not time telling
2. No "tyranny of the OR"
3. More than profits
4. Preserve the core/stimulate progress
5. Big hairy audacious goals
6. Cult-like cultures
7. Try a lot of stuff and see what works

8. Home-grown management
9. Good enough never is

The Discipline of Market Leaders by Michael Treacy and Fred Wiersema
(New York: Addison-Wesley, 1995)
1. Operational excellence
2. Customer intimacy
3. Product leadership

Good to Great by Jim Collins (New York: HarperBusiness, 2001)
1. Level 5 leadership
2. First who … then what
3. Confront the brutal facts
4. The hedgehog concept
5. A culture of discipline
6. Technology accelerators
7. The flywheel and the doom loop

The Agenda by Michael Hammer (New York: Random House, 2001)
1. Run your business for your customers
2. Give your customers what they really want
3. Put processes first
4. Create order where chaos reigns
5. Measure like you mean it
6. Manage without structure
7. Focus on the final customer
8. Knock down your outer walls
9. Extend your enterprise

What Really Works by William Joyce, Nitin Nohria and Bruce Roberson
(New York: HarperBusiness, 2003)
PRIMARY
1. Make your strategy clear and focused
2. Develop and maintain flawless operational execution
3. Develop and maintain a performance-based culture
4. Build and maintain a fast, flexible, flat organization
SECONDARY
1. Hold onto talented employees and find more
2. Keep leaders and directors committed to the business

3. Make innovations that are industry transforming
4. Make growth happen with mergers and partnerships

Great by Choice by Jim Collins and Morten Hansen (New York: HarperBusiness, 2011)

1. 10X leadership
2. 20-mile march
3. Fire bullets, then cannonballs
4. Leading above the death line
5. SmaC
6. Return on luck

Vanguard Management by James O'Toole (New York: Doubleday, 1985)

James O'Toole was of the view that "the best way to deal with a subjective issue is to ask a subjective question." So he asked some 200 people, "If you could choose to work in any *large* American corporation, which one would it be?" Most cited at least one of the following eight companies: Atlantic Richfield, Control Data, Dayton-Hudson, Deere, Honeywell, Levi Strauss, Motorola, and Weyerhauser.

With the help of 60 graduate students of his, O'Toole then looked for reasons why these "Vanguard companies" stood out, and came up with a list of seven characteristics (Figure A).

He also produced a list of eight "Old Guard" behaviours, arguing that corporations practising one or more of these "almost always fail."

Figure A

The Vanguard	The Old Guard
1. People-oriented	1. Insensitive to the realities of the external environment
2. Leaders are visible	2. Diversify out of their expertise and thus lose sight of the basics
3. Plan for employment stability	3. Make facile assumptions about the future
4. Have a consumer orientation	4. Become smug and complacent
5. Future-oriented	5. Become overly action-oriented and insufficiently thoughtful
6. Provide a sense of ownership	6. Repeat past successes and ignore the need for change
7. Are a link with entrepreneurial small businesses	7. Think short-term
	8. Behave as if the only purpose of a corporation is to maximize shareholder wealth

Staying Power by Michael A. Cusumano (Oxford: Oxford University Press, 2010)
1. Platforms, not just products
2. Services, not just products (or platforms)
3. Capabilities, not just strategy
4. Pull, don't just push
5. Flexibility, not just efficiency

ARTICLES

"The 4 Principles of Enduring Success" by Christian Stadler (*Harvard Business Review*, July–August 2007)
1. Exploit before you explore
2. Diversify your business portfolio
3. Remember your mistakes
4. Be conservative about change

"Three Rules for Making a Company Truly Great" by Michael E. Raynor and Mumtaz Ahmed (*Harvard Business Review*, April 2013)
1. Better before cheaper – in other words, compete on differentiators other than price
2. Revenue before cost – that is, prioritize increasing revenue over reducing costs
3. There are no other rules – so change anything you must to follow Rules 1 and 2

NOTES

INTRODUCTION

1 "Russell Ackoff-systems-based improvement," http://www.youtube.com/watch?v=_pcuzRq-rDU

2 Richard P. Rumelt, "What in the World is Competitive Advantage?" Policy Working Paper 2003–105, The Anderson School, UCLA, 5 August 2003

3 Rakesh Khurana, *Searching for a Corporate Savior*, Princeton: Princeton University Press, 2002

4 Barbara Kellerman, *The End of Leadership*, New York: Harper Business, 2012

5 Mary Yoko Brannen and Yves Doz, "Corporate Languages and Strategic Agility," *California Management Review*, Vol. 54, No. 3, Spring 2012

6 Edgar Schein, "SMR Forum: Does Japanese Management Style Have a Message for American Managers?" *Sloan Management Review*, Fall 1981

7 Anna Canato, Davide Ravasi, and Nelson Philips, "Coerced Practice Implementation in Cases of Low Cultural Fit: Cultural Change and Practice Adaptation During the Implementation of Six Sigma at 3M," *Academy of Management Journal*, Vol. 50, No. 6, 2013

8 Peter F. Drucker, *The Frontiers of Management*, New York: Truman Talley Books, 1986

9 Peter F. Drucker, *The Practice of Management*, New York: Harper & Row, 1954

10 John Tarrant, *Drucker: The Man Who Invented the Corporate Society*, New York: Cahners Books, 1976

11 John A. Byrne, "Management's New Gurus," *Businessweek*, 30 August 1992

12 Richard Webster, richardwebster.net, 2002

CHAPTER 1

1 Andrew S. Grove, *Only the Paranoid Survive*, New York: Doubleday, 1996

2 Fiona Czerniawska, "2013: The Bells Toll for the Old Thought Leadership Model," *The Source Blog*, 7 February 2013

3 Max H. Bazerman and Michael D. Watkins, *Predictable Surprises*, Boston: Harvard Business School Press, 2004

4 Thomas J. Peter and Robert H. Waterman, *In Search of Excellence*, New York: Harper & Row, 1982

5 James C. Collins and Jerry I. Porras, *Built to Last*, New York: HarperBusiness, 1994

6 Michael Treacy and Fred Wiersema, *The Discipline of Market Leaders*, New York: Addison-Wesley Publishing, 1995

7 Jim Collins, *Good to Great*, New York: HarperBusiness, 2001

8 Jim Collins, *Great by Choice*, New York: HarperCollins, 2011

9 Michael A. Cusumano, *Staying Power*, New York: Oxford University Press, 2010

10 William Joyce, Nitin Nohria, and Bruce Roberson, *What Really Works*, New York: HarperBusiness, 2003

11 James O'Toole, *Vanguard Management*, New York: Doubleday, 1985

12 Michael Hammer, *The Agenda*, New York: Random House, 2001

13 Christian Stadler, "The 4 Principles of Enduring Success," *Harvard Business Review*, July–August 2007

14 Michael E. Raynor and Mumtaz Ahmed, "Three Rules for Making a Company Truly Great," *Harvard Business Review*, April 2013

15 Paul R. Carlile and Clayton M. Christensen, "The Cycles of Theory Building in Management Research," Harvard Business School working paper 05-057, February 2005; Clark G. Gilbert and Clayton M. Christensen, "Anomaly-Seeking Research: Thirty Years of Development in Resource Allocation Theory," in Joseph L. Bower and Clark G. Gilbert, Editors, *From Resource Allocation to Strategy*, Oxford: Oxford University Press, 2005; Clayton M. Christensen, "The Ongoing Process of Building a Theory of Disruption," *The Journal of Product Innovation Management*, 2006

16 Craig C. Lundberg, "Is There Really Nothing So Practical as a Good Theory?" *Harvard Business Review*, 1 September 2004

17 John J. Tarrant, *Drucker: The Man Who Invented Corporate Society*, New York: Cahners Books, 1976

18 Dorothy Leonard and Walter Swap, *Deep Smarts*, Boston: Harvard Business School Press, 2005

19 John Gardner, *Changing Minds*, Boston: Harvard Business School Press, 2004

20 Peter F. Drucker, "Thinking Ahead: The Potentials of Management Science," *Harvard Business Review*, January–February 1959

CHAPTER 2

1 Peter Schwartz, Peter Leyden, and Joel Hyatt, *The Long Boom*, Reading, Massachusetts: Perseus Books, 1999

2 "World Economy: The Gated Globe," *The Economist*, 12 October 2013

3 Chris Giles, "Productivity Growth Haunts Global Economy," *Financial Times*, 14 January, 2014

4 "The Hard Truth is That the Economy is Recovering, But Productivity Isn't," *The Observer*, 9 March 2014

5 Stephen D. King, "When Wealth Disappears," *The New York Times*, 6 October 2013

6 Sandrine Rastello & Jeanna Smialek, "IMF Cuts Global Outlook, Warns of U.S. Default Threat," Bloomberg.com, 8 October 2013

7 Larry Summers, 14th Annual IMF Research Conference: Crises Yesterday and Today, 8 November 2013

8 Paul Krugman, "A Permanent Slump?" *The New York Times*, 17 November 2013

9 Robert J. Gordon, "Is U.S. Economic Growth Over? Faltering Innovation Confronts the Six Headwinds," NBER Working Paper No. 18315, August 2012

10 Edmund Phelps, *Mass Flourishing*, Princeton: Princeton University Press, 2013

11 Joseph E. Stiglitz, "The Innovation Enigma," Project Syndicate, 9 March 2014

12 "The United States, Falling Behind," *New York Times*, 22 October 2013; "Time for the U.S. to Reskill?: What the Survey of Adult Skills Says," OECD Publishing, 2013

13 Kenneth Rogoff, "Malthus, Marx, and Modern Growth," Project Syndicate, 4 March 2014

14 Ambrose Evans-Pritchard, "World's Biggest Investor Blackrock Says US Rally Nearing Exhaustion," *The Telegraph*, 9 December 2013

15 Sumantra Ghoshal, Christopher A. Bartlett, and Peter Moran, "A New Manifesto for Management," *Sloan Management Review*, Spring 1999

16 Alvin Toffler, *Future Shock*, London: The Bodley Head, 1970

17 Peter F. Drucker, *Post-Capitalist Society*, Oxford: Butterworth-Heinemann, 1993

18 Jeffrey Immelt, speech to the Canadian Club, 10 February 2009

19 Tim Harford, *Adapt*, London: Little, Brown and Company, 2011

20 Richard Foster and Sarah Kaplan, *Creative Destruction*, New York: Currency Doubleday, 2001

21 Clayton M. Christensen and Michael E. Raynor, *The Innovator's Solution*, Boston: Harvard Business School Press, 2003

22 Janamitra Devan, Matthew B. Klusas, and Timothy W. Ruefli, "The Elusive Goal of Corporate Outperformance," *McKinsey Quarterly*, Web exclusive, May 2007

23 Toni C. Langlinais and Marco A. Merino, "Special Report: How to Sustain Profitable Growth," *Outlook*, September 2007

24 "The Tightening Tether," *The Economist*, 30 March 2008

25 John Hagel III, John Seely Brown, and Duleesha Kulasooriya, *The 2011 Shift Index: Measuring the Forces of Long-term Change*, Deloitte Centre For The Edge, 2011

26 John Hagel, John Seely Brown, Tamara Samoylova, and Michael Lui, "Success or Struggle: ROA as a Measure of Business Performance," *Report 3 of the 2013 Shift Index*, Deloitte Centre For The Edge, 2013

27 Thomas S. Kuhn, *The Structure of Scientific Revolutions*, Chicago: University of Chicago Press, 1962

28 Walter Kiechel III, "The Management Century," *Harvard Business Review*, November 2012

29 Gary Hamel with Bill Breen, *The Future of Management*, Boston: Harvard Business School Press, 2007; Gary Hamel, "Moonshots for Management," *Harvard Business Review*, February 2009

30 Donella H. Meadows, Dennis L. Meadows, Jorgen Randers, and William W. Behrens III, *The Limits to Growth*, New York: Universe Books, 1972

31 John Kay, "The Startling Human Progress That Economists Fail to See," *Financial Times*, 4 March 2014

32 Peter F. Drucker, "Thinking Ahead: The Potentials of Management Science," *Harvard Business Review*, January–February 1959

33 Henry Ford, *My Life and Work*, London: William Heinemann, 1922

34 Robert Lacey, *Ford: The Man and the Machine*, London: William Heinemann, 1986

35 David Halberstam, *The Reckoning*, London: Bantam Books, 1987

36 Ibid.

37 Henry Ford, *My Life and Work*, London: William Heinemann, 1922

38 David Halberstam, *The Reckoning*, London: Bantam Books, 1987

39 Henry Ford, *My Life and Work*, London: William Heinemann, 1922

40 Henry Ford, *Today and Tomorrow*, New York: Doubleday Page, 1926

41 Ibid.

42 Ibid.

43 Ibid.

44 Ibid.

45 Henry Ford, *My Life and Work*, London: William Heinemann, 1922

46 Ibid.

47 Ibid.

48 Ibid.

49 Henry Ford, *Today and Tomorrow*, New York: Doubleday Page, 1926

50 Robert Lacey, *Ford: The Man and the Machine*, London: William Heinemann, 1986

51 Henry Ford, *My Life and Work*, London: William Heinemann, 1922

52 Henry Ford, *Today and Tomorrow*, New York: Doubleday Page, 1926

53 Robert Lacey, *Ford: The Man and the Machine*, London: William Heinemann, 1986

54 P. Ranganath Nayak and John M. Ketteringham, *Breakthroughs! How Leadership and Drive Created Commercial Innovations That Swept the World*, London: Mercury Books, 1986

55 Alfred D. Chandler, *Strategy and Structure: Chapters in the History of the American Industrial Enterprise*, Boston: The MIT Press, 1962

56 Bruce E. Kaufman, "Strategic Human Resource Management Research in the United States: A Failing Grade After 30 Years?" *Academy of Management Perspectives*, May 2012

57 Ibid.

58 Clark G. Gilbert and Clayton M. Christensen, "Anomaly-Seeking Research: Thirty Years of Development in Resource Allocation Theory," in Joseph L. Bower and Clark G. Gilbert, Editors, *From Resource Allocation to Strategy*, Oxford: Oxford University Press, 2005

59 Viktor E. Frankl, *Man's Search for Meaning*, London: Edbury Publishing, 2004

60 Art Kleiner, *The Age of Heretics*, San Francisco: Josse-Bass, 2008

61 Gary Hamel and Aimé Heene, Editors, *Competence-Based Competition*, New York: John Wiley & Sons, 1994

62 Gary Hamel, "The Dirty Little Secret of Strategy," *Financial Times*, 24 April 1997

63 "Call for papers for a special issue," *Strategic Management Journal* website, http://smj.strategicmanagement.net/strategy_design.php, accessed June 2014

64 Larry E. Greiner, Arvind Bhambri, and Thomas G. Cummings, "Searching for a Strategy to Teach Strategy," *Academy of Management Learning and Education*, 2003, Vol. 2, No. 4

65 Paul R. Lawrence, "Historical Development of Organizational Behavior," in Jay W. Lorsch, Editor, *Handbook of Organizational Behavior*, Engelwood Cliffs NJ: Prentice-Hall, 1987

66 Jeff Immelt, chairman and CEO of General Electric, speaking to the Canadian Club, 10 February 2009; Richard Florida, *The Great Reset*, New York: HarperCollins, 2010

CHAPTER 3

1 Daniel Kahneman, *Thinking Fast and Slow*, New York: Farrar, Strauss and Giroux, 2011

2 Fiona Czerniawska, "The Sacred Cows of Thought Leadership," The Source Blog, 27 November 2012

3 Rajshree Agarwal and Glenn Hoetker, "A Faustian Bargain? The Growth of Management and Its Relationship with Related Disciplines," *Academy of Management Journal*, Vol. 50, December 2007

4 Fiona Czerniawska, "Do Strategy Firms Still Lead the Thinking?" *Management Consulting News*, http://www.managementconsultingnews.com/articles/czerniawska_strat_firm.php, accessed 6 June 2007

5 http://www.sourceforconsulting.com/whitespace/

6 Harold Koontz, "The Management Theory Jungle," *Academy of Management Journal*, December 1961

7 Harold Koontz, "The Management Theory Jungle Revisited," *Academy of Management Review*, Vol. 5, No. 2, 1980

8 Harold Koontz, 1961

9 Joel Best, *Flavor of the Month: Why Smart People Fall for Fads*, Berkeley and Los Angeles, California: University of California Press, 2006

10 Richard Tanner Pascale, *Managing on the Edge*, New York: Simon & Schuster, 1990

11 books.google.com/ngrams

12 www.bain.com

13 Simon London, "Why Are Fads Falling Away?" *Financial Times*, 12 June 2003

14 Bain & Company, *Management Tools and Trends 2009*

15 Darrell Rigby, *Management Tools 2001*, Bain & Company

16 Chris Zook, *Profit from the Core*, Boston: Harvard Business School Press, 2001

17 Bain & Company, *Management Tools and Trends 2009, 2011, 2013*

18 Bain & Company: *Management Tools and Trends 2005*

19 Bain & Company, *Management Tools 2000*

20 Bain & Company, *Management Tools 2007*

21 Robert S. Kaplan and David P. Norton, "The Balanced Scorecard: Measures That Drive Performance," *Harvard Business Review*, January–February 1992

22 Ralph J. Cordiner, *New Frontiers for Professional Managers*, New York: McGraw-Hill, 1956

23 Robert G. Eccles, "The Performance Management Manifesto," *Harvard Business Review*, January–February 1991

24 Peter F. Drucker, *The Practice of Management*, New York: Harper & Row, 1954

25 William G. Ouchi, *Theory Z*, New York: Addison-Wesley, 1981

26 Michael E. Porter, *Competitive Strategy*, New York: The Free Press, 1980

27 Richard G. Hamermesh, *Making Strategy Work*, New York: John Wiley & Sons, 1986

28 Arthur M. Schneiderman, *The First Balanced Scorecard*, ebook, Analog Devices: 1986–1992

29 Darrell Rigby and Barbara Bilodeau, "Selecting Management Tools Wisely," *Harvard Business Review*, December 2007

30 Email from Darrell Rigby, Bain & Company, 4 December 2007

31 Philipp M. Nattermann, "Best Practice ≠ Best Strategy," *McKinsey Quarterly*, No. 2, 2000

32 Michael Hammer, "Reengineering Work: Don't Automate, Obliterate," *Harvard Business Review*, July–August 1990

33 Michael Hammer and James Champy, *Reengineering the Corporation: A Manifesto for Business Revolution*, New York: HarperBusiness, 1993

34 James Champy, *Reengineering Management: The Mandate for New Leadership*, New York: HarperBusiness, 1995

35 Michael Hammer, *The Agenda*, New York: Random House, 2001

36 Darrell Rigby, *Management Tools 2001*, Bain & Company

37 Darrell Rigby, *Management Tools & Trends 2003*, Bain & Company

38 Darrell Rigby and Barbara Bilodeau, *Management Tools & Trends 2009*, Bain & Company

39 Darrell Rigby and Barbara Bilodeau, *Management Tools & Trends 2013*, Bain & Company

CHAPTER 4

1 Stuart Crainer, *Corporate Man to Corporate Skunk: The Tom Peters Phenomenon*, London: Capstone, 1997

2 Richard Tanner Pascale and Anthony G. Athos, *The Art of Japanese Management*, New York: Simon and Schuster, 1981

3 Lowell Bryan, "Enduring Ideas: The 7S Framework," *McKinsey Quarterly*, March 2009

4 D. Quinn Mills, *Rebirth of the Corporation*, New York: John Wiley, 1991

5 Tom Peters, "Tom Peter's True Confessions," *Fast Company*, Issue 53, November 2001

6 Ibid.

7   "Oops. Who's Excellent Now?" *Business Week*, 5 November 1984

8   Daniel T. Carroll, "A Disappointing Search for Excellence," *Harvard Business Review*, November–December 1983

9   Michael A. Hitt and R. Duane Ireland, "Peters and Waterman Revisited: The Unended Quest for Excellence," *Academy of Management Executive*, Vol. 1, No. 2, 1987

10 Michael A. Cusumano, *Staying Power*, New York: Oxford University Press, 2010

11 Tom Peters, "Tom Peter's True Confessions," *Fast Company*, Issue 53, November 2001

12 Matthew Stewart, *The Management Myth*, New York: W.W. Norton & Company, 2009

13 Julia Kirby, "Toward a Theory of High Performance," *Harvard Business Review*, July–August 2005

14 Tom Peters, *Thriving on Chaos: Handbook for a Management Revolution*, New York: Harper & Row, 1987

15 James C. Collins and Jerry I. Porras, *Built to Last*, New York: HarperBusiness, 1994

16 Jim Collins, *Good to Great*, New York: HarperBusiness, 2001

17 Bruce Niendorf and Kristine Beck, "*Good to Great*, or just good?" *Academy of Management Perspectives*, November 2008

18 Bruce G. Resnick and Timothy L. Smunt, "From Good to Great to …," *Academy of Management Perspectives*, November 2009

19 Michael A. Cusumano, *Staying Power*, New York: Oxford University Press, 2010

20 Stefan Stern, "The Question All Leaders Should Ask Themselves," *Financial Times*, 1 December 2009

21 Jennifer Reingold and Ryan Underwood, "Was 'Built to Last' built to last?" *Fast Company*, 9 May 1992

22 Daniel Kahneman, *Thinking Fast and Slow*, London: Penguin Books, 2011

23 Tom Peters, *Re-imagine*, London: Dorling Kindersley, 2003

24 Starting with an article in *Business Week*, "Oops. Who's Excellent Now?" 5 November 1984

25 Emma Jacobs, "20 Questions: Tom Peters, Management Guru," *Financial Times*, 17 September 2010

26 "Good to Great Expectations: Jim Collins on Getting to the Next Level," *Business Week*, 14 August 2008

27 Leon Gettler, "Guru Peters Still Taking No Prisoners," www.the.age.co.au, 21 November 2003, accessed 27 December 2009

28 Bain & Company, *Management Tools and Trends 2007*

29 "What Witch Doctors?" *The Economist*, 13 November 2007

30 Stefan Stern, "The Write Stuff to Ensure a Winning Management Book," *Financial Times*, 16 May 2008

31 Paula Jarzabkowski, Monica Giulietti, and Bruno Oliveira, *Building a Strategy Toolkit*, report from the Advanced Institute of Management Research, 2009

32 Jennifer Reingold and Ryan Underwood, "Was 'Built to Last' built to Last?" *Fast Company*, 9 May 1992

33 Paula Jarzabkowski, Monica Giulietti, and Bruno Oliveira, *Building a Strategy Toolkit*, report from the Advanced Institute of Management Research, 2009

34 Lucy Kellaway, "The Return of Managerial Bone-Headedness," *Financial Times*, 15 November 2009

35 Walter Kiechel III, "The Management Century," *Harvard Business Review*, November 2012

36 Stefan Stern, "Lunch with the FT: Tom Peters," *Financial Times*, 21 November 2008

37 Emma Jacobs, "20 Questions: Tom Peters, Management Guru," *Financial Times*, 17 September 2010

38 John Mickelthwaite and Adrian Wooldridge, *The Witch Doctors*, New York: Times Books, 1996

39 Jeffrey Pfeffer and Robert I. Sutton, "Evidence-Based Management," *Harvard Business Review*, January 2006

40 Clark G. Gilbert and Clayton M. Christensen, "Anomaly-Seeking Research: Thirty Years of Development in Resource Allocation Theory," in Joseph L. Bower and Clark G. Gilbert, Editors, *From Resource Allocation to Strategy*, Oxford: Oxford University Press, 2005

41 Thomas H. Davenport and Lawrence Prusak with H. James Wilson, *What's the Big Idea?* Boston: Harvard Business School Press, 2003

42 Richard Hamermesh, *Fad-Free Management*, Santa Monica: Knowledge Exchange, 1996

43 Eileen Shapiro, *Fad Surfing in the Boardroom*, Oxford: Capstone Publishing, 1996

CHAPTER 5

1 Thomas H. Davenport and Laurence Prusak with H. James Wilson, *What's the Big Idea?* Boston: Harvard Business School Press, 2003

2 Sumantra Ghoshal, "Bad Management Theories Are Destroying Good Management Practices," *Academy of Management Learning & Education*, Vol. 4, No. 1, 2005

3 John Roberts, *The Modern Firm*, Oxford: Oxford University Press, 2004

4 Thomas H. Davenport and Lawrence Prusak with H. James Wilson, *What's the Big Idea?* Boston: Harvard Business School Press, 2003

5 Stefan Stern, "Lunch with the FT: Tom Peters," *Financial Times*, 21 November 2008

6 Donald L. Sull, "Strategy as Active Waiting," *Harvard Business Review*, September 2005

7 Rajshree Agarwal and Glenn Hoetker, "A Faustian Bargain? The Growth of Management and Its Relationship with Related Disciplines," *Academy of Management Journal*, Vol. 50, No. 6, 2007

8 Friederich August von Hayek, "The Pretence of Knowledge," Lecture to the memory of Alfred Nobel, 11 December 1974

9 Steven Wheeler, quoted in Bridget Finn, "The Life Cycle of Great Business Ideas," *Strategy+Business*, 30 September 2008

10 Albert A. Cannella Jr, "Upper Echelons: Donald Hambrick on Executives and Strategy," *Academy of Management Executive*, 2001, Vol. 15, No. 3

11 Clayton M. Christensen and Michael E. Raynor, "Why Hard-Nosed Executives Should Care about Management Theory," *Harvard Business Review*, September 2003

12 James O'Toole, *Vanguard Management*, New York: Doubleday, 1985

13 Ralph H. Kilmann, *Beyond the Quick Fix*, San Francisco, Jossey-Bass, 1985

14 Richard Tanner Pascale, *Managing on the Edge*, New York: Viking, 1990

15 John Kay, *Foundations of Corporate Success*, Oxford: Oxford University Press, 1993

16 Frederick Hilmer and Lex Donaldson, *Management Redeemed*, New York: The Free Press, 1996

17 Clayton M. Christensen & Michael E. Raynor, "Why Hard-Nosed Executives Should Care About Management Theory," *Harvard Business Review*, September 2003

18 Clayton M. Christensen, "The Ongoing Process of Building a Theory of Disruption," *The Journal of Product Innovation Management*, 2006

19 Suzanne Berger and the MIT Industrial Performance Centre, *How We Compete*, New York: Currency, 2005

20 Phil Rosenzweig, *The Halo Effect*, New York: The Free Press, 2007

21 Nick Bloom, Stephen Dorgan, John Dowdy, and John Van Reenen, "Management Practice &

Productivity: Why They Matter," *Management Matters*, paper published by the Centre for Economic Performance, London School of Economics, in collaboration with McKinsey & Co., November 2007

22 Theodore Levitt, "The Globalization of Markets," *Harvard Business Review*, May–June 1983

23 Jeffrey K. Liker, *The Toyota Way*, New York: McGraw-Hill 2004; Taiichi Ohno, *Taiichi Ohno's Workplace Management*, Tokyo: Gemba Press, 2007

24 David Halberstam, *The Reckoning*, London: Bantam Books, 1987

25 Ibid.

26 Peter Christie, Ronnie Lessem, and Lovemore Mbigi, Editors, *African Management*, Johannesburg: Knowledge Resources, 1994; Lovemore Mbigi and Jeremy Maree, *Ubuntu*, Johannesburg: Knowledge Resources, 1995; Mike Boon, *The African Way*, Cape Town: Zebra Press, 1996; Reuel J. Khoza, *Attuned Leadership*, Johannesburg: Penguin Books, 2011

27 Andrew Hill, "Managerial Techniques Remade in China," *Financial Times*, 8 July 2013

28 Thomas Hout and David Michael, "A Chinese Approach to Management," *Harvard Business Review*, September 2014; Peter J. Williamson and Eden Yin, "Accelerated Innovation: The New Challenge from China," *Sloan Management Review*, Summer 2014

29 Jeffrey Pfeffer, *The Human Equation*, Boston: Harvard Business School Press, 1988

30 Nick Bloom, Stephen Dorgan, John Dowdy, and John Van Reenen, "Management Practice & Productivity: Why They Matter," *Management Matters*, paper published by the Centre For Economic Performance, London School of Economics, in collaboration with McKinsey & Co., November 2007

31 Ibid.

32 Nicholas Bloom and John Van Reenen, "Why Do Management Practices Differ Across Firms and Countries?" *Journal of Economic Perspectives*, Vol. 24, No. 1, Winter 2010

33 Nicholas Bloom, Raffaella Sadun and John Van Reenen, "Does Management Really Work?" *Harvard Business Review*, November 2012

34 Paul R. Lawrence and Jay W. Lorsch, *Organization and Environment*, Boston: Harvard Business School Press, 1967

35 "Crossing the Divide," *The Economist*, 13 October 2013

36 Pankaj Ghemawat, *Redefining Global Strategy*, Boston: Harvard Business School Press, 2007

37 H. Fayol, *General and Industrial Management*, London: Pitman, 1949

38 Alfred P. Sloan Jr, *My Life with General Motors*, London: Sidgwick and Jackson, 1965

39 Peter F. Drucker, *The Effective Executive*, London: William Heinemann Ltd, 1967

40 Lex Donaldson and Frederick G. Hilmer, "Management Redeemed: The Case Against Fads That Harm Management," *Organization Dynamics*, Spring 1998

41 Nelson P. Repenning and John D. Sterman, "Nobody Ever Gets Credit for Fixing Problems That Never Happened," *California Management Review*, Summer 2001

CHAPTER 6

1 Jeffrey Pfeffer and Christina T. Fong, "The End of Business Schools? Less Success Than Meets the Eye," *Academy of Management Learning and Education*, Vol. 1, No. 1, September 2002

2 Video interview with Della Bradshaw, *Financial Times*, 26 January 2014

3 Jeffrey Pfeffer and Christina T. Fong, "The End of Business Schools? Less Success Than Meets the Eye," *Academy of Management Learning and Education*, Vol. 1, No. 1, September 2002; Warren G. Bennis and James O'Toole, "How Business Schools Lost Their Way," *Harvard Business Review*, May 2005

4   Andrew H. Van de Ven and Paul E. Johnson, "Knowledge for Theory and Practice," *Academy of Management Review*, Vol. 31, No. 4, 2006

5   Mie Augier and David J. Teece, "Reflections On (Shumpeterian) Leadership: A Report on a Seminar on Leadership and Management Education," *California Management Review*, Vol. 47, No. 2, Winter 2005

6   Rakesh Khurana, *From Higher Aims to Hired Hands*, Princeton: Princeton University Press, 2007

7   J. Sterling Livingston, "The Myth of the Well-Educated Manager," *Harvard Business Review*, May–June 1971

8   Quoted in Benjamin M. Oviatt and Warren D. Miller, "Irrelevance, Intransigence, and Business Professors," *The Academy of Management Executive*, Vol. III, No. 4, 1989

9   Warren G. Bennis and James O'Toole, "How Business Schools Lost Their Way," *Harvard Business Review*, May 2005

10 Richard Schmalensee, "Where's The 'B' In B-Schools?" *Business Week*, 27 November 2006

11 Denise M. Rousseau, "Is There Such a Thing as 'Evidence-Based Management'?", 2005 Presidential Address to the Academy of Management, *Academy of Management Review*, Vol. 31, No. 2, 2006

12 Donald Hambrick, "The Field of Management's Devotion to Theory: Too Much of a Good Thing," *Academy of Management Journal*, Vol. 50, No. 6, 2007

13 Art Kleiner, "Pankaj Ghemawat: The Thought Leader Interview," *Strategy+Business*, Issue 50, Spring 2008

14 Murray Steel, "Research Must Prove Its Worth in Practice," *Financial Times*, 9 February 2009

15 Freek Vermeulen, "Weak Teaching Formula Needs Research Injection," *Financial Times*, 24 January 2011

16 Peter Tufano, "Business Schools are Stuck in a Self-Reinforcing Bubble," *Bloomberg BusinessWeek*, 14 February 2014

17 Srikant M. Datar, David A. Garvin, and Patrick G. Cullen, *Rethinking the MBA*, Boston: Harvard Business Press, 2010

18 Rakesh Khurana, "The Multipolar MBA," *Strategy+Business*, 21 January 2013

19 Clive Cookson and Andrew Jack, "Science Stifled," *Financial Times*, 12 June 2008

20 "Practically Irrelevant," *The Economist*, 28 August 2007

21 "New Graduation Skills," *The Economist*, 10 May 2007

22 Rita Gunther McGrath, "No Longer a Stepchild: How the Management Field Can Come into Its Own," *Academy of Management Journal*, Vol. 50, No. 6, 2007

23 Tim Hughes, David Bence, Louise Grisoni, Nicholas O'Regan, and David Wornham, "Scholarship That Matters: Academic-Practitioner Engagement in Business and Management," *Academy of Management Learning & Education*, Vol. 10, No. 1, March 2011

24 Marvin D. Dunnette and Zita Marie Brown, "Behavioral Science Research and the Conduct of Business," *Academy of Management Journal*, June 1968

25 "Editor's Comments: Publishing Theory," *Academy of Management Review*, Vol. 31, No. 2, 2006

26 Clayton M. Christensen, in the Foreword to Steven J. Spear, *The High-Velocity Edge*, New York: McGraw-Hill, 2009

27 Gerard George, "Rethinking Management Scholarship," *Academy of Management Journal*, Vol. 57, No. 1, February 2014

28 "Practically Irrelevant," *The Economist*, 28 August 2007

29 Jean M. Bartunek and Sara L. Rynes, "The Construction and Contributions of 'Implications for Practice': What's in Them and What Might They Offer?" *Academy of Management Learning & Education* Vol. 9, No. 1, 2010

30 Jone L. Pearce and Laura Huang, "The Decreasing Value of Research to Management Education," *Academy of Management Learning & Education*, Vol. 11, No. 2, 2012

31 Jone L. Pearce and Laura Huang, "The Decreasing Value of Research to Management Education," *Academy of Management Learning & Education*, Vol. 11, No. 2, 2012

32 Steven Pinker, *How the Mind Works*, New York: W.W. Norton, 1997

33 Mie Augier and David J. Teece, "Reflections On (Shumpeterian) Leadership: A Report on a Seminar on Leadership and Management Education," *California Management Review*, Vol. 47, No. 2, Winter 2005

34 Roy Suddaby, Cynthia Hardy, and Quy Nguyen Huy, "Where Are the New Theories of Organization?" *Academy of Management Review*, Vol. 36, No. 2, 2011

35 Sean Silverthorne, "Q&A With Geoffrey G. Jones," *Harvard Business School Working Knowledge*, 17 March 2008

36 Paul R. Carlile and Clayton M. Christensen, "The Cycles of Theory Building in Management Research," Harvard Business School Working Paper 05-057, 27 October 2004

37 "Practically Irrelevant," *The Economist*, 28 August 2007

38 Ben Schiller, "Academia Strives For Relevance," *Financial Times*, 25 April 2011

39 Ibid.

40 Herman Aguinis, Isabel Suárez-González, Gustavo Lannelonge, and Harry Joo, "Scholarly Impact Revisited," *Academy of Management Perspectives*, 2012

41 John A. Pearce II, "The Value of University Tenure," *BizEd*, September/October 2013

42 Lokman I. Meho, "The Rise and Rise of Citation Analysis," *Physics World*, January 2007

43 Jason A. Colquitt and Cindy P. Zapata-Phelan, "Trends in Theory Building and Theory Testing: A Five-Decade Study of the *Academy of Management Journal*," *Academy of Management Journal*, Vol. 50, No. 6, 2007

44 Donald C. Hambrick, "The Field of Management's Devotion to Theory: Too Much of a Good Thing," *Academy of Management Journal*, Vol. 50, No. 6, 2007

45 George Lăzăroiu, "The Influence of Scientific Articles on the Accumulation of Knowledge," *Economics, Management, and Financial Markets*, Vol. 6, No. 4, 2011

46 Per O. Seglen, "Why the Impact Factor of Journals Should Not Be Used for Evaluating Research," *British Medical Journal*, Vol. 314, 15 February 1997

47 Emma Bell and Richard Thorpe, *A Very Short, Fairly Interesting and Reasonably Cheap Book about Management Research*, London: Sage Publications, 2013

48 Timothy M. Devinney, "What is the Role of Scholarship in Business Schools?" *Financial Times*, 14 November 2013

49 John Mickelthwait and Adrian Wooldridge, *The Witch Doctors*, London: William Heinemann, 1996

50 Lewis Pinault, *Consulting Demons: Inside the Unscrupulous World of Global Corporate Consulting*, New York: HarperBusiness, 2000

51 James O'Shea and Charles Madigan, *Dangerous Company: The Consulting Powerhouses and the Business They Save and Ruin*, New York: Times Business, 1997

52 Jeffrey Pfeffer, *Power*, New York: HarperCollins, 2010

CHAPTER 7

1 Pankaj Ghemawat, "Competition and Business Strategy in Historical Perspective," *The Business History Review*, The President and Fellows of Harvard College, Spring 2002

2 Jeffrey Bracker, "The Historical Development of the Strategic Management Concept," *Academy of Management Review*, Vol. 5, No. 2, 1980

3   C. Roland Christensen, Kenneth R. Andrews, Joseph L. Bower, Richard G. Hamermesh, Michael E. Porter, *Business Policy Text and Cases*, Fifth Edition, New York: Richard D. Irwin Inc., 1982

4   Kenneth R. Andrews, *The Concept of Corporate Strategy*, New York: Richard D. Irwin, 1980

5   Rakesh Khurana, *From Higher Aims to Hired Hands*, Princeton: Princeton University Press, 2007

6   Peter F. Drucker, *The Practice of Management*, New York: Harper & Row, 1954

7   Milton Leontiades, "The Confusing Words of Business Policy," *Academy of Management Review*, Vol. 7, No. 1, 1982

8   Bruce D. Henderson, *The Logic of Business Strategy*, Cambridge, Massachussetts: Ballinger, 1984

9   Bruce D. Henderson, *Henderson on Corporate Strategy*, Cambridge, Massachusetts: Abt Books, 1979

10 The Staff of the Boston Consulting Group, *Perspectives on Experience*, Boston: The Boston Consulting Group, 1972

11 Anne B. Fisher, "Is Long-Range Planning Worth It?" *Fortune*, 23 April 1990

12 Peter F. Drucker, *The Practice of Management*, New York: Harper & Row, 1954

13 H. Igor Ansoff, "Strategies for Diversification," *Harvard Business Review*, September–October 1957

14 Philip Kotler, *Marketing Management: Analysis, Planning and Control*, Engelwood Cliffs, New Jersey: Prentice-Hall, 1980

15 Derek F. Abell, *Defining the Business*, Engelwood Cliffs, New Jersey: Prentice-Hall, 1980

16 Costas Markides, *All the Right Moves*, Boston: Harvard Business School Press, 2000

17 Jay Barney and Trish Gorman Clifford, *What I Didn't Learn in Business School*, Boston: Harvard Business Review Press, 2010

18 Richard Rumelt, *Good Strategy, Bad Strategy*, New York: Crown Business, 2011

19 Cynthia A. Montgomery, *The Strategist*, New York: HarperBusiness, 2012

20 Michael E. Porter, "How Competitive Forces Shape Strategy," *Harvard Business Review*, March–April 1979

21 Michael E. Porter, *Competitive Strategy*, New York: The Free Press, 1980

22 Ibid.

23 Michael E. Porter, "What is strategy?" *Harvard Business Review*, June 1996

24 Ibid.

25 Henry Mintzberg, *The Rise and Fall of Strategic Planning*, New York: The Free Press, 1994

26 Gary Hamel and C.K. Prahalad, "Corporate Imagination and Expeditionary Marketing," *Harvard Business Review*, July–August 1991; Gary Hamel and C.K. Prahalad, "Competing for the Future," *Harvard Business Review*, July 1994; Richard A. D'Aveni, *Hypercompetition: Managing the Dynamics of Strategic Maneuvering*, New York, NY: The Free Press, 1994; Richard T. Pascale, Mark Milleman, and Linda Gioja, *Surfing the Edge of Chaos*, New York: Crown Business, 2000; Rita Gunther McGrath and Ian MacMillan, *The Entrepreneurial Mindset*, Boston: Harvard Business School Press, 2000; Richard D'Aveni, Giovanni Battista Dagnino, and Ken G. Smith, Guest Editors, "The Age of Temporary Advantage, Special Edition," *Strategic Management Review*, December 2010

27 Theodore Levitt, "Marketing Myopia," *Harvard Business Review*, May 1960

28 Theodore Levitt, "Marketing Success Through Differentiation – Of Anything," *Harvard Business Review*, January–February 1980

29 Gary Hamel and C.K. Prahalad, "Corporate Imagination and Expeditionary Marketing," *Harvard Business Review*, July–August 1991

30 Jeffrey F. Rayport and John J. Sviokla, "Managing in the Marketspace," *Harvard Business Review*, November 1994

31 W. Kim Chan and Renèe Mauborgne, "Creating New Market Space," *Harvard Business Review*, January–February 1999

32 Peter Weill and Michael R. Vitale, *Place to Space*, Boston: Harvard Business School Press, 2001

33 W. Kim Chan and Renèe Mauborgne, "Value Innovation," *Harvard Business Review*, July–August 2004

34 W. Kim Chan and Renèe Mauborgne, *Blue Ocean Strategy*, Boston: Harvard Business School Press, 2005

35 www.blueoceanstrategy.com, 24 December 2013

36 Peter F. Drucker, *Managing for Results*, London: William Heinemann, 1964

37 Kenichi Ohmae, *The Mind of the Strategist*, New York: McGraw-Hill, 1982

38 Kenichi Ohmae, "Getting Back to Strategy," *Harvard Business Review*, November–December 1988

39 Among them, Clayton M. Christensen, *The Innovator's Dilemma*, Boston: Harvard Business School Press, 1997; Clayton M. Christensen and Michael E. Raynor, *The Innovator's Solution*, Boston: Harvard Business School Press, 2003

40 Kenichi Ohmae, "Getting Back to Strategy," *Harvard Business Review*, November–December 1988

41 Theodore Levitt, *The Marketing Imagination*, New York: The Free Press, 1983

42 Gary Hamel and C.K. Prahalad, "The Core Competence of the Corporation," *Harvard Business Review*, May–June 1989

43 Walter Kiechel III, *The Lords of Strategy*, Boston: Harvard Business Press, 2010

44 Peter F. Drucker, *Concept of the Corporation*, New York: The John Day Company, 1946

45 Peter F. Drucker, *Managing for Results*, London: William Heinemann, 1964

46 Philip Selznick, *Leadership in Administration*, Evanston: Row Peterson & Co., 1957

47 Deborah Blagg, "Chris Christensen: Legend of the Classroom," *Harvard Business School Working Knowledge*, 16 April 2008, http://hbswk.hbs.edu/item/5901.html, accessed 22 April 2008

48 Edith Penrose, *The Theory of the Growth of the Firm*, New York: Oxford University Press, 1959

49 H. Igor Ansoff, *Corporate Strategy*, New York: McGraw-Hill, 1965

50 Birger Wernerfelt, "A Resource-Based View of the Firm," *Strategic Management Journal*, No. 5, 1984

51 Hiroyuki Itami, *Mobilizing Invisible Assets*, Boston: Harvard University Press, 1987

52 Gary Hamel and C.K. Prahalad, "Strategy as Stretch and Leverage," *Harvard Business Review*, March 1993

53 Gary Hamel and C.K. Prahalad, "Competing for the Future," *Harvard Business Review*, July 1994; Gary Hamel and C.K. Prahalad, *Competing for the Future*, Boston: Harvard Business Press, 1994

54 Nicholas Argyres and Anita McGahan, "An Interview with Michael Porter," *Academy of Management Executive*, Vol. 16, Issue 2, May 2002

55 Priyanka Sangan, "Strategies That Change with Trends Aren't Strategies: Michael Porter, Harvard University," *The Economic Times*, 20 May 2011

56 Joseph L. Bower and Clayton M. Christensen, "Disruptive Technologies: Catching the Wave," *Harvard Business Review*, January 1995

57 Larissa MacFarquhar, "When Giants Fail," *The New Yorker*, 14 May 2012

58 Richard A. D'Aveni, *Hypercompetition: Managing the Dynamics of Strategic Maneuvering*, New York, NY: The Free Press, 1994

59 John Caples, *Tested Advertising Methods*, New York: Prentice-Hall, 1932

60 Peter F. Drucker, *The Practice of Management*, New York: Harper & Row, 1954

61 Peter F. Drucker, *Management Challenges for the 21st Century*, New York: HarperCollins, 1999

62 Theodore Levitt, "Marketing Myopia," *Harvard Business Review*, May 1960

63 Theodore Levitt, *The Marketing Imagination*, New York: The Free Press, 1983

64 Philip Kotler, *Marketing Management: Analysis, Planning and Control*, Engelwood Cliffs, New Jersey: Prentice-Hall, 1980

65 Kenichi Ohmae, "Getting Back to Strategy," *Harvard Business Review*, November–December 1988

66 Theodore Levitt, *The Marketing Imagination*, New York: The Free Press, 1983

67 Theodore Levitt, "The Globalization of Markets," *Harvard Business Review*, May–June 1983

68 Walter Isaacson, *Steve Jobs*, New York: Simon and Schuster, 2011

69 Peter F. Drucker, *The Age of Discontinuity*, New York: Harper & Row, 1968

70 Tony Manning, "Assets and Allies," *The Executive*, March 1990

71 Jill Lepore, "The Disruption Machine," *The New Yorker*, 23 June 2014

72 Drake Bennett, "Clayton Christensen Responds to New Yorker Takedown of 'Disruptive Innovation,'" *Bloomberg Businessweek*, 20 June 2014

73 Larry E. Greiner, Arvand Bhambri, and Thomas G. Cummings, "Searching for a Strategy to Teach Strategy," *Academy of Management Learning & Education*, Vol. 2, No. 4, 2003

74 Robert S. Kaplan and David P. Norton, "Mastering the Management System," *Harvard Business Review*, January 2008

75 Thomas A. Stewart, "Great Enterprise," *Harvard Business Review*, January 2008

76 H. Igor Ansoff, *Corporate Strategy*, New York: McGraw-Hill, 1965

77 Henry Mintzberg, "Crafting Strategy," *Harvard Business Review*, July–August 1987

78 H. Igor Ansoff, "Toward a Strategic Theory of the Firm," *Economies et Societes*, Vol. 2, No. 3, 1968, reprinted in H. Igor Ansoff, Editor, *Business Strategy*, London: Penguin Books, 1969

79 H. Igor Ansoff, *Implanting Strategic Management*, Englewood Cliffs, NJ: Prentice Hall, 1984

80 H. Igor Ansoff, *The New Corporate Strategy*, New York: John Wiley & Sons, 1988

81 Joseph L. Bower, "Business Policy in the 1980s," *Academy of Management Review*, Vol. 7, No. 4, 1982

82 Michael J. Mol and Julian Birkinshaw, *Giant Steps*, London: FT Prentice Hall, 2008

83 H. Igor Ansoff, *The New Corporate Strategy*, New York: John Wiley & Sons, 1988

84 Paula Jarzabkowski, Monica Giulietti, and Bruno Oliveira, *Building a Strategy Toolkit*, report from the Advanced Institute of Management Research, December 2009

85 Roger Martin, *The Opposable Mind*, Boston: Harvard Business School Press, 2007

86 Henry Mintzberg, "Planning on the Left Side and Managing on the Right," *Harvard Business Review*, July 1976

87 Warren G. Bennis and James O'Toole, "How Business Schools Lost Their Way," *Harvard Business Review*, May 2005

88 Russell L. Ackoff, *A Concept of Corporate Planning*, New York: Wiley-Interscience, 1970

89 Gary Kasparov and Diane Coutu, "Strategic Intensity," *Harvard Business Review*, April 2005

90 Walter Isaacson, *Steve Jobs*, New York: Simon and Schuster, 2011

91 Peter F. Drucker, *The Practice of Management*, New York: Harper & Row, 1954

92 Thomas P.M. Barnett, *The Pentagon's New Map*, New York: Penguin, 2004

93 Joseph S. Nye Jr, *Bound to Lead: The Changing Nature of American Power*, New York: Basic Books, 1990; Joseph S. Nye Jr, *Soft Power*, New York: Public Affairs, 2004

94 Mark Owen with Kevin Maurer, *No Easy Day*, New York: Dutton Adult, 2012; Rorke Denver and Ellis Henican, *Damned Few*, New York: Hyperion, 2013

95 Alvin and Heidi Toffler, *War and Anti-War*, New York: Little, Brown and Company, 1993

96 Marilyn Darling, Charles Parry, and Joseph Moore, "Learning in the Thick of It," *Harvard Business Review*, July–August 2005

CHAPTER 8

1 Charles H. Fine, *Clockspeed*, New York: Little, Brown and Company, 1998

2 George Stalk Jr, "Time – The Next Source of Competitive Advantage," *Harvard Business Review*, July–August 1988

3 James P. Womack, Daniel T. Jones, and Daniel Roos, *The Machine That Changed the World*, New York: Rawson Associates, 1990; Bennett Harrison, *Lean And Mean*, New York: Basic Books, 1994

4 John Naisbitt, *Megatrends*, New York: Warner Books, 1982

5 John Seely Brown and Paul Duguid, *The Social Life of Information*, Boston: Harvard Business School Press, 2000

6 See David S. Pugh and David Hickson, "Henri Fayol," *Writers on Organizations*, London: Penguin Books, Sixth Edition, 2007

7 Peter F. Drucker, *The Practice of Management*, New York: Harper & Row, 1954

8 Henry Mintzberg, *Managing*, San Francisco: Berrett-Kohler Publishers, 2009

9 Michael E. Porter and Nitin Nohria, "What Is Leadership?" *Handbook of Leadership Theory and Practice*, Edited by Nitin Nohria and Rakesh Khurana, Boston: Harvard Business Press, 2010

10 Alfred P. Sloan Jr, *My Life with General Motors*, London: Sidgwick and Jackson, 1965

11 Michael S. Malone, *Bill & Dave: How Hewlett and Packard Built the World's Greatest Company*, New York: Portfolio, 2007

12 Ram Charan, Stephen Drotter, and James Noel, *The Leadership Pipeline*, San Francisco: Jossey-Bass, 2001

13 Peter Capelli, "Talent Management for the Twenty-First Century," *Harvard Business Review*, March 2008

14 Robert G. Eccles and Nitin Nohria, *Beyond the Hype*, Boston: Harvard Business School Press, 1992

15 "The New Organization: A Survey of the Company," *The Economist*, 21 January 2006

16 "The Mix Manifesto," Management Innovation eXchange, http://www.managementexchange.com/about-the-mix, accessed November 2014

17 Peter F. Drucker, "New Templates for Today's Organizations," *Harvard Business Review*, January–February 1974

18 John Sculley, with John A. Byrne, *Odyssey, Pepsi to Apple*, London: Collins, 1987

19 Jeremy Main, "The Winning Organization," *Fortune*, 26 September 1988

20 Rosabeth Moss Kanter, "The New Managerial Work," *Harvard Business Review*, November 1989

21 Robert Kanigel, *The One Best Way*, New York: Little, Brown and Company, 1997

22 Henry Ford, *My Life and Work*, London: William Heinemann, 1922

23 Peter F. Drucker, *Post-Capitalist Society*, London: Butterworth-Heinemann, 1993

24 Peter F. Drucker, "The Coming Rediscovery of Scientific Management," *Conference Board Record*, 1976

25 Henry Ford, *My Life and Work*, London: William Heinemann, 1922

26 Allan Nevins with Frank Ernest Hill, *Ford: The Times, the Man, The Company*, New York: Scribner's, 1954, cited in Bruce E. Kaufman, "Strategic Human Resource Management Research in the United States: A Failing Grade after 30 Years?" *Academy of Management Perspectives*, May 2012

27 Ronald Heifetz, *Leadership Without Easy Answers*, Boston: The Belknap Press, Harvard University Press, 1998

28 Sylvia Nasar, *Grand Pursuit*, New York: Simon & Schuster, 2011

29 Frederick W. Taylor, "Shop Management," lecture to meeting of mechanical engineers held at the United States Hotel, Saratoga, June 1903

30 Fritz Machlup, *The Production and Distribution of Knowledge in the United States*, Princeton: Princeton University Press, 1962; John J. Tarrant, *Drucker, the Man Who Invented the Corporate Society*, New York: Cahners Books, 1976

31 Peter F. Drucker, *The Age of Discontinuity*, New York: Harper & Row, 1968

32 James Surowiecki, *The Wisdom of Crowds*, New York: Little, Brown and Company, 2004

33 Tom Peters, "The Brand Called You," *Fast Company*, August–September 1997; *The Brand You 50*, New York: Alfred A. Knopf, 1999

34 Thomas A. Stewart, "A New Way to Think About Employees," *Fortune*, 13 April 1998

35 George H. Litwin and Robert A. Stringer Jr, *Motivation and Organization Climate*, Boston: Division of Research, Graduate School of Business Administration, Harvard University, 1968

36 Ibid.

37 Daniel R. Denison, *Corporate Culture and Organizational Effectiveness*, New York: John Wiley, 1990; Michael Beer, Russell A. Eisenstadt, and Bert Spector, *The Critical Path to Corporate Renewal*, Boston: Harvard Business School Press, 1990

38 Rodd Wagner and James K. Harter, "The Heart of Great Managing," *Gallup Management Journal*, June 2008

39 *Towers Perrin European Talent Survey*, 2004

40 "Gallup Study: Feeling Good Matters in the Workplace," *Gallup Management Journal*, 12 January 2006

41 *Towers Perrin Global Workforce Study*, 2007

42 Martin Dewhurst, Matthew Guthridge, and Elizabeth Mohr, "Motivating People: Getting Beyond Money," *McKinsey Quarterly*, November 2009

43 Susan Sorenson and Keri Garman, "How to Tackle U.S. Employees' Stagnating Engagement," *Gallup Business Journal*, 11 June 2013

44 Marco Nink, "Low Employee Wellbeing and Engagement Hurt German Companies," *Gallup Business Journal*, 26 April 2013

45 David MacLeod and Chris Brady, *The Extra Mile*, London: FT Prentice Hall, 2008

46 Andrew Revkin, "A New Measure of Well-Being from a Happy Little Kingdom" *The New York Times*, 4 October 2005; "Economics Discovers Its Feelings," *The Economist*, 19 December 2006; *How's Life*, OECD, November, 2011; Jeffrey Kluger, "The Happiness of Pursuit," *Time*, 8–15 July 2013

47 Thomas A. Wright and Russell Cropanzano, "Well-Being, Satisfaction and Job Performance: Another Look at the Happy/Productive Worker Thesis," *Academy of Management Best Papers Proceedings*, 1997; Fred Luthans and Alan H. Church, "Positive Organizational Behavior: Developing and Managing Organizational Strengths," *Academy of Management Executive*, February 2002, Vol. 16, Issue 1; Cynthia Fisher, "Happiness at Work," *International Journal of Management Reviews*, Vol. 12, Issue 4, December 2010; Christine Riordan, "The Positive Returns of a Happy Workforce," *Financial Times*, 19 May 2013; Nancy Cook, "The Corporate Pursuit of Happiness," *Fast Company*, March 2011; *Mlab Mnotes*, February 2008, Issue 07; "The Secrets of Happiness," http://www.managementlab.org/files/site/publications/labnotes/mlab-labnotes-007.pdf

48 Nancy Rothbard, "Put on a Happy Face. Seriously." *The Wall Street Journal*, 24 October 2011

49 Rensis Likert, "Measuring Organizational Performance," *Harvard Business Review*, March–April 1958

50 R. Likert, *New Patterns of Management*, New York: McGraw-Hill, 1961; Rensis Likert, *The Human Organization*, Tokyo: McGraw-Hill, 1967

51 Abraham H. Maslow with Deborah C. Stephens and Gary Heil, *Maslow on Management*, New York: John Wiley & Sons, 1998

52 A.H. Maslow, *The Farther Reaches of Human Nature*, New York: The Viking Press, 1971

53 Daniel Goleman, Richard Boyatzis, and Annie Mckee, "Primal Leadership," *Harvard Business Review*, December 2001

54 Bill Breen, "The 6 Myths of Creativity," *Fast Company*, Issue 89, December 2004

55 Rosabeth Moss Kanter, *Confidence*, New York: Crown Business, 2004

56 Steven Wheeler, Walter McFarland, and Art Kleiner, "A Blueprint for Strategic Leadership," *Strategy+Business*, Issue 49, Winter 2007

57 Theresa Welbourne, "Dear Workforce: How Important is an Overall Measure of Employee Satisfaction?" *Workforce Management*, 24 September 2002, http://www.workforce.com/archive/article/23/45/28.php?ht=employee%20satisfaction

58 Jessica Marquez, "Halo Effect: The Myth of Employee Satisfaction," Workforce Management Online, 26 July 2007

59 Howard Gardner, *Changing Minds*, Boston: Harvard Business School Press, 2004

60 K. Anders Ericsson, "The Influence of Experience and Deliberate Practice on the Development of Superior Performance," in K. Anders Ericsson, Neil Charness, Paul J. Feltovitch, and Robert R. Hoffman, Editors, *The Cambridge Handbook of Expertise and Expert Performance*, New York: Cambridge University Press, 2006; Malcolm Gladwell, *Outliers*, New York: Little, Brown and Company, 2008; Daniel Coyle, *The Talent Code*, New York: Bantam Books, 2009; Steven J. Spear, *The High-Velocity Edge*, New York: McGraw-Hill, 2009

61 Christian Kiewitz, "Happy Employees and Firm Performance: Have We Been Putting the Cart Before the Horse?" *Academy of Management Executive*, February 2004

62 Frederick Herzberg, *Work and the Nature of Man*, New York: World Publishing Co., 1966, cited in Derek S. Pugh, Editor, *Organization Theory: Selected Classic Readings*, Fifth Edition, London: Penguin Books, 2007

63 Mihaly Csikszentmihalyi, *Living Well*, New York: Basic Books, 1997

64 Matthew Stewart, *The Management Myth*, New York: W.W. Norton & Company, 2009

65 W. Edwards Deming, *Out of the Crisis*, Cambridge: University of Cambridge, 1982

66 Douglas McGregor, *The Human Side of Enterprise*, New York: McGraw-Hill, 1960

67 Ibid.

68 *Towers Perrin Global Workforce Study*, 2007

69 Teresa M. Amabile and Steven J. Kramer, "What Really Motivates Workers," *Harvard Business Review*, January–February 2010

70 David C. McClelland, *The Achieving Society*, New York: Irvington, 1968

71 Frederick Herzberg, "One More Time: How Do You Motivate Employees?" *Harvard Business Review*, January–February 1968

72 Peter F. Drucker, *The Age of Discontinuity*, New York: Harper & Row, 1968

73 Kenneth Blanchard and Spencer Johnson, *The One Minute Manager*, New York: William Morrow, 1982

74 Jack and Suzy Welch, "The Biggest Dirty Little Secret in Business," *The Welch Way* website, www.welchway.com

75 Douglas S. Sherwin, "Strategy for Winning Employee Commitment," *Harvard Business Review*, May–June 1972

76 Duff McDonald, *The Firm*, New York: Simon & Schuster, 2013

77 Richard Beckhard, *Organization Development*, New York: Addison-Wesley Publishing Company, 1969

78 Michael Beer, Russell A. Eisenstadt, and Bert Spector, *The Critical Path to Corporate Renewal*, Boston: Harvard Business School Press, 1990

79 Edgar H. Schein, *Organizational Culture and Leadership*, San Francisco: Jossey-Bass, 1985; Edgar H. Schein, *The Corporate Culture Survival Guide*, San Francisco: Jossey-Bass, 1999; Edgar H. Schein, interview with the author, May 2005

80 Edgar H. Schein, *Organizational Culture and Leadership*, San Francisco: Jossey-Bass, 1985

81 Sarah Kaplan and Paula Jarzabkowski, "Using Strategy Tools in Practice – How Tools Mediate Strategizing and Organizing," Advanced Institute of Management Research, Paper No. 047, August 2006

82 Interview with the author, 2004

83 Daniel Goleman, Richard Boyatzis, and Annie McKee, "Primal Leadership," *Harvard Business Review*, December 2001

CHAPTER 9

1 James McGregor Burns, *Leadership*, New York: HarperCollins, 1978

2 Warren Bennis and Burt Nanus, *Leaders*, New York: Harper & Row, 1985

3 Barbara Kellerman, *The End of Leadership*, New York: HarperCollins, 2012

4 Peter F. Drucker, *The Practice of Management*, New York: Harper & Row, 1954

5 Rakesh Khurana, *Searching for a Corporate Savior*, Princeton: Princeton University Press, 2002

6 Bruce Aviolo, Fred Walumba, and Todd J. Weber, "Leadership: Current Theories, Research, and Future Directions," *Management Department Faculty Publications*, University of Nebraska, Paper 37, 1 January 2009

7 Michael E. Porter and Nitin Nohria, "What is Leadership?" *Handbook of Leadership Theory and Practice*, Edited by Nitin Nohria and Rakesh Khurana, Boston: Harvard Business Press, 2010

8 Barbara Kellerman, *The End of Leadership*, New York: HarperCollins, 2012

9 Oliver Staley, "Harvard Business School Hires Manchester United's Alex Ferguson," Bloomberg, 4 April 2014

10 Peter F. Drucker, *Management Tasks, Responsibilities, Practices*, London: William Heinemann, 1974

11 Abraham Zaleznik, "Managers and Leaders, Are They Different?" *Harvard Business Review*, May–June 1977

12 John P. Kotter, "What Leaders Really Do," *Harvard Business Review*, May–June 1990

13 John P. Kotter, *A Force for Change*, New York: The Free Press, 1990

14 Stephen R. Covey, *The 7 Habits of Highly Successful People*, New York: Simon & Schuster, 1989

15 John P. Kotter, *The New Rules*, New York: The Free Press, 1995

16 Henry Mintzberg, *Managing*, San Francisco: Berrett-Koehler Publishers, 2009

17 Jay Lorsch, "A Contingency Theory of Leadership," *Handbook of Leadership Theory and Practice*, Edited by Nitin Nohria and Rakesh Khurana, Boston: Harvard Business Press, 2010

18 Peter F. Drucker, *The Practice of Management*, New York: Harper & Row, 1954

19 Daniel Goleman, Richard Boyatzis, and Annie McKee, "Primal Leadership," *Harvard Business Review*, December 2001

20 *Emerson's Essays*, London: J.M. Dent & Sons, 1978

21 Wayne Dyer, *Your Erroneous Zones*, New York: Funk & Wagnalls, 1976

22 Stephen R. Covey, *The 7 Habits of Highly Effective People*, New York: The Free Press, 1989

23 Fred Fiedler, *A Theory of Leadership Effectiveness*, New York: McGraw-Hill, 1967

24 Paul R. Lawrence and Jay W. Lorsch, *Organization and Environment*, Boston: Harvard Business School Press, 1967

25 Robert R. Blake and Jane S. Mouton, *The Managerial Grid*, Houston: The Gulf Publishing Co., 1964

26 http://psychology.wikia.com/wiki/Social_style#cite_ref-0

27 P. Hersey and K.H. Blanchard, "Life Cycle Theory of Leadership," *Training and Development Journal*, 23 (2), 1969; P. Hersey, K.H. Blanchard, and W.E. Natemeyer, "Situational Leadership, Perception, and the Impact of Power," *Group and Organization Management* 4, No. 4, 1979; Paul Hersey and Kenneth H. Blanchard, *The Management of Organizational Behavior*, New Jersey: Prentice-Hall, 1984

28 Dale Carnegie, *How to Win Friends and Influence People*, New York: Simon & Schuster, 1936

29 Ronald Heifetz, *Leadership Without Easy Answers*, Boston: Harvard University Press, 1998

30 Jim Collins, *Good to Great*, New York: HarperBusiness, 2001

31 Peter Salovey and John D. Mayer, "Emotional Intelligence," Bayport Publishing, 1990

32 Daniel Goleman , *Emotional Intelligence*, New York: Bantam Books, 1995

33 Dana L. Joseph and Daniel A. Newman, "Emotional Intelligence: An Integrative Meta-Analysis and Cascading Model," *Journal of Applied Psychology*, Vol. 95, No. 1, 2010; Adam Grant, "The Dark Side of Emotional Intelligence," *The Atlantic*, 2 January 2014

34 Herminia Ibarra, "Beware the Navel-Gazing Leader," *Financial Times*, 8 February 2015

35 John R. Wells, *Strategic IQ*, San Francisco: Jossey-Bass, 2012

36 Michael Blanding, "Strategic Intelligence: Adapt or Die," *HBS Working Knowledge*, 6 August 2012

37 John R. Wells, *Strategic IQ*, San Francisco: Jossey-Bass, 2012; www.exed.hbs.edu/programs/sa/Pages/curriculum.aspx

38 Tony Manning, *Making Sense of Strategy*, Cape Town: Zebra Press, 2001

39 Anthony D. Manning, *The New Age Strategist*, Johannesburg: Southern Book Publishers, 1988

40 Tony Manning, "Questions Of Strategy," *Directorship*, September 1998; reprinted in *The Management Challenge: South Africa in the New World: A Selection of Articles*, 1998, available on www.tonymanning.com

41 David Ogilvy, *Confessions of an Advertising Man*, New York: Athenium, 1963

42 Tony Manning, *Making Sense of Strategy*, Cape Town: Zebra Press, 2001

43 Warren Bennis and Burt Nanus, *Leaders: The Strategies for Taking Charge*, New York: Harper & Row, 1985

44 John W. Gardner, *On Leadership*, New York: The Free Press, 1990

45 Malcolm S. Knowles, *The Modern Practice of Adult Education*, Cambridge: The Adult Education Company, 1980

CHAPTER 10

1 Alvin Toffler, *The Third Wave*, London: Collins, 1980

2 Peter F. Drucker, "The Coming of the New Organization," *Harvard Business Review*, January–February 1988

3 Harold J. Leavitt, "Why Hierarchies Thrive," *Harvard Business Review*, March 2003

4 Gary Hamel, "Bringing Silicon Valley Inside," *Harvard Business Review*, September–October 1999

5 Gary Hamel, "Innovation as a Deep Capability," *Leader to Leader*, No. 27, Winter 2003

6 Gary Hamel with Bill Breen, *The Future of Management*, Boston: Harvard Business School Press, 2007

7 Gary Hamel, "The Why, What, and How of Management Innovation," *Harvard Business Review*, February 2006

8 Joanna Barsh, "Innovative Management: A Conversation with Gary Hamel and Lowell Bryan," *The McKinsey Quarterly*, No. 1, 2008

9 Gary Hamel, "Moonshots for Management," *Harvard Business Review*, February 2009

10 Peter F. Drucker, *Concept of the Corporation*, New York: The John Day Company, 1946

11 Douglas McGregor, *The Human Side of Enterprise*, New York: McGraw-Hill, 1960

12 John W. Gardner, *Self-Renewal: The Individual and the Innovative Society*, New York: Harper & Row, 1963

13 Alvin Toffler, *Future Shock*, London: The Bodley Head, 1970

14 Alvin Toffler, *The Adaptive Corporation*, New York: McGraw-Hill, 1985

15 Alvin Toffler, *Future Shock*, London: The Bodley Head, 1970

16 Alvin Toffler, *The Third Wave*, London: Collins, 1980

17 Alvin Toffler, *Powershift*, New York: Bantam Books, 1990

18 Robert L. Schwartz, *The Tarrytown Letter*, No. 33, November 1983

19 William G. Ouchi, *Theory Z*, New York: Addison-Wesley, 1981

20 John Naisbitt and Patricia Aburdene, *Re-inventing the Corporation*, New York: Warner Books, 1985

21 Tom Peters, "Get Innovative or Get Dead, (Part One)" *California Management Review* Vol. 33, No. 1, Fall 1990; and Tom Peters, "Get Innovative or Get Dead, (Part Two)" *California Management Review*, Vol. 33, No. 2, Winter 1991

22 Interview with Rowan Gibson, Editor, *Rethinking the Future*, London: Nicholas Brealey, 1996

23 James O'Toole, "Coming Attractions: The New *New Management*," *New Management*, Vol. 6, No. 1, Summer 1988

24 Geoffrey Colvin, "Managing in the Info Era," *Fortune*, 6 March 2000

25 Joanna Barsh, "Innovative Management: A Conversation with Gary Hamel and Lowell Bryan," *The McKinsey Quarterly*, No. 1, 2008

26 Peter F. Drucker, "The Coming Rediscovery of Scientific Management," *Conference Board Record*, 1976

27 Robert Townsend, *Up the Organization*, London: Michael Joseph, 1970

28 Jeanne M. Liedtka and John W. Rosenblum, "Shaping Conversations: Making Strategy, Managing Change," *California Management Review*, Vol. 39, No. 1, Fall 1996

29 Ronald E. Purser and Steven Cabana, *The Self Managing Organization*, New York: The Free Press, 1998

30 Tom Peters and Nancy Austin, *A Passion for Excellence*, New York: Random House, 1985

31 Tom Peters, *Liberation Management*, New York: Alfred A. Knopf, 1992

32 Ricardo Semler, "Managing Without Managers," *Harvard Business Review*, September–October 1989

33 Ricardo Semler, *Maverick*, New York: Warner Books, 1993

34 Ricardo Semler, *The Seven-Day Weekend*, New York: Penguin/Portfolio, 2004

35 Frederick G. Hilmer and Lex Donaldson, *Management Redeemed*, New York: The Free Press, 1996

36 For a sampling, see Robert Townsend, *Up the Organization*, London: Michael Joseph, 1970; John Diebold, *Making the Future Work*, New York: Simon & Schuster, 1984; John Naisbitt and Patricia Aburdene, *Re-inventing the Corporation*, New York: Warner Books, 1985; Steven C. Brandt, *Entrepreneuring in Established Companies*, Homewood, Illinois: Dow Jones-Irwin, 1986;

John J. Nora, C. Raymond Rogers, and Robert J. Stramy, *Transforming the Workplace*, Princeton, NJ: Princeton University Press, 1986; Stanley M. Davis, *Future Perfect*, New York: Addison Wesley, 1987; Rosabeth Moss Kanter, *When Giants Learn to Dance*, New York: Simon & Schuster, 1989; Kevin Barham and Clive Rassam, *Shaping the Corporate Future*, London: Unwin Hyman, 1989; Robert B. Reich, *The Work of Nations*, New York: Alfred A. Knopf, 1991; D. Quinn Mills, *Rebirth of the Corporation*, New York: John Wiley, 1991; Gifford Pinchot III, *Intrapreneuring*, New York: Harper & Row, 1985; Gifford and Elizabeth Pinchot, *The End of Bureaucracy and the Rise of the Intelligent Enterprise*, San Francisco: Berret-Koehler, 1993; David Birchall and Laurence Lyons, *Creating Tomorrow's Organization*, London: Pitman, 1995; Rowan Gibson, Editor, *Rethinking the Future*, London: Nicholas Brealey, 1996; Art Kleiner, *The Age of Heretics*, New York: Doubleday, 1996; Rosabeth Moss Kanter, *Frontiers of Management*, Boston: Harvard Business School Press, 1997; Rick Levine, Christopher Locke, Doc Earls, and David Weinberger, *The Cluetrain Manifesto*, Cambridge: Perseus Books, 2000; Subir Chowdhury, *Management 21C*, London: Pearson Education, 2000; Philip Evans and Thomas S. Wurster, *Blown to Bits*, Boston: Harvard Business School Press, 2000; Tom Brown, Stuart Crainer, Des Dearlove, and Jorge N. Rodrigues, *Business Minds*, London: Pearson Education, 2002; Frances Cairncross, *The Company of the Future*, London: Profile Books, 2002; Thomas W. Malone, Robert Laubacher, and Michael S. Scott Morton, *Inventing the Organizations of the 21st Century*, Boston: MIT Press, 2003; Thomas W. Malone, *The Future of Work*, Boston: Harvard Business School Press, 2004

37 Stanley M. Davis, *Future Perfect*, New York: Addison-Wesley, 1987

38 Tom Brown, "Innovation Station," *Business Strategy Review*, Vol. 18, Issue 2, Summer 2007

39 Henry Mintzberg, *Tracking Strategies*, Oxford: Oxford University Press, 2007

40 Julian Birkinshaw, "The Reinvention of Management," www.london.edu/newsandevents/news/ 2009/10/The_reinvention_of_management_1035.html, accessed 8 December 2009

41 David K. Hurst, "Books in Brief," *Strategy+Business*, Issue 50, Spring 2008

42 www.managementlab.org, 26 October 2011

43 "Are We Going 'Back to the Future' in Researching Management," Harvard Business School *Working Knowledge*, 3 February 2011

44 Andrew Hill, "Still on the Cusp of a Revolution," *Financial Times*, 4 March 2012

45 The Mix Manifesto, http://www.managementexchange.com

46 http://www.managementexchange.com

47 Rob Cross and Andrew Parker, *The Hidden Power of Social Networks*, Boston: Harvard Business School Press, 2004

48 Nitin Nohria and Sumantra Ghoshal, *The Differentiated Network*, San-Francisco: Jossey-Bass, 1997

49 D. Quinn Mills, *Rebirth of the Corporation*, New York: John Wiley, 1991

50 Charles Handy, *The Age of Unreason*, London: Business Books, 1989

51 Lars Kolind, *The Second Cycle*, London: Pearson Prentice-Hall, 2006

52 Harold J. Leavitt, "Why Hierarchies Thrive," *Harvard Business Review*, March 2003

53 Alfred D. Chandler, *Strategy and Structure: Chapters in the History of the American Industrial Enterprise*, Boston: The MIT Press, 1962; Henry Mintzberg, *The Structuring of Organizations*, Englewood Cliffs, NJ: Prentice-Hall, 1979; Frederick G. Hilmer and Lex Donaldson, *Management Redeemed*, New York: The Free Press, 1996; David A. Nadler and Michael L. Tushman, *Competing by Design*, New York: Oxford University Press, 1997; Russell L. Ackoff, *Re-creating the Corporation*, New York: Oxford University Press, 1999; Eric D. Beinhocker, *The Origin of Wealth*, New York: Random House, 2006; Harold J. Leavitt, "Why Hierarchies Thrive," *Harvard*

Business Review, March 2003; Harold J. Leavitt, *Top Down*, Boston: Harvard Business School Press, 2005

CHAPTER 11

1   Peter F. Drucker, *The Practice of Management*, New York: Harper & Row, 1954; Pankaj Ghemawat, *Commitment: The Dynamic of Strategy*, New York: The Free Press, 1991; Michael E. Porter, "What Is Strategy?" *Harvard Business Review*, June 1996

2   Scott E. Page, "Path Dependence," *Quarterly Journal of Political Science*, Vol. 1, 2006

3   Karl E. Weick, *Sensemaking in Organizations*, Thousand Oaks, California: Sage Publications, 1995; Karl E. Weick and Kathleen M. Sutcliffe, *Managing the Unexpected*, San Francisco: Jossey-Bass, 2001; Richard Normann, *Reframing Business*, Chichester: John Wiley & Sons, 2001; Sarah Kaplan and Paula Jarzabkowski, "Using Strategy Tools in Practice – How Tools Mediate Strategizing and Organizing," Advanced Institute of Management Research, Paper No. 047, August 2006; James March, *The Ambiguities of Experience*, New York: Cornell University Press, 2010; Sarah Kaplan, "Strategy and Powerpoint," *Organization Science*, 2011; Sarah Kaplan and Wanda J. Orlikowski, "Temporal Work in Strategy Making," *Organizational Science*, 2013; JP Eggers and Sarah Kaplan, "Cognition and Capabilities," *The Academy of Management Annals*, Vol. 7, No.1, May 2013

4   Chester I. Barnard, *The Functions of the Executive*, Cambridge, Massachusetts: Harvard University Press, 1938

5   Richard Rumelt, *Good Strategy, Bad Strategy*, New York: Crown Business, 2011

6   Ibid.

7   Gary Hamel & C.K. Prahalad, "Strategic Intent," *Harvard Business Review*, May–June, 1989

8   Christopher A. Bartlett and Sumantra Ghoshal, "Changing the Role of Top Management: Beyond Strategy to Purpose," *Harvard Business Review*, November 1994; Tony Manning, *Making Sense of Strategy*, Cape Town: Zebra Press, 2001; Rick Warren, *The Purpose-Driven Life*, Grand Rapids Michigan: Zondervan, 2002; Nikos Mourkogiannis, *Purpose*, New York: Palgrave Macmillan, 2006

9   Tony Manning, *Making Sense of Strategy*, Cape Town: Zebra Press, 2001

10 Robert Simons, "The Business of Business Schools: Restoring a Focus on Competing to Win," *Capitalism and Society*, Vol. 8, Issue 1, 2013

11 Milton Friedman, "The Social Responsibility of Business is to Increase Its Profits," *The New York Times Magazine*, 13 September 1970

12 Jeff Madrick, "Why Jack Welch Knows About Changing Numbers," *Harper's*, 10 October 2012

13 "The Jack Welch MBA," *The Economist*, 23 June 2009

14 "Jack Welch Cracks the Whip Again," *Business Week*, 14 December 1997

15 Francesco Guerrera, "Welch Condemns Share Price Focus," *Financial Times*, 12 March 2009

16 Michael E. Porter and Mark R. Kramer, "Strategy and Society," *Harvard Business Review*, December 2006

17 Michael E. Porter and Mark R. Kramer, "Creating Shared Value," *Harvard Business Review*, January–February 2011

18 Martin Neil Baily and Frank Comes, "Prospects for Growth: An Interview with Robert Solow," *McKinsey Quarterly*, September 2014

19 Charles A. O'Reilly III and Michael L. Tushman, "Organizational Ambidexterity: Past, Present And Future," Research paper No. 2130, Stanford Graduate School of Business, June 2013

20 Louis V. Gerstner, *Who Says Elephants Can't Dance?* New York: HarperCollins, 2002

21 Richard A. D'Aveni, *Beating the Commodity Trap*, Boston: Harvard Business Press, 2010

22 "Historically Speaking: A Roundtable with Alfred D. Chandler, Nancy F. Koehn, Debora L. Spar, and Richard S. Tedlow," *Leading Research*, Harvard Business School, http://www.leadingresearch.hbs.edu/story02.html, accessed 4 April 2008

23 Kenneth R. Andrews, *The Concept of Corporate Strategy*, Homewood, Illinois: Richard D. Irwin Inc., 1980

24 Martin Neil Baily and Frank Comes, "Prospects for Growth: An Interview with Robert Solow," *McKinsey Quarterly*, September 2014

25 Fred Gluck, Michael G. Jacobides, and Dan Simpson, "Synthesis, Capabilities, and Overlooked Insights: Next Frontiers for Strategists," *McKinsey Quarterly*, September 2014

26 Richard Rumelt, *Good Strategy, Bad Strategy*, New York: Crown Business, 2011

27 Michael E. Porter, "What is Strategy?" *Harvard Business Review*, November–December 1996

28 Michael E. Porter, "CEO As Strategist," *Leadership Excellence*, September 2005

29 Eric Van den Steen, "A Theory of Explicitly Formulated Strategy," Working Paper 12-102, Harvard Business School, May 2012

30 Thomas J. Peters and Robert H. Waterman, *In Search of Excellence*, New York: Harper & Row, 1982

31 Henry Mintzberg, Bruce Ahlstrand, and Joseph Lampel, *Strategy Safari*, New York: The Free Press, 1990

32 Kurt Lewin, "Frontiers in Group Dynamics," in D. Cartwright, Editor, *Field Theory in Social Science*, London: Social Science Paperbacks, 1952; Richard Beckhard and Reuben T. Harris, *Organizational Transitions*, New York: Addison-Wesley, 1987; W. Warner Burke, *Organization Development*, New York, Addison-Wesley, 1987

33 Abraham Zaleznick, "Managers and Leaders: Are They Different?" *Harvard Business Review*, March–April 1977; John P. Kotter, "What Leaders Really Do" *Harvard Business Review*, March 1990; John Kotter, *John Kotter on What Leaders Really Do*, Boston: Harvard Business School Press, 1999

34 Henry Mintzberg, *Managers Not MBAs*, San Francisco: Berrett-Koehler Publishers, 2004; Cynthia A. Montgomery, *The Strategist*, New York: HarperBusiness, 2012

35 Ellen F. Goldman, "Strategic Thinking at the Top," *Sloan Management Review*, Vol. 48, No. 4, Summer 2007

36 William Duggan, *Strategic Intuition*, New York: Columbia Business School Publishing, 2007

37 Dorothy Leonard & Walter Swap, *Deep Smarts*, Boston: Harvard Business School Press, 2005; K. Anders Ericsson, 2006; Malcolm Gladwell, 2008

38 Eugen Herrigel, *Zen in the Art of Archery*, London: Routledge & Kegan Paul, 1953

39 Steven J. Spear, "Learning to Lead at Toyota," *Harvard Business Review*, May 2004

CHAPTER 12

1 Peter F. Drucker, "Thinking Ahead: The Potentials of Management Science," *Harvard Business Review*, January–February 1959

2 William A. Sherden, *The Fortune Sellers*, New York: John Wiley, 1998

3 Peter Cornelius, Alexander Van de Putte & Mattia Romani, "Three Decades of Scenario Planning at Shell," *California Management Review*, Vol. 48, No. 1, Fall 2005

4 Nate Silver, *The Signal and the Noise*, New York: Allen Lane, 2012

5 Ben Lauderdale, "What We Got Wrong in Our 2015 U.K. General Election Model," 8 May 2015, fivethirtyeight.com

6 Nassim Nicholas Taleb, *The Black Swan*, New York: Random House, 2007

7 Tim Harford, *Adapt*, London: Little, Brown and Company, 2011

8 George Stalk Jr, "Time – The Next Source of Competitive Advantage," *Harvard Business Review*, July–August 1988; Tony Manning, *The Race to Learn*, Cape Town: Juta & Co, 1991; Yves Doz and Mikko Kosonen, *Fast Strategy*, London: Pearson Education, 2008; Steven J. Spear, *The High-Velocity Edge*, New York: McGraw-Hill, 2009; Jocelyn R. Davis, Henry M. Frechette Jr, Edwin H. Boswell, *Strategic Speed*, Boston: Harvard Business Press, 2010

9 Sumantra Ghoshal and Christopher A. Bartlett, "Changing the Role of Top Management: Beyond Strategy to Purpose," *Harvard Business Review*, November–December 1994; Sumantra Ghoshal and Christopher A. Bartlett, "Changing the Role of Top Management: Beyond Structure to Processes," *Harvard Business Review*, January–February 1995; Sumantra Ghoshal and Christopher A. Bartlett, "Changing the Role of Top Management: Beyond Systems to People," *Harvard Business Review*, May–June 1995

10 Tony Manning, "A New Model for Strategists," *Tony Manning's Strategy Letter*, Issue No. 9, July 1994

11 Tony Manning, "Beyond Strategy to Purpose," *Tony Manning's Strategy Letter*, Issue No. 12, April 1995

12 Hiroyuki Itami, *Mobilizing Invisible Assets*, Boston: Harvard University Press, 1987

13 Donald N. Sull, *Revival of the Fittest*, Boston: Harvard Business School Press, 2003

14 Liisa Välikangas, *The Resilient Organization*, New York: McGraw-Hill, 2010

15 David J. Collis and Cynthia A. Montgomery, "Competing on Resources," *Harvard Business Review*, July 2008

16 Steven P. Schnaars, *Managing Imitation Strategies*, New York: The Free Press, 1994; Paul Geroski, *Fast Second*, San Francisco: Jossey-Bass, 2004

17 Mehrdad Baghai, Stephen C. Coley, and David White with Charles Conn and Robert J. McLean, "Staircases to Growth," *McKinsey Quarterly*, November 1996; Mehrdad Baghai, Stephen Coley, and David White, *The Alchemy of Growth*, New York: Perseus Publishing, 1999.

18 Lawrence G. Hrebiniak, *Making Strategy Work*, New Jersey: Wharton Publishing, 2005; Michael C. Mankins and Richard Steele, "Turning Great Strategy into Great Performance," *Harvard Business Review*, July 2005; Donald Sull, Rebecca Homkes, and Charles Sull, "Why Strategy Execution Unravels – and What to Do About It," *Harvard Business Review*, March 2015

19 Mark Morgan, Raymond E. Levitt, and William Malek, *Executing Your Strategy*, Harvard Business School Press, 2007

20 Paddy Miller, *Mission Critical*, Maidenhead: McGraw-Hill, 2001

21 Ian I. Mitroff, Can M. Alpaslan, and Richard O. Mason, "The Messy Business of Management," *Sloan Management Review*, Vol. 54, No. 1, Fall 2012

22 Tom Peters, "Tom Peter's True Confessions," *Fast Company*, Issue 53, November 2001

23 Frederick W. Taylor, "Shop Management," lecture to meeting of mechanical engineers held at the United States Hotel, Saratoga, June 1903

24 James P. Womack, Daniel T. Jones, and Daniel Roos, *The Machine That Changed the World*, New York: Rawson Associates, 1990

CHAPTER 13

1 Walter Kiechel, "The Management Century," *Harvard Business Review*, November 2012

2 "Change Management: The MBA Is Being Transformed, for Better or for Worse," *The Economist*, 13 October 2013

3 "Build It and They May Come," *The Economist*, 18 January 2014

4   Earl F. Cheit, "Business Schools and Their Critics," *California Management Review*, Vol. XXVII, No. 3, Spring 1985; Jeffrey Pfeffer and Christina T. Fong, "The End of Business Schools? Less Success than Meets the Eye," *Academy of Management Learning and Education*, Vol. 1, No. 1, September 2002; Henry Mintzberg, *Managers Not MBAs*, San Francisco: Berrett-Koehler, 2004; Warren G. Bennis and James O'Toole, "How Business Schools Lost Their Way," *Harvard Business Review*, May 2005; Harry DeAngelo, Linda DeAngelo, and Jerold L. Zimmerman, "What's Really Wrong with U.S. Business Schools?" *SSRN Network*, accessed 3 May 2008; Diane Parente, John Stephan, and Randy C. Brown, "Understanding the Big Picture: An Explanatory Model of Strategic Management Skills Acquisition," Academy of Management Best Conference Paper, 2006; Stan Abraham and Robert J. Allio, "The Troubled Strategic-Business-Advice Industry: Why It's Failing Decision Makers," *Strategy & Leadership*, Vol. 34, No. 3, 2006; Manfred Kets De Vries, "Creating Transformational Executive Education Programs," *Academy of Management Learning & Education*, 2007, Vol. 6, No. 3; David A. Garvin; "Teaching Executives and Teaching MBAs," *Academy of Management Learning & Education*, 2007, Vol. 6, No. 3; Jonathan P. Doh and Stephen A. Stumpf, "Executive Education, A View from the Top," *Academy of Management Learning & Education*, 2007, Vol. 6, No. 3; Jim Heskett, "Are Elite Business Schools Fostering the Deprofessionalization of Management?" *Harvard Business School Working Knowledge* online forum, 7 September 2007; Rakesh Khurana, *From Higher Aims to Hired Hands*, Princeton: Princeton University Press, 2007; Sharon K. Clinebell and John M. Clinebell, "The Tension in Business Between Academic Rigor and Real-World Relevance: The Role of Executive Professors," *Academy of Management Learning & Education*, Vol. 7, No. 1, 2008; Peter Navarro, "The MBA Core Curricula of Top-Ranked U.S. Business Schools: A Study in Failure?" Academy of Management Learning & Education, Vol. 7, No. 1, 2008

5   Della Bradshaw, "Moot But Advantageous," *Financial Times*, 7 April 2008

6   Schumpeter, "Those Who Can't, Teach," *The Economist*, 8 February 2014

7   Emma Boyde, "Is an MBA Worth the Cost?" *Financial Times*, 26 January 2014

8   Lawrence Delevingne and Henry Blodget, "The World's Best Business Schools," *Business Insider*, 24 March 2010

9   Adam Palin, "Poll Shows That Alumni Networks Really Do Lead to Job Offers," *Financial Times*, 28 January 2013

10 Aaron A. Gottesman and Matthew R. Morey, "Does a Better Education Make for Better Managers? An Empirical Examination of CEO Educational Quality and Firm Performance," 21 April 2006, http://papers.ssrn.com/sol3/papers.cfm?abstract_id=564443

11 Spencer Stuart, *2007 Route to the Top*, 1 November 2007

12 Menachem Wecker, "Where the Fortune 500 CEOs Went to School," *US News & World Report*, 14 May 2012

13 Delece Smith-Barrow, "Where America's Top CEOs Went to School," *US News & World Report*, 22 May 2013

14 Adam Palin, "Aiming for the Stars ... Then Get a Top MBA," *Financial Times*, 19 January 2014

15 Valeria Calderon and Preety Sisdhu, "Business Leaders Say Knowledge Trumps College Pedigree," www.gallup.com, 25 February 2014

16 David A. Garvin and Srikant M. Datar, "Business Education in the 21st Century," Harvard University Centennial Global Business Summit, 2008

17 Kit Gillet, "In China, Executives Flock Back to School for Unfinished Business," *New York Times*, 16 March 2013

18 Peter Tufano, "Business Schools are Stuck in a Self-Reinforcing Bubble," *Bloomberg BusinessWeek*, 14 February 2014

19 Robert Hayes and William Abernathy, "Managing Our Way to Economic Decline," *Harvard Business Review*, July–August 1980

20 Jack N. Behrman and Richard I. Levin, "Are Business Schools Doing Their Job?" *Harvard Business Review*, January–February, 1984

21 Sumantra Ghoshal, "Bad Management Theories Are Destroying Good Management Practices," *Academy of Management Learning & Education*," Vol. 4, No. 1, 2005

22 Mary C. Gentile and Judith F. Samuelson, "Keynote Address to the AACSB Conference, 10 February 2003: The State of Affairs for Management Education and Social Responsibility," *Academy of Management Learning & Education*, Vol. 4, No. 4, 2005

23 Anita McGahan, "An Agenda for Business Schools," *Competitive Strategy Newsletter*, Strategic Management Society, Vol. 4, No. 1, Spring 2011

24 Rakesh Khurana and Nitin Nohria, "It's Time to Make Management a True Profession," *Harvard Business Review*, October 2008

25 www.mbaoath.org

26 Robert Simons, "The Business of Business Schools: Restoring a Focus on Competing to Win," *Capitalism and Society*, Vol. 8, Issue 1, 2013

27 Richard Schmalensee, "Where's the 'B' in B-Schools?" *Business Week*, 27 November 2006

28 Rebecca Knight, "Looming Threat of Faculty Shortage as Phd Entrants Fall," *Financial Times*, 5 May 2008

29 D.C. Denison, "Modernizing the Harvard MBA Program," *The Boston Globe*, 15 July 2012

30 Tamar Lewin, "After Setbacks, Online Courses Are Rethought," *New York Times*, 10 December 2013; "Penn GSE Study Shows MOOCs Have Relatively Few Active Users, with Only a Few Persisting to Course End," Penn GSE Press Room, 5 December 2013

31 www.openeducationeurope.eu

32 Jessica Leber, "In the Developing World, MOOCs Start to Get Real," *MIT Technology Review*, 15 March 2013

33 Matthew Poyiadgi, "Accreditation Will Be Central to the Success of MOOCs," *Financial Times*, 9 March 2014

34 Yann Zopf, "World Economic Forum launches Forum Academy in partnership with edX," http://www.weforum.org/news/world-economic-forum-launches-forum-academy-partnership-edx

35 John Gapper, "Davos Thought: Disruption Comes to Education," *Financial Times*, 23 January 2014

36 Antonio Regalado, "The Most Important Education Technology in 200 Years," *MIT Technology Review*, 2 November 2012

37 Adam Palin, "The No-Cost Option: Moocs are Starting to Offer MBA Content," *Financial Times*, 26 January 2014

38 David A. Garvin, speaking on "Business Education in the 21st Century," Global Business Summit, Harvard Business School, 14 October 2008

39 David A. Garvin; "Teaching Executives and Teaching MBAs: Reflections on the Case Method," *Academy of Management Learning & Education*, Vol. 6, No. 3, 2007

40 Michael L. Tushman, Charles A. O'Reilly, Amy Fenollosa, Adam M. Kleinbaum, and Dan McGrath, "Relevance and Rigor: Executive Education as a Lever in Shaping Practice and Research," *Academy of Management Learning & Education*, Vol. 6, No. 3, 2007

41 Rakesh Khurana, "The Multipolar MBA," *Strategy+Business*, 21 January 2013

42 David A. Garvin and Srikant M. Datar, "Business Education in the 21st Century," Harvard University Centennial Global Business Summit, 2008; www.som.yale.edu

43 Ken Bain, *What the Best College Teachers Do*, Boston: Harvard University Press, 2004

44 Jeffrey Pfeffer and Robert I. Sutton, "Evidence-Based Management," *Harvard Business Review*, January 2006

45 Della Bradshaw, "MBAs Focus on New Horizons," *Financial Times*, 14 April 2008

46 D.C. Denison, "Modernizing the Harvard MBA Program," *The Boston Globe*, 15 July 2012

47 Jeffrey Pfeffer and Robert I. Sutton, *The Knowing-Doing Gap*, Boston: Harvard Business School Press, 1999

48 Theodore Levitt, *The Marketing Imagination*, New York: The Free Press, 1983

49 www.africanmanagers.org

50 Vasant Dhar, "Caught Between a Rock and a Hard Place," *Financial Times*, 23 March 2014

51 Clayton M. Christensen and Harry J. Eyring, *The Innovative University*, San Francisco: Jossey_Bass, 2011

INDEX